Peter Angermann ———— Licht am Horizont

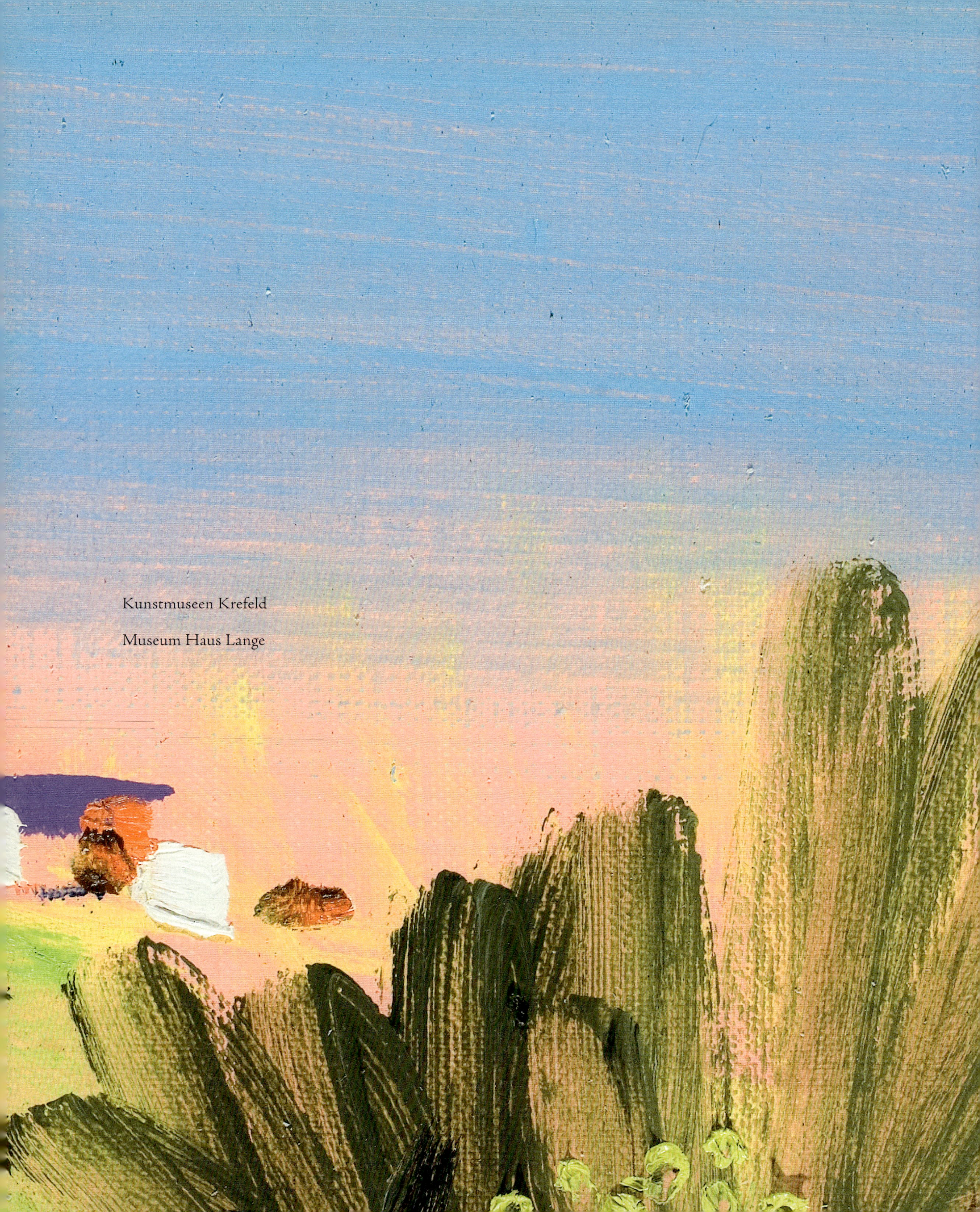

Kunstmuseen Krefeld
Museum Haus Lange

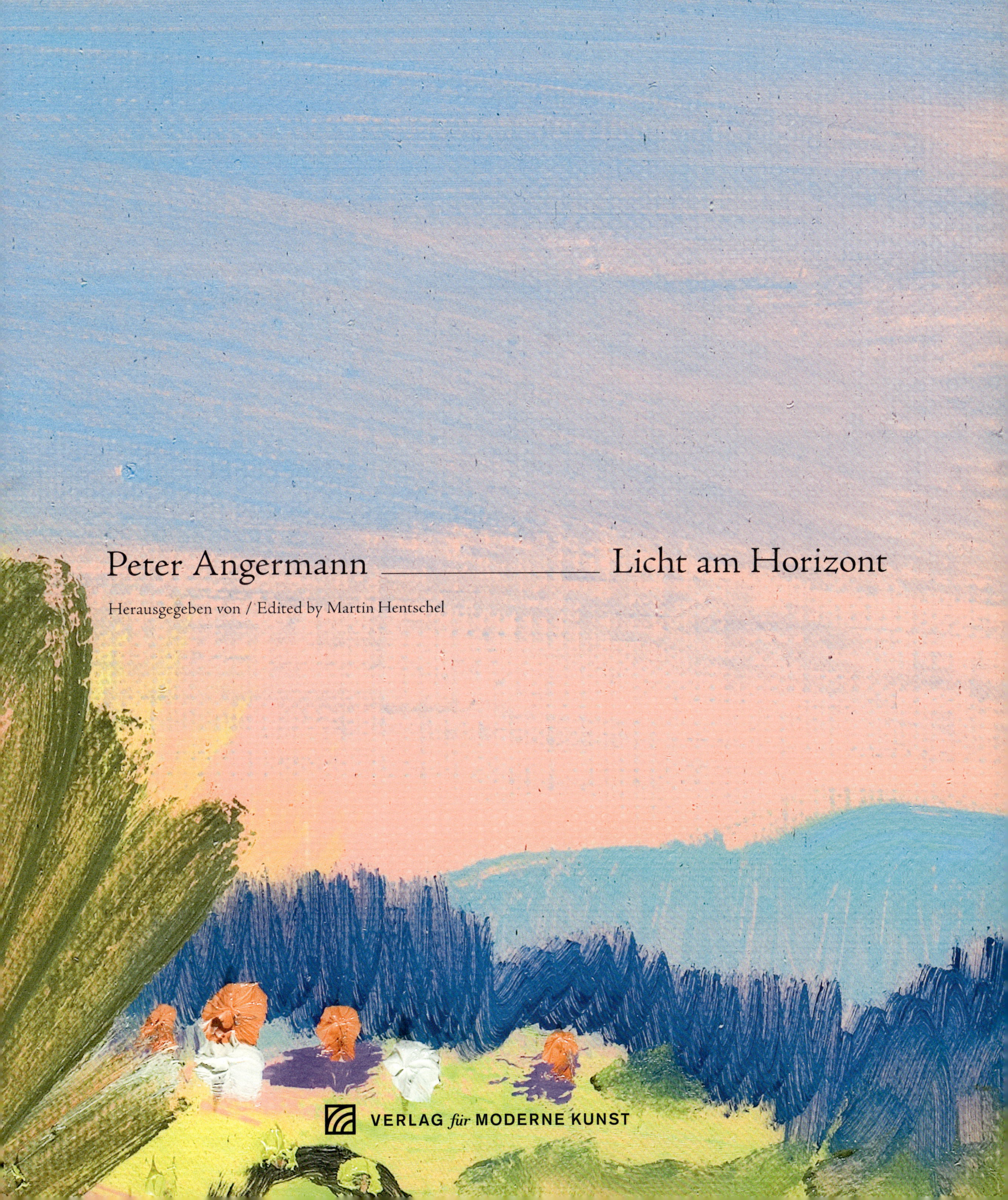

Peter Angermann ———————— Licht am Horizont

Herausgegeben von / Edited by Martin Hentschel

VERLAG *für* MODERNE KUNST

Inhalt / Contents

Foreword

This book is about a rediscovery: the rediscovery of an artist who had already started to paint before he came to enjoy the benefits of an academic education, and who afterwards – since 1973 – has worked consistently away at a painterly oeuvre that today, after forty years, comprises several thousand works.

Initially, from 1966 to 1968, Peter Angermann, who was born in 1945 in Rehau, a small town in Upper Franconia in Bavaria, studied at the Academy of Fine Arts in Nuremberg. Then, in autumn 1968, he was drawn to the class run by Joseph Beuys at the Düsseldorf Art Academy. Constantly showered with his teacher's praise, he nevertheless – or perhaps precisely for that reason – became co-founder of the legendary YIUP group, which from 1969 on attracted attention inside the academy, and above all in the Beuys class, through provocative actions that were directed even against Beuys himself. On leaving the academy in 1972, Angermann saw that in artistic terms, he had come away empty-handed; his passion for painting had not exactly been fostered by Beuys. Not until a year later, once he had largely jettisoned Beuys's ideas, did Angermann make a new start in the field of painting. A meeting with his former classmate Milan Kunc proved exceptionally fruitful in this situation. Together they developed a new visual language that was closely oriented to everyday life, while simultaneously being fired by a witty, anarchic impulse. In 1979 Jan Knap joined the two friends, and group NORMAL was born. They championed the rejection of individualism and, in line with this, created a large number of joint works – paintings that in some cases were done in public. By 1981, however, each of the three members had progressed so far in his own artistic development that it was decided to disband the group.

Standing now on his own two feet, Peter Angermann has retained the socio-critical impulse from his earlier works – coupled with that provocative and at times absurdist humour that marks many of his paintings to this day. In 1976 he surprised the world with the first of his "bear paintings" and what was to be the beginning of a series that has kept on expanding. In fact these are paintings of family life which, while sharpening our eye for the human condition under the strict use of the bear guise, do not baulk at depicting idylls. Ten years later Angermann pulled another surprise out of the hat – at first through the sheer joy of exploring a genre which at that time was frowned on: en plein air painting. In the meantime, this group of works has found a permanent place in his oeuvre and has led him to discover a virtuosity as colourist that also distinguishes his mature, themed works. The two of them – his themed works and his landscapes – alternate without more ado in Angermann's work, and it is this liaison that makes Ackermann so unique in today's art scene.

Parallel to this, Peter Angermann has also passed his artistic experience on to a new generation of artists, at first through guest professorships at Reykjavik and Kassel, followed

Vorwort

Dieses Buch gilt einer Wiederentdeckung: der Wiederentdeckung eines Künstlers, der schon zu malen begann, noch bevor er eine akademische Ausbildung genoss, und der danach – seit 1973 – konsequent an einem malerischen Œuvre gearbeitet hat, das heute, nach vierzig Jahren, auf mehrere tausend Arbeiten angewachsen ist.

Peter Angermann, 1945 in Rehau, einer kleinen Stadt in Oberfranken, Bayern, geboren, studierte zunächst von 1966 bis 1968 an der Akademie der Bildenden Künste in Nürnberg, bevor es ihn im Herbst 1968 in die Klasse von Joseph Beuys an der Kunstakademie Düsseldorf zog. Von seinem Lehrer stets mit Lob bedacht, wurde er dennoch – und womöglich gerade deshalb – zum Mitbegründer der legendären YIUP-Gruppe, die seit 1969 innerhalb der Akademie und vor allem in der Beuys-Klasse mit provokanten Aktionen auch gegen Beuys selbst auf sich aufmerksam machte. Als Angermann 1972 die Akademie verließ, stand er künstlerisch gesehen zunächst mit leeren Händen da; denn seine Leidenschaft für Malerei war in der Beuys-Klasse nicht gerade befördert worden. Erst ein Jahr später, nachdem er die Lehren von Beuys weitgehend über Bord geworfen hatte, wagte Angermann einen Neuanfang in Sachen Malerei. Das Zusammentreffen mit dem Ex-Kommilitonen Milan Kunc wirkte sich in dieser Situation äußerst fruchtbar aus. Gemeinsam entwickelten sie eine neue Bildsprache, die nah am alltäglichen Leben orientiert war und zugleich von einem anarchisch-witzigen Impetus befeuert wurde. 1979 gesellte sich Jan Knap zu den Freunden: Die Gruppe NORMAL war geboren. Sie propagierte die Ablehnung des Individualismus und artikulierte sich folgerichtig in einer Vielzahl von gemeinschaftlich erarbeiteten Werken – Gemälden, die teilweise auch in der Öffentlichkeit entstanden. 1981 war allerdings die künstlerische Entwicklung jedes einzelnen der drei Mitglieder so weit fortgeschritten, dass man sich zur Auflösung der Gruppe entschloss.

Gänzlich auf eigenen Füßen stehend, hat Peter Angermann den gesellschaftskritischen Impuls seiner frühen Arbeiten beibehalten – gepaart mit jenem provokanten, teilweise absurden Witz, der aus vielen seiner Gemälde bis heute hervorsticht. 1976 überraschte der Künstler mit dem ersten seiner „Bärenbilder", dem Beginn einer Werkgruppe, die immer noch fortgeschrieben wird. Es sind eigentlich Bilder aus dem Familienleben, die durch ihre stringente Verkleidung im Bärenkostüm den Blick auf die *conditio humana* schärfen und auch vor der Idylle nicht zurückschrecken. Zehn Jahre später überraschte Angermann erneut, als er – zunächst aus purer Freude am damals verpönten Genre – mit Pleinairmalerei aufwartete. Mittlerweile nimmt diese Werkgruppe ebenfalls einen festen Platz in seinem Œuvre ein, und in ihr hat er zu einer koloristischen Virtuosität gefunden, die auch seine reifen thematischen Werke auszeichnet. Beides – thematische Werke und Landschaftsmalerei – wechselt sich heutzutage zwanglos in Angermanns Werk ab, und dieser Liaison verdankt sich, was den Künstler im heutigen Kunstgeschehen so unverwechselbar macht.

from 1996 to 2002 by a professorship at the Städelschule, Frankfurt/Main, and then from 2002 to 2010 at the Academy of Fine Arts in Nuremberg. In 1995, Angermann made his home one hour's car drive away from Nuremberg, in Thurndorf, where, far removed from the turmoil of the art business, he continues to dedicate himself enthusiastically to the medium that holds every possibility of artistic development open to him: painting.

We would like to thank Peter Angermann for all his commitment to the present publication, which has been exquisitely designed by the graphic artist Ernst Christian Dümmler. Thanks are also due to the English art historian Julian Spalding for his comprehensive essay, no less illuminating than it is polemical, on Peter Angermann's art. Moreover we wish to thank Peter Angermann for the great effort he put into preparing the exhibition. Last but not least, our thanks go to all of the lenders, who were willing to part from their works for the duration of the exhibition.

Dr. Martin Hentschel
Director Kunstmuseen Krefeld

Daneben hat Peter Angermann seine gesammelte künstlerische Erfahrung auch einer jüngeren Künstlergeneration vermittelt, zunächst durch Gastprofessuren in Reykjavik und Kassel, dann von 1996 bis 2002 als Professor an der Städelschule, Frankfurt am Main, und schließlich von 2002 bis 2010 an der Akademie der Bildenden Künste in Nürnberg. Eine Autostunde von Nürnberg entfernt hat sich der Künstler 1995 in Thurndorf niedergelassen, wo er sich – fernab vom ruhelosen Kunstbetrieb – nach wie vor enthusiastisch dem Medium widmet, das ihm alle Möglichkeiten künstlerischer Entfaltung offenhält: der Malerei.

Wir danken Peter Angermann für seine engagierte Mitarbeit an der vorliegenden Publikation, die durch den Grafiker Ernst Christian Dümmler vorzüglich gestaltet wurde. Gedankt sei auch dem britischen Kunsthistoriker Julian Spalding für seinen umfangreichen, gleichermaßen erhellenden wie streitbaren Essay zur Kunst von Peter Angermann. Schließlich danken wir dem Künstler dafür, dass er die Vorbereitung der Ausstellung mit großem Einsatz begleitet hat. Nicht zuletzt gilt unser Dank allen Leihgebern, die sich für die Dauer der Ausstellung von ihren Werken getrennt haben.

Dr. Martin Hentschel
Direktor Kunstmuseen Krefeld

How He Became What He Is: Peter Angermann, the Painter

Martin Hentschel

Beginnings with YIUP

How did Peter Angermann come to be the painter that we know? After starting out in Gerhard Wendland's painting class in Nuremberg, in 1968 he entered Joseph Beuys's class at the Düsseldorf Art Academy. But painting there was not exactly *au fait*. Norbert Tadeusz and Blinky Palermo had already left Beuys's class, and the cool minimalist works that Imi Knoebel was producing – at that time in room 19 together with Imi Giese[1] – did not really interest the student from southern Germany. Jörg Immendorff, who was already active then as an art educator, set up a LIDL class in December 1968 in the hallway of the academy as a branch of the LIDL room he had previously founded in Düsseldorf's Blücherstrasse; it served as a forum for political agitation and art actions.[2] One of the chief aims of the LIDL class was to radically question the relationship between tutor and taught. The months-long tumult that subsequently arose between professors and students actually brought the academy into discredit in the national newspapers.[3] While LIDL finally withdrew from the academy in May 1969 after being repeatedly banned from the premises, a few months later Peter Angermann, Robert Hartmann, Hans Heininger, Hans Henin and Hans Rogalla (the last two had also been involved in LIDL) founded the YIUP group ("YIUP" was pronounced "yupp", like Beuys's first name when spoken in the regional dialect).[4] It was directed not so much at social critique as at representing a critical counterweight to Beuys's teaching and his extended concept of art. Although class war was ostensibly part of their programme, the struggle only took place within the walls of the academy classes. Through a diversity of actions they not only stirred up the Beuys class but also those run by the other professors and heightened the already sizzling tension between Beuys's champions and opponents. Little painting was done, but all the more drawing; each action was announced with specially made silk-screen prints, as for instance for the "Akademie-Erstbesteigung" [First Mounting of the Academy] on 1 December 1970 (ill. 1).

 With his painted aporia *Hört auf zu malen* [*Stop Painting*] (1966) – the title is an integral part of the picture – Immendorff had already conveyed the pettiness of painting that relates to nothing beyond its own self. *Ehepaar mit Futter* and *Ehepaar in Tierhandlung* [*Married Couple with Animal Feed* and *Married Couple in a Pet Shop*] (both 1968)[5] were two of

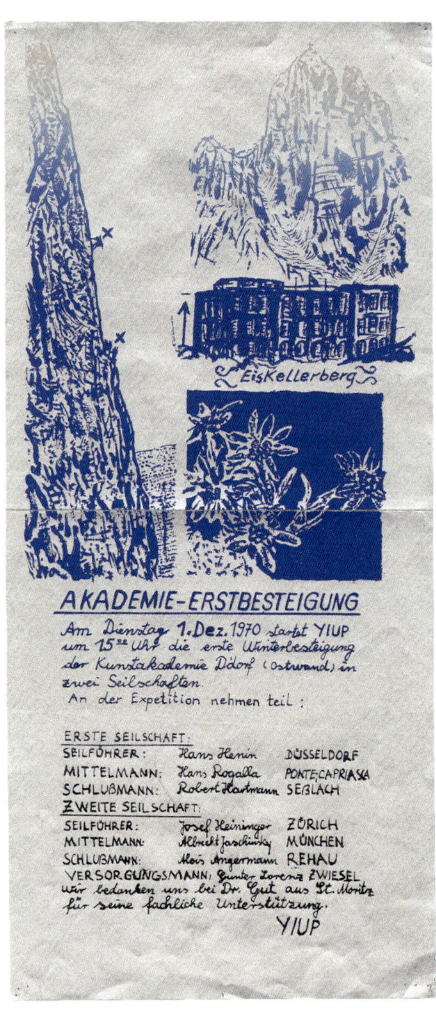

1 *Akademie-Erstbesteigung / First Mounting of the Academy*, 1970, Siebdruck auf Papier / silk screen on paper

Wie er wurde, was er ist: Peter Angermann, der Maler

Martin Hentschel

Anfänge mit YIUP

Wie wurde Peter Angermann zu dem Maler, als den wir ihn kennen? Als er sich 1968, nach den Anfängen in der Malerklasse von Gerhard Wendland in Nürnberg, in die Klasse von Joseph Beuys an der Kunstakademie Düsseldorf begibt, ist Malerei nicht gerade eine angesagte Disziplin. Norbert Tadeusz und Blinky Palermo haben die Beuys-Klasse bereits verlassen, und die coolen minimalistischen Arbeiten, die Imi Knoebel – damals in Raum 19 zusammen mit Imi Giese – produziert,[1] interessieren den Studenten aus Süddeutschland nicht wirklich. Jörg Immendorff, der seinerzeit bereits auch als Kunsterzieher tätig ist, richtet im Dezember 1968 eine LIDL-Klasse im Flur der Akademie ein, als Dependance seines zuvor gegründeten LIDL-Raums in der Düsseldorfer Blücherstraße; er dient als Forum für politische Agitation und Kunstaktionen.[2] Ziel der LIDL-Klasse ist es unter anderem, grundsätzlich das Verhältnis von Lehrenden und Lernenden infrage zu stellen. Die anschließenden monatelangen Tumulte zwischen Professoren und Studenten bringen die Akademie gar in der überregionalen Presse in Misskredit.[3] Während sich LIDL nach mehrfach ausgesprochenem Hausverbot schließlich im Mai 1969 aus der Akademie zurückzieht, gründen Peter Angermann, Robert Hartmann, Hans Heininger, Hans Henin und Hans Rogalla (die beiden Letzteren haben bereits bei LIDL mitgemacht) wenige Monate später die YIUP-Gruppe (YIUP – wie „Jupp" gesprochen, die Abkürzung von Beuys' Vornamen im rheinischen Dialekt).[4] Sie ist weniger gesellschaftskritisch orientiert, sondern versteht sich vielmehr als kritische Instanz gegenüber der Lehrtätigkeit von Beuys und seinem erweiterten Kunstbegriff. Zwar gibt man sich durchaus klassenkämpferisch, tatsächlich spielt sich der Kampf aber ausschließlich in den Akademieklassen ab. Mit diversen Aktionen mischt man sowohl die Beuys-Klasse als auch die Klassen der übrigen Professoren auf und verschärft die ohnehin vorhandene Spannung zwischen Beuys-Befürwortern und Beuys-Gegnern. Es wird wenig gemalt, dafür umso mehr gezeichnet; eigens gefertigte Siebdrucke kündigen jeweils Aktionen an, wie etwa die der „Akademie-Erstbesteigung" vom 1. Dezember 1970 (Textabb. 1).

Mit seiner gemalten Aporie *Hört auf zu malen* (1966) – der Titel ist integraler Bestandteil des Bildes – hat Immendorff bereits die Beschränktheit einer Malerei, die sich auf nichts außerhalb ihrer selbst bezieht, zum Ausdruck gebracht. *Ehepaar mit Futter* und *Ehepaar in Tierhandlung* (beide 1968)[5] heißen zwei seiner ersten, ungelenken Versuche, sich künstlerisch der Arbeiterklasse und ihrem Alltag zu nähern. Sie münden, wie wir wissen, in den Folgejahren in handfester Agitprop-Malerei. Der Legitimationsdruck, sich überhaupt malerisch zu betätigen, lastet um 1970 insbesondere auch auf der Beuys-Klasse. Nicht von ungefähr widmen sich die ersten Ölgemälde, die Peter Angermann während der YIUP-Zeit anfertigt, der

his first, clumsy attempts to draw close as an artist to the working class and their daily lives. As we know, his paintings developed over the next few years into strident agitprop. The onus of having to legitimise the very wish to paint also exerted a pressure on the students around 1970, especially in the Beuys class. It is no accident that the first oils that Peter Angermann did during this YIUP period were dedicated to everyday life – because that at least lent them some legitimacy. These works present the first indications of a style that later distinguished Angermann's paintings.

Image of the Foe (1970, p. 41), for instance: an itinerant labourer with his face lit up a sickly yellow raises his arms in his helplessness. He is being attacked by, simultaneously, a broken bottle and a barking dog – both tools wielded by an all-powerful capitalist (Mafioso?); the latter is visible only on the outermost margin of the painting and identifiable by a black suit. This striking mixture of crime story and class struggle takes place outside of town on a field. The ascending flock of crows and the worker's clearly accentuated ear trigger associations with the despair that once beset van Gogh. The quickly dashed off brushstrokes, which steer the whole towards a crude Verism, were later to be adopted by Angermann to far more decisive effect. Or *Chicken* (1971, p. 42), only 31 × 45 cm: a glimpse into a fried-chicken shop stands out by virtue of its strong use of light contrasts, which at the same time receive an art-historical reference through a depiction within the painting of a reproduction of Rembrandt's *The Man with the Golden Helmet*.[6] Here we also see the inception of those bright colours that from then on accompanied Angermann's imagery. No less astonishing is the tiny oil painting *Little Murder* (1970, p. 40): it scarcely hides its borrowings from van Gogh but also anticipates Angermann's later plein-air paintings.

An "Art for the People"?

Around 1973, after the artist had become friends with his comrade-in-arms Milan Kunc[7], the characteristic features by which we now identify Angermann's art finally emerged. As of now he painted large canvases with content ranging from ironic digs at capitalism to exuberantly anarchic grotesques. As is shown for instance by his *Magpie Painting* (1974, p. 53) and *Large Frog Painting* (1974, p. 51): both paintings adopt a casual, comic-strip-like style, although the latter is more ornamental in structure and the former delights in sophisticated perspectives. Also attributable to the realms of the grotesque[8] is a solitary painting whose strangeness and caustic wit are still curiously moving almost forty years after it was painted. The picture is *Schwarzenbach* (1974, p. 49): a small town located in Upper Franconia, whose name – directly translated: "black brook" – is victim here to a literal but uncanny interpretation: all of the inhabitants are black. Milan Kunc participates in the picture in a number of details, while Martin Figuli, at that time friend and inspiration to the two artists, is immortalised in the work as a shop-keeper. The painting has lost none of its humour over the years, because a scene such as this, projected mentally onto any German small town one would care to mention, would seem every bit as shocking today: all the fine words about integrating immigrants would be quashed in one fell swoop. Unlike the previously

alltäglichen Lebenswelt – ist doch damit wenigstens eine Art der Legitimation gegeben. Diese Arbeiten lassen zum ersten Mal Ansätze jener Malweise erkennen, die Angermann später auszeichnen wird.

Feindbild (1970, S. 41) etwa: Ein Gastarbeiter mit kränklich gelb leuchtendem Gesicht hebt hilflos die Arme hoch. Er wird gleichermaßen von einer zerbrochenen Flasche wie von einem kläffenden Köter attackiert – beides Werkzeuge, die aus der Hand eines übermächtigen Kapitalisten (Mafioso?) hervorspringen; dieser ist – extrem vom Bildrand angeschnitten – nur an seinem schwarzen Anzug zu erkennen. Die denkwürdige Mischung aus Krimi und Klassenkampf spielt sich auf einem Acker draußen vor der Stadt ab. Die aufsteigenden Krähen und das deutlich herausgehobene Ohr des Arbeiters lassen jene Verzweiflung assoziieren, die einst van Gogh befiel. Die schnell hingeworfenen Pinselstriche, die das Ganze auf einen kruden Verismus zuspitzen, wird Angermann später weitaus entschiedener einsetzen. Oder *Hähnchen* (1971, S. 42), nur 31 × 45 cm groß: Der Blick in die Hähnchenbackstube zeichnet sich durch seine kontrastreiche Lichtregie aus, die zugleich in der innerbildlichen Darstellung einer Reproduktion von Rembrandts Gemälde *Der Mann mit dem Goldhelm* mit einer kunsthistorischen Referenz bedacht wird.[6] Hier deutet sich schon die satte Lichtfarbigkeit an, die Angermanns Bilderwelten fortan begleiten wird. Ebenso verblüffend ist das winzige Ölbild *Kleiner Mord* (1970, S. 40): Es verbirgt kaum seine Anleihen bei der Malerei van Goghs, weist aber ebenso auf Angermanns spätere Pleinair-Bilder voraus.

Eine „Kunst fürs Volk"?

Um 1973, nachdem unser Künstler seinen Mitstreiter Milan Kunc[7] kennengelernt hat, kristallisiert sich endgültig heraus, was wir ohne Weiteres als Angermanns Kunst identifizieren können. Nunmehr entstehen großformatige Gemälde, deren inhaltliche Spannweite von ironischer Kapitalismuskritik bis zu anarchischen, überbordenden Grotesken reicht. Dafür mögen *Elsternbild* (1974, S. 53) und *Großes Froschbild* (1974, S. 51) einstehen: Beide Gemälde operieren mit einer lässigen, comicartigen Handschrift, wobei das letztere stärker ornamental strukturiert ist, während das erstere mit perspektivischer Raffinesse aufwartet. In das Reich des Grotesken[8] gehört auch ein solitäres Gemälde, dessen Fremdartigkeit und beißender Humor auch heute noch, fast vierzig Jahre nach der Entstehung, auf eigentümliche Weise berühren. Es ist die Rede von *Schwarzenbach* (1974, S. 49): ein real existierender Ort in Oberfranken, dessen Name aber durch das Bild einer unheimlichen, buchstäblichen Interpretation anheimfällt – sämtliche Einwohner des Ortes sind als Schwarze dargestellt. Milan Kunc ist mit einigen Details daran beteiligt, während Martin Figuli, seinerzeit Freund und Inspirationsquelle der beiden Künstler, als Geschäftsinhaber im Bild verewigt ist. Der Witz des Bildes ist keineswegs gealtert, denn ein derartiges Szenario, als Vorstellung auf jede beliebige deutsche Kleinstadt projiziert, würde heute nicht weniger schockieren als damals: Alle Sonntagsreden über die Integration von Migranten wären mit einem Schlag ausgehebelt. Anders als in den bisher erwähnten Arbeiten zitiert Angermann hier bewusst Darstellungsformen der Volkskunst, vor

discussed works, here Angermann consciously employs the means used in folk art, above all in the discontinuity of the perspectives and in the wilful naivety of the detailed drawing. These elements have continued to appear right up to his latest works. And when combined with the topics in his paintings, they lend the whole an astonishingly self-evident quality which must have stuck in the craw of both the art lover and Joe "the Philistine" Public.

Karl Schawelka is quite right in noting that "for all his intellectualism, Angermann cannot clearly be categorised as part of the art establishment and makes a splendid game out of the question of which audience he actually paints for"[9]. In fact, around 1973 Angermann and Kunc envisaged something like "art for the people"[10], and this idea was to bear at least some signs of fruit in the public painting actions staged by the group NORMAL[11] they founded in 1979 (with Jan Knap as the third in the trio).

On the way there another painting catches the eye, which conversely extends into the innermost realms of private life while nevertheless allowing us to feel a hint of something like folk art: *For Renate* (1973/76, p. 55) is a large-scale painted declaration of love. As in *Schwarzenbach*, the representation of perspective is discontinuous. The painting contains all the ingredients that make up a town, neatly bundled together from a couple of houses and even an airport, and all drawn in red. It is evidently not meant to be a small town. That the scene nevertheless mutates into an idyll is due in part to the dark blue stripe in the foreground – in which a deer, a butterfly and a dwarf bound about in perfect harmony. And partly because we and the picture's inhabitants are looking at an oversized heart nestling in an aureole of clouds, while up above in the night sky (sic!) the stars are twinkling. Here the artist has ventured for the first time to take a kitsch motif that would have honoured the great master of the discipline, Sigmar Polke. The real cheek of it consists however in the way Angermann, freshly in love with his new girlfriend, Renate, has simply crossed out the name of his previous flame and rededicated the work – which explains the two dates that are given. For the idyll, the magic has been dispelled in an outrageous, frivolous way, but for the composition it marks a clear improvement – because with the new inscription the colours of the foreground, background (sky) and centre of the picture go together beautifully.

During the years 1976/77, which is to say before the official formation of group NORMAL, Peter Angermann came up with some of his most daring creations. He laid here the foundation stone for his later "bear pictures" (which I shall look at later), and with, for instance, *Gregor Samsa's Friends 1* (1976, p. 56) painted a truly magical capriccio replete with allusions to "sex and drugs and rock 'n' roll," which in a trice turns the pessimism of Franz Kafka's novella *The Metamorphosis* into its opposite. Or *Necropolis* (1976, p. 58), a reverse glass painting: the depiction of a town full of walking skeletons that is witty and macabre in equal measure, and in no way inferior to the images from the Mexican Day of the Dead cult. In *Poverty, Wealth, Sex* (1977, p. 59) the artist has produced a sterling orgy on top of a cake. The painting is utterly obscene, not merely on account of the blatant pornography, which far exceeds the forerunners created by Otto Dix and George Grosz. Far more pornographic – and with that, absolute taboo – are the crass comparisons between the rich and their venal sex, and the poor folks outside the window

allem in der Diskontinuität der Perspektive, aber auch in der forciert naiven Detailzeichnung. Diese Elemente werden auch in späteren Arbeiten immer wieder auftauchen. Bezogen auf die Thematik des Bildes verleihen sie dem Ganzen eine stupende Selbstverständlichkeit, die damals dem Kunstliebhaber ebenso wie dem kunstfernen Durchschnittsbürger sauer aufstoßen musste.

Mit Recht hat Karl Schawelka darauf aufmerksam gemacht, dass „Angermann bei all seiner Intellektualität nicht eindeutig dem Kunstbetrieb zuzuordnen ist und ein schillerndes Spiel damit betreibt, für welches Publikum er eigentlich malt"[9]. Tatsächlich schwebt Angermann und Kunc um 1973 so etwas vor wie eine „Kunst fürs Volk"[10], und in den öffentlichen Malaktionen der 1979 gegründeten Gruppe NORMAL[11] (mit Jan Knap als Drittem im Bunde) sollte diese Idee zumindest ansatzweise fruchten.

Auf dem Weg dorthin fällt ein weiteres Gemälde ins Auge, das umgekehrt ins Innerste des Privaten reicht und dennoch etwas von einer Art Volkskunst erahnen lässt: *Für Renate* (1973/76, S. 55) ist eine gemalte Liebeserklärung im großen Format. Wie bei *Schwarzenbach* ist die perspektivische Darstellung diskontinuierlich. Das Bild enthält alle Ingredienzien einer Stadt, zusammengeschnurrt auf wenige Gebäude, einschließlich Flughafen – alle in Rot gezeichnet. Es ist offensichtlich keine Kleinstadt gemeint. Dass die Szene trotzdem zur Idylle mutiert, liegt zum einen an dem tiefblauen Streifen im Vordergrund – hier tummeln sich Reh, Schmetterling und Zwerg in trauter Eintracht. Zum anderen blicken wir mit diesen Bildbewohnern auf ein überdimensionales Herz, eingebettet in eine Aureole aus Wolken, während oben am Nachthimmel (sic!) die Sterne blinken. Hier hat sich der Künstler zum ersten Mal an ein Kitschmotiv gewagt, das dem damaligen Großmeister in dieser Disziplin, Sigmar Polke, zur Ehre gereicht hätte. Die eigentliche Chuzpe besteht allerdings darin, dass Angermann, nachdem er sich frisch in seine neue Freundin Renate verliebt hat, den Namen der vorhergehenden Flamme durchstreicht und das Bild einfach umwidmet – daher die zweifache Jahreszahl. Auf der Ebene der Idylle bedeutet das eine unerhörte, frivole Entzauberung, auf der Ebene des Bildes dagegen eine klare Verbesserung – insofern, als mit dem neuen blauen Schriftzug Vordergrund, Bildmitte und Hintergrund (Himmel) farblich aufs Schönste korrespondieren.

In den Jahren 1976/77, also noch vor der offiziellen Gründung der Gruppe NORMAL, gelingt Peter Angermann eine Reihe seiner gewagtesten Bildfindungen. Hier legt er den Grundstein für seine späteren „Bärenbilder" (auf die ich noch eingehen werde), hier entsteht zum Beispiel *Gregor Samsas Freunde 1* (1976, S. 56), ein wahrhaft märchenhaftes Capriccio voller Anspielungen auf „Sex and Drugs and Rock 'n' Roll", das den Pessimismus von Franz Kafkas Erzählung *Die Verwandlung* schlagartig ins Gegenteil umstülpt. Oder *Nekropolis* (1976, S. 58), ein Hinterglasbild: die ebenso witzige wie makabre Darstellung einer Stadt der wandelnden Skelette, die den szenischen Bildern im mexikanischen Totenkult in nichts nachsteht. In *Armut, Wohlstand, Sex* (1977, S. 59) entwickelt der Künstler auf einer riesigen Torte eine handfeste Orgie. Das Gemälde ist durch und durch obszön, nicht allein wegen seiner offensichtlichen Pornografie, deren Drastik die Vorbilder von Otto Dix und George Grosz

who are starved to the bones. Is that what the new folk art is supposed to be? Once again the question about who Angermann actually paints for rears its head. At any rate, the artist's success with these images may be gauged from the fact that he later returned to all three motifs in modified form.

The Group NORMAL – Painted Social Critique

The joint works by the group NORMAL, which they first began in 1979, were doubt-lessly inspired by the idea of a folk-like art, for the rejection of individualism is the first point on the manifesto that the group members, Angermann, Kunc and Knap, squeezed onto an A4 page (ill. 2). Georg Bussmann has aptly described the new experiences they encountered in their joint work: "In a curious blend of mixed emotions and experiences: inquisitiveness, closeness, uncertainty and desire to assert themselves, the responsibility for the picture seemed to be reassigned with every new moment. That produced an awareness of commonalty but also of conflict. What does one say for instance when in the joint painting *Champs-Élysées* (1980) [ill. 3] one has painted a crutch under the right arm of the injured heart that is leading the parade of hearts (Paris, the city of love), and then returns from the café to see that the crutch has now been turned into a pair of baguettes? Is that really an improvement? Yes, it must be, at any rate people are painting together not because it's quicker but because this complicated working with and against each other brings greater intensity, a wealth of ideas and ultimately a gain for the others." [12] At the same time the mixture of styles means that the joint paintings always differ slightly from the individual oeuvres of the artists involved. Although the idea is to abolish individualism, the artists' signature styles keep breaking out; they cannot be eliminated on command.

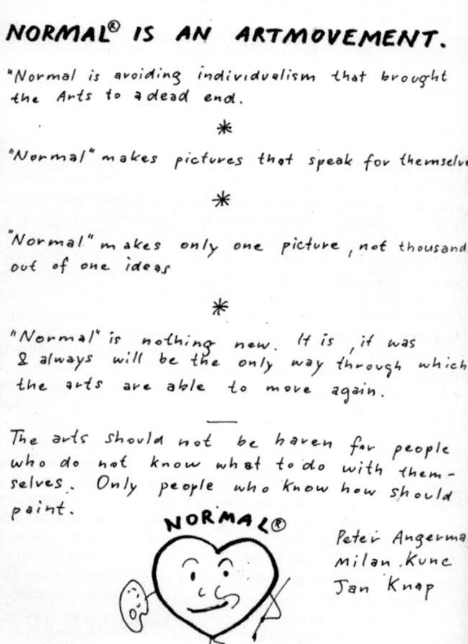

2   NORMAL manifesto, 1981

One example of a really harmonious collaboration between Angermann and Knap is to be found in the painting *Flight into Egypt* (1981, p. 68). Although it may be surmised that the majority of the Christian motifs (on genuine gold backgrounds!) and all the more delicate elements came from Jan Kap, everything fits into perfect order. This piece is one of many dedicated to the "Holy Family" that were done between 1979 and 1981 with changing partners within the group. [13] In each case Christian iconography has been transported to the present. This obsession earned the group NORMAL its dismissive title the "Neo-Nazarenes" from former YIUP member Robert Hartmann. [14] On the other hand, these motifs probably come very close to the dream of an "art for the people".

Be that as it may – the dream of "contact with the people" has also been dreamt by a number of artists in the past – not least Marcel Duchamp [15], the Dadaists, Piet Mondrian [16], and finally Claes Oldenburg [17]. Their failure was due less to their artistic ideas than to that extreme-ly influential institution called Art: the capitalist-oriented system of the art market, museums and art critics, with all its ramifications. Even the members of group NORMAL were sooner or later to be absorbed by it, even if it was not to their own disadvantage.

deutlich übertrifft. Tiefergehend pornografisch – und damit tabubrechend – ist vielmehr die krasse Gegenüberstellung zwischen dem gekauftem Sex der Reichen und den bis zum Skelett ausgemergelten Armen draußen vor dem Fenster. Sollte das etwa die neue Volkskunst sein? Hier wird die Frage, für welches Publikum Angermann eigentlich malt, noch einmal virulent. Jedenfalls spricht für den Erfolg dieser Bildfindungen, dass der Künstler alle drei Motive später noch einmal in abgewandelten Formen aufgreift.

Die Gruppe NORMAL – gemalte Gesellschaftskritik

Die Gemeinschaftsarbeiten der Gruppe NORMAL, die ab 1979 entstehen, folgen zweifellos dem Impetus einer volksnahen Kunst, ist doch die Ablehnung des Indivi- dualismus der erste Punkt des knapp auf eine DIN-A4-Seite gepressten Manifests der Gruppenmitglieder Angermann, Kunc und Knap (Textabb. 2). Georg Bussmann hat die neuen Erfahrungen, die mit dem gemeinschaftlichen Arbeiten einhergingen, tref- fend beschrieben: „In einem seltsamen Gemenge gemischter Erfahrungen und Gefühle: Neugier, Nähe, Unsicherheit und Behauptungswillen, erscheint die Verantwortung für das Bild jeden Augenblick neu verteilt. Das ergibt ein Bewusstsein für Gemein- samkeit, aber auch für Gegeneinander. Was sagt man zum Beispiel, wenn man in dem Gemeinschaftsbild *Champs-Élysées* (1980) [Textabb. 3] dem Invalidenherz, das die Parade der Herzen (Paris, die Stadt der Liebe) anführt, eine Krücke unter den rechten Arm gemalt hat, und man kommt aus dem Café zurück und aus der Krücke sind zwei Baguettes geworden. Ist das nun wirklich besser? Ja, muß wohl, jedenfalls, man malt zusammen, nicht weil's schneller geht, sondern weil das komplizierte Mit- und Ge- geneinander ein Mehr an Intensität, einen Überschuss an Einfällen, schließlich einen Gewinn für die anderen bringt.“[12] Andererseits fallen die Gemeinschaftswerke durch ihren Stilmix immer ein wenig aus dem jeweiligen Œuvre der einzelnen Künstler heraus. Man will zwar den Individualismus abschaffen, aber die individuelle künstlerische Handschrift bricht sich immer wieder die Bahn; sie lässt sich nicht per Dekret eliminieren.

Ein Beispiel für eine durchaus harmonische Zusammenarbeit zwischen Angermann und Knap findet sich in dem Gemälde *Flucht nach Ägypten* (1981, S. 68). Man ahnt zwar, dass die Mehrzahl der christlichen Motive (mit echtem Goldgrund!) und alle sonstigen feingliedrigen Elemente von Jan Kap stammen, dennoch fügt sich alles zu schöner Ordnung. Die Arbeit stellt eine aus einer ganzen Serie mit dem Thema der „Heiligen Familie“ dar, die zwischen 1979 und 1981 mit wechselnden Partnern der Gruppe entstehen.[13] Immer wird dabei die christliche Ikonografie in die Gegenwart transportiert. Diese Obsession bringt der Gruppe NORMAL den vom ehemaligen YIUP-Mitglied Robert Hartmann erfundenen abschätzigen Titel „Neonazarener“ ein.[14] Auf der anderen Seite kommen diese Motive dem Traum einer „Kunst fürs Volk“ womöglich recht nahe.

Wie auch immer – den Traum vom „Kontakt mit dem Volk“ hat zuvor schon eine Rei- he von Künstlern geträumt – unter ihnen Marcel Duchamp[15], die Dadaisten, Piet Mondrian[16]

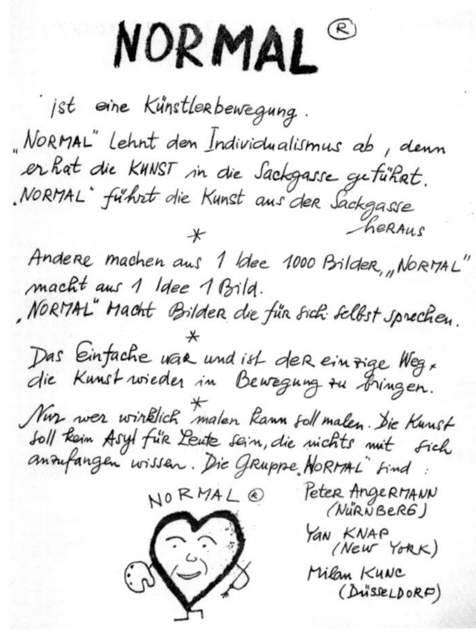

2   NORMAL-Manifest, 1981

The failure of a new folk art has not spelt however the end of
the socio-critical impulse. It has accompanied Peter Angermann to this
day, and even his plein-air paintings may be regarded in certain respects
as socio-critical because they flaunt as ever one of the unspoken jud-
gements of high art. Paintings such as *Force Majeure* (1981, p. 67), *The
Final Second* (1983, p. 75), *Tower of Babylon 1* (1989, p. 125), *Ghost Driver*
(1989, p. 128), *Fountain of Youth 1* (1991, p. 143), *Deaf in Bischofsheim*
(2007, p. 199), *Autonomoney 2* (2007, p. 201) and *Behind, Far Away…*
(2008, p. 205) all allude to the fears and self-delusions inherent in the
middle-class self-image and thus aim at the heart of our society. The
fact that these kinds of themed works have grown fewer in recent years
is not due to a dearth of ideas. It comes rather from the scruples that
Angermann has developed while looking back on his work. Some of
the work he painted without so much as a second thought during the
group NORMAL period no longer seems sufficiently viable and durable
to him – and no one will deny that his powers of reflection have grown
after three more decades of artistic production. His en plein air painting
since 1987 has provided a welcome opportunity to yield to his work
drive without getting caught up in self-doubts.

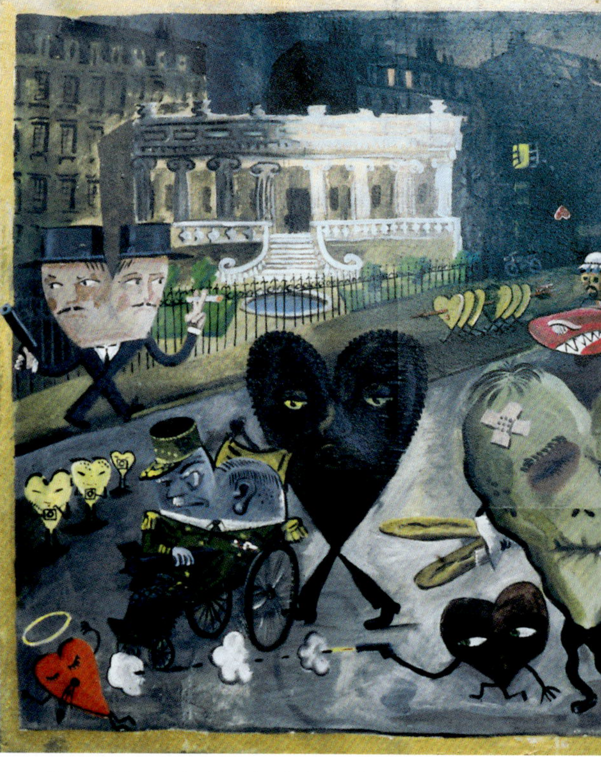

3   *Champs-Élysées*, 1980, öffentliche Malaktion / public painting
action, 11. Biennale de Paris, mit / with Milan Kunc und / and Jan Knap

The "Bear Paintings"

The "bear paintings" occupy a special place in Peter Angermann's oeuvre. Bears are by far his
most common motif; since 1976, he has done around sixty to date, in paintings, drawings and
silk-screen prints. The overture to this was an image that some would doubtless dismiss as
kitsch; and yet it moves us in a curious way. *Bear Picture 1* (1976, p. 57) shows two bears in
a tight embrace on a field at the forest edge, gazing at a giant red sun that has immersed the
meadow in front of them along with the entire forest in brilliant red light. Even the pitched tent
is aglow with red, and warming them from behind is a campfire. This little painting, like the
larger *For Renate* from the same year, is a painted declaration of love. Even the two bicycles have
been affected: their two front wheels are interlocked in what is clearly a symbolic form.

The metamorphosis from human to animal has a long history. Grandville was one of
the first artists to depict the society of his day in the form of animals – including bears – in
human situations.[18] And within the anthropomorphised animal world, the bear assumes an
outstanding place. It is regarded as extremely affable, protective and strong – although without
exploiting its strength in the manner of lions, wolves or tigers. These attributions have earned
it a permanent place in the nursery, as the teddy bear, Yogi Bear, Winnie-the-Pooh, Captain
Bluebear and so on – and all the other versions which allow us humans to try to make up for
the disappearance of real animals from our lives.[19]

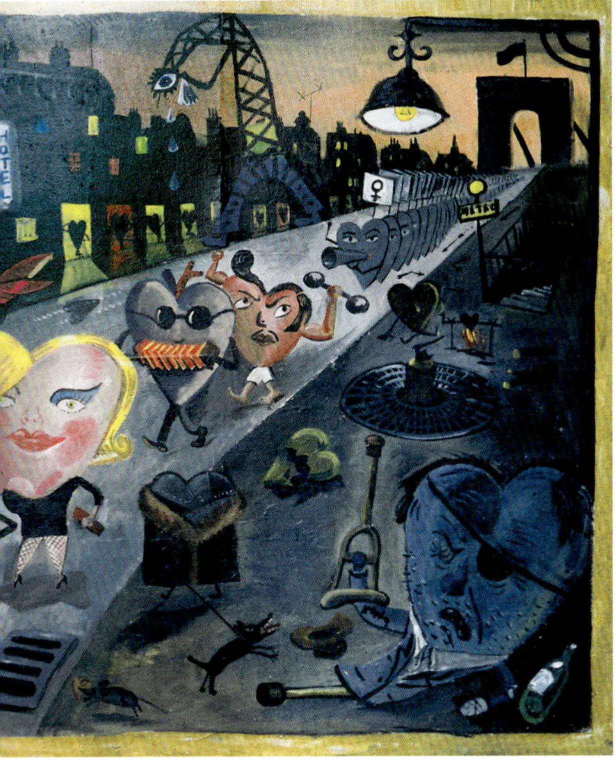

und nicht zuletzt Claes Oldenburg[17]. Sie scheiterten weniger an ihren künstlerischen Einfällen, als vielmehr an der äußerst wirkungsmächtigen Institution Kunst: dem kapitalistisch geprägten System von Kunstmarkt, Museum und Kunstkritik mit all seinen Verästelungen. Auch die Mitglieder der Gruppe NORMAL sollten über kurz oder lang davon absorbiert werden, was ihnen persönlich freilich nicht zum Nachteil gereichte.

Das Scheitern einer neuen Volkskunst bedeutet hingegen nicht das Ende des gesellschaftskritischen Impetus. Dieser begleitet Peter Angermann bis heute, und selbst seine Pleinairmalerei kann unter bestimmten Gesichtspunkten als gesellschaftskritisch betrachtet werden, verstößt sie doch nach wie vor gegen ein unausgesprochenes Verdikt der Hochkunst. Gemälde wie *Höhere Gewalt* (1981, S. 67), *Die Jüngste Sekunde* (1983, S. 75), *Turmbau zu Babel 1* (1989, S. 125), *Geisterfahrer* (1989, S. 128), *Jungbrunnen 1* (1991, S. 143), *Taub in Bischofsheim* (2007, S. 199), *Autonomoney 2* (2007, S. 201) oder *Hinten, fern…* (2008, S. 205) spielen allesamt mit den Ängsten und Selbsttäuschungen des bürgerlichen Selbstverständnisses und zielen damit mitten ins Herz unserer Gesellschaft. Dass solche thematischen Arbeiten in den letzten Jahren seltener geworden sind, liegt nicht an mangelnden Einfällen. Diese Verringerung ist den Skrupeln geschuldet, die Angermann im Rückblick auf sein eigenes Werk entwickelt hat. Einiges, was zu Zeiten der Gruppe NORMAL ohne Bedenken auf die Leinwand gebracht wurde, erscheint ihm heute nicht mehr tragfähig und langlebig genug – und dass sein Reflexionsvermögen nach drei weiteren Jahrzehnten künstlerischer Arbeit gewachsen ist, will ihm niemand absprechen. Die Pleinairmalerei bietet ihm seit 1987 eine willkommene Gelegenheit, seinem Arbeitsdrang nachzukommen, ohne sich in Selbstzweifeln zu verfangen.

Die „Bärenbilder"

Im Werk von Peter Angermann nehmen die „Bärenbilder" eine besondere Stellung ein. Bären sind das bei Weitem durchgängigste Motiv; von 1976 bis heute hat er etwa sechzig ins Bild gesetzt, in Gemälden, Zeichnungen und Siebdrucken. Den Auftakt bildet ein Motiv, das mancher Betrachter zweifellos als Kitsch abzutun bereit ist. Dennoch berührt es auf eigentümliche Weise. *Bärenbild 1* (1976, S. 57) zeigt uns ein Bärenpaar, eng umschlungen auf einer Wiese am Waldrand, mit Blick auf die riesige rote Sonne, die den Weiher vor dem Paar und den gesamten Wald in strahlend rotes Licht taucht. Selbst das aufgeschlagene Zelt glüht rot,

Angermann's *Bear Picture 1* is the painted response to the question of how one can still depict the joys of love without being consigned once and for all to artistic oblivion. Evidently the artist is not the slightest bit bothered about exposing himself to accusations of kitsch-mongering. On the contrary: every element is deliberately kitschy, so much so that industrially manufactured kitsch pales by comparison. Works on or with kitsch are certainly nothing new in art. Francis Picabia's elegant nudes (1940–43) and René Magritte's wild paintings from the *période vache* (around 1948) must be included, as must Sigmar Polke's *Reiherbilder* [*Heron Paintings*] (1968/69); the theme runs through the whole of Martin Kippenberger's oeuvre and certainly has not found its end in the kitschy motifs of Martin Eder. These excursions into kitsch always contain an appreciable amount of provocation directed at the dictates of high art and its recipients. But what is so provocative about Angermann's *Bear Picture 1* is that it doesn't even try to provoke; it wishes to be nothing more than a declaration of love in a totally convincing and fitting form. With his courage to transport a feeling that everyone knows into painting, albeit a feeling that is normally relegated to private realms or the gutter press, Angermann broke a taboo that from then on was to grant him a hitherto unknown freedom in his choice of motifs.

From then on he could project the bear theme onto every imaginable family situation, and once again a conceptual rigour manifests here in that he has reserved the topic solely for the pictures of his own family. We see the bear family out in the rain, under a capsized rowboat, or crouching in front of the fire (*Warm and Dry 1*, 1983, p. 77), at their home where Father Bear is at the computer, Mother Bear is busy doing the cooking and the children are romping about (*Bears at Home*, 1988, p. 120); or during an unintended break while travelling across the United States while Father Bear repairs the camper (*Yermo*, 1988, p. 121); during a hefty *Family Row 1* (1991, p. 141); or at the house of the grandparents, who look on happy and attentive while their grandchildren learn to ride a bike (*Grandparents Picture*, 2007, p. 200) – a picture that once again is graced by the evening sun, which is casting violet shadows onto the bright village street. All of these pictures, however cute they are at times, testify to Angermann's deep understanding of the human condition; they are in fact pictures of people, in the guise of bears, that are concerned with family life. Afterwards one asks oneself: in what way other than this could a contemporary artist even begin to think up a coherent family picture? It is precisely because Angermann has chosen an unusual form of defamiliarisation as his means that the pictures are so convincing and touching. No question, the majority of these painted images are idylls; as such, they are always under suspicion of conveying a false impression. But that is exactly where the artistic licence lies that Angermann has struggled to attain over all the years: he simply chooses to lend the image of the family such a peaceable if not blithe aura, one that strikes many of his contemporaries as being so remote that it is absurd.

Sprezzatura and Landscape Painting

In *The Book of the Courtier*, first published in 1528, the author Baldassare Castiglione draws up a canon of rules by means of a number of conversations that are intended to instruct the

und von hinten wärmt ein Lagerfeuer. Das kleine Gemälde ist, wie das größere *Für Renate* aus demselben Jahr, eine gemalte Liebeserklärung. Selbst die beiden Fahrräder sind davon affiziert: Die Art, wie ihre Vorderreifen ineinandergreifen, ist nichts anderes als eine symbolische Form.

Die Metamorphose von Mensch zu Tier hat eine lange Vorgeschichte. Grandville war wohl der erste Künstler, der die gesamte menschliche Gesellschaft seiner Zeit in Form von Situationen mit Tieren darstellte – Bären eingeschlossen.[18] Innerhalb der vermenschlichten Tierwelt nimmt der Bär wiederum einen herausragenden Platz ein. Er gilt als ausgesprochen gutmütig, beschützend, stark, aber ohne seine Stärke auszunutzen wie etwa der Löwe, der Tiger oder der Wolf. Diese Zuschreibungen haben ihm einen dauerhaften Platz im Kinderzimmer gesichert, als Teddybär, Yogi Bär, Pu der Bär, Käpt'n Blaubär usw. – wie auch immer die Varianten heißen, mit denen wir Menschen das Verschwinden der Tiere aus unserem Leben zu kompensieren suchen.[19]

Angermanns Gemälde *Bärenbild 1* ist die gemalte Antwort auf die Frage, wie man heutzutage noch Liebesglück darstellen kann, ohne sich rettungslos ins Abseits zu begeben. Offenbar kümmert es den Künstler nicht im Geringsten, sich dem Kitschvorwurf auszusetzen, im Gegenteil: Alle Elemente sind gezielt kitschig, gar so kitschig, dass jedes industriell gefertigte Kitschprodukt daneben verblasst. Nun ist die Arbeit am Kitsch oder mit Kitsch gewiss keine Neuigkeit in der Kunst. Francis Picabias elegante Frauenakte (1940–1943) und René Magrittes wüste Gemälde der *période vache* (um 1948) gehören dazu, ebenso wie Sigmar Polkes *Reiherbilder* (1968/69); sie zieht sich durch das gesamte Werk von Martin Kippenberger und findet sicherlich in den kitschigen Motiven von Martin Eder kein Ende. Immer ist mit diesen Referenzen auf Kitsch eine gehörige Portion Provokation gegenüber den Diktionen der Hochkunst und ihren Rezipienten im Spiel. Das Provokante an Angermanns *Bärenbild 1* aber liegt darin, dass es gar nicht provozieren will; es will nichts anderes sein als eine völlig glaubwürdige und angemessene Form der Liebeserklärung. Mit diesem Mut, ein Gefühl in die Malerei zu transportieren, das jeder kennt, das aber ansonsten durchgängig in den Bereich des Privaten oder der Regenbogenpresse verbannt ist, begeht Angermann einen Tabubruch, der ihm von nun an eine Anzahl ungeahnter neuer Freiheiten in der Motivwahl bescheren wird.

Fortan kann er das Bärenthema auf alle möglichen Familiensituationen projizieren, und es liegt wiederum eine konzeptuelle Konsequenz darin, das Sujet ausschließlich den Bildern der eigenen Familie vorzubehalten. Wir sehen die Bärenfamilie im Regen unter einem umgedrehten Ruderboot vor dem Feuer kauernd (*Warm und Trocken 1*, 1983, S. 77), im eigenen Heim, wo Vaterbär mit dem Computer und Mutterbär mit Kochen beschäftigt ist, während die Kinder herumtollen (*Bären daheim*, 1988. S. 120), bei unfreiwilliger Rast auf der Reise durch die Vereinigten Staaten, während Vaterbär das Wohnmobil repariert (*Yermo*, 1988, S. 121), beim handfesten *Familienkrach 1* (1991, S. 141) oder bei den Großeltern, die beglückt und aufmerksam zuschauen, wie dem Enkel das Fahrradfahren beigebracht wird (*Großelternbild*, 2007, S. 200) – auch dieses Bild ziert wieder die rote Abendsonne, und sie wirft violette Schatten auf die leuchtende Dorfstraße. All diese Bilder, so putzig sie teilweise daherkommen mögen, bezeugen Angermanns tiefes Verständnis für die *conditio humana*; es sind eigentlich

untitled courtier as to how to become a *gentiluomo* – a universally educated person. In these didactic discussions, the Count of Canossa gives the following advice: "But having before now often considered whence this grace springs, laying aside those men who have it by nature, I find one universal rule concerning it, which seems to me worth more in this matter than any other in all things human that are done or said: and that is to avoid affectation to the uttermost and as it were a very sharp and dangerous rock; and, to use possibly a new word, to practise in everything a certain 'nonchalance' that shall conceal design and show that what is done and said is done without effort and almost without thought." [20]

The key word in this translation is "nonchalance" – *sprezzatura*. It contrasts with "affectation" (*affettazione*); recently a German author translated *sprezzatura* as "Leichtigkeit" – "levity" – and *affettazione* as "Affektiertheit" – "affectedness". [21] The history of art contains a host of examples that demonstrate this kind of lofty composure. To name one famous painting: in Rembrandt's *Nightwatch* (1642, detail ill. 4) we see to the front on the right of the lieutenant a dog barking in the shadows. On closer inspection, we see that it is made up solely of a few fleeting brushstrokes which nevertheless give a convincing image of an irritable dog. The *sprezzatura* of the dog comes across as particularly effective inasmuch as all the other sections of the painting – as for instance the depiction of the lieutenant – have been done with painstaking accuracy. The representation of the dog is no less lifelike, just that Rembrandt seems to have concealed his artistic gifts at this point. In fact the *sprezzatura* is as apt for this moving, casual dog motif as is the precision that has been used for the central but motionless figures. In this way the apparent nonchalance here demonstrates the outstanding abilities of the artist as painter.

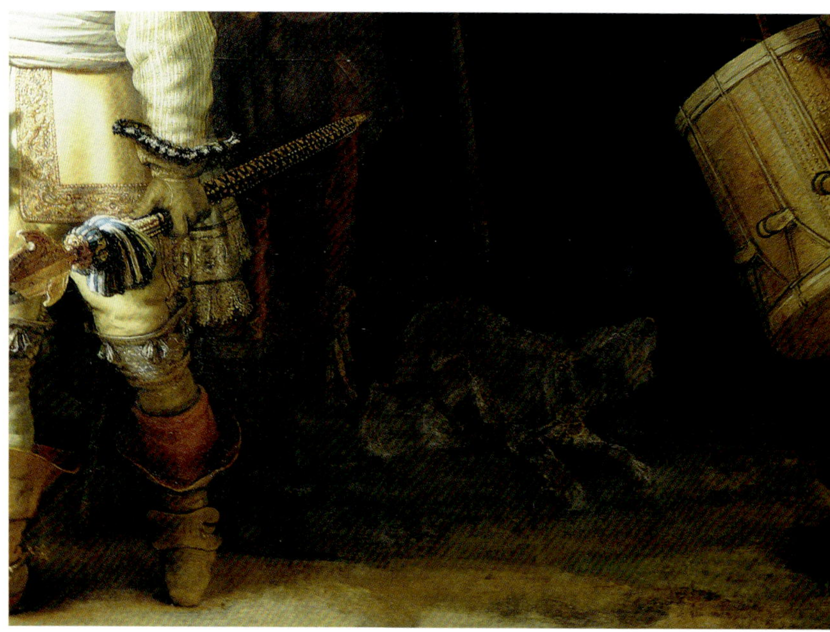

4   Rembrandt Harmensz. van Rijn, *Nachtwache / Nightwatch*, 1642 (Detail / detail), Rijksmuseum Amsterdam

When we now look at Peter Angermann's painting, we encounter the experience of *sprezzatura* time and again: the apparent lightness and effortlessness that actually conceal the artist's creative power, but simultaneously seem the only appropriate means for the subject matter. And it likewise manifests *in nuce* in all the plein-air paintings, which are not bound to any particular subject.

A lot has already been written on the anachronism of sitting today outdoors at the easel and painting what one sees. [22] Doubtless this kind of art practice amounts to yet another freedom which Angermann the artist has permitted himself, despite all the taboos; and he has done so ever since 1987. Our concern here however is mainly with the nature of the representation, and in this respect the term *sprezzatura* seems very instructive.

Menschenbilder im Bärenkostüm, die vom Familienleben handeln. Im Nachhinein fragt man sich: Wie anders als hier könnte überhaupt ein zeitgenössischer Künstler ein stimmiges Familienbild entwerfen? Gerade weil Angermann das Mittel einer ungewöhnlichen Verfremdung wählt, wirken die Bilder so glaubwürdig und anrührend. Fraglos sind die Mehrzahl dieser Bildfindungen gemalte Idyllen; als solche sind sie immer dem Verdacht des falschen Scheins ausgesetzt. Aber gerade darin liegt die künstlerische Freiheit, die Angermann sich über viele Jahre erkämpft hat: dass er es sich einfach herausnimmt, das Bild der Familie mit einer derart friedfertigen, ja glücklichen Aura zu versehen, die für viele Zeitgenossen so weit entfernt scheint, dass sie ihnen geradezu abwegig vorkommt.

Sprezzatura und Landschaftsmalerei

Im *Buch vom Hofmann*, 1528 veröffentlicht, entfaltet dessen Autor Baldassare Castiglione in Form von Gesprächen einen Regelkanon, anhand dessen der Höfling bürgerlicher Herkunft zu einem *gentiluomo* – einem universal versierten Menschen –ausgebildet werden soll. In diesen Lehrgesprächen erteilt der Graf Canossa folgenden Ratschlag: „Ich habe nun des öfteren bei mir nachgedacht, woher die Anmut mit Ausnahme der durch die Gunst der Gestirne erhaltenen eigentlich stamme, und eine Regel gefunden, die mir allgemein gültig zu sein scheint bei allen menschlichen Taten und Reden: man muß jede Ziererei gleich einer spitzigen und gefährlichen Klippe vermeiden und, um eine neue Wendung zu gebrauchen, eine gewisse Nachlässigkeit zur Schau tragen, die die angewandte Mühe verbirgt und alles, was man tut und spricht, als ohne die geringste Kunst und gleichsam absichtslos hervorgebracht erscheinen lässt." [20]

Das Stichwort dieser Übersetzung ist „Nachlässigkeit" – *sprezzatura*. Sie steht im Gegensatz zur „Ziererei" (*affettazione*); jüngst hat eine Autorin *sprezzatura* mit „Leichtigkeit" übersetzt, *affettazione* mit „Affektiertheit".[21] Die Geschichte der Kunst ist reichlich gefüllt mit Beispielen für diese Art von Souveränität. Um ein berühmtes Gemälde zu zitieren: In Rembrandts *Nachtwache* (1642, Detail Textabb. 4) sehen wir vorne rechts neben dem Leutnant einen kläffenden Hund im Schatten der Szenerie. Aus der Nähe betrachtet, gewahren wir, dass sich seine Gestalt bloß aus wenigen flüchtigen Pinselstrichen zusammensetzt, die aber dennoch das gültige Bild eines gereizten Hundes ergeben. Die *sprezzatura* in der Gestaltung des Hundes kommt insbesondere dadurch zur Geltung, dass andere Partien des Bildes – wie zum Beispiel die Darstellung des Leutnants – mit akribischer Detailgenauigkeit ausgeführt sind. Die Darstellung des Hundes ist nicht weniger naturgetreu, nur verbirgt Rembrandt scheinbar sein malerisches Können an dieser Stelle. Tatsächlich ist die *sprezzatura* im Hinblick auf das bewegte, beiläufige Motiv des Hundes ebenso angemessen wie die Präzision im Hinblick auf die unbewegten Hauptfiguren. Die scheinbare Nachlässigkeit in diesem Bereich erweist sich solchermaßen als Beleg der überragenden malerischen Fähigkeiten des Künstlers.

Wenn wir nun die Malerei von Peter Angermann ins Auge fassen, stellt sich immer wieder das Erlebnis der *sprezzatura* ein: die scheinbar mühelose Leichtigkeit, die des Künstlers malerische Potenz eigentlich verbirgt, doch gleichzeitig der jeweiligen Thematik einzig

Let us look for instance at the painting *Streit* (2012, p. 216)
– the title is taken from the name of a north Bavarian village. In
some places the pink of the ground can be seen; but instead of being
covered over, it has been allowed to participate quite naturally in
the things that make up the painting. In the region of the sky it
conveys the impression of warmth and light, in the middle ground it
represents the fields and meadows, and in the foreground it grows up
through the grass. Finally, the same pink appears as a surface colour
in the stream, where it acts as part of the water's reflection. The lightness with which the picture ground is drawn into the finished image
is astonishing. It lends an unmistakable coherence to the whole that
could never have been achieved by naturalistic means. Let us look
at the stream: a simple zigzag describes the passage of the water.
Additional, coarser zigzags: the forest. A couple of dabs of white,
extending more or less lengthways: the clouds. Three loose, in some cases wafer-thin lines:
vapour trails from aeroplanes. All of this with a nonchalance that astonishes, precisely because
when viewed as a whole, it convinces on all counts. And when as here we also have the fortune
to have the actual model for the picture in front of us in the form of a photo, we realise how
unprepossessing the stretch of countryside actually was where the artist set up his easel – and
how different from the painting (ill. 5). Viewed in this way, Angermann's outdoor paintings
are anything but *vedute* – that genre of landscape painting that aspires to topographical
fidelity. They are the result rather of a complex painting procedure in which the artist's mental
alacrity, imagination and artistic abilities interact with his perception of the world outside.
Angermann's en plein air painting is interior picture and exterior picture to the same degree, as
achieved by years of painterly practice.

We find this inside-outside relationship depicted metaphorically in the painting *Self as
Klein Bottle* (1987, p. 118). The artist is depicted lying on the beach in the company of other
sun-worshippers, while the image of the beach simultaneously leaps up into his own eye. An
enthusiast of mathematics and physics, Angermann has based his painting on the famous
model devised by the mathematician Felix Klein: a geometrical object that disallows any un-
equivocal distinction between inside and out.[23] And therein lies the secret of Angermann's en
plein air painting.

It is no accident that the artist himself observed that it was outdoor painting that first
turned him into a "colourist"[24]; his knowledge of the possibilities of colourism has only first
matured through this activity. What is surprising about this development in the intrinsic
value of colour is that we as viewers even take what seem to be randomly chosen colours to be
quite normal. The violet of the motorway in *A9* (1998, p. 157) looks totally realistic, although
asphalt never appears in this colour. The realistic impression is communicated however by the
colour scheme of the entire painting. Or let us look at the bright green sections at the front of
Oak Tree on Deutes Hill (2010, p. 213), which mutate in the region of the violet-grey street into

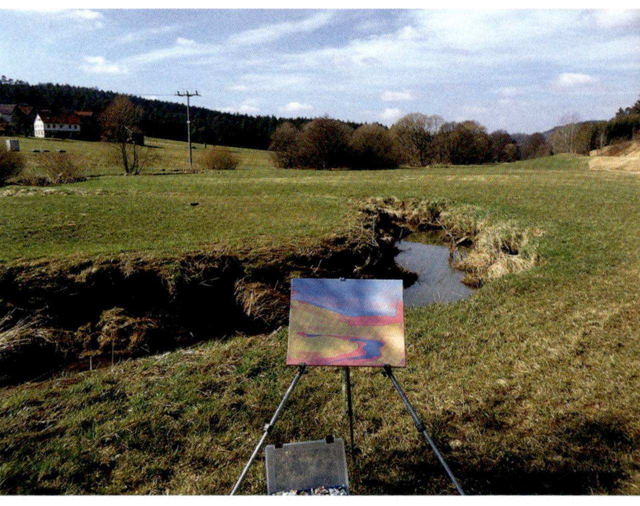

5   Pleinairmalerei in der Nähe von / Plein-air painting made near Streit, 2012

angemessen erscheint. Und sie zeigt sich bei den Pleinair-Gemälden, die ja keiner bestimmten Thematik verpflichtet sind, sozusagen *in nuce*.

Über den Anachronismus, sich heute noch mit der Staffelei nach draußen zu begeben, um zu malen, was man sieht, ist bereits mehrfach geschrieben worden.[22] Zweifellos bedeutet diese Art der Kunstausübung eine weitere Freiheit, die der Künstler Angermann sich gegen alle vermeintlichen Tabus herausnimmt, und er tut dies schon seit 1987. Uns geht es hier aber vorrangig um die Art und Weise der Darstellung, und hier erscheint der Terminus *sprezzatura* sehr erhellend.

Betrachten wir etwa das Gemälde *Streit* (2012, S. 216) – der Titel benennt ein Dorf in Nordbayern. An manchen Stellen tritt das Rosa des Bildgrundes hervor. Anstatt kaschiert zu sein, partizipiert der Bildgrund völlig selbstverständlich an den Bilddingen. Im Bereich des Himmels vermittelt er den Eindruck von Wärme und Licht, im Mittelgrund stellt er Feld und Weide dar, im Vordergrund wächst er durch das Gras hindurch. Schließlich taucht dasselbe Rosa als Oberflächenfarbe im Bereich des Baches auf, wo es als Teil der Spiegelung des Wassers fungiert. Diese Leichtigkeit, mit der der Bildgrund in die fertige Bildgestalt einbezogen wird, ist frappierend. Sie verleiht dem Ganzen eine unverwechselbare Stimmigkeit, die mit naturalistischen Mitteln niemals erreichbar wäre. Schauen wir auf den Bach: Eine einfache Zickzacklinie beschreibt die Bewegung des Wassers. Weitere, gröbere Zickzacklinien: der Wald. Ein paar weiße Tupfer, mehr oder minder langgezogen: die Wolken. Drei lose, teils hauchdünne Striche: Kondensstreifen von Flugzeugen. All das ist mit einer Nonchalance vorgetragen, die in Staunen versetzt, gerade weil sie im Ganzen gesehen in jeder Hinsicht überzeugt. Und wenn wir noch, wie in diesem Fall, das Glück haben, der realen Bildvorlage in Form eines Schnappschusses habhaft zu werden, wird uns bewusst, wie unscheinbar das Stück Landschaft, vor dem der Künstler seine Staffelei aufgebaut hat, in Wirklichkeit ist – und wie verschieden von dem Gemälde (Textabb. 5). So gesehen sind Angermanns Freilichtbilder alles andere als Veduten – jene Gattung der Landschaftsdarstellung, die sich um topografische Genauigkeit bemüht. Sie sind vielmehr Resultate eines komplexen Malvorgangs, bei dem Auffassungsgabe, Vorstellungskraft und künstlerische Kompetenz mit der Wahrnehmung der Außenwelt zusammenspielen. Angermanns Pleinairmalerei ist im selben Maße Innenbild wie Außenbild, vermittelt durch viele Jahre malerischer Praxis.

Metaphorisch dargestellt finden wir dieses Innen-Außen-Verhältnis in dem Gemälde *Selbst als Kleinsche Flasche* (1987, S. 118). Der Künstler liegt am Strand in Gesellschaft anderer Sonnenanbeter, während das Bild des Strandes zugleich seinen eigenen Augen entspringt. Mathematik- und physikbegeistert wie Angermann ist, hat der das Bild nach dem bekannten Modell des Mathematikers Felix Klein entworfen: ein geometrisches Objekt, das keine eindeutige Orientierung zwischen Innen und Außen zulässt.[23] Eben darin liegt auch das Geheimnis von Angermanns Pleinair-Bildern.

Nicht von ungefähr hat der Künstler selbst festgestellt, dass ihn erst die Freilichtmalerei zum „Koloristen" gemacht habe.[24] Seine Kenntnis koloristischer Möglichkeiten ist erst mit dieser Beschäftigung gereift. Das überraschendste Moment an dieser Entwicklung

pink-coloured patches: a colouristic trifle, but one that radiates an enormous influence over the picture as a whole. Or the painting *Heron* (1995, p. 152): a few dabs of brown in the area of the stream are enough to give the perfect impression of a water reflection. All of this freedom as a painter, done with such facility, belongs to the realm of *sprezzatura*.

It is in the nature of en plein air painting that the formats are always small. Angermann has constructed for this express purpose a wooden box that enables him to paint two pictures size 40 × 50 cm and to transport them at the same time on a bicycle – even while they are still wet. With this baggage he tours the district, which grants him closer contact with the countryside and its potential images than if he were to drive around in a car.

On the basis of the works done in the countryside, Angermann has also regularly painted large landscapes in his studio. These include such outstanding works as *August 1* (1989, p. 131), *December 1* (1990, p. 138) and *May (Walberla)* (1990, p. 133). Painted with loose gestures, they give a convincing idea of the seasons, however anachronistic the subject might seem. But what other contemporary paintings really convey to the viewer that he is completely at home here and at one with himself? That is a quality which, in an age when people are almost literally perforated by the omnipresence of the mass media, once again assumes a utopian character. Or *Nocturne* (1990, p. 137) – done simply with the paint left on his palette, which mixed together yielded those grey tones that dominate the picture. It goes without saying that Angermann is aware that this tonal reduction recalls James A. M. Whistler's chromatics; indeed, the title indicates that the piece is an homage to Whistler's famous painting *Nocturne: Blue and Gold – Old Battersea Bridge* (c. 1872–75, ill. 6). Be that as it may, Angermann's loose-wristed version is a contemporary painting *par excellence*.

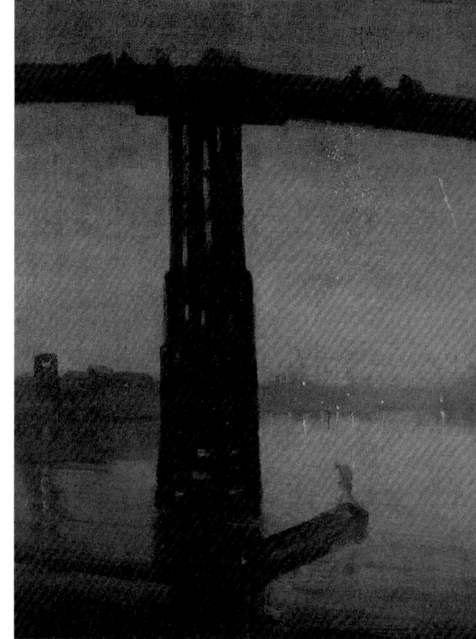

6   James A. M. Whistler, *Nocturne: Blue and Gold – Old Battersea Bridge*, ca. 1872–1875, Tate Gallery, London

The *Tertium Comparationis*

In view of his growing number of plein-air paintings over the last thirty years, some writers have noted a dichotomy between Angermann's themed paintings and his landscapes – two threads in his oeuvre that are apparently hard to reconcile. For which reason we shall look at this juncture for the *tertium comparationis*, for the missing link between the two directions.

In his painting *World Picture* (1997, p. 156) the artist manages to give a kind of résumé of his landscape paintings. Starting from his own village of Thurndorf, he has painted a bird's-eye landscape – a view that in reality could only be seen from a balloon. But the painting goes one step beyond: the horizon curves to form a globe, taking the whole landscape with it. In this way the village becomes the centre of the world, and its horizon ends as a consequence on the border to the Upper Palatinate – as indicated by the topographical names inscribed on the canvas. We see the artist in person, floating high above in the sky – and simultaneously in outer space – busily painting the stars on the red canopy of the heavens. Angermann is watching his own self at work, and with this self-observation the picture bursts the bounds of the landscape painting.

des Eigenwerts der Farbe besteht darin, dass wir als Betrachter auch scheinbar willkürliche
Farbsetzungen als völlig selbstverständlich empfinden. Das Violett der Autobahn in *A9* (1998,
S. 157) wirkt geradezu realistisch, obwohl der Asphalt diese Farbe gar nicht hergibt. Der rea-
listische Eindruck wird aber durch die Farbkomposition des Bildes insgesamt vermittelt. Oder
betrachten wir jene lichtgrünen Partien vorne in *Eiche am Deutes* (2010, S. 213), die im Bereich
der violett-grauen Straße zu rosafarbenen Flecken mutieren: eine koloristische Petitesse, die
aber eine enorme Wirkung für das Bildganze ausstrahlt. Oder das Bild *Reiher* (1995, S. 152):
Wenige braune Tupfer im Bereich des Baches genügen, um den vollkommenen Eindruck einer
Wasserspiegelung zu entfalten. All diese malerischen Freiheiten, die so leichthändig daherkommen, gehören in den Bereich der *sprezzatura*.

Es liegt in der Natur der Sache, dass die Pleinair-Bilder stets im kleinen Format gemalt
werden. Angermann hat eigens für diesen Zweck eine Holzkiste gebaut, die es ihm ermöglicht,
zwei Bilder im Format 40 × 50 cm gleichzeitig mit dem Fahrrad zu transportieren – auch im
noch nassen Zustand. Mit diesem Gepäck durchstreift er die Gegend, was ihm einen engeren
Kontakt mit der Natur und ihren möglichen Sujets erlaubt, als wenn er mit dem Auto führe.

Ausgehend von den in der freien Natur entstandenen Arbeiten realisiert Angermann
immer wieder auch großformatige Landschaftsbilder im Atelier. Dazu gehören so herausragende
Werke wie *August 1* (1989, S. 131), *Dezember 1* (1990, S. 138) oder *Mai (Walberla)* (1990,
S. 133). Mit lockerer Geste gemalt, geben sie überzeugende Vorstellungen von den Jahreszeiten,
so unzeitgemäß das Thema auch anmuten mag. Aber welche anderen zeitgenössischen Gemälde
vermitteln schon dem Betrachter, hier sei er ganz zu Hause und ganz bei sich selbst? Das ist eine
Qualität, die in einer Zeit, da die Menschen von der Allgegenwart der Massenmedien geradezu
perforiert werden, schon wieder utopische Züge annimmt. Oder *Nocturno* (1990, S. 137) –
gemalt bloß aus Resten auf der Farbpalette, die vermischt jenen grauen Grundton ergeben,
der die gesamte Bildgestalt beherrscht. Dass die tonige Farbigkeit an James A. M. Whistlers
Farbarrangements erinnert, ist Angermann selbstverständlich bewusst, und auch der Titel deutet
darauf hin, dass die Arbeit als Hommage an Whistlers berühmtes Gemälde *Nocturne: Blue and
Gold – Old Battersea Bridge* (ca. 1872–1875, Textabb. 6) zu verstehen ist. Nichtsdestoweniger ist
Angermanns leichthändige Version ein zeitgenössisches Bild *par excellence*.

Das *Tertium comparationis*

Angesichts der wachsenden Zahl von Pleinair-Bildern in den letzten dreißig Jahren tut sich
für manche Rezipienten eine Dichotomie zwischen thematischen Bildern einerseits und Land-
schaftsbildern andererseits auf – zwei Stränge im Œuvre von Peter Angermann, die scheinbar
nur schwer miteinander in Einklang zu bringen sind. Daher suchen wir an dieser Stelle nach
dem *Tertium comparationis*, nach dem Missing Link zwischen beiden Werkgruppen.

In dem Gemälde *Weltbild* (1997, S. 156) gelingt es dem Künstler, eine Art Resümee
seiner Landschaftsmalerei zu ziehen. Ausgehend von seinem Wohnort Thurndorf malt er
hier eine Übersichtslandschaft – eine Ansicht, die in Wirklichkeit wohl nur vom Ballon aus

Another work, *Landscape with Blind Spot* (1999, p. 160), picks up this thread of self-observation. As alluded to by the inscription in the painting, the idea came in its inception from the sociologist Niklas Luhmann. In his systems theory, Luhmann discusses the concept of observation, "defined as an operation of distinguishing and denoting" [25]. He comes to the conclusion that "observation alone is not capable of distinguishing between true and false" [26]. This inability to reflect on one's own observation outside of itself is referred to by Luhmann as the "blind spot". It can only be eliminated by a "second-order observation": "This second-order observation assumes that one distinguishes the observed observer, uses a different distinction to the one for oneself." [27] Nevertheless, "however great the interest in refutation or correction … the second-order observer … remains an aspect of the same systems of recursive observation of observations" [28].

Angermann's painting amounts to an ingenious implementation of Luhmann's notion of observation. Once again the scene is Thurndorf, but now we as observers are on the ground. At the centre of the picture we see the characteristic silhouette of Joseph Beuys as an elided surface (which nevertheless casts shadows). As the painter of the landscape, Angermann assumes the position of observer, who distinguishes between trees, fields, meadows, village, sky, etc. But then he introduces a second-order observation: the result is Beuys's silhouette, which does not enter his gaze as landscape painter because it acts as a blind spot in his role as prime observer. In this way he succeeds in integrating his own past as Beuys student as an unconsciously conscious element, which in this case means: embodying this Other in the painting.

We can also find further works where Angermann experiments with the aim of wresting new facets from the landscape painting. One of his earliest attempts has been preserved in a sketchbook that the artist did during a trip round the USA in 1982/83. *Dry Lagoon* (1983, ill. 7) shows a landscape consisting solely of words. Seeing and reading, we get an idea of the whole, which must however remain vague because our minds have constantly to switch back and forth between concept and perceptual image. This experiment has an echo in a painting that languished, unfinished, for a long while in the depot, until recently when the artist tackled it again. In *Vapour Trails* (2013, p. 217) the title inscribed on the painting develops as writing from the painted vapour trail in the sky, and correspondingly we see "junge Kartoffeln" [new potatoes] unexpectedly revealed by the field. And by the reverse token, the writing transforms seamlessly into the ornamentation in the picture.

Likewise the painting *Curve (Winter)* (2013, p. 221), an image that is shown here in its sixth incarnation at least, is in fact a landscape painting, but without any reference to a particular location. The idea behind the work comes from a productive misunderstanding about the curvature of space that is mentioned in the Theory of Relativity – and presumably the only landscape in the world that permits itself to be hung from two different sides. What

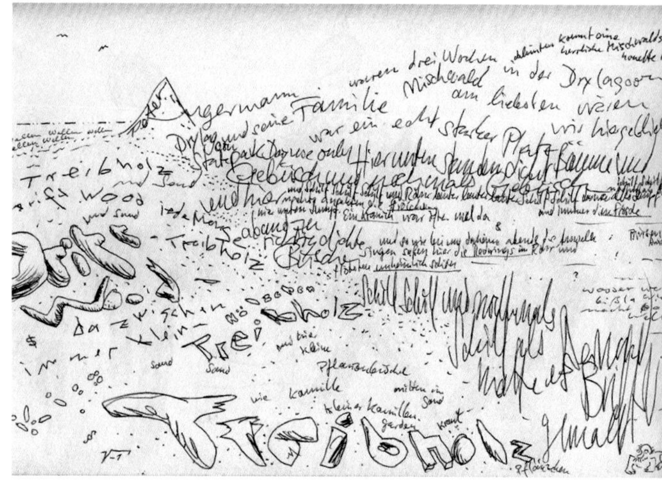

7 *Dry Lagoon*, 1983, Kugelschreiber auf Papier / ballpoint pen on paper

sichtbar wäre. Aber das Gemälde geht noch darüber hinaus: Der Horizont krümmt sich zum Erdball und mit ihm die ganze Landschaft. Solchermaßen gerät das Dorf zum Zentrum der Welt, und deren Horizont endet folgerichtig an der Grenze der Oberpfalz; darauf deuten die ins Bild geschriebenen topografischen Namen. Wir sehen den Künstler selbst hoch oben in der Luft – und gleichzeitig im All – schweben, damit beschäftigt, die Sterne am roten Firmament zu malen. Angermann sieht sich hier also selbst bei der Arbeit zu, und in dieser Selbstbeobachtung sprengt das Bild den Rahmen des Landschaftsbildes.

Ein weiteres Werk, *Landschaft mit Blindem Fleck* (1999, S. 160), nimmt den Faden der Selbstbeobachtung auf. Wie die Inschrift im Bild andeutet, verdankt sich die Idee im Ansatz der Lektüre des Soziologen Niklas Luhmann. In seiner Systemtheorie spricht Luhmann über den Begriff des Beobachtens, „definiert als Operation des Unterscheidens und Bezeichnens"[25]. Er kommt zu dem Schluss, „dass die Beobachtung selbst nicht in der Lage ist, in ihrem Vollzug zwischen wahr und unwahr zu unterscheiden"[26]. Diesen Mangel, die eigene Beobachtung nicht außerhalb ihrer selbst reflektieren zu können, nennt Luhmann den „blinden Fleck". Er kann nur durch eine „Beobachtung zweiter Ordnung" eliminiert werden: „Diese Beobachtung zweiter Ordnung setzt voraus, dass man den beobachteten Beobachter unterscheidet, also eine andere Unterscheidung verwendet als er selbst."[27] Dennoch bleibt der „Beobachter zweiter Ordnung […] bei allem Interesse an Widerlegung oder Korrektur […] Moment desselben Systems rekursiven Beobachtens von Beobachtungen"[28].

Angermanns Gemälde initiiert eine höchst geistreiche Umsetzung des Luhmann'schen Beobachtungskonzepts. Wieder ist der Schauplatz Thurndorf, nur dass wir uns als Betrachter nunmehr auf dem Boden befinden. Inmitten des Bildes sehen wir die charakteristische Silhouette von Joseph Beuys wie eine ausgesparte Fläche (die nichtsdestotrotz Schatten wirft). Als Maler der Landschaft nimmt Angermann die Position des Beobachters ein, er unterscheidet zwischen Bäumen, Feld, Wiese, Dorf, Himmel usf. Dann aber führt er eine Beobachtung zweiter Ordnung ein: Das Ergebnis ist die Silhouette von Beuys, die ihm als Landschaftsmaler nicht in den Blick fällt, weil sie in dieser ersten Beobachterrolle als blinder Fleck fungiert. So gelingt es ihm, seine eigene Vergangenheit als Schüler von Beuys als unbewusst-bewusstes Element zu integrieren, und das bedeutet in diesem Fall: dieses Andere dem Bild einzuverleiben.

Auch sonst finden wir bei Angermann Experimente, die darauf abzielen, dem Landschaftsbild neue Facetten abzuringen. Einer der frühesten Versuche ist in einem Skizzenbuch aufbewahrt, das der Künstler während seiner Reise durch die USA 1982/83 angefertigt hat. *Dry Lagoon* (1983, Textabb. 7) zeigt eine Landschaft, die ausschließlich aus Worten besteht. Sehend-lesend bekommen wir eine Vorstellung vom Ganzen, die allerdings vage bleibt, weil unser Gehirn ständig zwischen Begriff und Anschauung hin und her springen muss. Dieses Experiment findet seinen Niederschlag in einem Gemälde, das lange Zeit unvollendet im Depot geschlummert hat, bis der Künstler es jüngst nochmals in Angriff nahm. In *Kondensstreifen* (2013, S. 217) entwickelt sich der Titel als Schrift im Bild aus dem gemalten Kondensstreifen am Himmel, und auf dem Boden korrespondieren dazu „junge Kartoffeln",

is so astonishing about this composition is that the picture's inhabitants are not in the slightest aware of this painted nightmare. Everything follows its normal course, as if this village were the most ordinary place on the planet. Here Angermann's *heimat* paintings have literally been turned on their head.

Similarly the painting *Streetview* (2011, p. 219) – which is also a special kind of landscape painting – operates with unusual curvatures of space. And once again it comes under Luhmann's category of "observing the observation". The daily round of the grey suburb is gently disrupted by the curious presence of floating spheres: they show the same street, but suddenly in the most beautiful colours, under a radiant blue sky: a reference to the photos that are faded in during a virtual trip on Google Earth when one switches to the "Street View" mode. In Angermann's case, though, the balance between reality and virtuality has shifted in favour of the latter. The protagonist in the painting is looking quite enviously at the beautiful new world that is being proffered him – tellingly in the form of bright soap bubbles. But in painterly terms, both reality and virtuality are on the same level. As such the work not only contains a slice of media criticism; in the new paragone debate about the merits of painting versus new media, this idea clearly comes down on the side of the former.

These examples show that the themed paintings and landscape paintings in Angermann's work do not constitute a hard-and-fast dichotomy. We find rather a number of fluid transitions between the two. The pictorial experiences that the two yield in their respective areas are effortlessly absorbed by the other. Angermann's unreserved courage in working with such startling ideas corresponds to his courage in using *sprezzatura* for the form and colour of his landscapes. And conversely, the colourist experiments that have their traditional place there extend far into the themed works. Ultimately it is all the one and the same artist who is at home in both genres: his name is Peter Angermann.

die der Acker unversehens freigibt. Umgekehrt geht das Geschriebene übergangslos in das Ornament des Bildes über.

Auch das Gemälde *Krümmung (Winter)* (2013, S. 221), eine Bildfindung, die hier mindestens in der sechsten Fassung vorliegt, ist eigentlich ein Landschaftsbild, jedoch ohne Referenz auf eine bestimmte Topografie. Die Bildidee ist aus einem produktiven Missverständnis der durch die Relativitätstheorie zur Sprache gebrachten Raumzeitkrümmung geboren – und vermutlich das weltweit einzige Landschaftsbild, das eine Aufhängung an zwei verschiedenen Bildseiten erlaubt. Das Frappierende an dieser Komposition ist, dass der gemalte Alptraum seitens der Bewohner des Bildes nicht im Geringsten wahrgenommen wird. Alles geht seinen Gang, als sei dieses Dorf das allergewöhnlichste der Welt. Hier steht Angermanns Heimatmalerei buchstäblich Kopf.

Auch das Gemälde *Streetview* (2011, S. 219) – ebenfalls eine Sonderform des Landschaftsbildes – arbeitet mit ungewöhnlichen Raumkrümmungen. Und es fällt wiederum unter die Luhmann'sche Kategorie „Beobachtung der Beobachtung". Der alltägliche Gang durch die graue Vorstadt wird durch die merkwürdige Präsenz schwebender Kugeln irritiert: Sie zeigen dieselbe Straße mit einem Mal in schönster Farbigkeit und bei strahlend blauem Himmel: Referenz auf die eingeblendeten Fotos, die beim virtuellen Gang durch Google Earth auftauchen, wenn man dort den „Street View"-Modus anklickt. Bei Angermann hat sich allerdings die Gewichtung zwischen Realität und Virtualität zugunsten Letzterer verschoben. Der Protagonist des Bildes schaut geradezu neidisch auf die schöne neue Welt, die ihm sinnigerweise in Form von bunten Seifenblasen geboten wird. Beide aber – Realität und Virtualität – liegen malerisch gesehen auf derselben Ebene. Insofern beinhaltet das Bild nicht nur ein Stück Medienkritik; im Paragone-Streit zwischen Malerei und neuen Medien entscheidet diese Idee eindeutig zugunsten der Ersteren.

Diese Beispiele zeigen, dass sich thematische Bilder und Landschaftsbilder im Werk von Angermann nicht wirklich dichotomisch verhalten. Vielmehr finden wir eine Reihe von fließenden Übergängen. Die bildnerischen Erfahrungen, die jeweils in beiden Bereichen gewonnen werden, gehen zwanglos im Gegenüber auf. Angermanns unbedingter Mut, mit gnadenlos bestürzenden Ideen zu arbeiten, korrespondiert mit seinem Mut zur *sprezzatura* in Form und Farbe, was die Landschaftsmalerei angeht. Und umgekehrt reichen die koloristischen Experimente, die dort ihren angestammten Platz haben, weit in die thematischen Werke hinein. Es ist schlussendlich ein und derselbe Künstler, der in beiden Gattungen zu Hause ist: Er heißt Peter Angermann.

Notes

1 Cf. Johannes Stüttgen, *Der Ganze Riemen. Der Auftritt von Joseph Beuys als Lehrer – die Chronologie der Ereignisse an der Staatlichen Kunstakademie Düsseldorf 1966–1972*, ed. Hessisches Landesmuseum Darmstadt, Cologne, 2008, pp. 530 ff.

2 "LIDL" does not allude to the well-known supermarket chain; as Jörg Immendorff explained, "Lidl draws directly on 'baby art'. I was largely convinced that in terms of content, the changes in our society had to come through art. I took the word 'lidl' from baby language. Lidl-lidl-lidl-lidl and so on." Jörg Immendorff, *Hier und Jetzt: Das tun, was zu tun ist; Materialien zur Diskussion; Kunst im politischen Kampf. Auf welcher Seite stehst du, Kulturschaffender?*, Cologne and New York, 1973, p. 54.

3 Harald Szeemann writes on this at length in "Der lange Marsch oder Ausreizungen aus der Zeit heraus. Ein Kompilat", in *Immendorff*, exh. cat. Kunsthaus Zürich, 1983, pp. 8–34, and Stüttgen 2008 (see note 1), pp. 543 ff. and 582 ff.

4 Although a letter by Peter Angermann from 1982 dates the period when the group formed to summer semester 1969, Johannes Stüttgen writes that "according to the general opinion" it was not before the beginning of February 1970. Cf. Stüttgen, ibid., pp. 724 and 721 ff.; also contained there is further material on the YIUP group. Additional valuable reading: Stephan Schmidt-Wulffen, "Alles in allem – Panorama 'wilder' Malerei", in cat. *Tiefe Blicke. Kunst der achtziger Jahre aus der Bundesrepublik Deutschland, der DDR, Österreich und der Schweiz*, ed. Verein der Freunde und Förderer des Hessischen Landesmuseums Darmstadt, Cologne, 1985, pp. 17 ff. and ill. pp. 97 ff.

5 Ill. in Immendorff 1973 (see note 2), pp. 72 and 75.

6 Nowadays, the painting is no longer ascribed to Rembrandt.

7 On Milan Kunc see for instance *Milan Kunc. Neue Ikonen. Nieuwe Ikonen. Arbeiten 1979–1984*, exh. cat. Kunstverein für die Rheinlande und Westfalen, Düsseldorf; Groniger Museum, Groningen, 1984.

8 In his analysis of the grotesque, Wolfgang Kayser emphasises the contradictory mixture of the playfully cheerful and the oppressively uncanny, which leads him to conclude: "… the grotesque is the alienated world."

Wolfgang Kayser, *Das Groteske in Malerei und Dichtung*, Reinbek bei Hamburg, 1960, p. 136.

9 Karl Schawelka, "Ain't Misbehavin'. Die Malerei von Peter Angermann", in *Peter Angermann, Malerei 1973 bis 1995*, exh. cat. Kunsthalle Nürnberg; Galleria d'Arte Moderna e Contemporanea, Repubblica di San Marino, Nuremberg, 1995, pp. 36–43, here p. 37.

10 See the interview with Peter Angermann in this publication.

11 See *NORMAL: Peter Angermann, Jan Knap, Milan Kunc*, exh. cat. Neue Galerie – Sammlung Ludwig, Aachen, 1981.

12 Georg Bussmann, "Das Museum als Oase oder Normal-Revival", in *Von hier aus: Zwei Monate neue deutsche Kunst in Düsseldorf*, exh. cat., Cologne, 1984, pp. 218–24, here p. 219.

13 A number of reproductions of joint works are given in *Normal Group*, exh. cat. Prague Biennial; Trevi Flash Art Museum; MACI, Isernia, Milan, 2005.

14 See the interview with Peter Angermann in this publication.

15 Cf. Herbert Molderings, *Marcel Duchamp. Parawissenschaft, das Ephemere und der Skeptizismus*, Frankfurt/ Main and Paris, 1983, chap. VII, pp. 79 ff.: "Kontakt mit dem Volk".

16 In Mondrian's utopia, contact with the people was equated with the end of art: "In the same way, abstract-real painting in turn serves an evolution toward *nonart* – the end of art as we know it today – as something that *expresses life* but that is not yet life itself. Only when life is transformed into real life will our art come to an end." Piet Mondrian, "The New Plastic in Painting" (1917), cited in Harry Holtzman and Martin S. Jones (eds.), *The New Art – The New Life. The Collected Writings of Piet Mondrian*. London, 1987, pp. 27–74, here p. 64, note z.

17 One is reminded for instance of Oldenburg's project *The Store* (1961); cf. *Claes Oldenburg's Store Days*, ed. Claes Oldenburg and Emmett Williams, New York, 1967.

18 Grandville, *Public and Private Life of Animals*, London, 1977 (first published 1840–42).

19 See in this context John Berger's essay "Why Look at Animals?", in Berger, *Why Look at Animals*, Harmondsworth, 2009, pp. 12–39. In this context, the euphoria over the polar bear Knut at the Berlin zoo and the months-long and final cull of "Problem Bear Bruno" – both in 2006 – represent two sides of the same coin.

20 Baldassare Castiglione, *The Book of the Courtier* (1528), New York, 1903, p. 26.

21 Annika Blohm, "Baldassare Castigliones *sprezzatura* im beginnenden 21. Jahrhundert", http://www. anwesenheitsnotiz.de/juli-2012-nr-4/inhaltlicher-ueberblick/baldassare-castigliones-sprezzatura (accessed February 14, 2013).

22 See for instance Schawelka (see note 9), pp. 39 ff., and Thomas Heyden, "Keinen Jux will er sich machen", in *Peter Angermann. Pleinair*, exh. cat. Galerie Defet, Nuremberg, 2001, n.p.

23 The book the artist is holding is entitled *The Beauty of Fractals* and alludes simultaneously to the self-similarity of natural things, as shown in the formations of the beach close to his eyes. Angermann has returned to this subject in for instance his painting *Artificial Intelligence 2* (2001, p. 163). See H.-O. Peitgen, P. H. Richter, *The Beauty of Fractals: Images of Complex Dynamical Systems*, Berlin et. al., 1986.

24 See the interview with Peter Angermann in this publication.

25 Niklas Luhmann, *Die Wissenschaft der Gesellschaft*, Frankfurt/Main, 1992, p. 73.

26 Ibid., p. 85.

27 Ibid., p. 86.

28 Ibid.

Anmerkungen

1 Vgl. Johannes Stüttgen, *Der Ganze Riemen. Der Auftritt von Joseph Beuys als Lehrer – die Chronologie der Ereignisse an der Staatlichen Kunstakademie Düsseldorf 1966–1972*; hrsg. v. Hessischen Landesmuseum Darmstadt, Köln 2008, S. 530 ff.

2 LIDL spielt nicht etwa auf die bekannte Supermarktkette an, sondern in den Worten Jörg Immendorffs: „Lidl knüpfte direkt an die ,Babykunst' an. Inhaltlich war ich weiterhin davon überzeugt, dass die Veränderung in unserer Gesellschaft durch die Kunst stattfinden müsste. Das Wort Lidl nahm ich aus der Baby-Sprache. Lidl-lidl-lidl-lidl usw." Jörg Immendorff, *Hier und Jetzt: Das tun, was zu tun ist; Materialien zur Diskussion; Kunst im politischen Kampf. Auf welcher Seite stehst du, Kulturschaffender?*, Köln und New York 1973, S. 54.

3 Ausführlich dazu Harald Szeemann, „Der lange Marsch oder Ausreizungen aus der Zeit heraus. Ein Kompilat", in: *Immendorff*, Ausst.-Kat. Kunsthaus Zürich, 1983, S. 8–34, sowie Stüttgen 2008 (wie Anm. 1), S. 543 ff. u. 582 ff.

4 Während Peter Angermann in einem Brief von 1982 das Sommersemester 1969 als Gründungszeit der Gruppe benennt, datiert Johannes Stüttgen diese „nach übereinstimmenden Berichten" erst auf Anfang Februar 1970. Vgl. Stüttgen, ebd., S. 724 u. S. 721 ff.; dort auch weitere Materialien zur YIUP-Gruppe. Lesenswert auch: Stephan Schmidt-Wulffen, „Alles in allem – Panorama ,wilder' Malerei", in: Kat. *Tiefe Blicke. Kunst der achtziger Jahre aus der Bundesrepublik Deutschland, der DDR, Österreich und der Schweiz*, hrsg. v. Verein der Freunde und Förderer des Hessischen Landesmuseums Darmstadt, Köln 1985, S. 17 ff. u. Abb. S. 97 ff.

5 Abb. in Immendorff 1973 (wie Anm. 2), S. 72 u. S. 75.

6 Inzwischen wird das Gemälde nicht mehr Rembrandt zugeschrieben.

7 Zu Milan Kunc siehe zum Beispiel *Milan Kunc. Neue Ikonen. Nieuwe Ikonen. Arbeiten 1979–1984*, Ausst.-Kat. Kunstverein für die Rheinlande und Westfalen, Düsseldorf; Groniger Museum, Groningen, 1984.

8 In der Analyse des Grotesken, die Wolfgang Kayser vorgelegt hat, betont er die widersprüchliche Mischung zwischen Spielerisch-Heiterem und Beklemmendem, Unheimlichem, die ihn zu dem Schluss bringt: „[…] das Groteske ist die entfremdete Welt". Wolfgang Kayser, *Das Groteske in Malerei und Dichtung*, Reinbek bei Hamburg 1960, S. 136.

9 Karl Schawelka, „Ain't Misbehavin'. Die Malerei von Peter Angermann", in: Kat. *Peter Angermann. Malerei 1973 bis 1995*, Ausst.-Kat. Kunsthalle Nürnberg, Galleria d'Arte Moderna e Contemporanea, Repubblica di San Marino, Nürnberg 1995, S. 36–43, hier: S. 37.

10 Siehe das Interview mit Peter Angermann in dieser Publikation.

11 Siehe *NORMAL: Peter Angermann, Jan Knap, Milan Kunc*, Ausst.-Kat. Neue Galerie – Sammlung Ludwig, Aachen 1981.

12 Georg Bussmann, „Das Museum als Oase oder Normal-Revival", in: *Von hier aus: Zwei Monate neue deutsche Kunst in Düsseldorf*, Ausst.-Kat., Köln 1984, S. 218–224, hier: S. 219.

13 Eine Reihe von Abbildungen von Gemeinschaftsarbeiten findet sich in: *Normal Group*, Ausst.-Kat. Prague Biennale; Trevi Flash Art Museum; MACI, Isernia, Mailand 2005.

14 Siehe das Interview mit Peter Angermann in dieser Publikation.

15 Vgl. Herbert Molderings, *Marcel Duchamp. Parawissenschaft, das Ephemere und der Skeptizismus.* Frankfurt/Main und Paris 1983, Kap. VII, S. 79 ff.: „Kontakt mit dem Volk".

16 In Mondrians Utopie fällt der Kontakt mit dem Volk in Eins mit dem Ende der Kunst: „So wie die abstraktreale Malerei wiederum dazu dient, zur Nicht-Gestaltung zu gelangen: d. h. zum Ende der Kunst, wie wir sie jetzt kennen: zwar Gestaltung des Lebens, aber noch nicht das Leben selber. Wenn die Kunst sich in reales Leben verwandelt – dann erst ist das Ende unserer gegenwärtigen Kunst gekommen." Piet Mondrian, „Die neue Gestaltung in der Malerei" (1917), zit. n. Hans L. C. Jaffe, *Mondrian und De Stijl*, Köln 1967, S. 83.

17 Man denke etwa an Oldenburgs Ladenprojekt *The Store* (1961); vgl. *Claes Odenburg: Eine Anthologie*, Ausst.-Kat. Kunst- und Ausstellungshalle der Bundesrepublik Deutschland, Bonn 1996, S. 33 ff.

18 Grandville, *Bilder aus dem Staats- und Familienleben der Tiere*, 2 Bde., Frankfurt/Main 1976 (erstmals publiziert 1840–1842).

19 Vgl. dazu den Essay von John Berger, „Warum sehen wir Tiere an?", in: Ders., *Das Leben der Bilder oder die Kunst des Sehens*, Berlin 1981, S. 7–26. In diesem Zusammenhang erscheinen die Euphorie über den Berliner Zoobären Knut und die monatelange, finale Jagd nach dem „Problembären Bruno" – beides spielte sich 2006 ab – als zwei Seiten derselben Medaille.

20 Baldassare Castiglione, *Der Hofmann. Lebensart der Renaissance*, Berlin, 3. Aufl. 2008, Erstes Buch, S. 35.

21 Annika Blohm, „Baldassare Castigliones *sprezzatura* im beginnenden 21. Jahrhundert", http://www.anwesenheitsnotiz.de/juli-2012-nr-4/inhaltlicher-ueberblick/baldassare-castigliones-sprezzatura (abgerufen am 12.02.2013).

22 Siehe unter anderem Schawelka 1994 (wie Anm. 9), S. 39 ff., und Thomas Heyden, „Keinen Jux will er sich machen", in: *Peter Angermann. pleinair*, Ausst.-Kat. Galerie Defet, Nürnberg 2001, o. P.

23 Das Buch in der Hand des Künstlers mit dem Titel *The Beauty of Fractals* spielt zugleich auf die Selbstähnlichkeit natürlicher Dinge an, die sich in der Darstellung der Strandformation nahe den Augen zeigt. Diese Thematik nimmt Angermann beispielsweise in dem Gemälde *Artificial Intelligence 2* (2001, S. 163) wieder auf. Vgl. H.-O. Peitgen, P. H. Richter, *The Beauty of Fractals: Images of Complex Dynamical Systems*, Berlin u. a. 1986.

24 Siehe das Interview mit Peter Angermann in dieser Publikation.

25 Niklas Luhmann, *Die Wissenschaft der Gesellschaft*, Frankfurt/Main 1992, S. 73.

26 Ebd., S. 85.

27 Ebd., S. 86.

28 Ebd

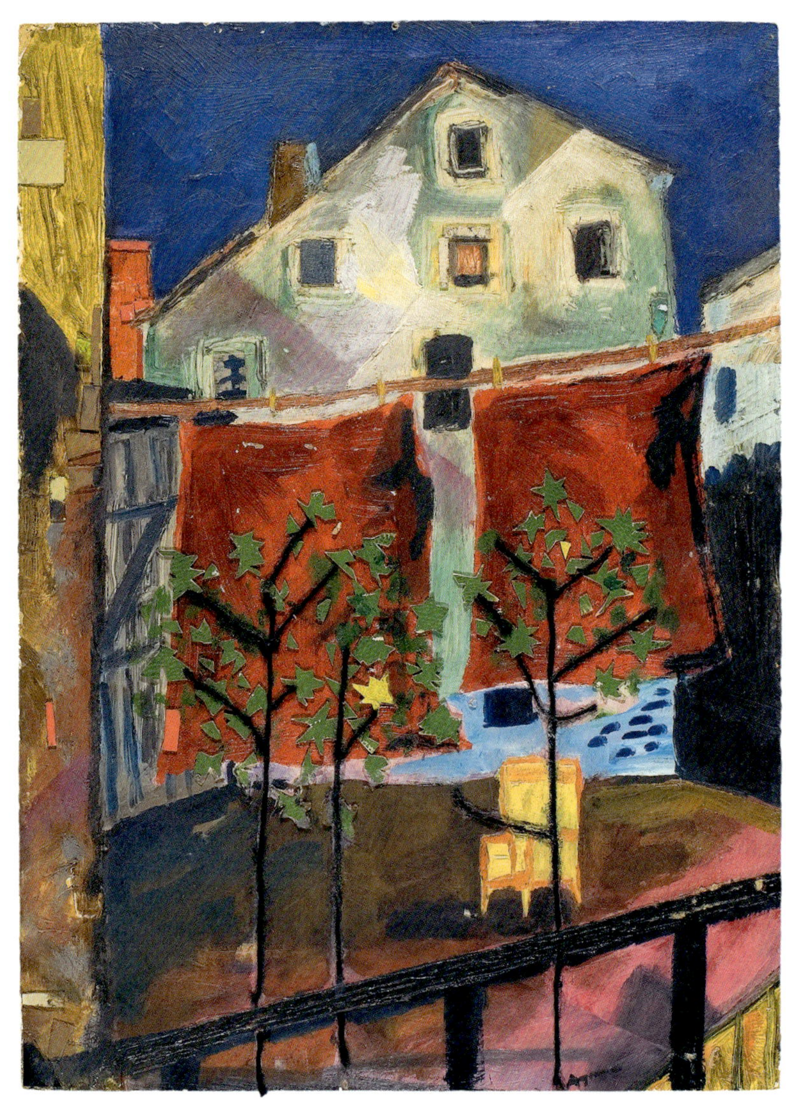

Drei junge Ahörner / Three Young Maples, 1959

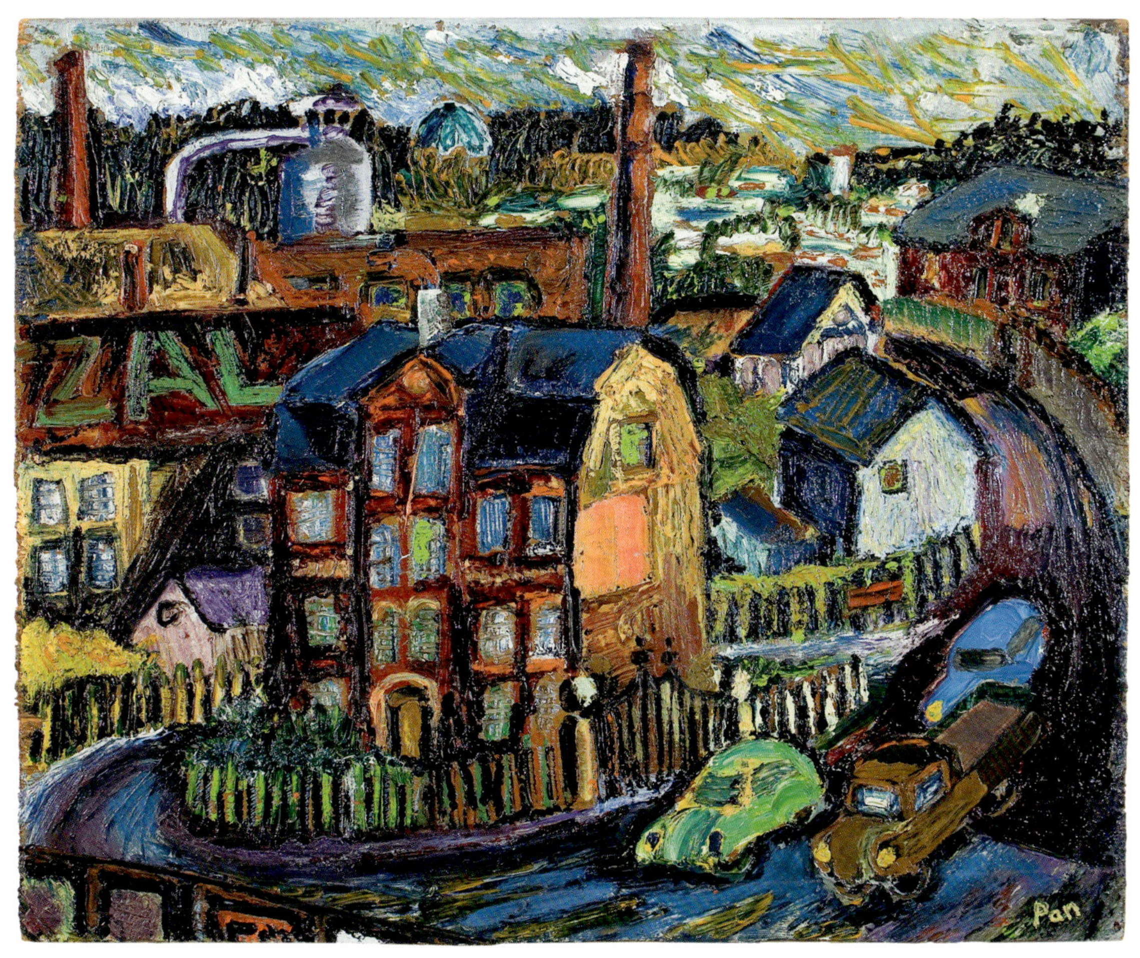

Selb, 1962

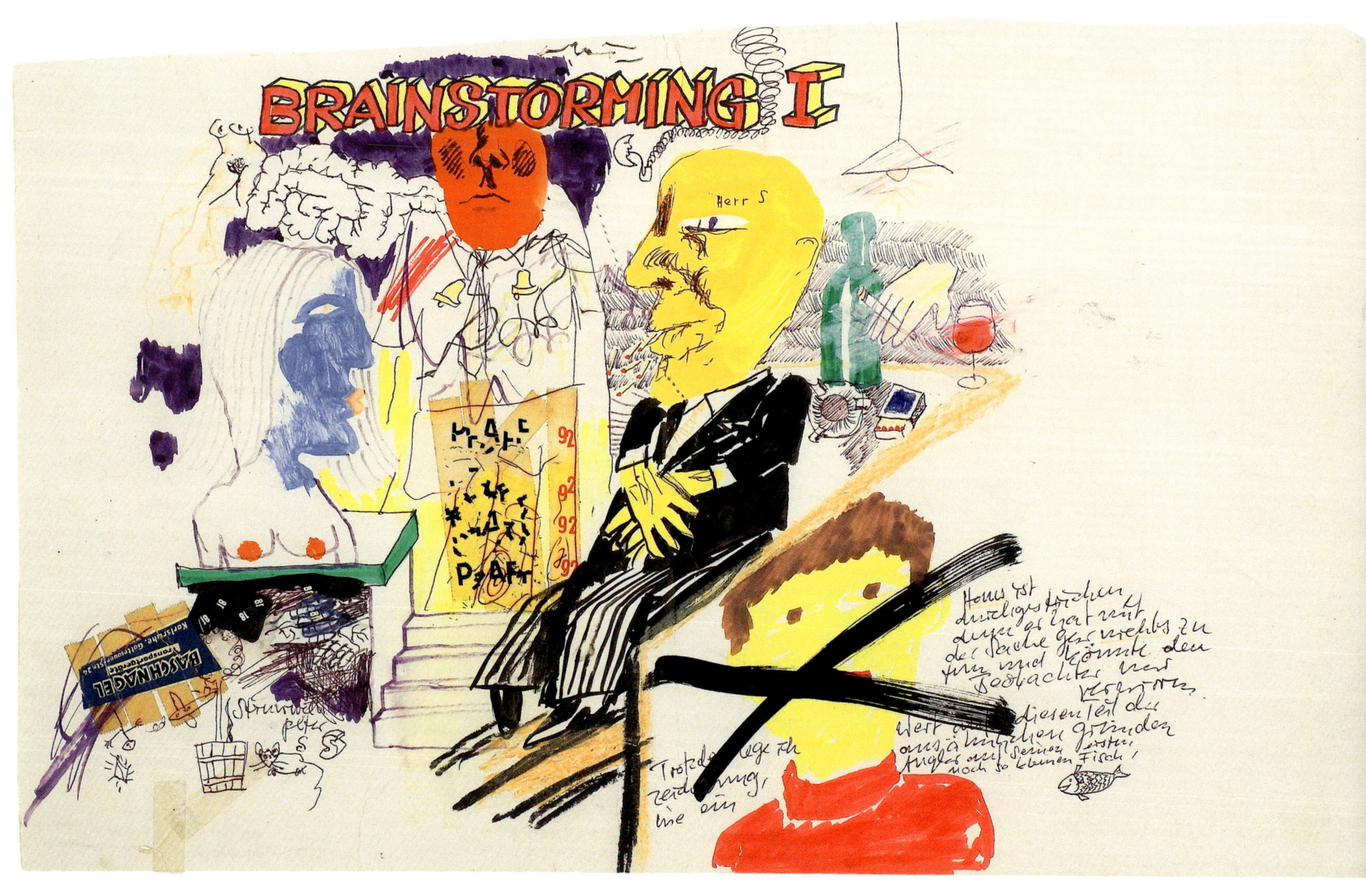

Brainstorming 1, 1968

36

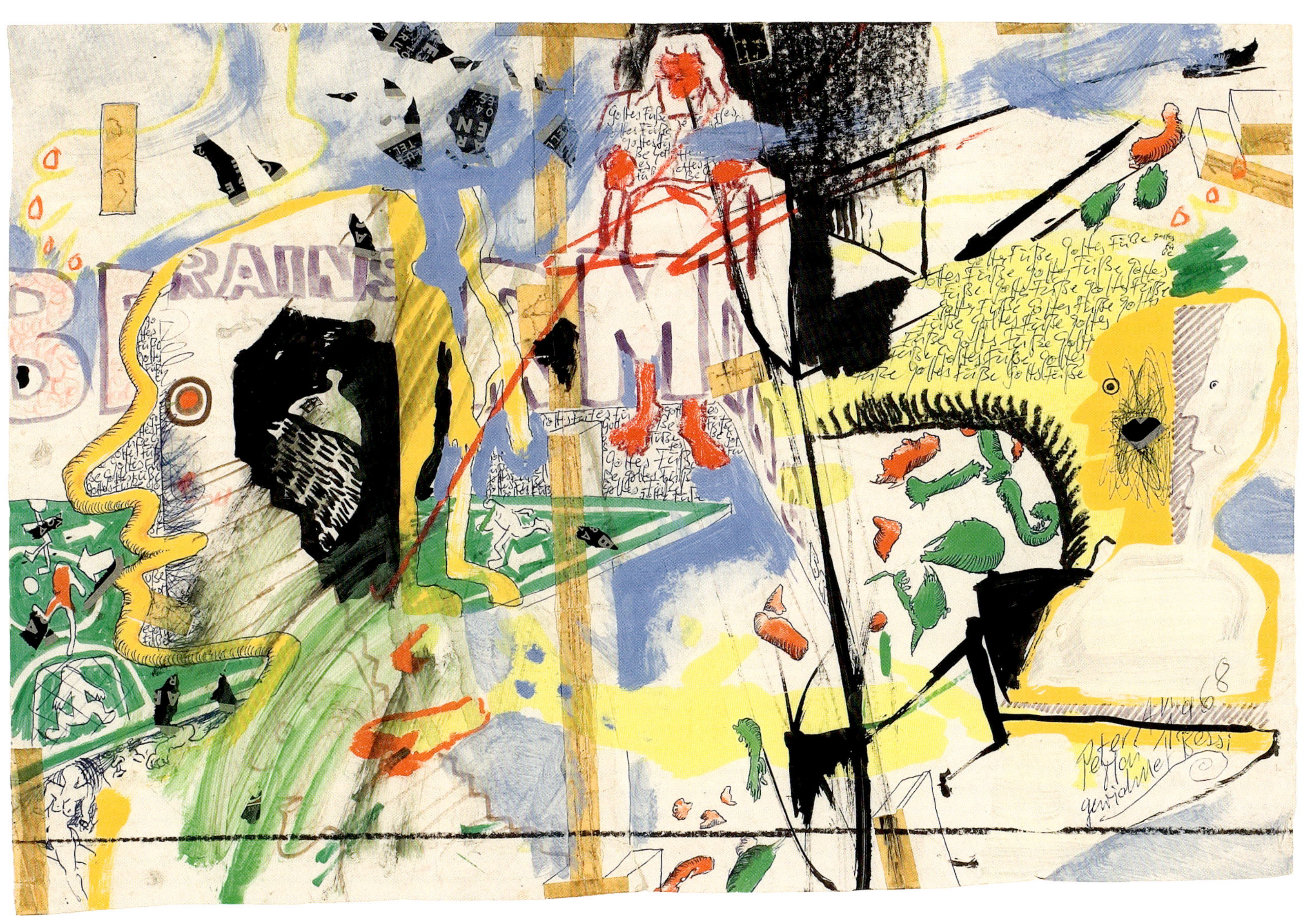

Brainstorming 5, 1968

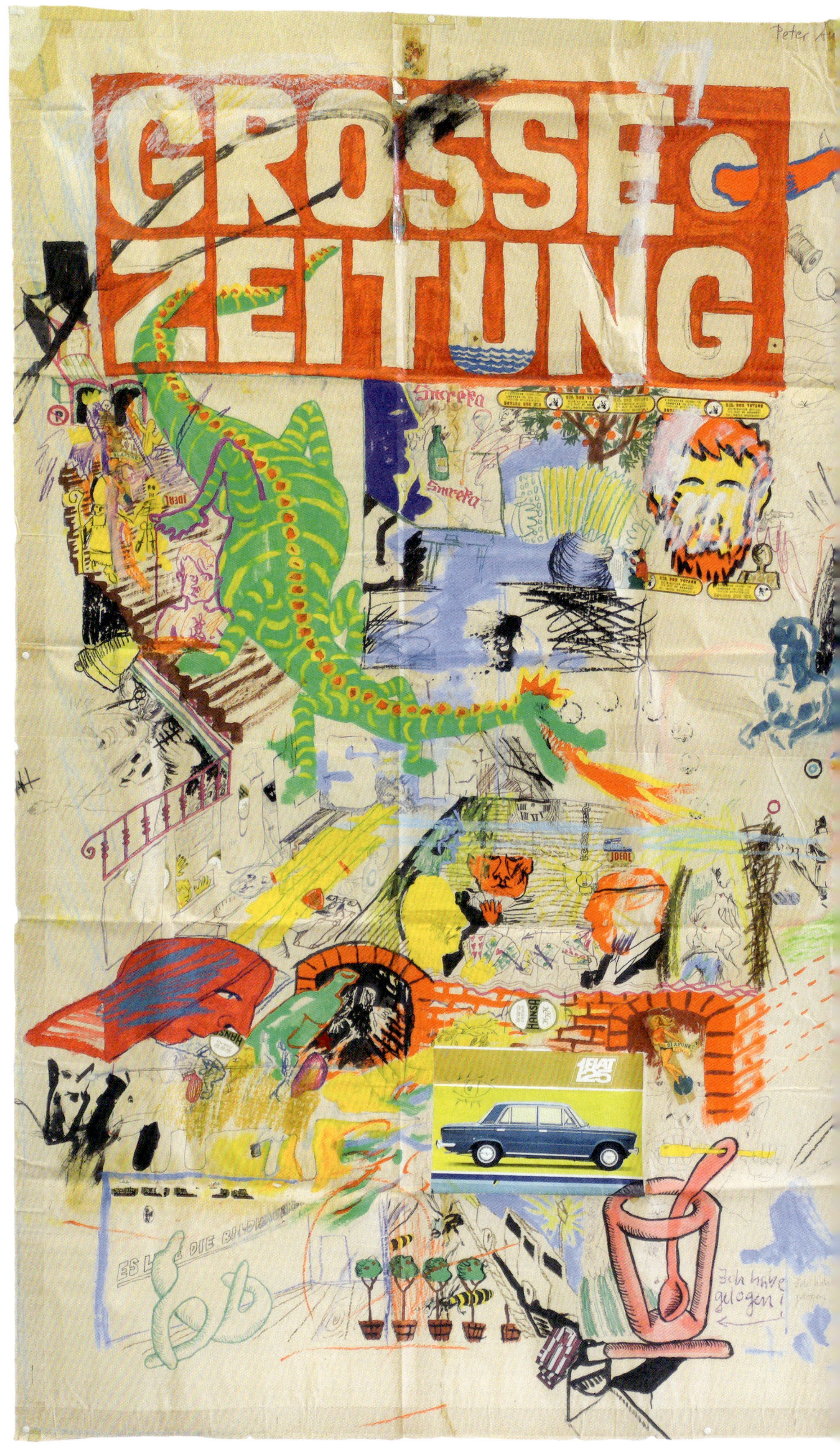

Große Zeitung / Large Newspaper, 1968

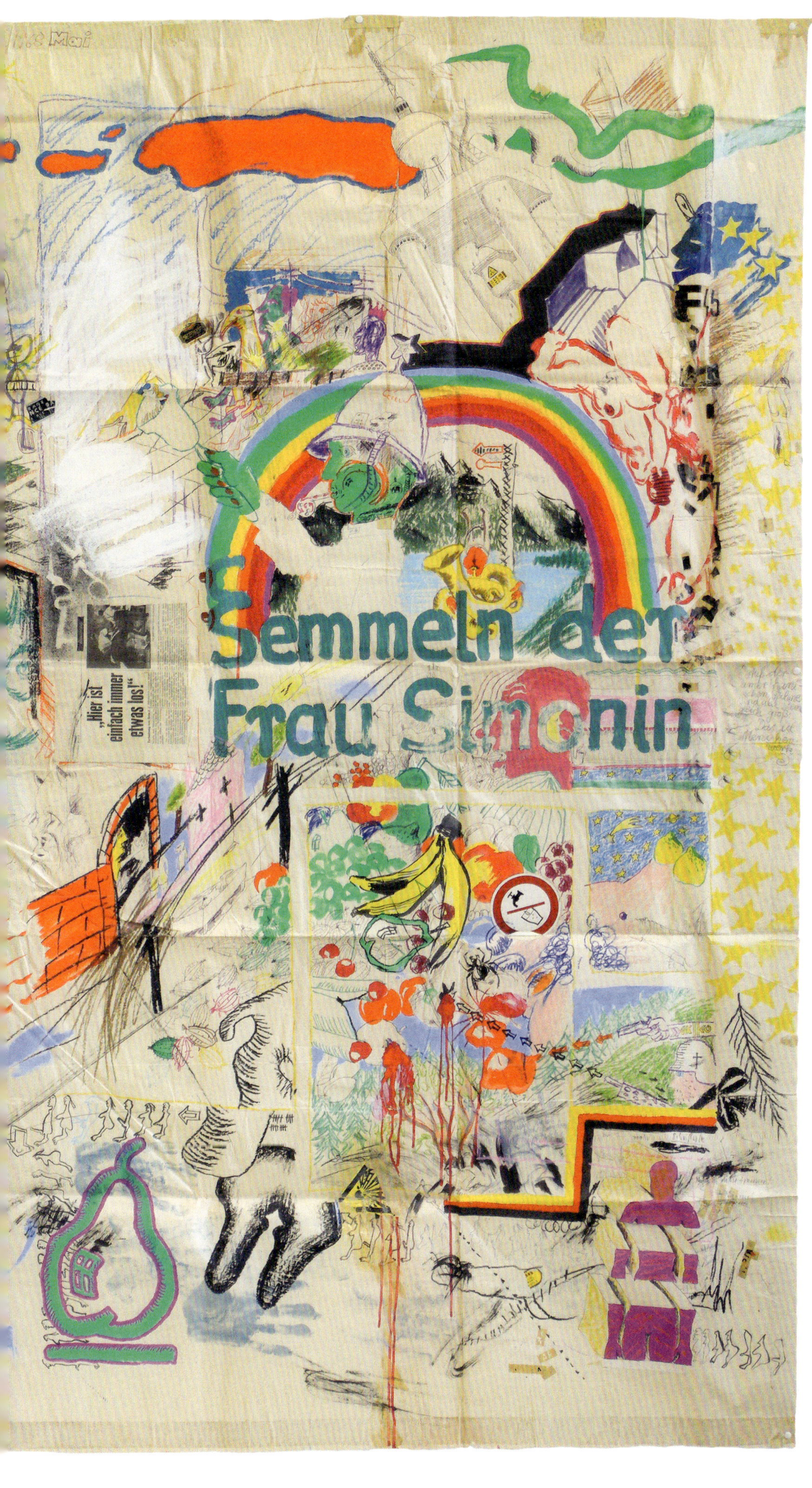
1. Mai
Semmeln der
Frau Simonin
Hier ist "einfach immer etwas los!"
F

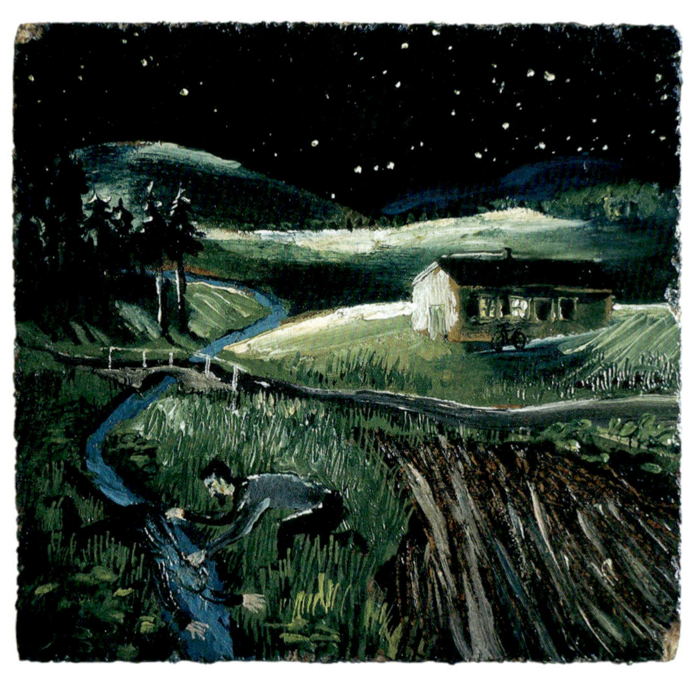

Kleiner Mord / Little Murder, 1970

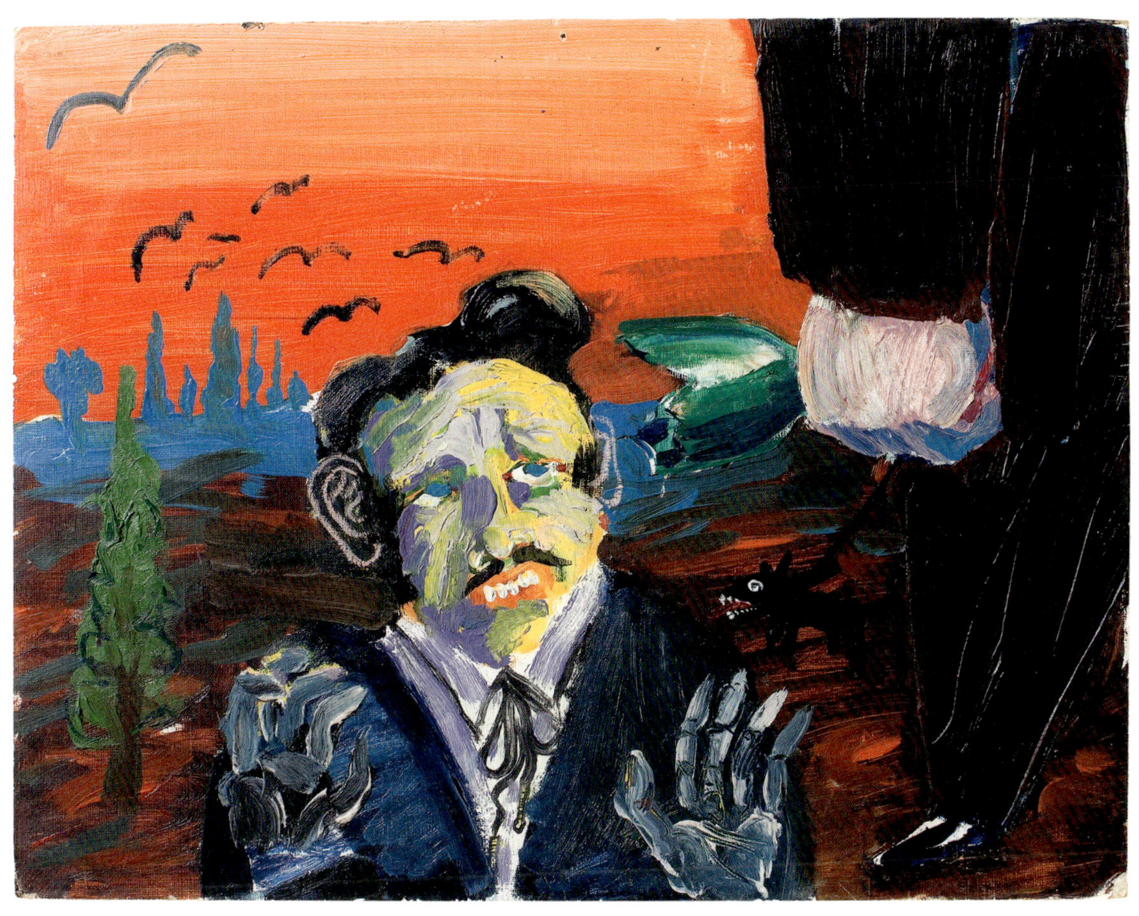

Feindbild / Image of the Foe, 1970

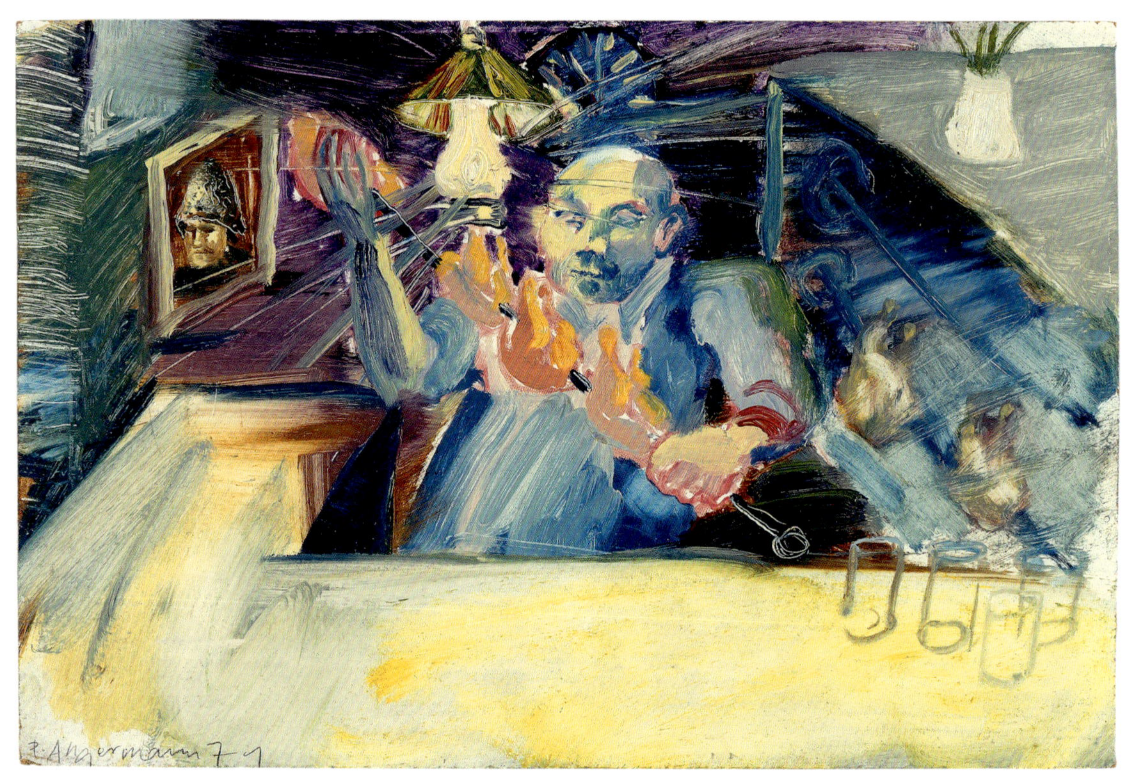

Hähnchen / Chicken, 1971

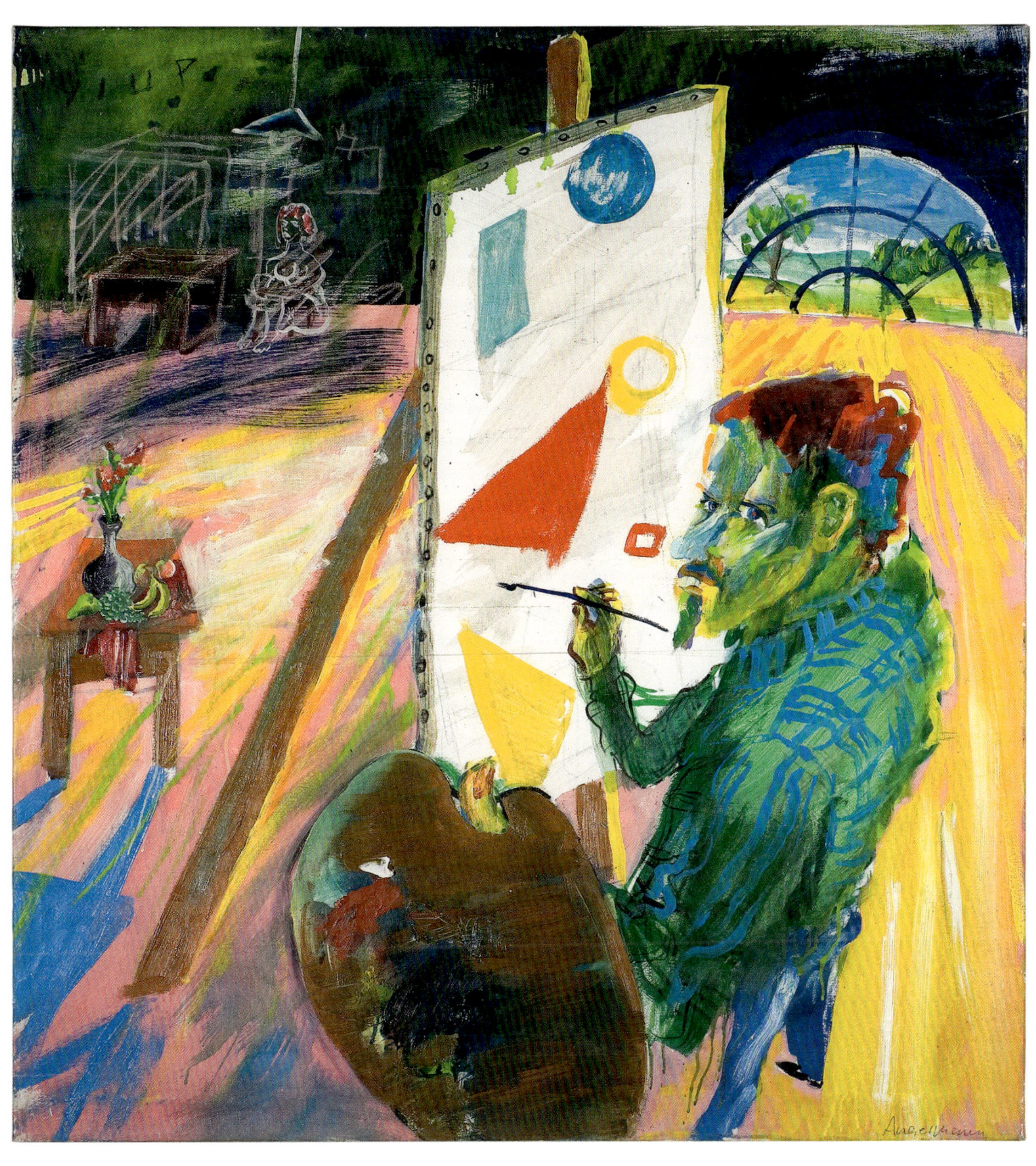

Selbstportrait im Raum 111 / Selfportrait in Room 111, 1971

43

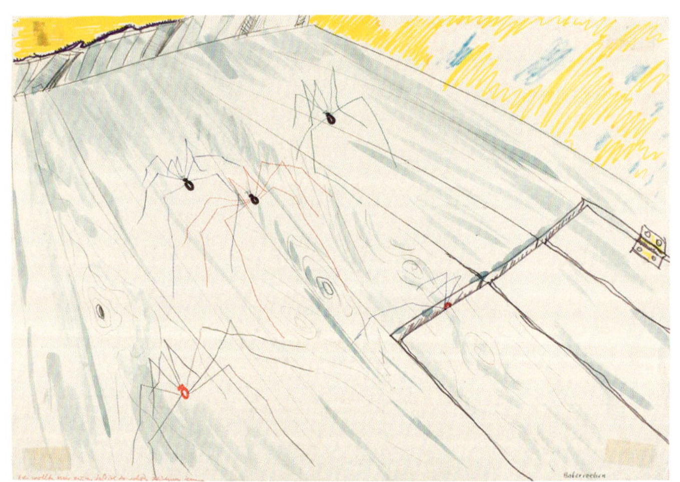
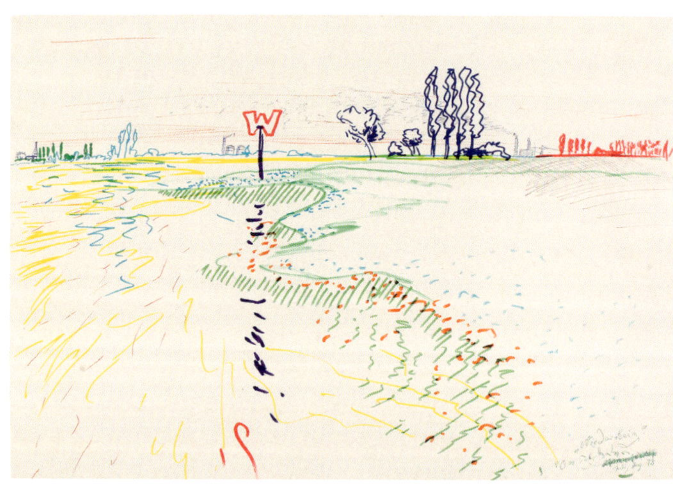
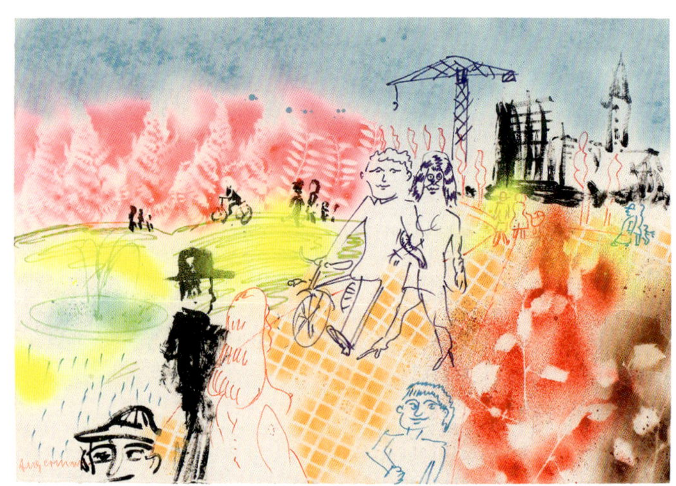
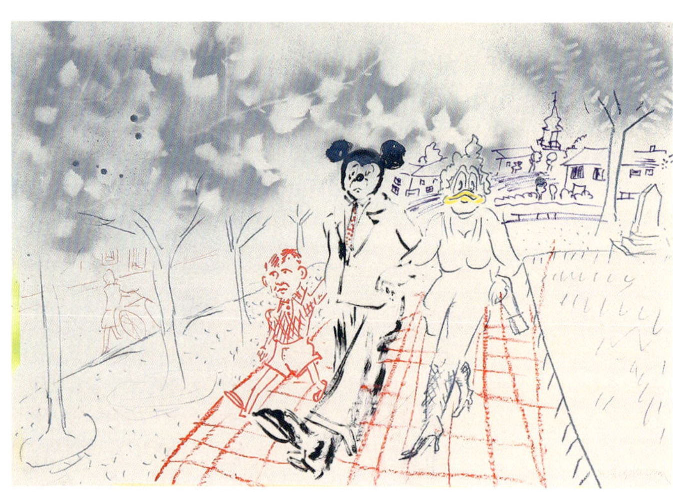
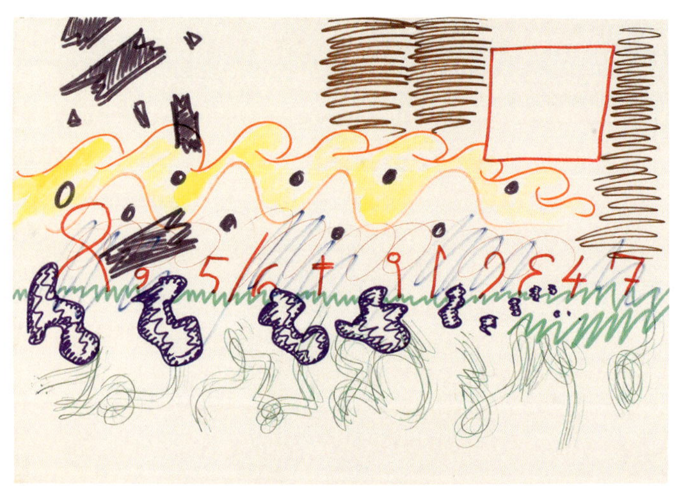
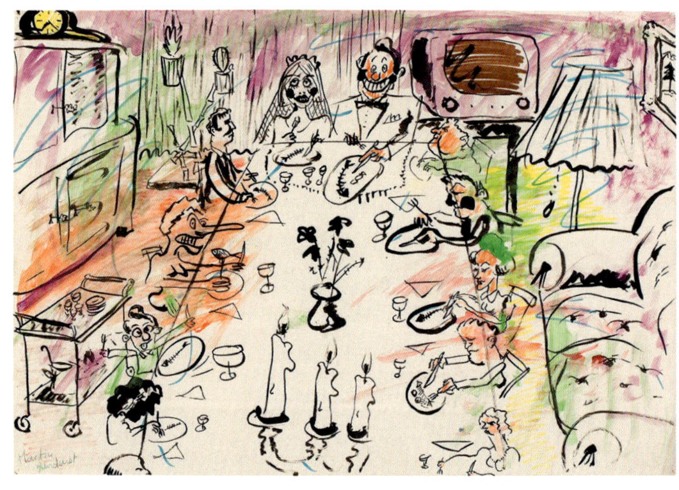

Zurück zur Kunst / Back to Art, 1973

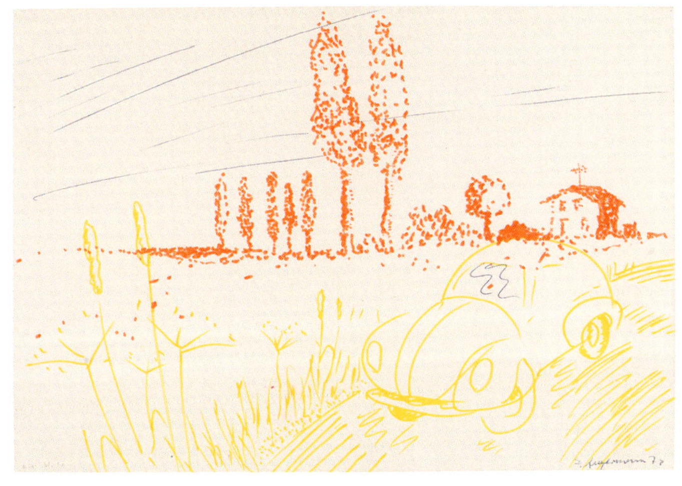

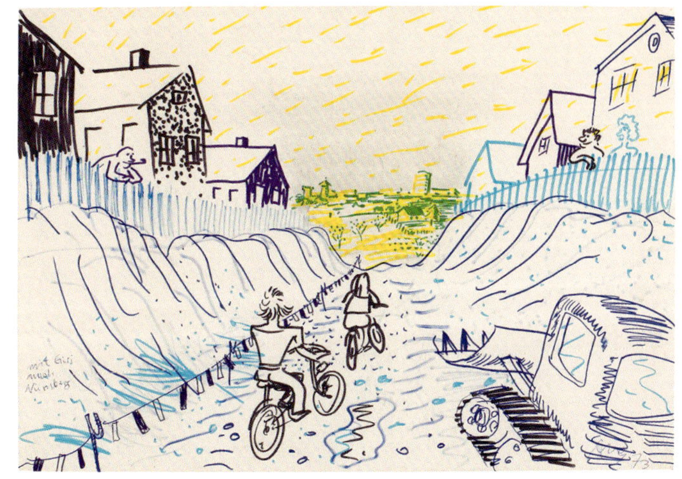

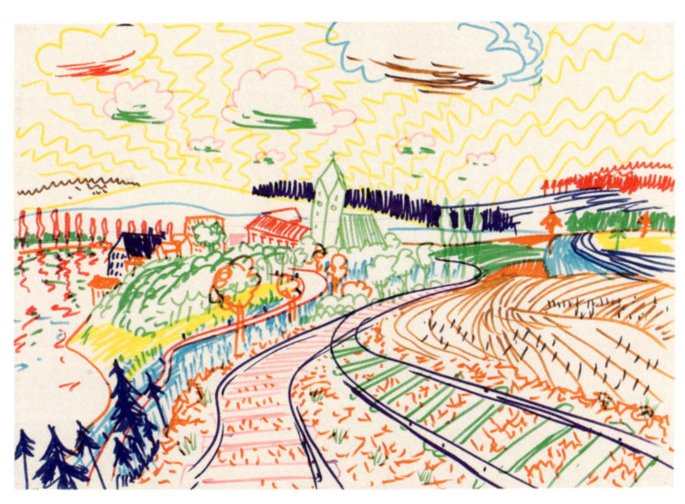

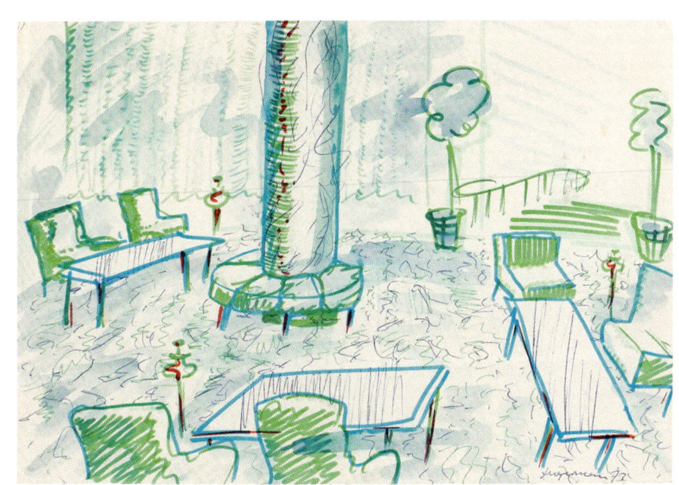

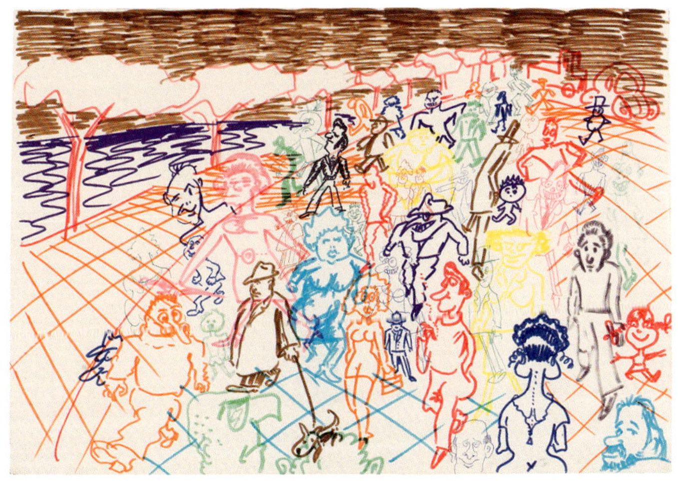

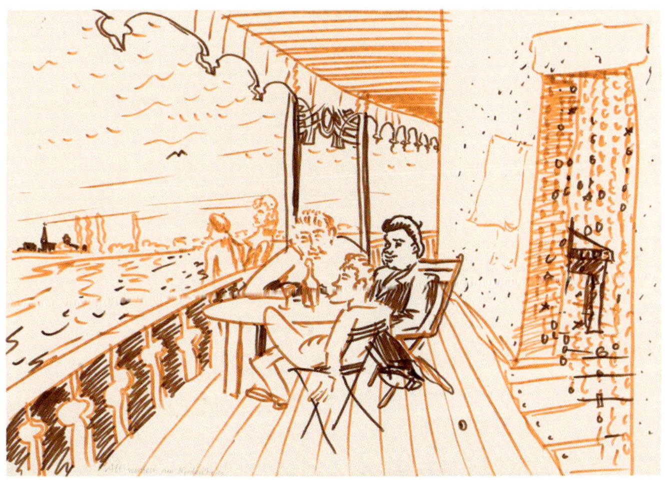

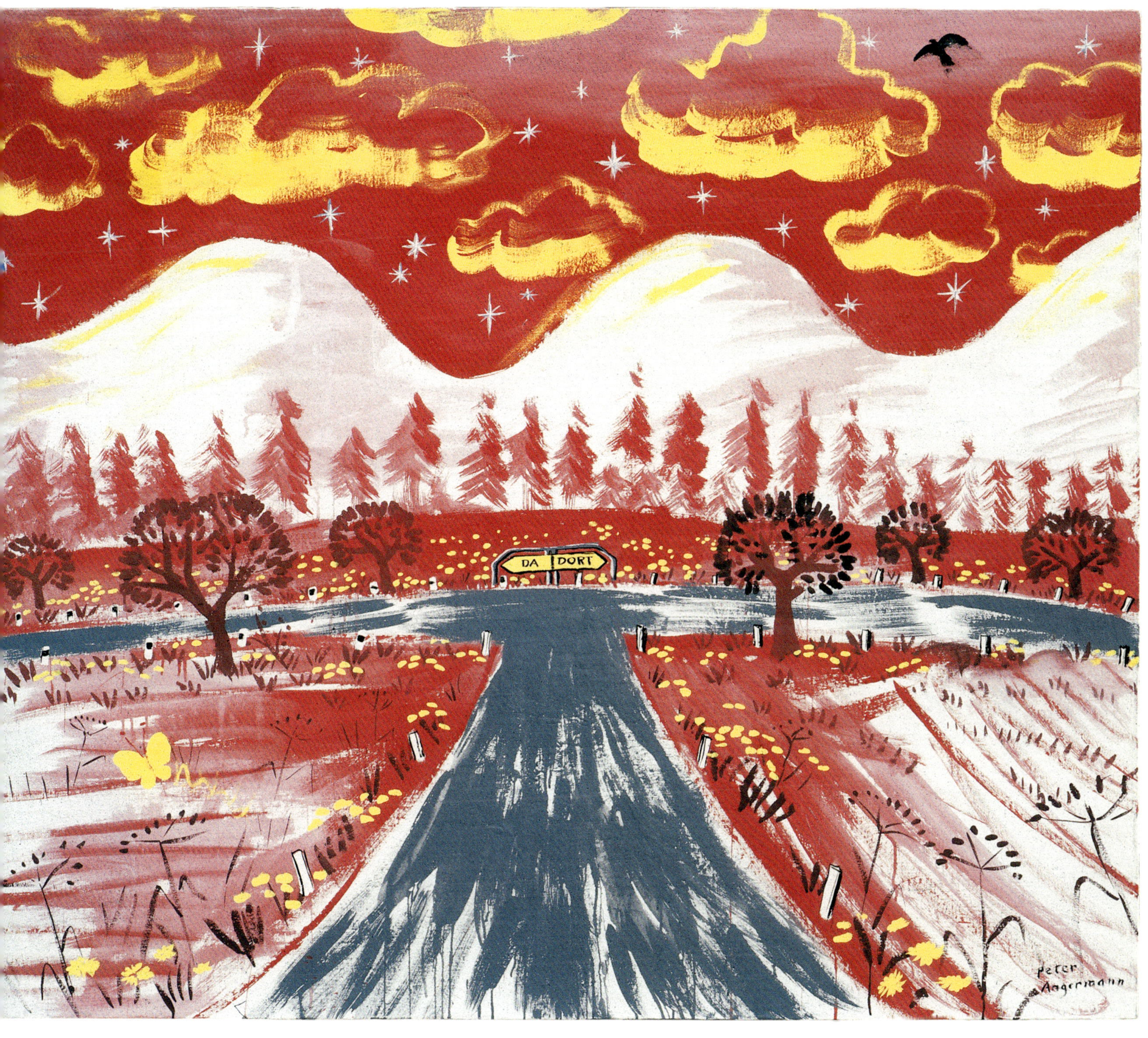

Tatort / Crime Scene, 1973

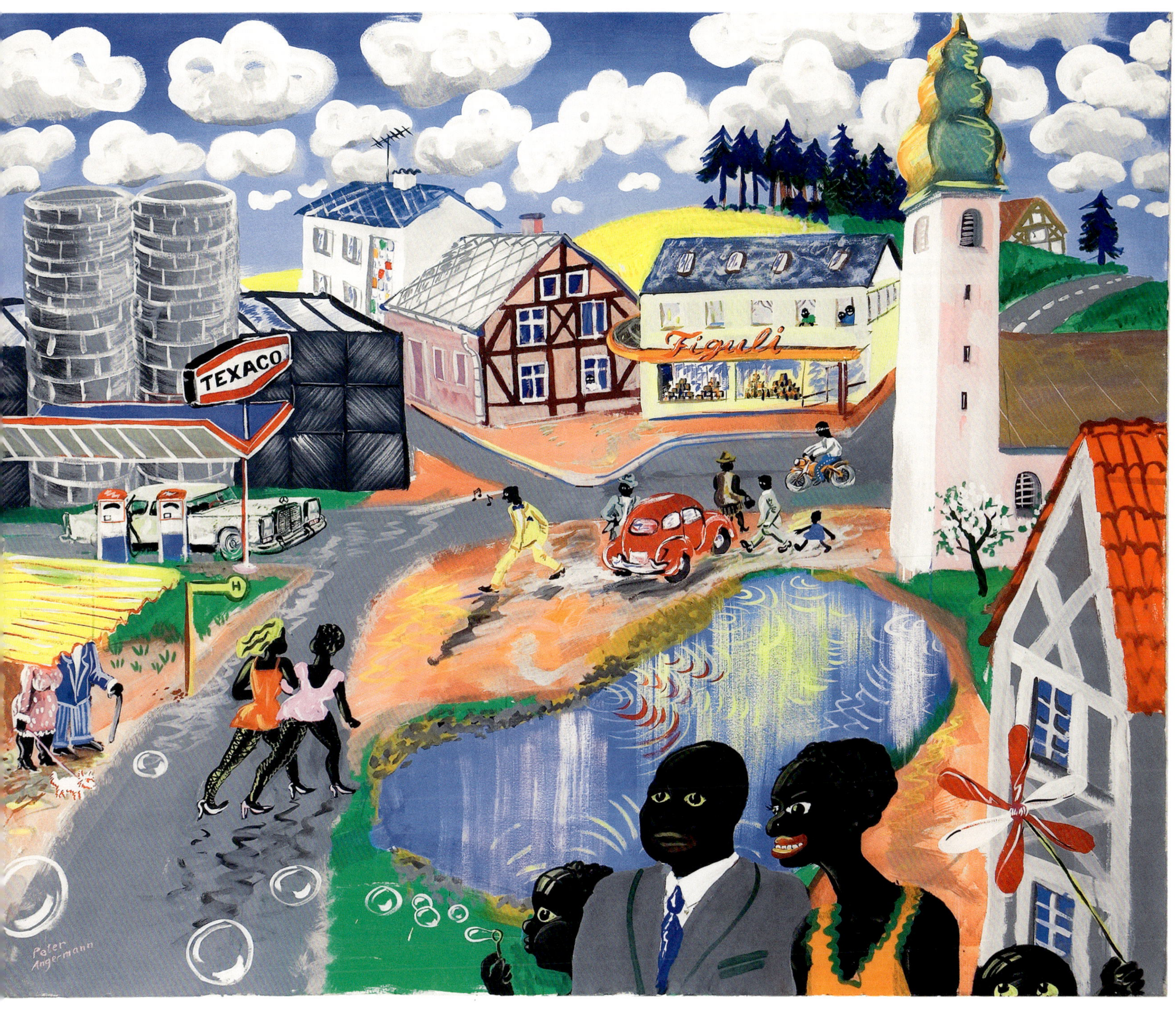

Schwarzenbach, 1974

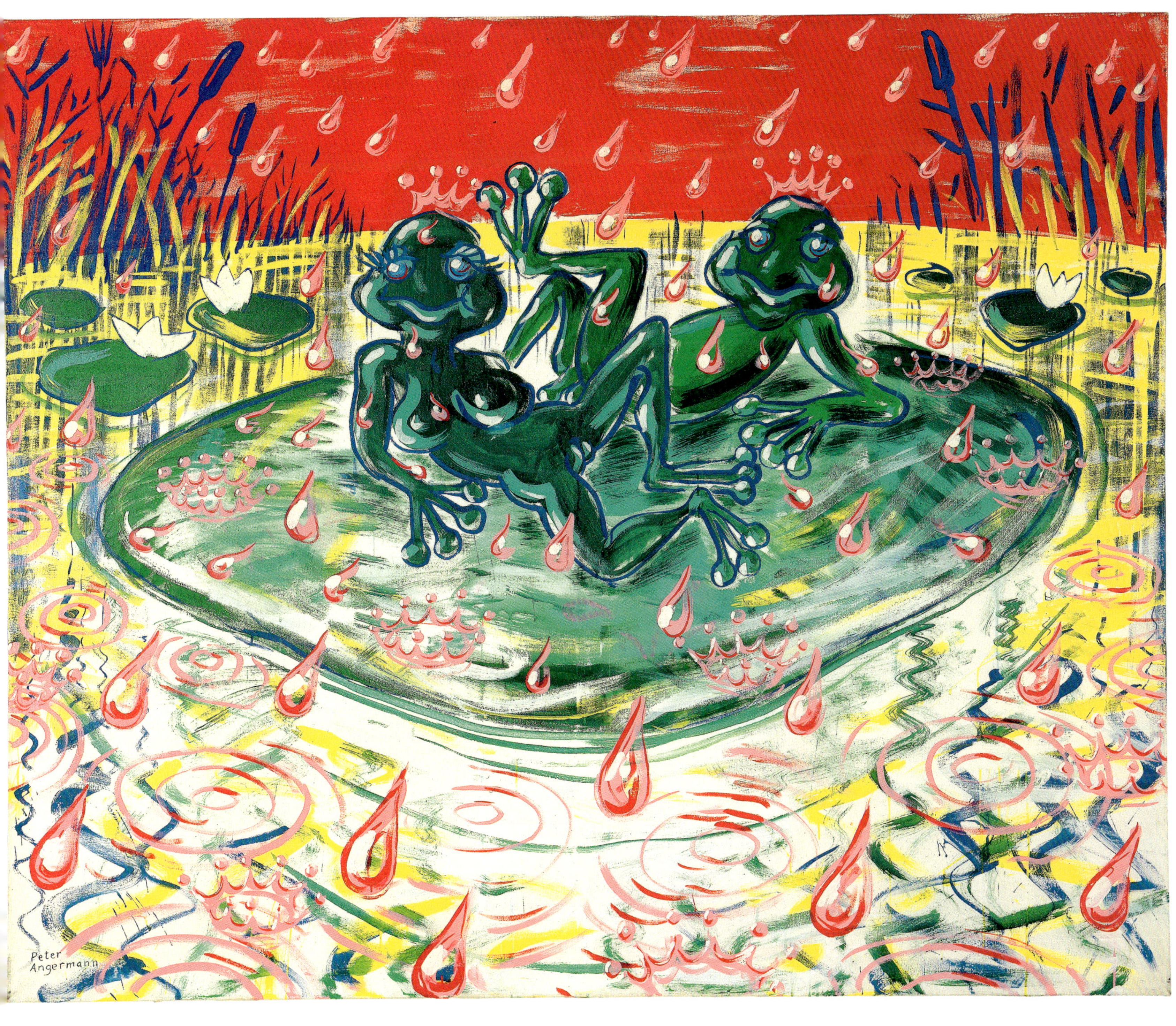

Großes Froschbild / Large Frog Painting, 1974

51

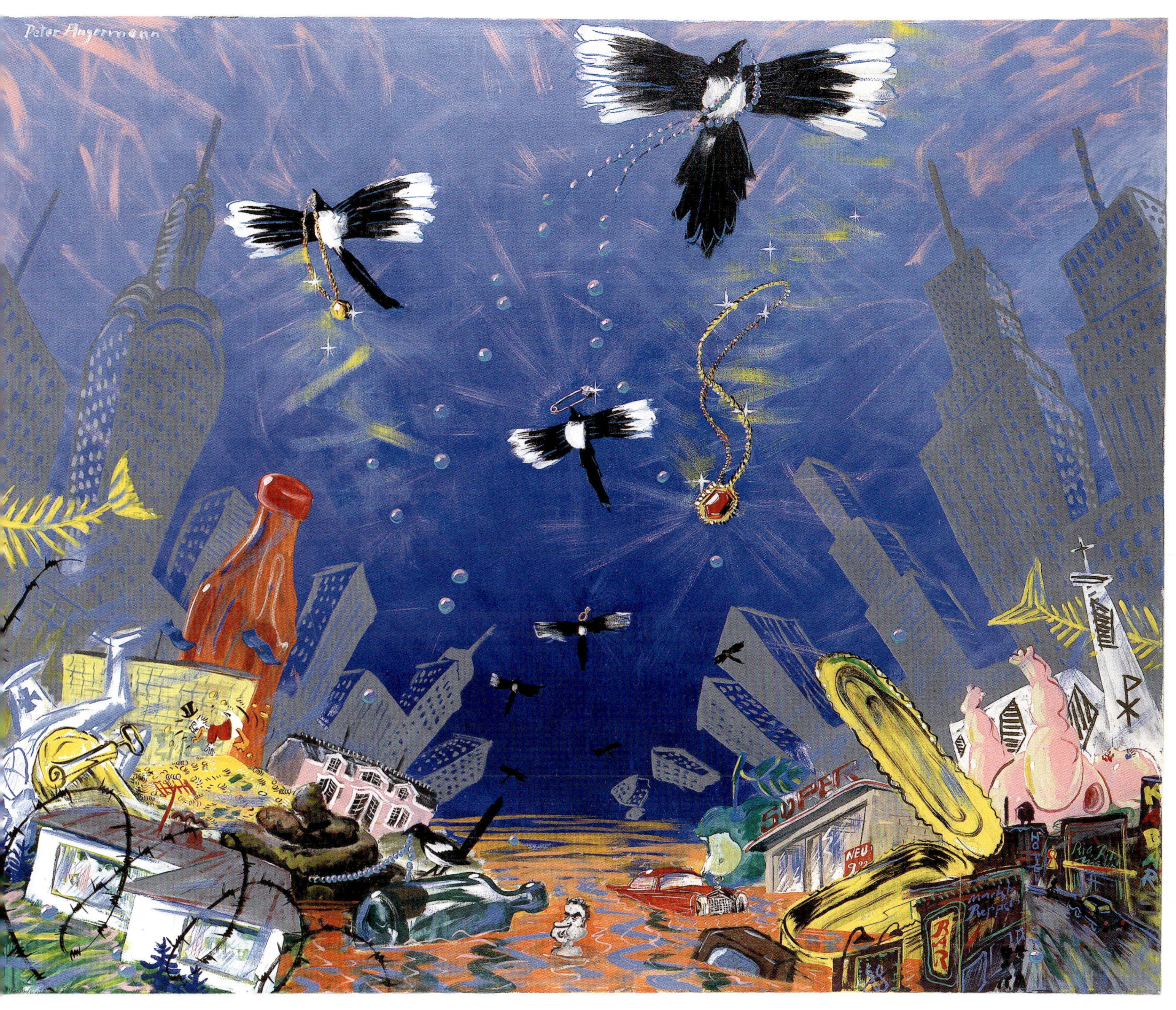

Elsternbild / Magpie Painting, 1974

53

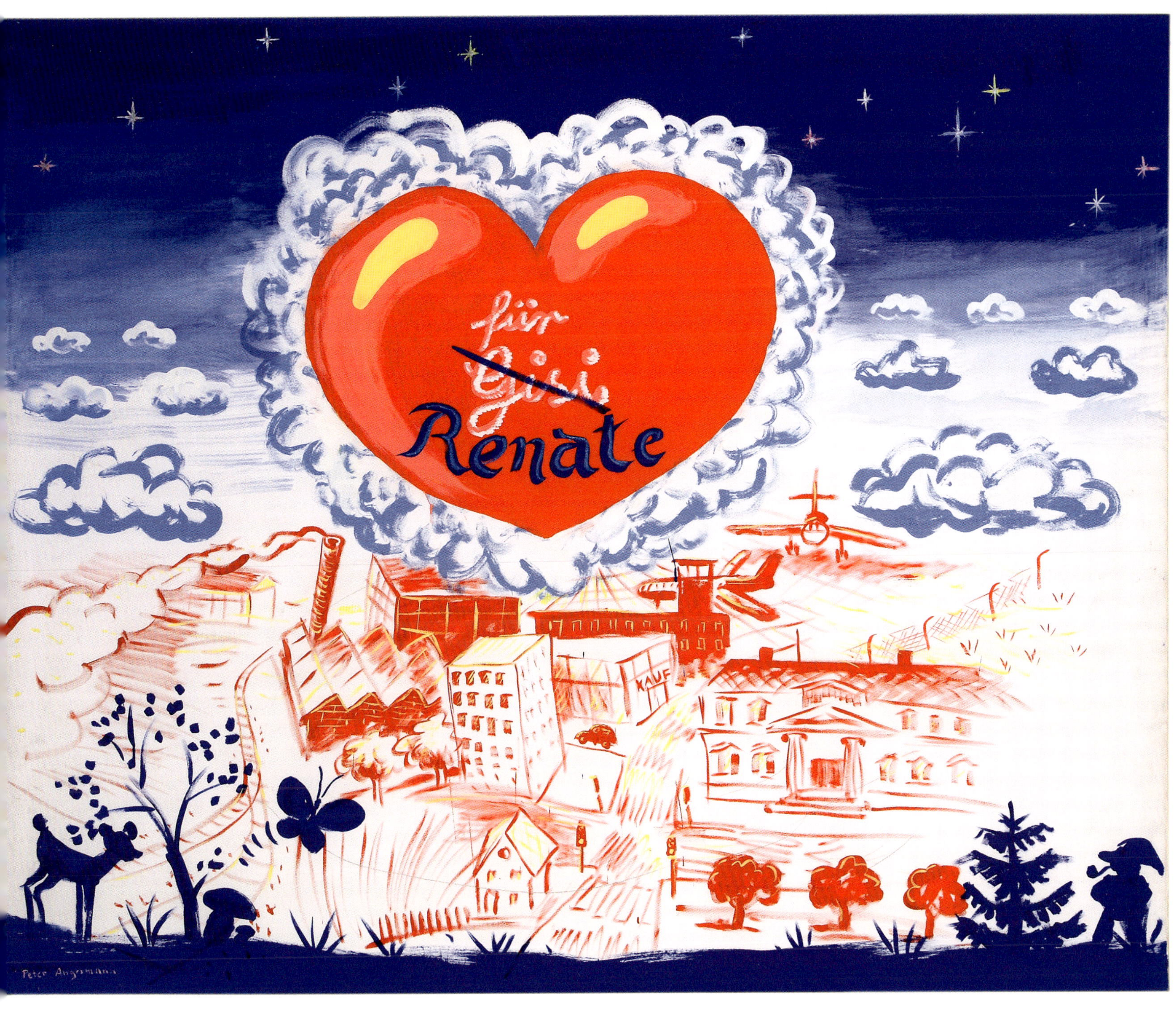

Für Renate / For Renate, 1973/76

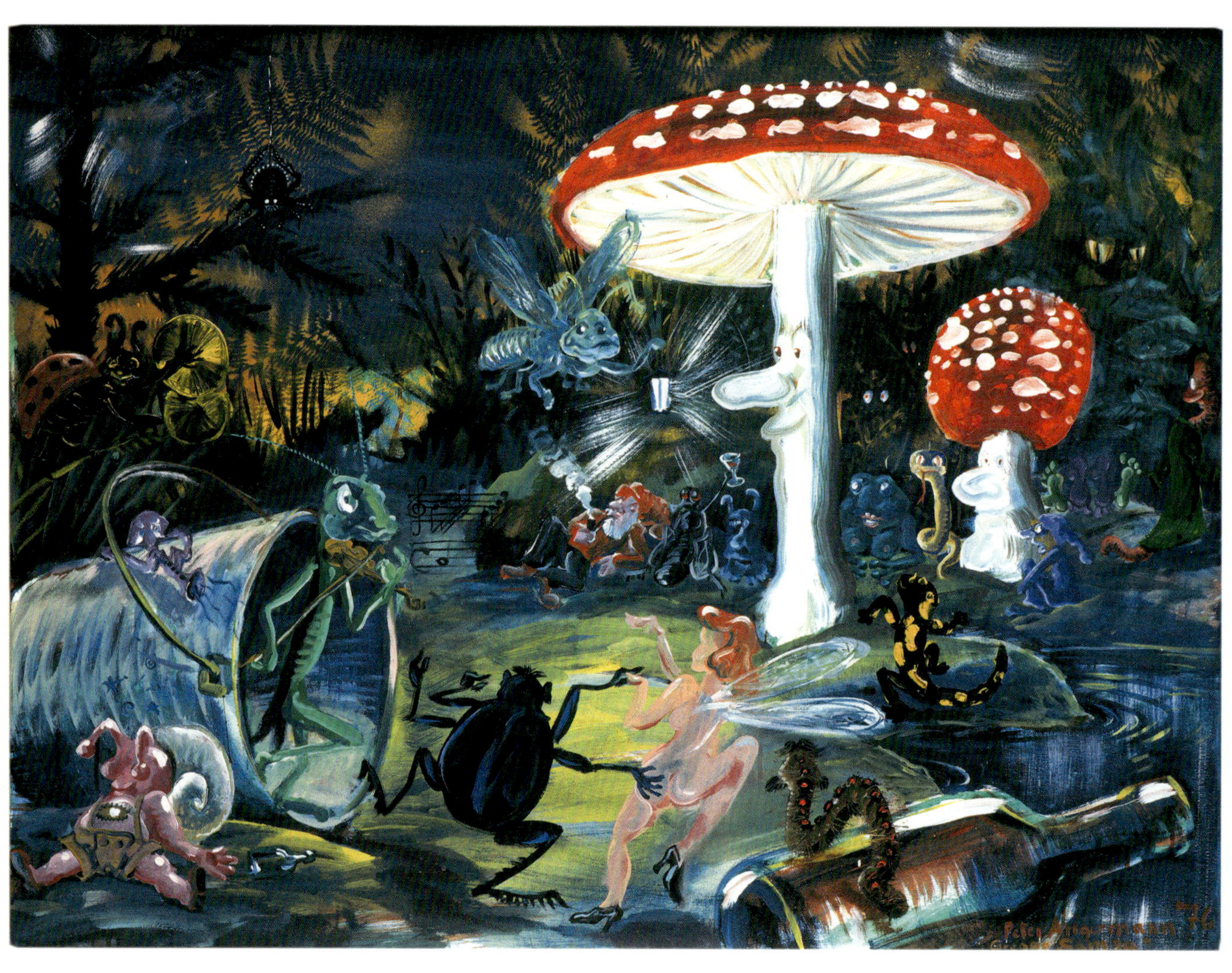

Gregor Samsas Freunde 1 / Gregor Samsa's Friends 1, 1976

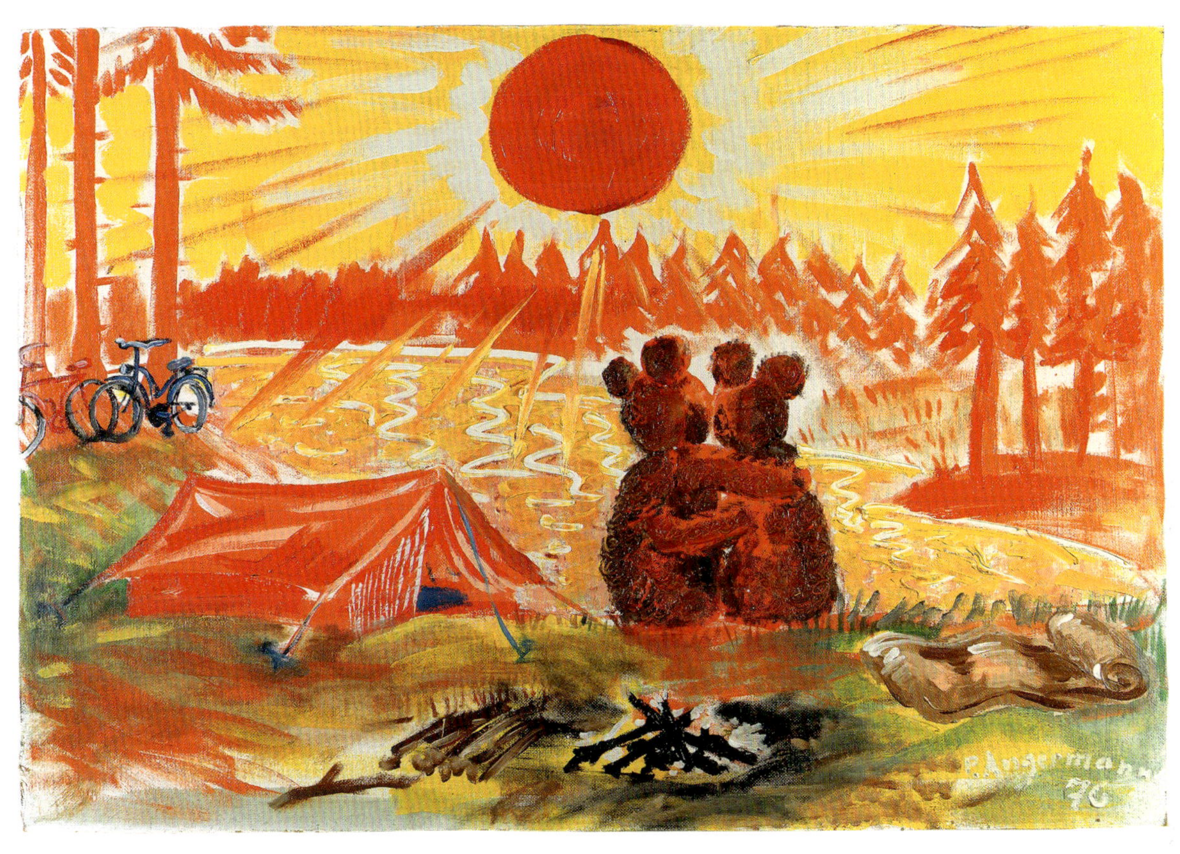

Bärenbild 1 / Bear Picture 1, 1976

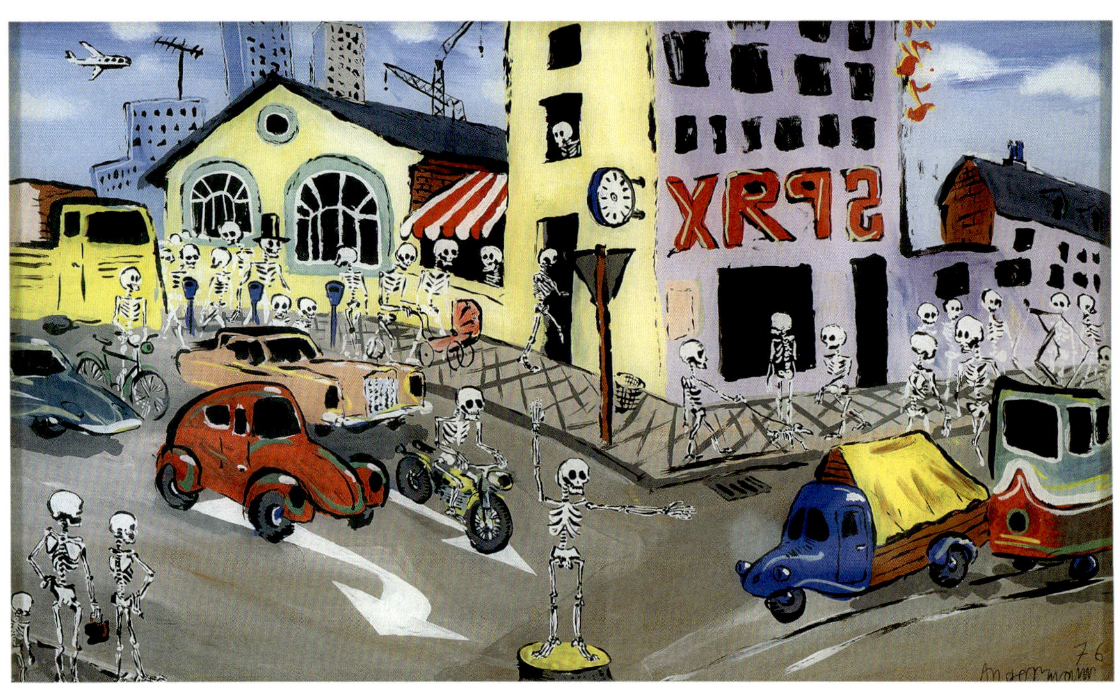

Nekropolis / Necropolis, 1976

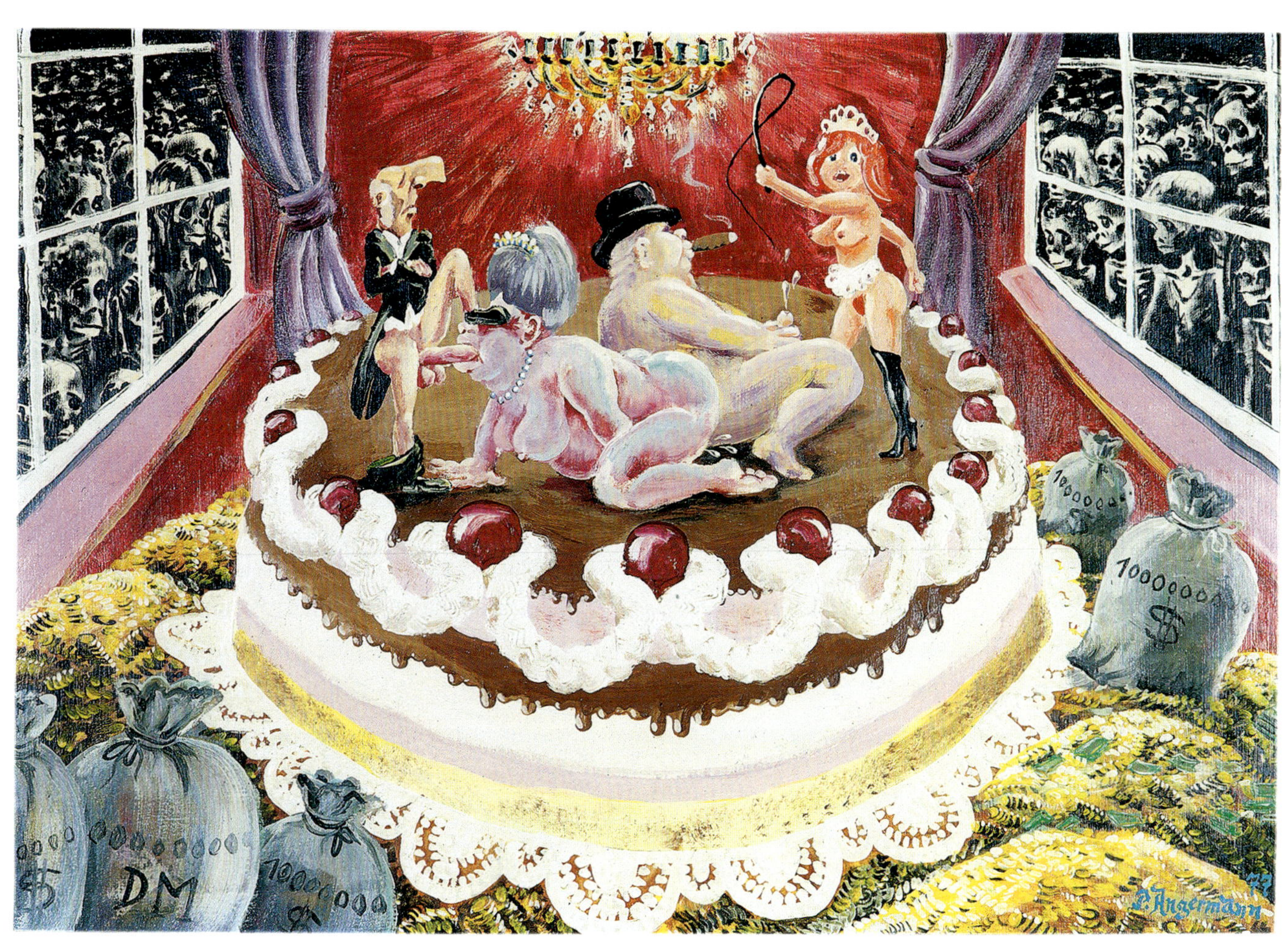

Armut, Wohlstand, Sex / Poverty, Wealth, Sex, 1977

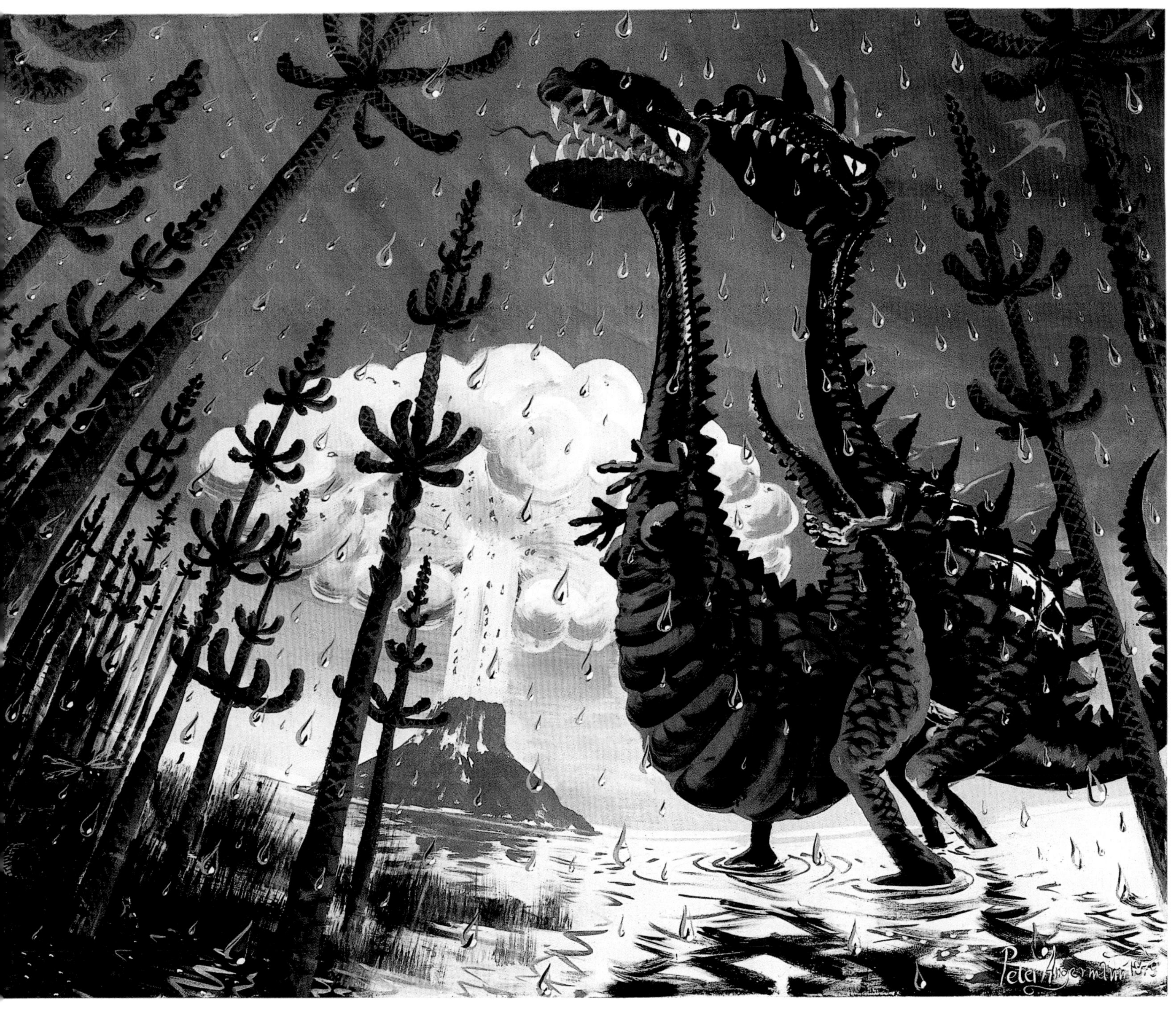

Aus grauer Vorzeit / From Time Immemorial, 1979

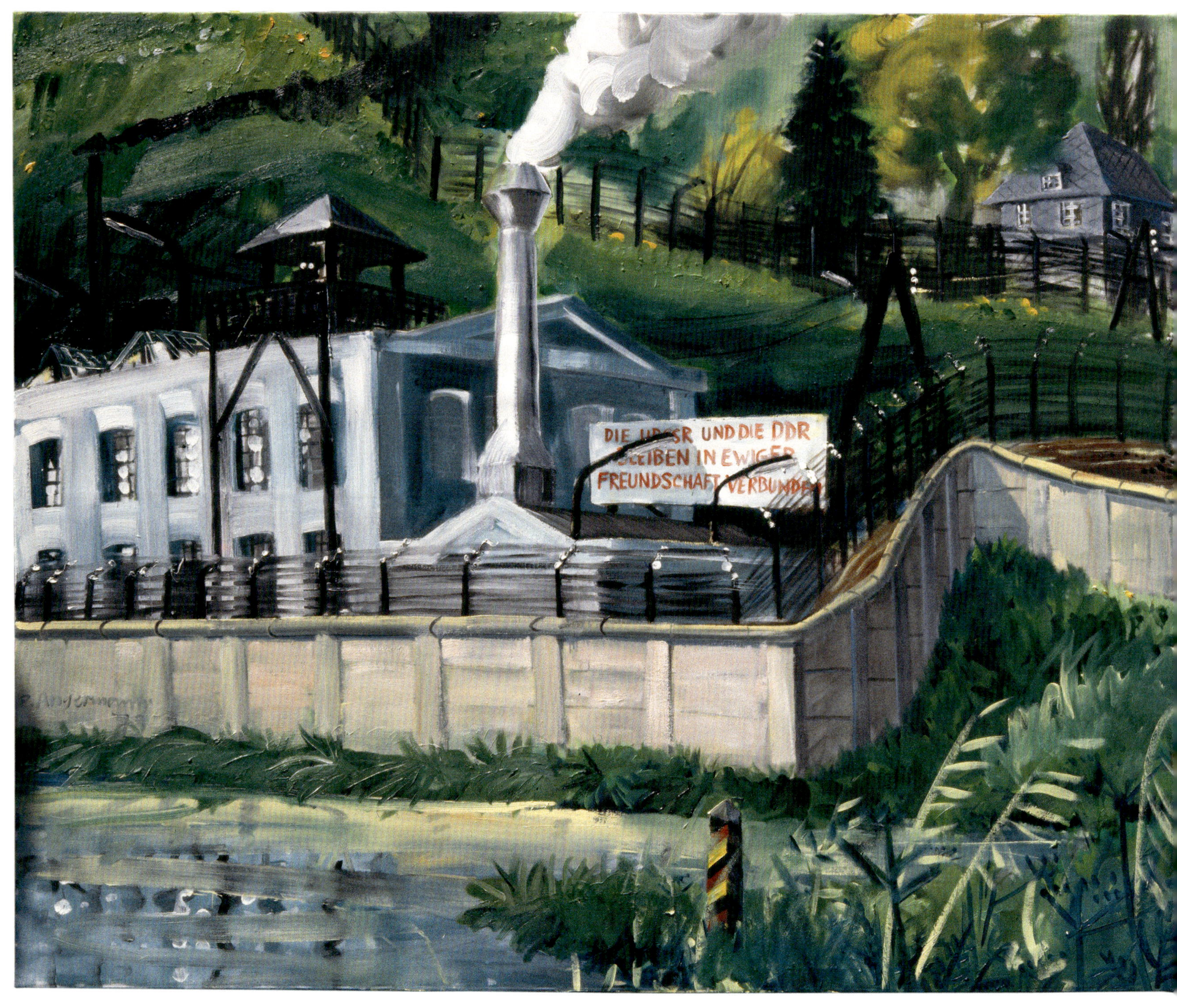

Saaletal 1, 1979

▷ *Saaletal 3, 1981*

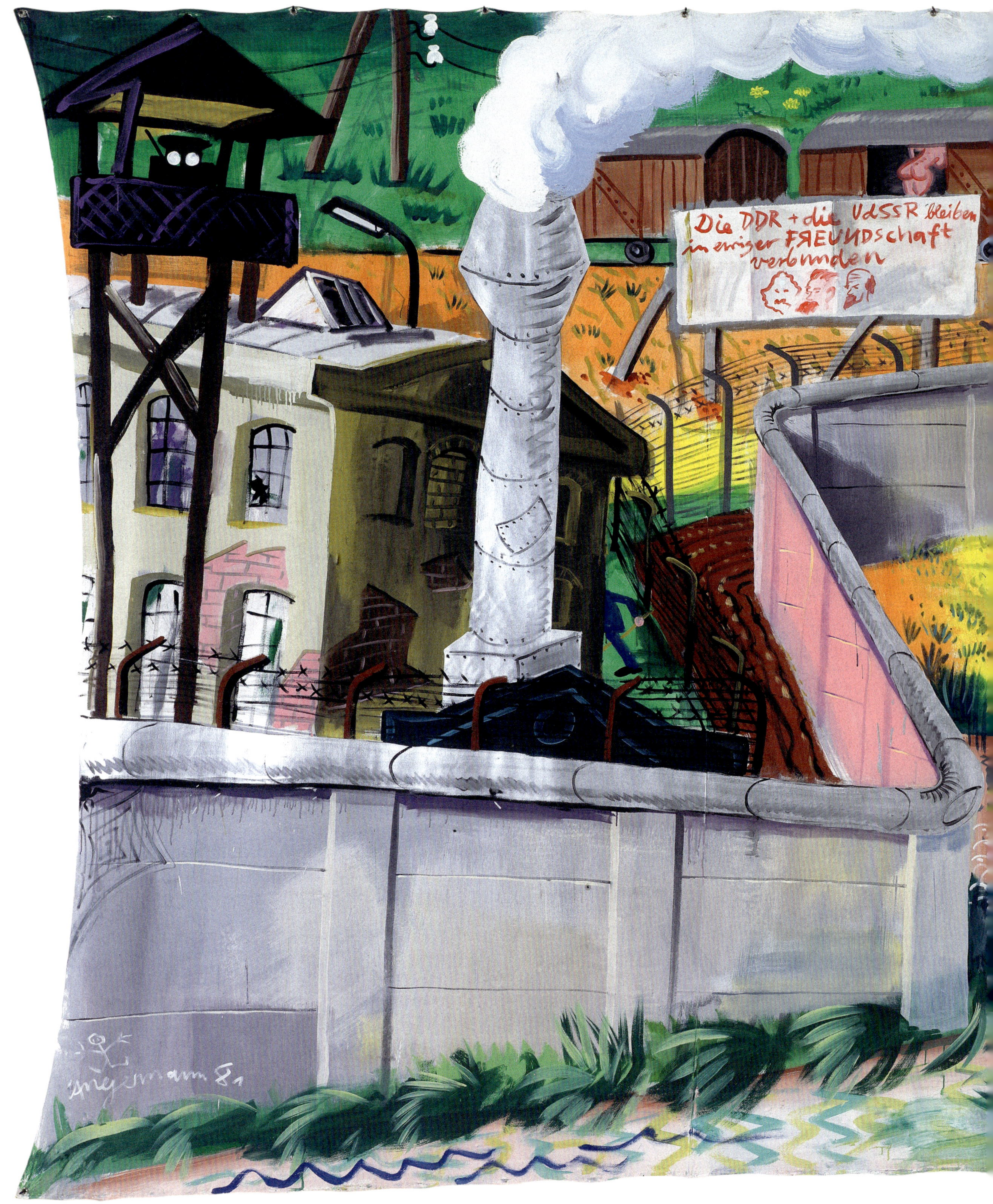

Die DDR + die UdSSR bleiben
in ewiger FREUNDschaft
verbunden

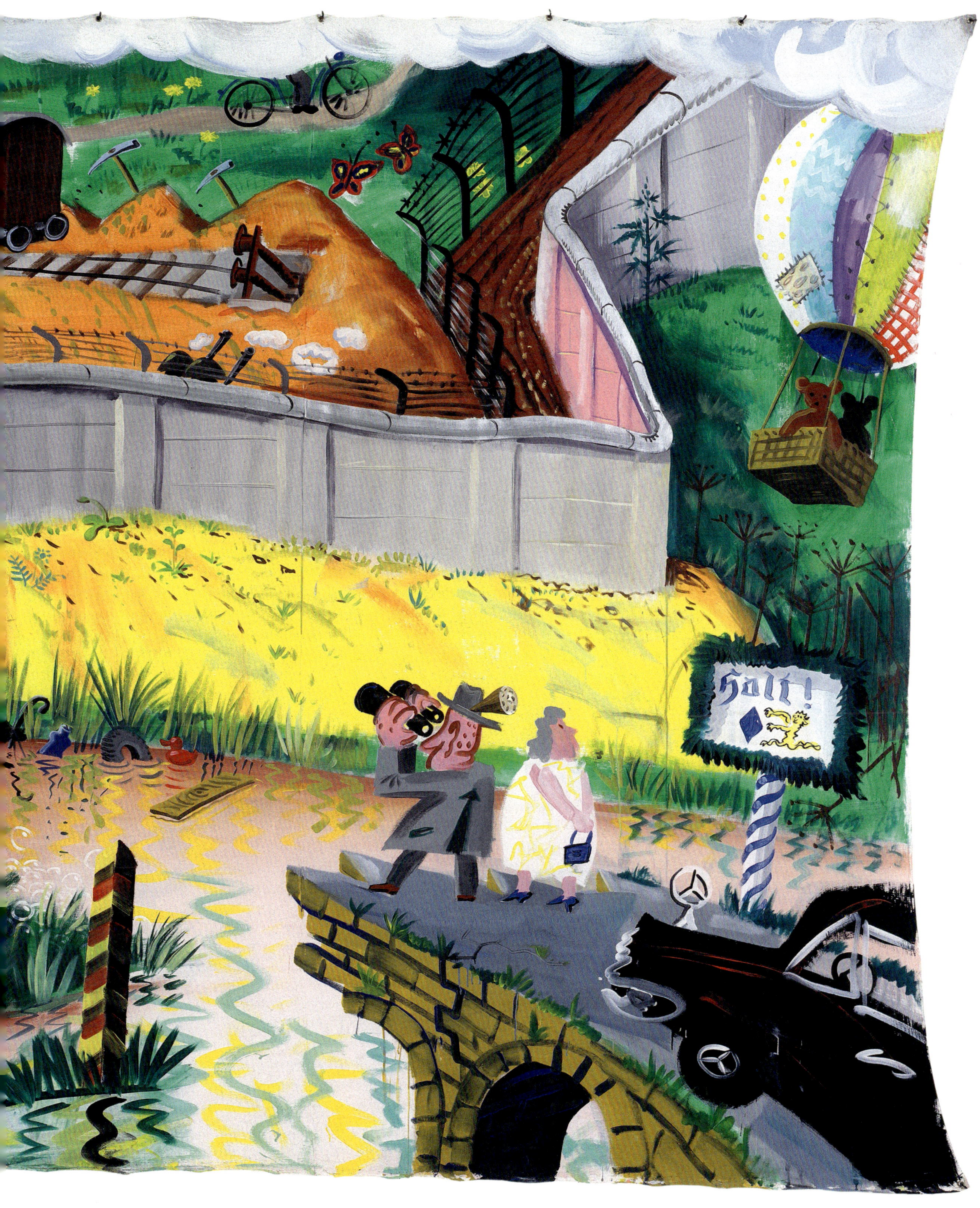
Halt!

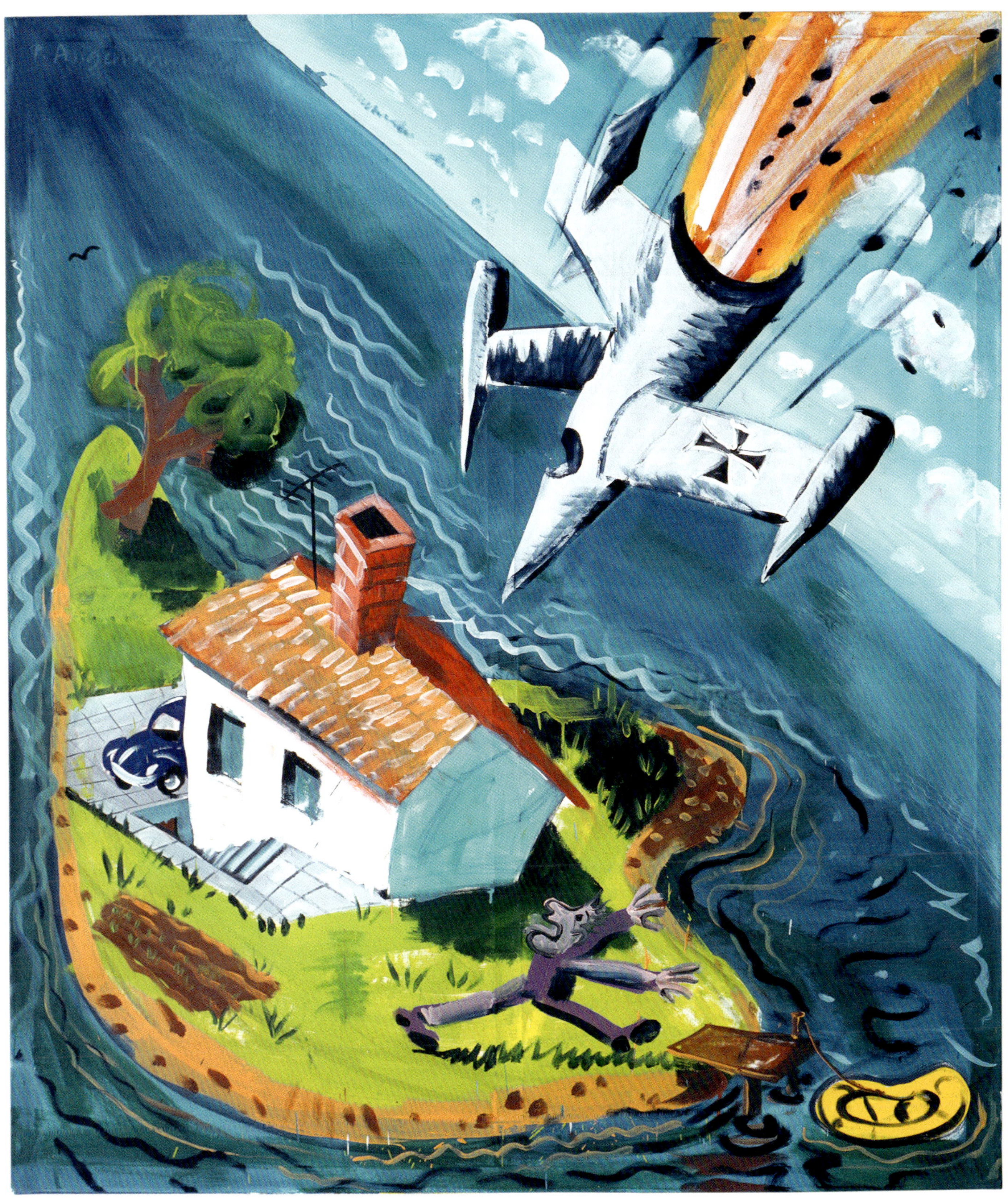

Höhere Gewalt / Force Majeure, 1981

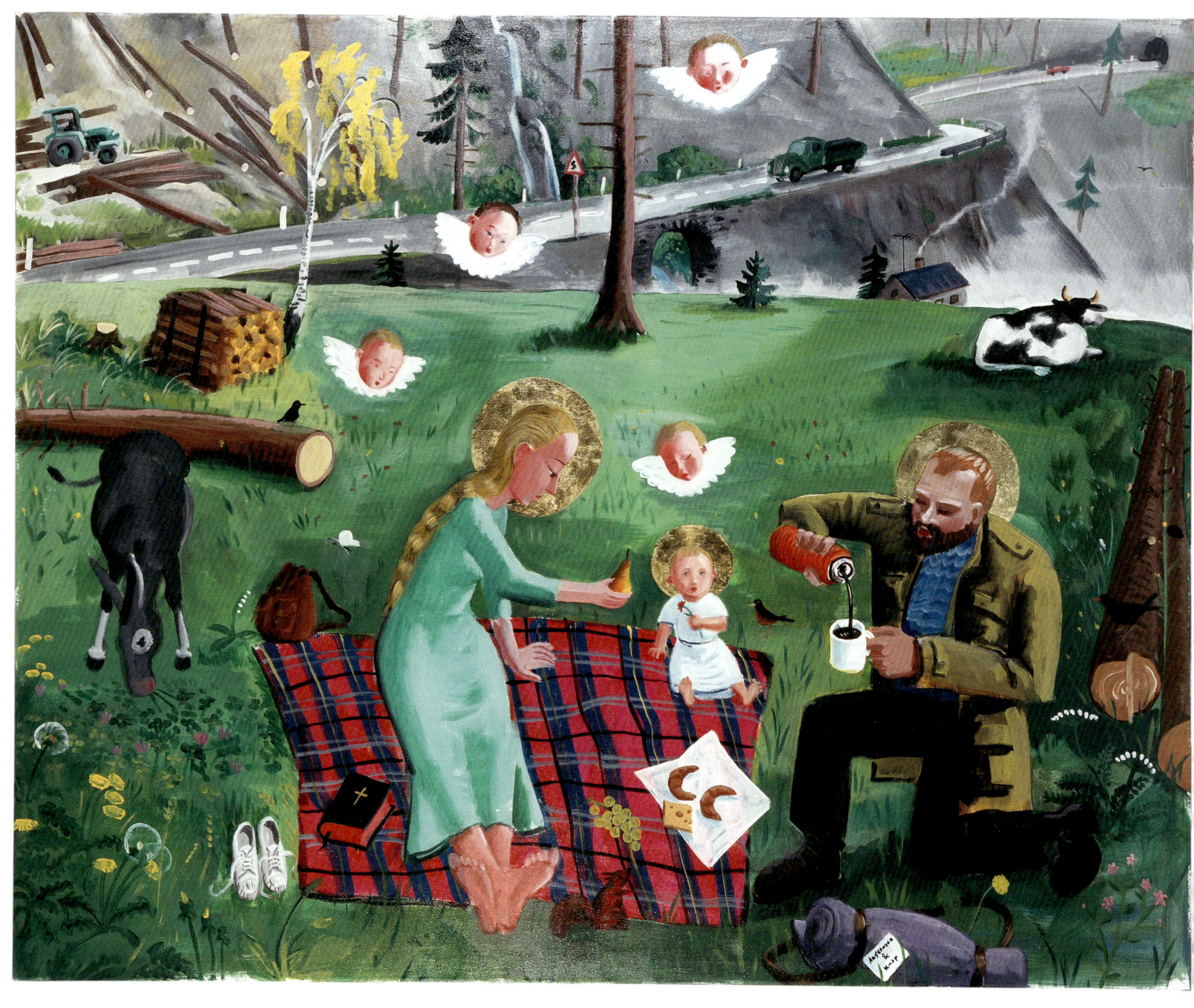

Flucht nach Ägypten / Flight into Egypt, 1981

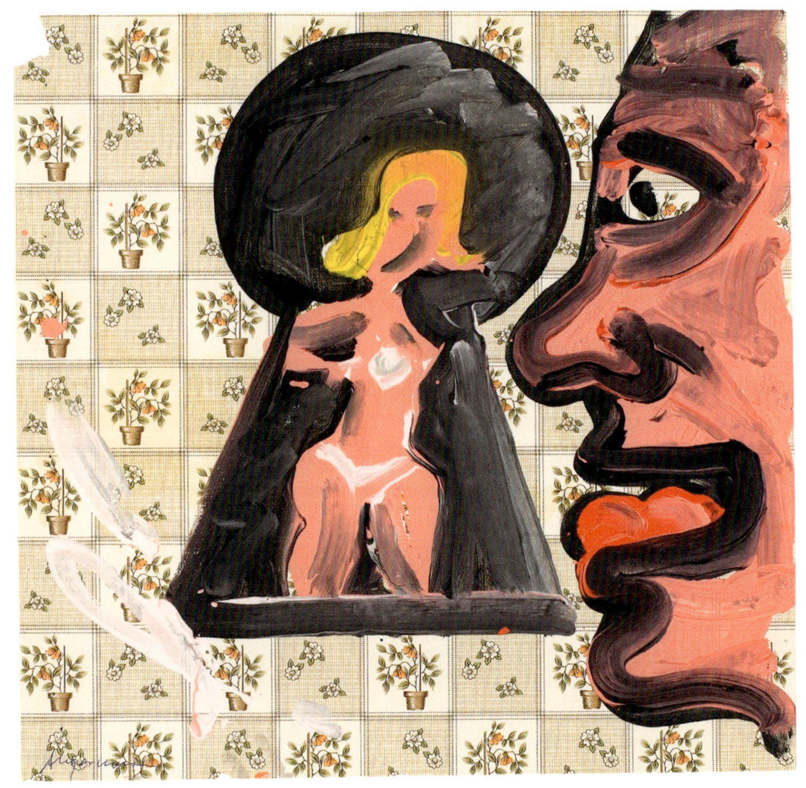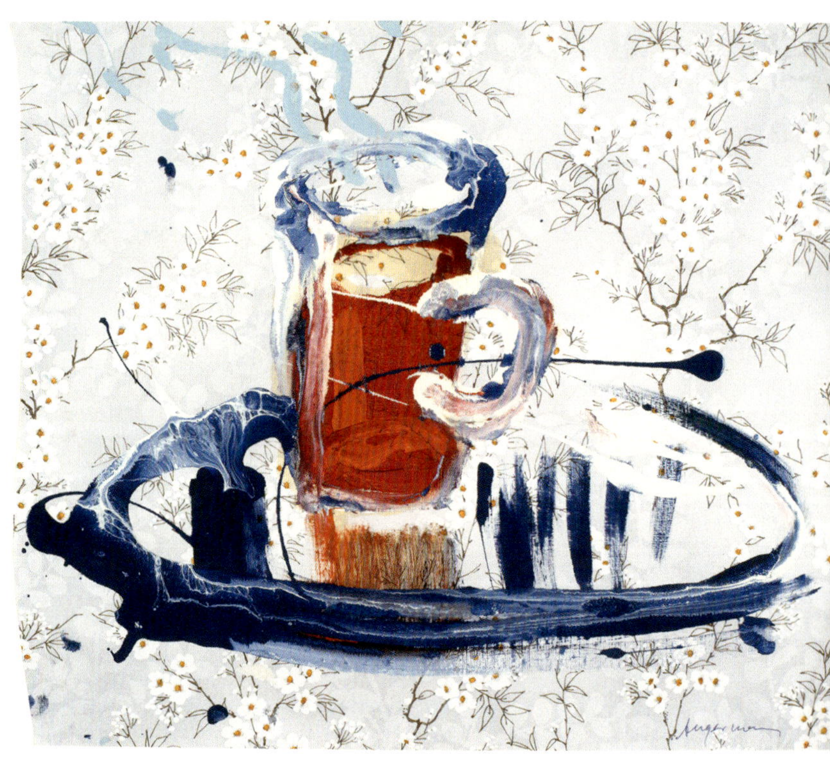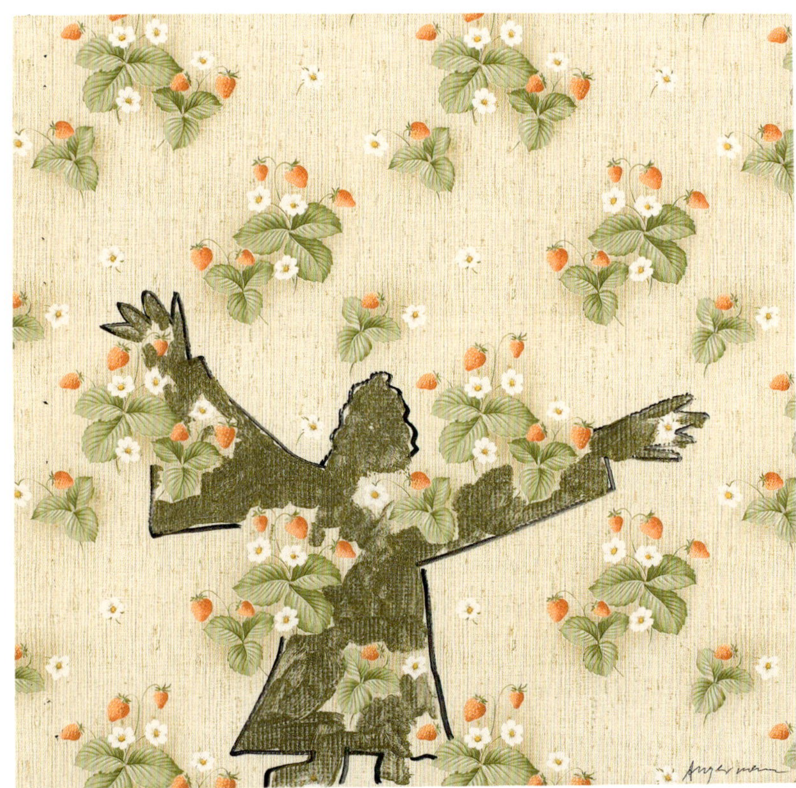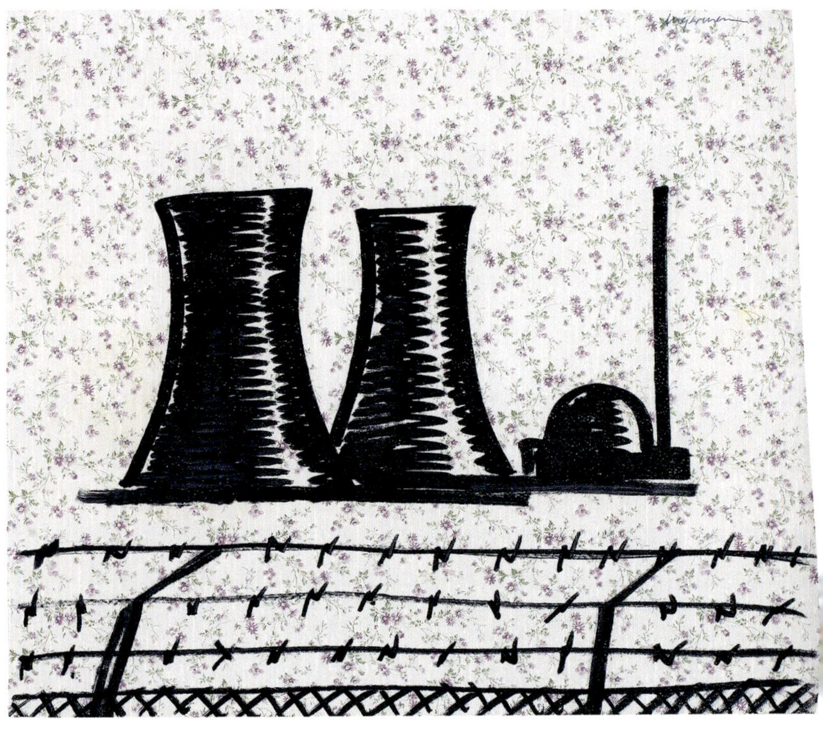

Tapeten / Wallpapers, 1983

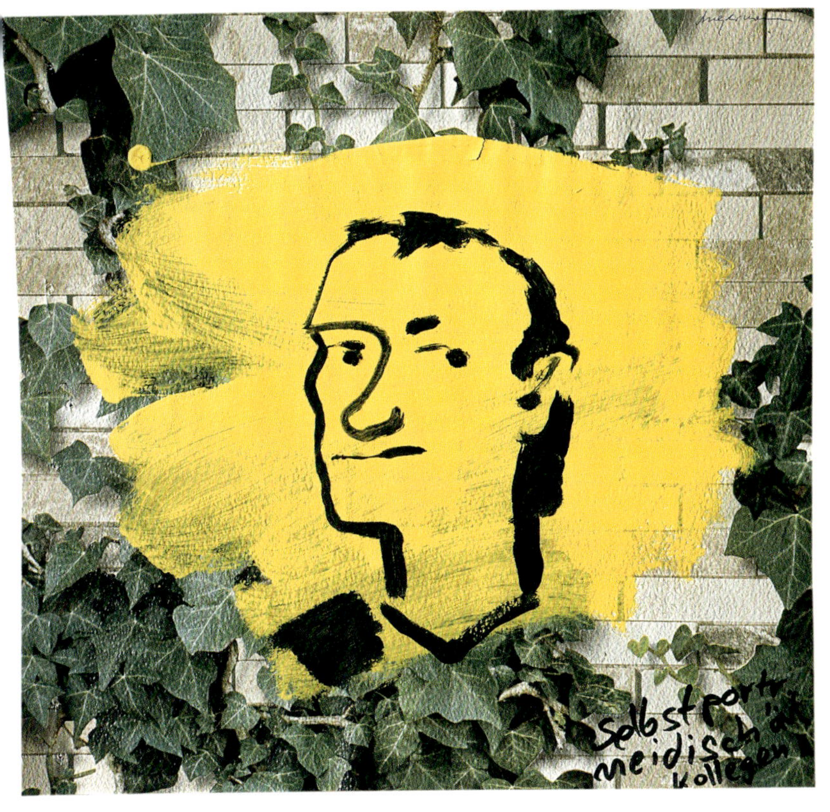

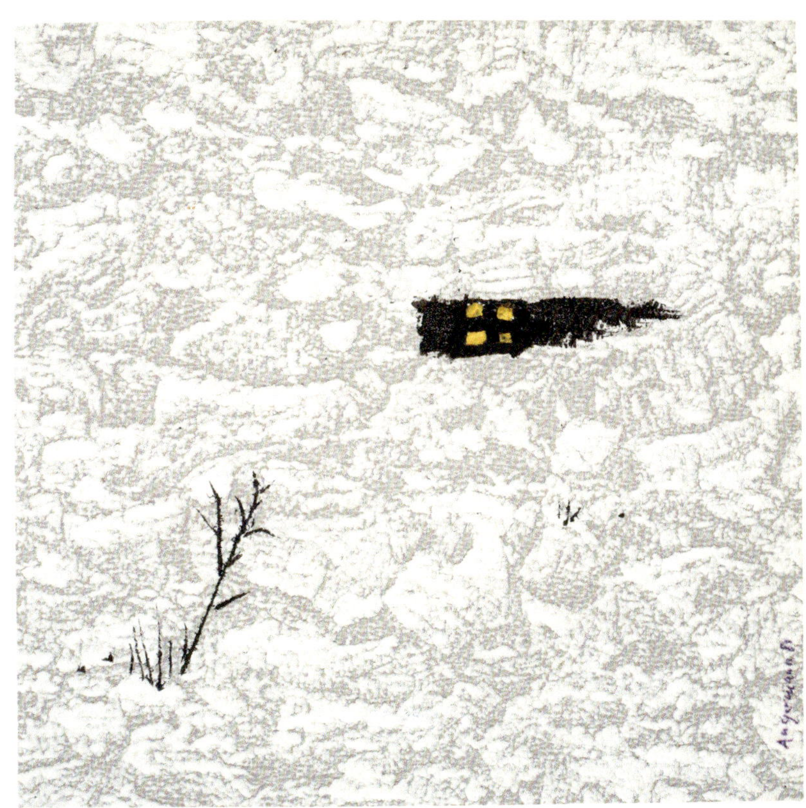

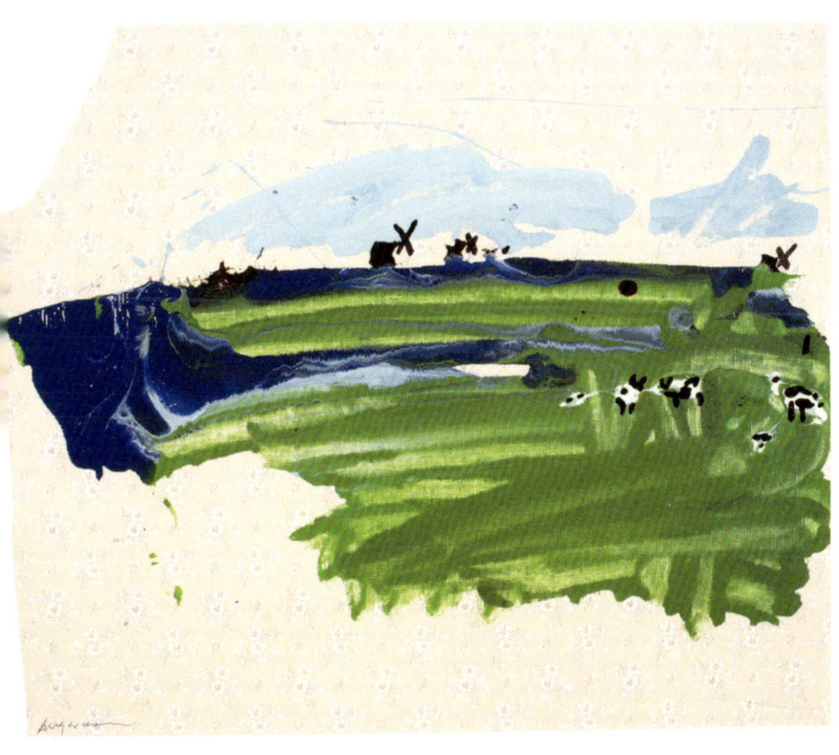

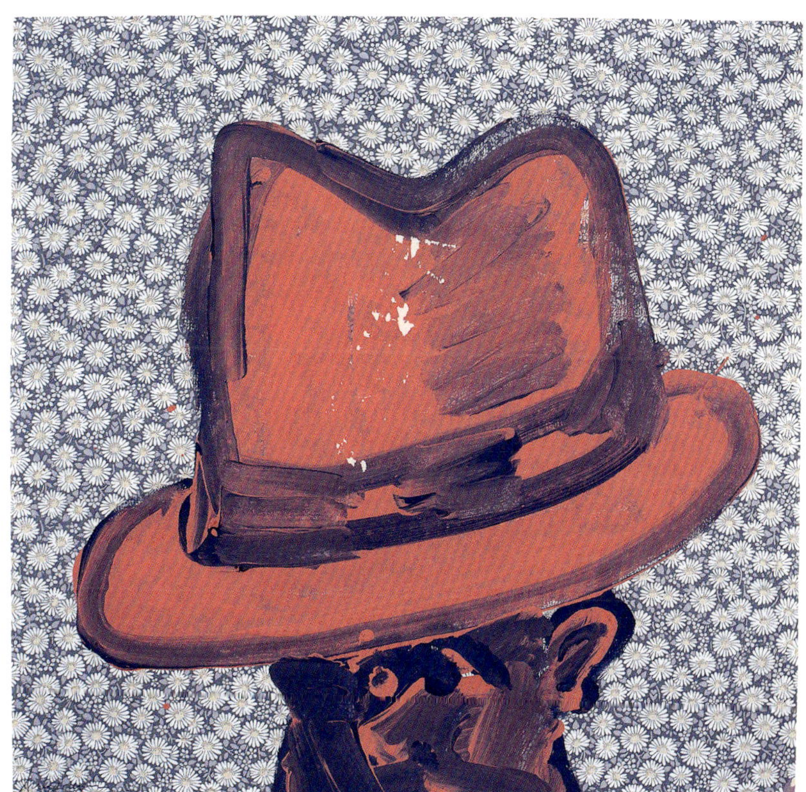

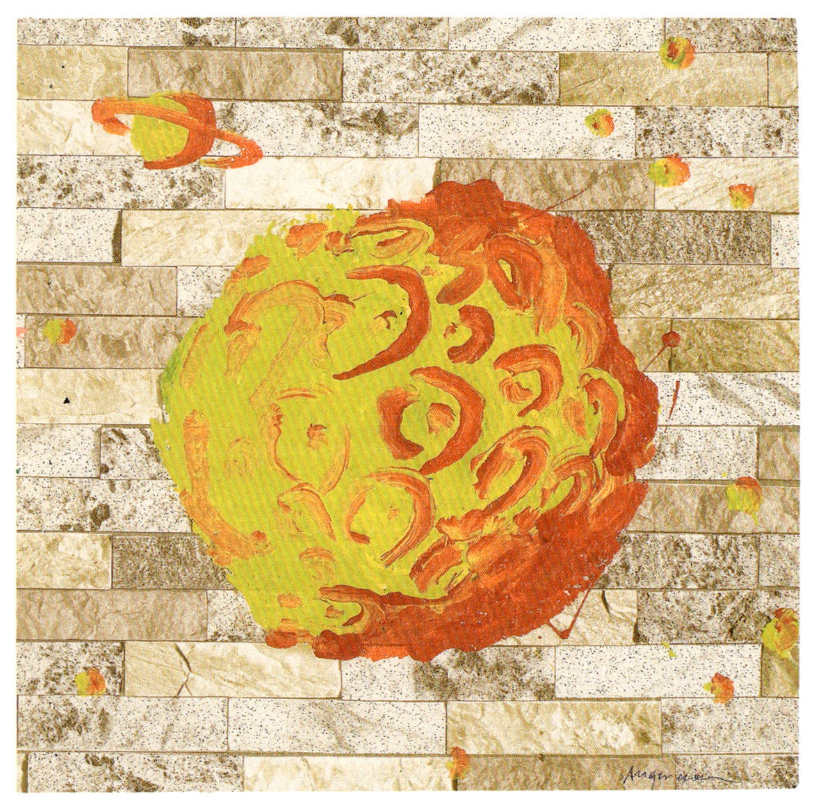
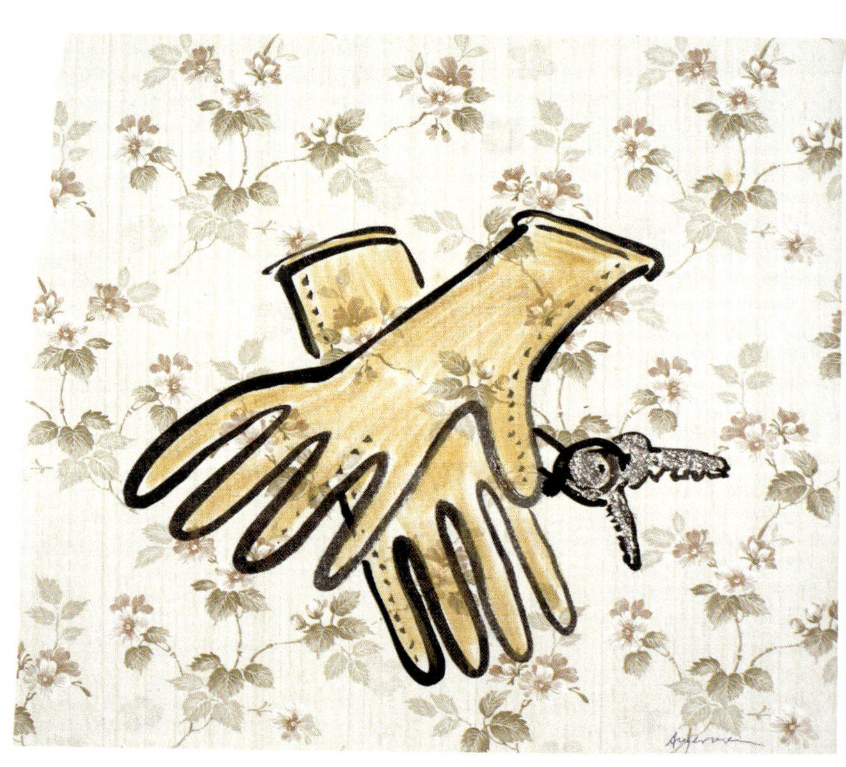
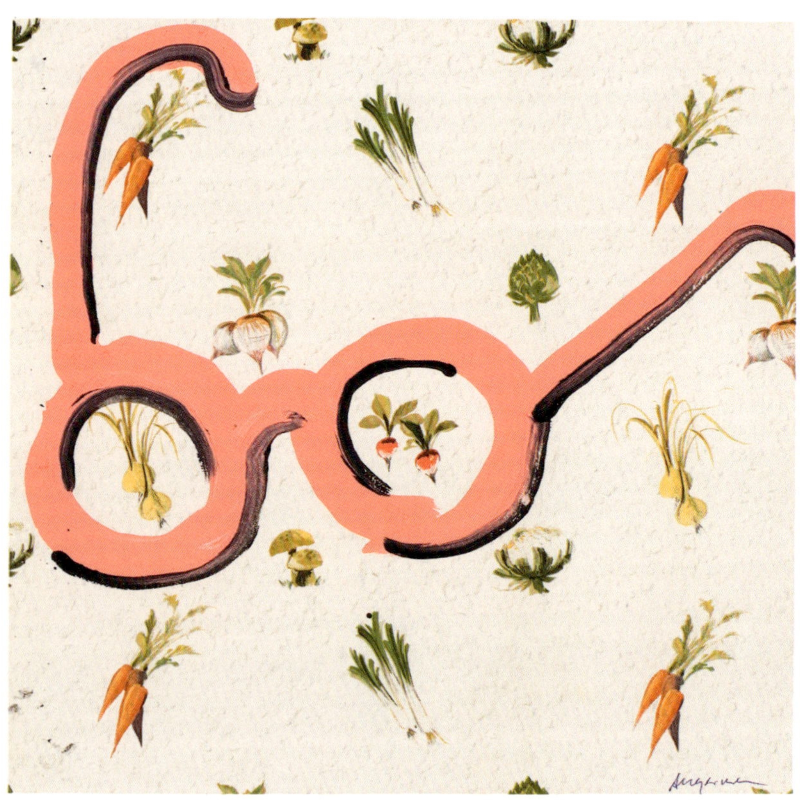
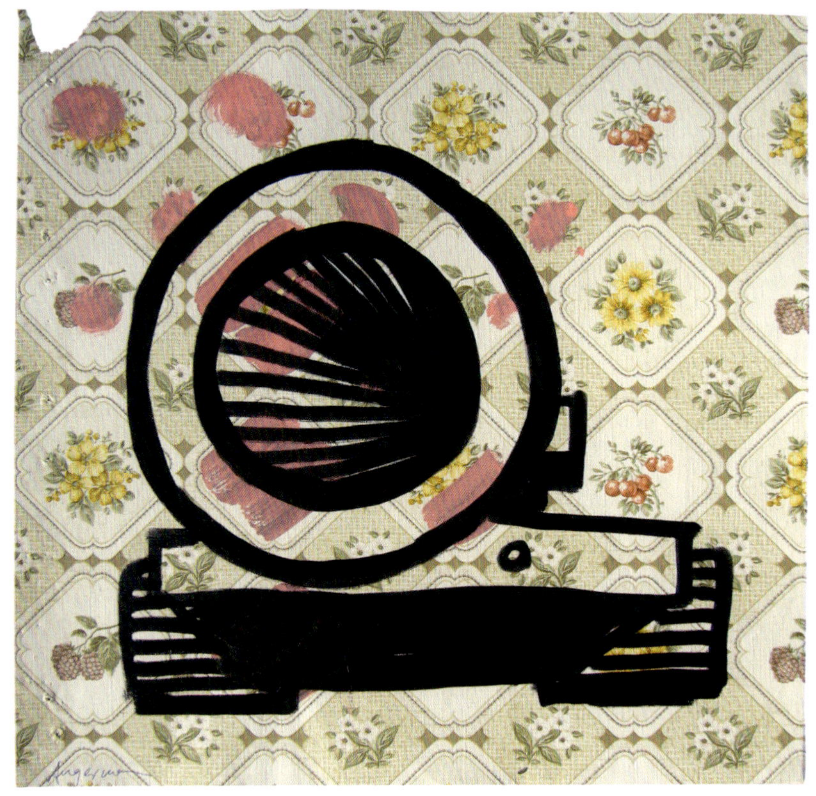

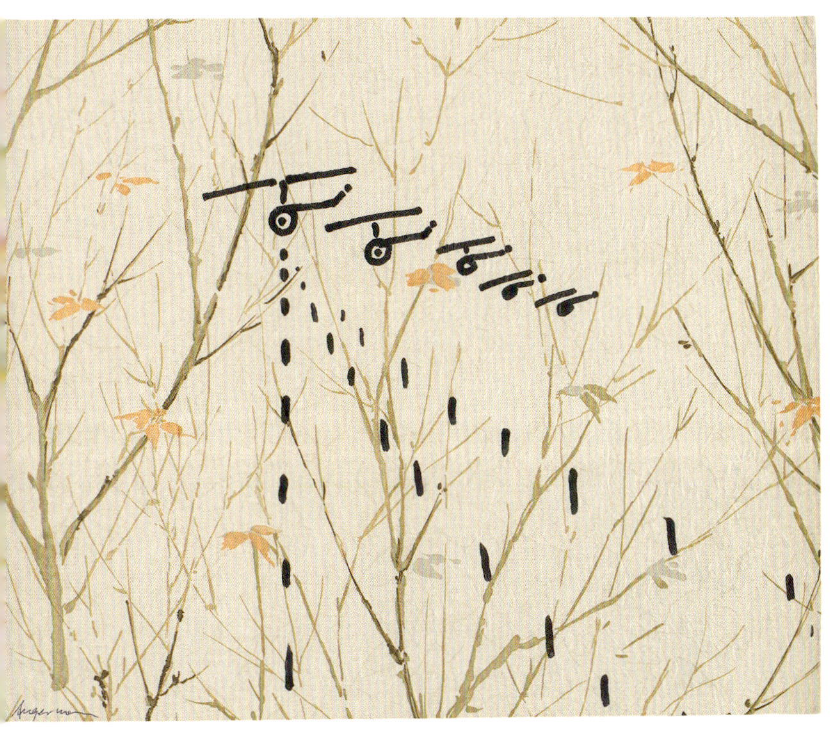

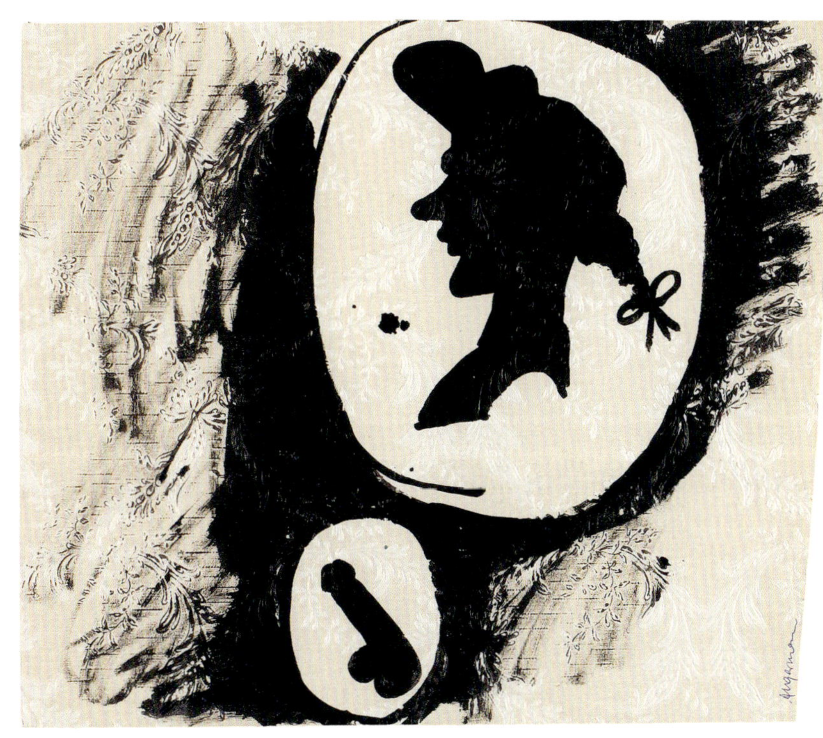

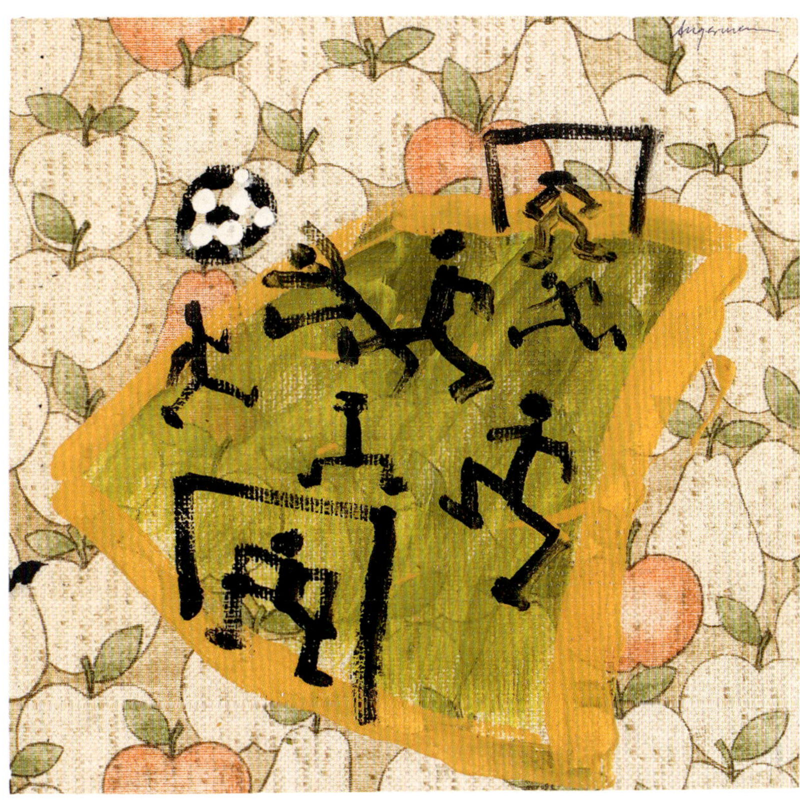

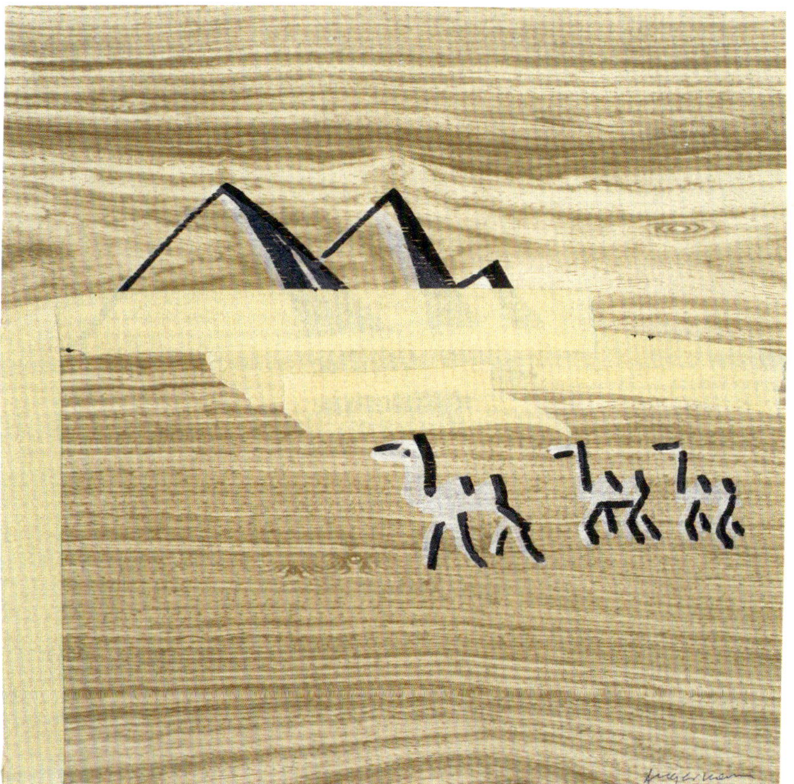

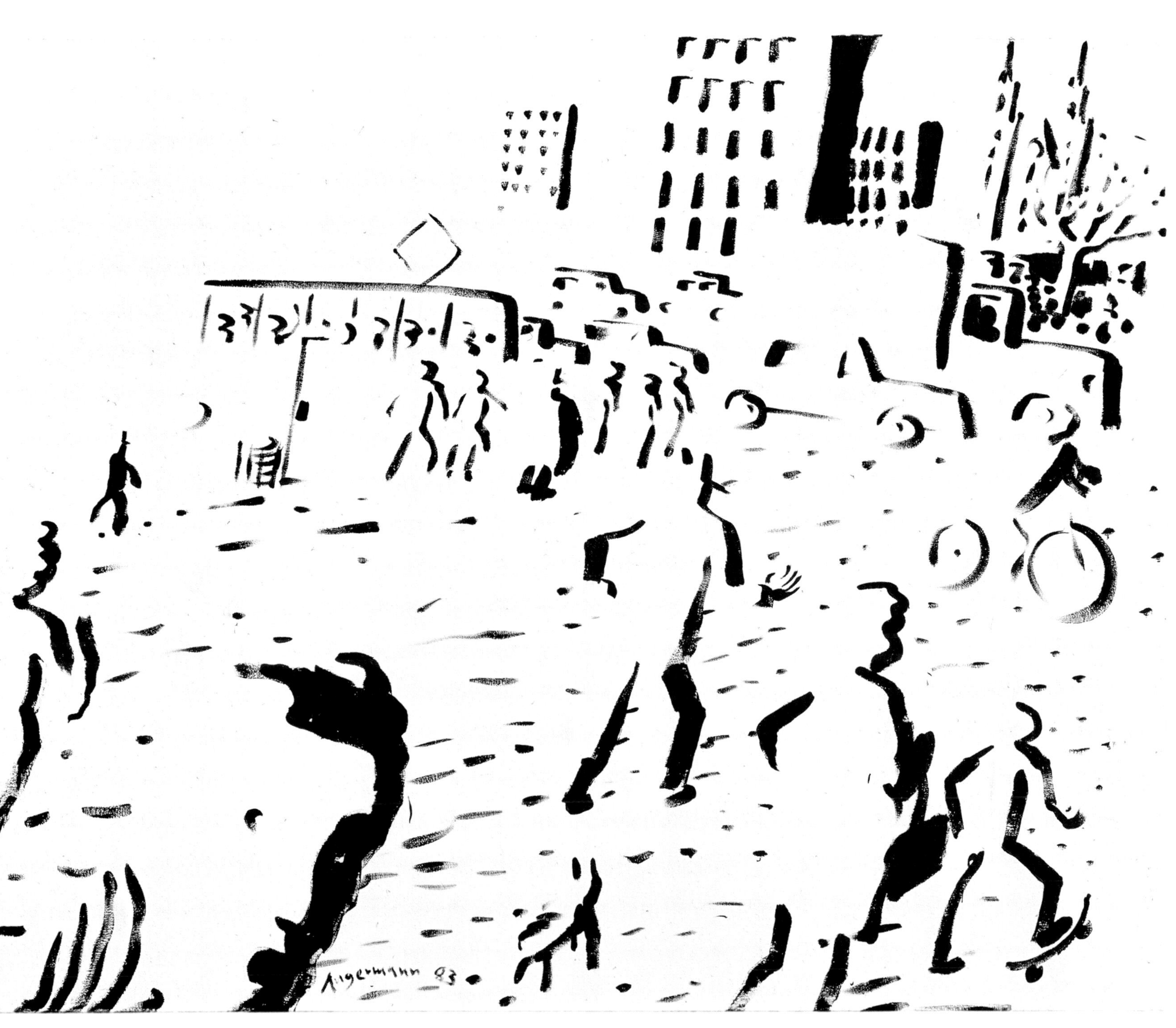

Die Jüngste Sekunde / The Final Second, 1983

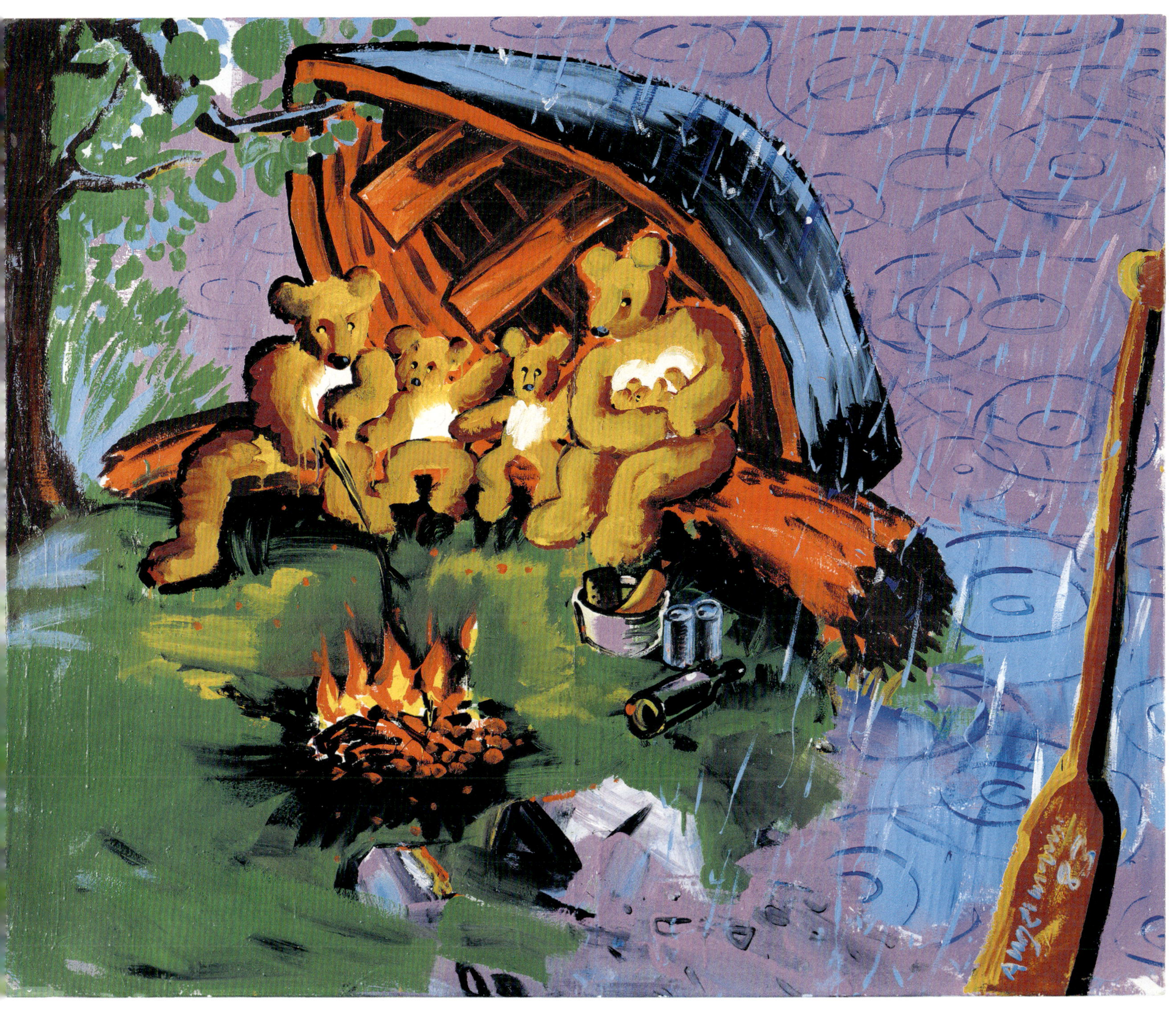

Warm und Trocken 1 / Warm and Dry 1, 1983

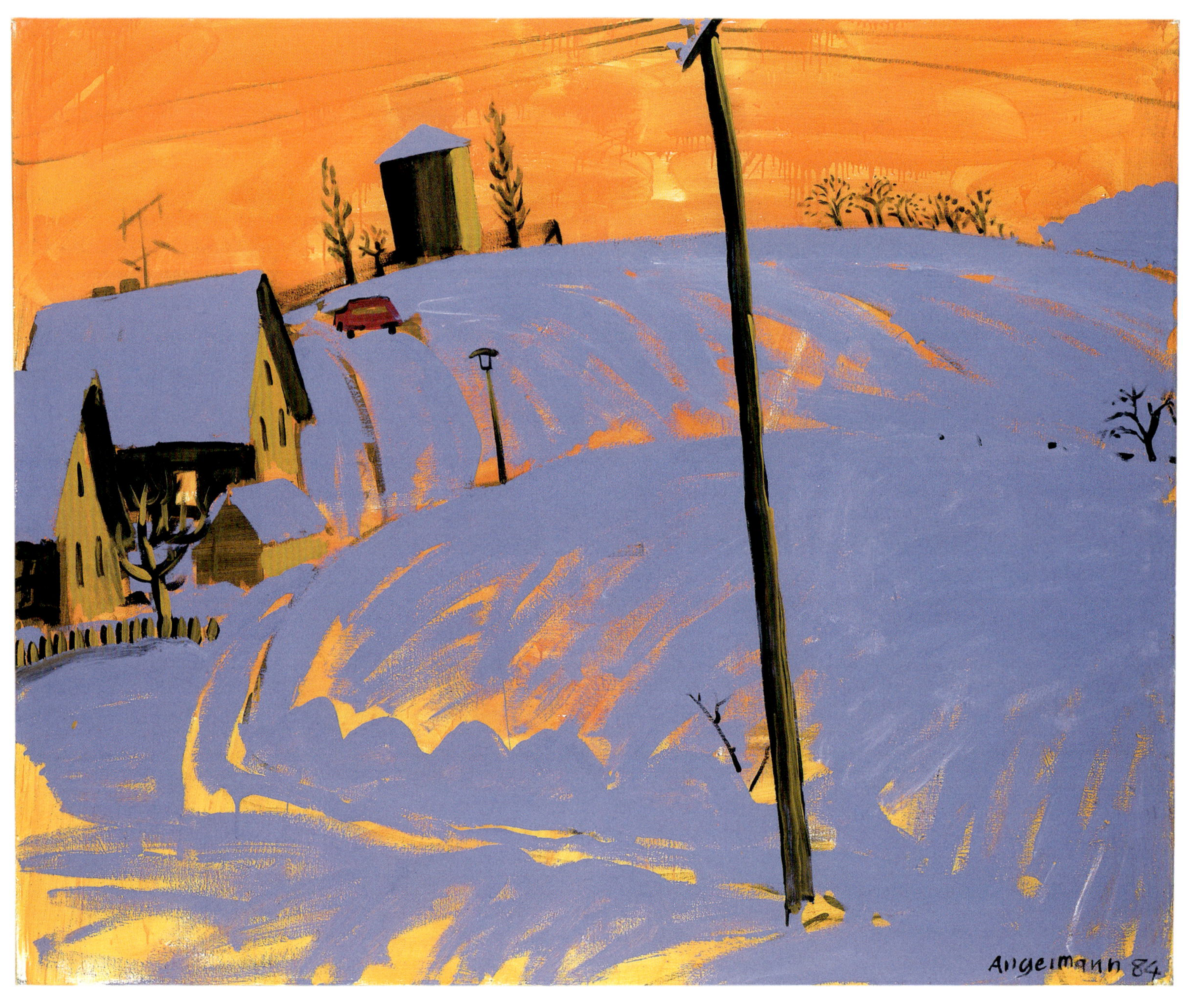

Kleingeschaidt, 1984

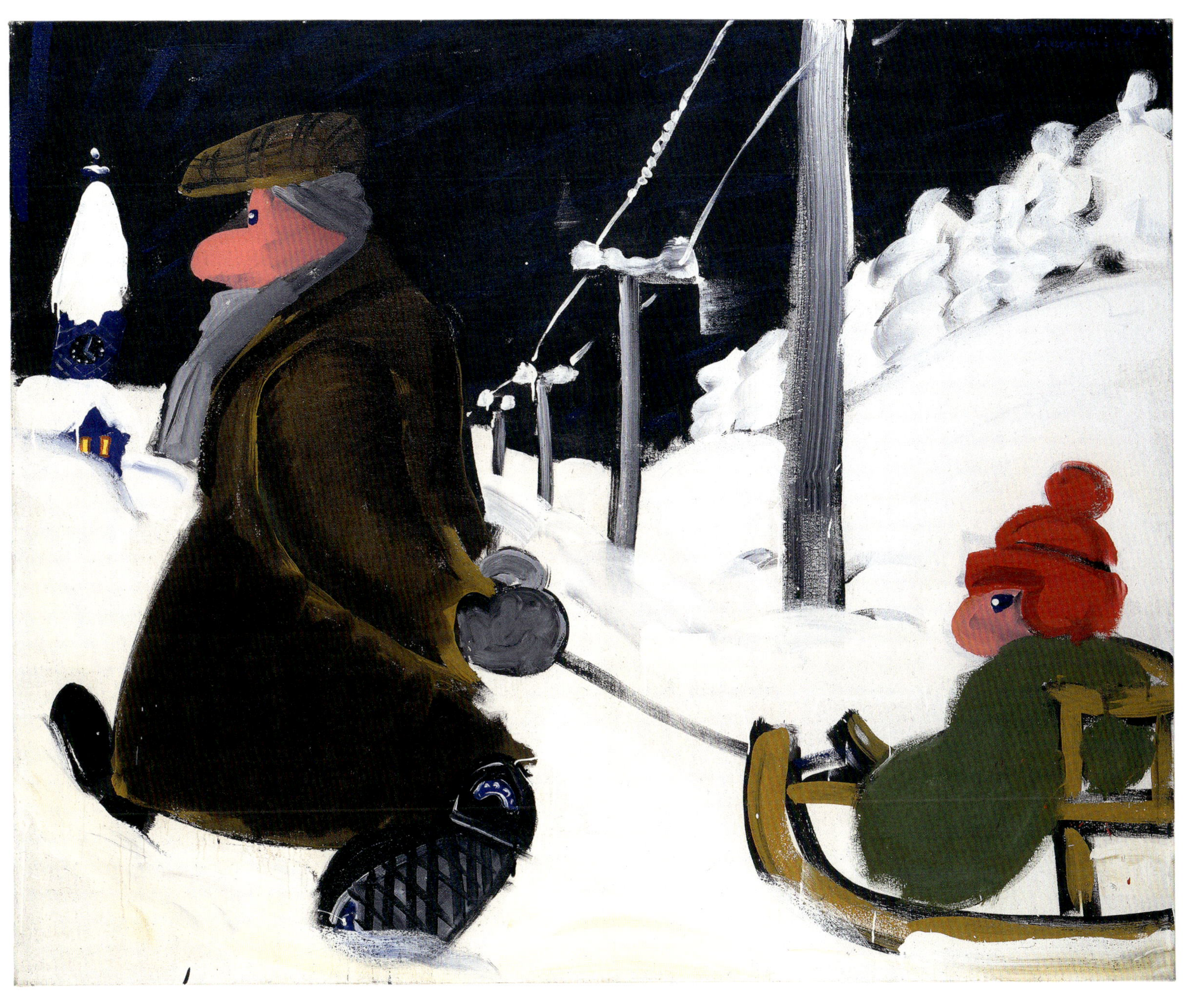

Selbst mit Opa / Self with Granddad, 1985

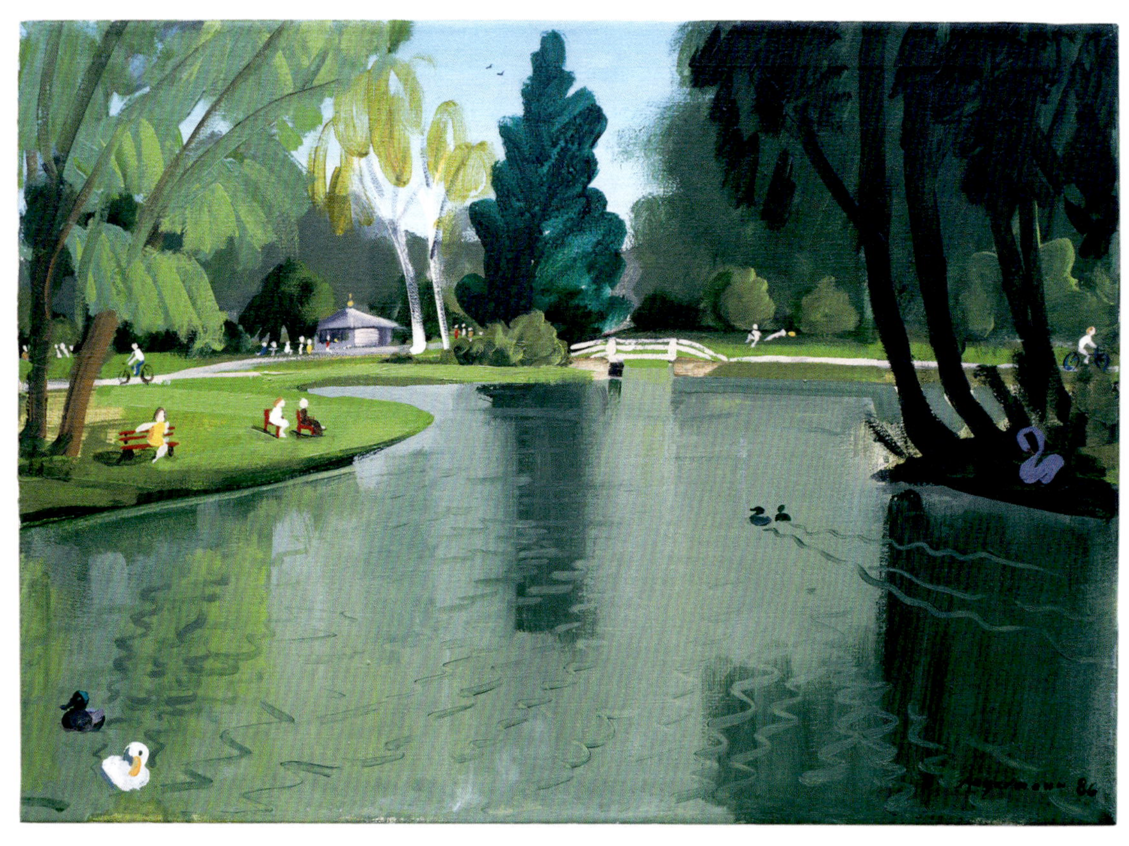

Stadtparkweiher in Nürnberg / Municipal Gardens in Nuremberg, 1986

Die Bäume schlagen aus – Die Malerei von Peter Angermann

Julian Spalding

Der Lieblingszeitvertreib des kleinen Peter Angermann war es erstens, ins Kino mitgenommen zu werden, und zweitens, mit seinen Margarine-Tierbildern zu spielen. Eine seiner frühesten und höchst lebendigen Erinnerungen ist der Versuch, beides miteinander zu verbinden. Er baute einen finsteren Tunnel aus Sofakissen und stellte seine Margarinebilder hinten hinein. Dann warf er mittels eines Spiegels das Sonnenlicht vom Fenster in die Höhle, so dass die Szene an der Rückwand wie eine Kinoleinwand aufleuchtete. Jahre später stellte er fest, dass es genau dies war, was er in seiner Malerei tat: Licht auf etwas zu werfen, das ihn faszinierte.

Platons berühmtes Höhlengleichnis fällt einem ein – nicht dass sich Angermann dessen damals bewusst gewesen wäre! Platon dachte, wir wären wie Leute, die auf dem Boden der Höhle sitzend die bewegten Schatten an der Wand beobachteten, welche von Leuten geworfen wurden, die draußen vor der Höhle und außer Sichtweite vor der verborgenen Lichtquelle vorbeigingen. Aber sie konnten diese Passanten reden hören, so dass sie glaubten, die Schatten sprächen. Sie mussten annehmen, die Schatten seien wirkliche Menschen. Platon stellte sich vor, jemand käme von draußen herein, der das Licht gesehen hatte und die Höhlenbewohner davon zu überzeugen suchte, dass das, was sie sahen, nur eine Täuschung sei, was diese dann wenig freundlich aufnahmen. Es ist das Schicksal aller Künstler mit tieferer Einsicht, zuerst auf Unverständnis zu stoßen. Und Angermann ist keine Ausnahme. Was an ihm überrascht, ist neben vielem anderen, dass er irgendwie von Anfang an fühlte, dass er ein Maler ist. Und dass er es trotz aller Hindernisse des Konzeptualismus, die ihm in den Weg geworfen wurden, schließlich schaffte, genau das zu werden: ein Maler unserer und für unsere Zeit, und zwar einer, der Licht auf das wirft, was wir oft nicht so gern wahrhaben möchten.

Peter Angermann wurde in der kleinen fränkischen Industriestadt Rehau geboren, wo es nach Gerbereien roch und die Tunnelöfen der Porzellanfabriken den Himmel verrußten, nördlich der Gegend, wo er heute lebt und arbeitet und die er kaum je verlässt. Sein Vater war ein Krankenkassen-Beamter. Es gab Musik im Haus, doch keine bildende Kunst. Weil man sich wegen der Aufnahmeprüfung für das Gymnasium glaubte Sorgen machen zu müssen, schickte man ihn zu Nachhilfestunden ins Haus einer hugenottischen Familie, das zu seiner Überraschung und Freude voller Malerei und Bücher über Malerei war – Dufy, Cézanne, van Gogh. Sein Lehrer, Gunther le Maire, nur wenig älter als er, sprach ihm für seine Begeisterung und seine frühen Anläufe Mut zu. Er gewann Selbstvertrauen, widerstand den Wünschen seiner Eltern, etwas Nützliches zu studieren (da Malerei in ihren Augen nur ein Hobby sein konnte), und ging zur Kunstakademie. Dort erweiterte sich sein Horizont: Er kam mit der Pop-Art in Berührung (Hockney bleibt ein fruchtbarer Einfluss), mit der Fluxus-Bewegung, und war bald auf der Höhe der Zeit angekommen. Frei ließ er Blatt für Blatt seine Gedanken und Gefühle wandern, was er „Brainstorming" (*Brainstorming 1* und 5, 1968, S. 36/37)

Painting's Spring – The Art of Peter Angermann

Julian Spalding

When Peter Angermann was a small boy, his two favourite pastimes were being taken to the cinema and playing with his farm-animal pictures. One of his earliest and most vivid memories was an attempt to combine these experiences. He made a dark tunnel on a sofa by leaning cushions together and balancing one on top. He propped up pictures of farm animals at the back and then, using a mirror, shone sunlight from the window into the cavern so that the scene at the end lit up like a cinema screen. Years later he realised that this was what he was doing in his painting, shining a light on something that fascinated him.

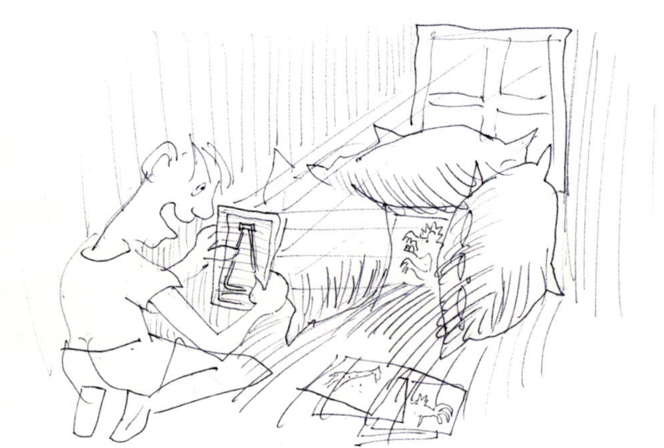

Heimkino / Home Cinema, 2011, Kugelschreiber auf Papier / ballpoint pen on paper

Plato's famous analogy of the cave comes to mind, not that Angermann was aware of this at the time! Plato thought we were like people sitting at the bottom of a cave watching shadows moving on a wall before them. These shadows were cast by people passing the mouth of the cave high up and behind the people's heads so that they couldn't see the source of the light. But they could hear these passers-by talking, so they thought the shadows were speaking. They assumed, naturally enough, that the shadows were real people. Plato imagines someone coming in from outside, who's seen the light, and trying to convince the cave-dwellers that what they're looking at is an illusion. The cave-dwellers don't take kindly to this suggestion. It's the fate of all artists with insight to be met at first with incomprehension. And Angermann is no exception. What is surprising, among many surprising things about him, is that he somehow sensed he was a painter from the beginning, and that despite all the obstacles of Conceptualism thrown in his path, he managed to become just that: a painter of and for our times, and one who has thrown light on what we often don't like to admit might well be true.

Peter Angermann was born and brought up in Bavarian Franconia, in the small industrial town of Rehau, smelling of tanneries, the sky darkened by the soot of the kilns of the porcelain factories, to the north of the countryside where he now lives and works, and which he hardly ever leaves. His father was a health-insurance clerk. There was music in the home, but no visual art. Thought to be a bit slow and in need of help in passing exams, he was sent for private lessons in a Huguenot home which, to his surprise and delight, was full of paintings and books about paintings – Dufy, Cézanne, van Gogh. His tutor Gunther le Maire, only a little older than him, encouraged his enthusiasm and early efforts. Gaining confidence, he resisted his parents' wishes to study something useful (since painting, for them, could only ever be a hobby) and went to art school. There his horizons widened: he came into contact with Pop art (Hockney has remained a seminal influence), and the Fluxus movement, and was soon in the

nannte, teils Malerei, teils Collage, teils automatisches Schreiben, gespickt mit Witzen und Kindereien, eine Nackte, ein Düsenjäger und Gottes fluoreszierende Füße – ein junger Geist in der Metamorphose, der sich instinktiv gegen das Erwachsenwerden sträubte. Wie so viele damals fing er an, wie besessen vergängliche, flüchtige Kunst zu machen: ein Kartenhaus, ein wackliges Drahtgebilde, das zusammenfallen musste, sobald jemand die Tür öffnete, ein traditionelles, wirklich hässliches Reiterstandbild, das immer auf die Knie fiel, so sehr man sich auch anstrengte, es aufzustellen. Das führte ihn folgerichtig in die Klasse für Monumentale Bildhauerei an der Kunstakademie Düsseldorf.

Peter Angermann spricht heute recht freundlich über Joseph Beuys. Er nennt ihn „keinen schlechten Künstler, was seine Zeichnungen und einige seiner Plastiken betrifft", und erinnert sich an sein Charisma und seinen politischen Instinkt. Mit einigen Kommilitonen hatte Angermann 1968, rebellierend wie so viele zu dieser Zeit – was lag bloß im Äther, was uns damals alle so drauf brachte? –, einige Künstler zu einem revolutionären Treffen in die Mensa der Nürnberger Akademie eingeladen, darunter HAP Grieshaber, Friedensreich Hundertwasser (der nicht kommen konnte, aber ein zweiseitiges Solidaritätstelegramm schickte) und Joseph Beuys. Die Studenten hatten dort einige Tage zuvor die Wände chaotisch mit einem ausufernden Angermann'schen „Brainstorming" bemalt, und ernste Probleme mit der Akademieleitung bekommen. Beuys kam als letzter, begriff instinktiv die gruppendynamische Situation, nahm unverzüglich auf dem Klavier Platz und war von da an der König. Der Hauch von Neid, den ich in Angermanns Schilderung dieser Szene zu vernehmen glaube, ist vielleicht ein letzter Rest uneingestandener Enttäuschung darüber, dass die kommende Revolution nicht von der Malerei geleitet werden sollte, sondern von Personen und Worten. Beuys hatte die Schlacht gekidnappt. Keiner interessierte sich für die Wände. Alles, was Angermann blieb, waren die wütenden Reaktionen der Professoren, des Präsidenten, des Kanzlers über die Entstellung ihres makellosen Interieurs. Malerei – das Schaffen visueller Botschaften – war marginalisiert worden. Trotz allem bewundert Angermann noch immer Beuys' Chuzpe. Wenn nur seine eigenen Bilder solch eine Wirkung gehabt hätten! Ich bin nicht so großzügig wie er, obwohl ich Beuys vergeben hätte, wenn er, statt auf dem Klavier zu sitzen, darauf gespielt hätte.

1984 traf Angermann seinen alten Professor in Düsseldorf wieder bei der Installation der Ausstellung *Von hier aus*; sie waren sich seit mehr als zehn Jahren nicht mehr begegnet. Sie sprachen, gaben sich die Hand. Angermann hatte ein Anliegen, das er offen ansprach: Er besaß eine unsignierte Beuys-Zeichnung, die er signieren lassen und verkaufen wollte. Beuys erklärte sich dazu bereit, doch Angermann versäumte es, sie ihm vor seinem Tod 1986 vorzulegen. Mit dem Treffen aber ist für Angermann eine spannungsvolle Phase seines Lebens zu Ende gegangen. Doch da war er längst dem Gefängnis des Modernismus entkommen, sah Beuys schon lange nicht mehr als dessen Aufseher. Zweifellos war er das gewesen, wenn auch das Gefängnis, dessen Schlüssel Beuys hütete, perverserweise ein Gefängnis grenzenloser Freiheit war. Verboten war jede Art von Grenze. In gewisser Hinsicht zeigt sich, dass Beuys Angermann einen Gefallen tat, indem er so strikt an seinen Grundsätzen festhielt. Angermann gab sich alle Mühe, aus der Beuys-Klasse geworfen zu werden. Mit einer kleinen Gruppe von

current of what was then thought to be modern art. He let his thoughts and feelings wander freely across sheet after sheet of what he called "Brainstormings" (*Brainstorming 1* and 5, 1968, pp. 36/37), part painting, part collage, part automatic writing, with jokes and juvenilia thrown in – a nude, a jet fighter and God's fluorescent feet – a young mind in metamorphosis, instinctively reluctant to fully grow up. He became obsessed, as so many did then, with making art which was ephemeral: a castle of cards, a balanced construction of stalks that would collapse as soon as someone opened the door, a traditional, truly ugly model of a horse and rider that would always fall over no matter how hard anyone tried to make it stand up. This led him, as naturally as water flows down a drain, to study under the professor of monumental sculpture at the Düsseldorf Art Academy.

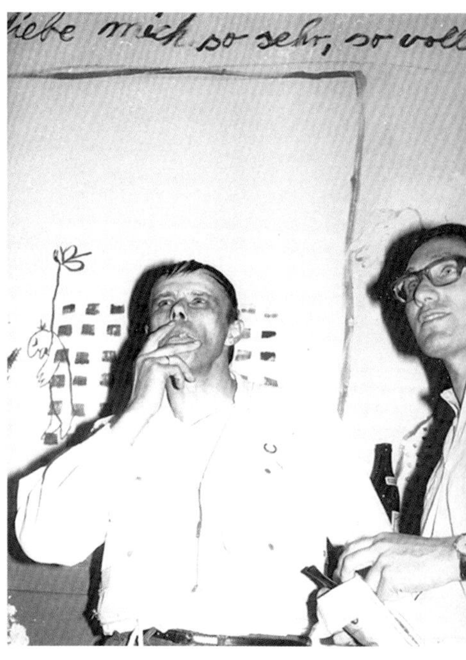

Joseph Beuys, Mensawand-Hearing, Akademie der Bildenden Künste in Nürnberg / refectory-wall hearing, Academy of Fine Arts in Nuremberg, 1968

Peter Angermann now speaks quite kindly about Joseph Beuys. He refers to him as "not a bad artist, as far as his drawings and some of his sculptures go", and remembers his charisma and political instinct. In 1968 Angermann and a group of students, rebelling like so many others at that time – what *was* it in the ether that made us all do that then? – had invited artists like HAP Grieshaber, Joseph Beuys and Friedensreich Hundertwasser (who couldn't come but sent a two-page telegram) to participate in a revolutionary meeting in the refectory of the Academy of Fine Arts in Nuremberg. The students, following the initiative of Angermann, had spent the previous couple of days painting chaotically all over the walls, improvising a massive Angermann "Brainstorming". This posed problems for the college authorities. Beuys was the last to arrive; instinctively assessing the whole situation and the group dynamics, he instantly went over and sat on top of the piano, ensuring that he was king from that moment on. The slight note of envy that I think can still be heard in Angermann's recounting of this incident is perhaps a residue of his own feeling of disappointment, not fully articulated at the time, or perhaps even now, that the coming revolution would be led not by painting, but by personalities and words. Beuys had hijacked the battle. No one looked at the walls. All Angermann was left with was the subsequent fury of the professors, president and director at the students' defacement of their pristine interior. Painting – creating visual messages – had been marginalised. Yet Angermann still admires Beuys's chutzpah. If only his own paintings could have had that effect! I'm not as generous as him, though I would have forgiven Beuys if instead of sitting on the piano, he had played it.

In 1984, during the installation of the big exhibition *Von hier aus* in Düsseldorf, Angermann met his old professor again; neither had crossed each other's path for over a decade. They spoke, shook hands. Angermann had a motive which he openly declared: he had an unsigned Beuys drawing which he wanted to sell. Beuys agreed to sign it, but Angermann failed to get the drawing to him before he died in 1986. With this encounter Angermann felt that a phase of tension in his life was over. But by then he had long been out of the prison of modernism, and no longer saw Beuys as its gaoler. That he was one is now not in doubt, although, perversely, the prison that Beuys held the keys to was a prison of unrestricted

Freunden (nur fünf Rebellen in einer Klasse von vierhundert!) zog er seine Schau ab unter dem geheimnisvollen, sloganartigen Namen YIUP (einem bedeutungslosen Wort, das wie „Jupp" gesprochen wird, die rheinische Kurzform von Joseph). So arg es nur ging, stilisierten sie sich zu Buhmännern, pissten in Ecken, zündeten Styroporbrocken an, die ganze Flügel der Akademie mit schwarzem, giftigem Rauch füllten. Doch Beuys stand zu seinen Prinzipien: Es gab für niemanden Aufnahmebedingungen in seiner Klasse, wie konnte es so Übertretungen geben, die zur Exmatrikulation führten? Beuys jedenfalls weigerte sich, Angermann rauszuwerfen, und leistete dadurch mit ausgleichender Gerechtigkeit, was ich als seinen einzig bleibenden, wenn auch völlig unfreiwilligen Beitrag zur Kunst betrachte.

Was Angermann mehr instinktiv als ausgeklügelt planvoll versuchte, war, den Umriss, den Rand, die Grenze von Beuys herauszufinden. Er fühlte auch damals schon, dass die Kunst so eine Grenze haben muss. Alles hat eine, denn ohne Rand ist nichts wahrnehmbar. Später erst entwickelte er seine Philosophie des Kontrasts, die jetzt sein Leben und seine Arbeit durchzieht, eine über Jahre des Schauens und Malens herausgearbeitete und ausgefeilte Theorie. Er liebt es, Wittgenstein zu zitieren: „Wenn alles rot ist, ist nichts rot." Würden wir ewig leben, lebten wir gar nicht. In seinem herrlich lustigen Bild *Jungbrunnen 1* (1991, S. 143) tapsen alte, graue menschliche Wracks in einen Teich, versinken und tauchen auf, rosig und feingliedrig, mit kecken Penissen und Brüsten, vor Freude hüpfend und kreischend: „Spaß und Sex für immer!" Angermann ist heutzutage das, was Hieronymus Bosch am nächsten kommt. Er hat die seltene Gabe, messerscharf zu sehen, wie wir sind, die Fähigkeit, die närrische rohe Energie auszudrücken, die durch unsere Leben tobt, unsere lächerliche unablässige Jagd nach Nahrung und Sex, die magnetische, elektrische Kraft, die, wie wir alle wissen, zwar lebenswichtig, aber irgendwie doch auch weniger ist als das eigentliche Leben in der ganzen Fülle seiner Möglichkeiten. Denn das Leben, wie wir es erfahren, wäre kein Leben ohne einen Gegensatz dazu. Und das ist der Tod. Also bricht donnernd in *Aus grauer Vorzeit* (1979, S. 61) ein Vulkan aus, chemische Lauge tropft vom Himmel, Baumfarne fingern sich hoch, und zwei Dinosaurier vögeln voller Hingabe. So war das am Anfang … wir alle kennen das Gefühl und müssen

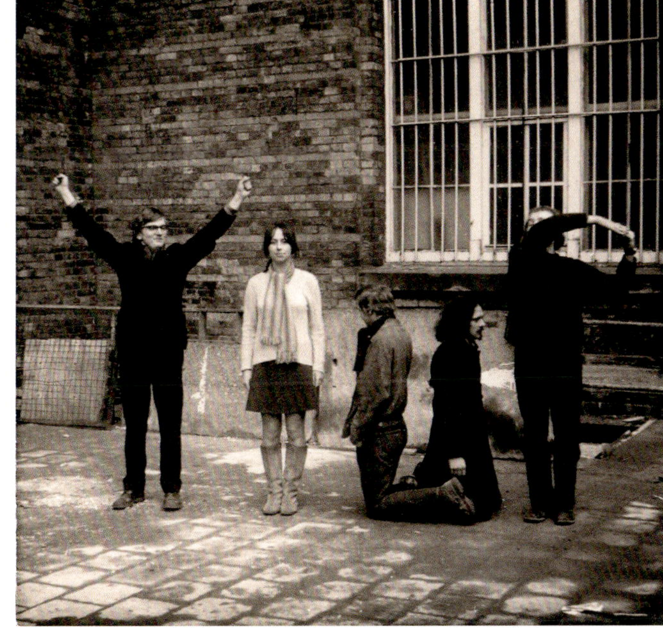

YIUP, 1969

lachen. Das ist es, was wir sind und was uns hierher getrieben hat und wie wir wohl enden werden – als Verwesungsflüssigkeit oder, wie es der britische Künstler David Kemp nennt: Dinosauriersaft. Und wie ist diese rohe Energie in Farbe umgesetzt? Durch den Kontrast von Schwarz und Weiß, *petrol and spirit*, Schatten und dem Schimmer von Augen und Zähnen. Farbe hätte dem eine andere Dimension hinzugefügt, eine regenbogene Andeutung, wohin die Reise gehen könnte, der umsichtigeren Liebe zum Leben, die der Todesangst entspringt. Das sollte Angermann später beschäftigen. In diesem frühen Bild kriegen wir eine grobe Portion Öl, mit plumpen Viechern, die sich ausgelassen der lächerlichen Notwendigkeit hingeben,

freedom. What was forbidden was any sort of limit. With hindsight, we can see that Beuys did Angermann a favour by sticking so strictly to his principles. Angermann did his damnedest to get thrown out of Beuys's class. Individually, and with a small group of friends (only five rebels out of a class of four hundred!) he performed his antics under the arcane, slogan-style name YIUP (a meaningless word derived from the name Jupp – a contraction of Joseph). They made themselves as not-nice-to-know as they possibly could, pissing in corners, setting light to polystyrene packing, filling whole wings of the college with black, poisonous fumes. But Beuys stuck to his principles: there were no entry requirements for anyone to join his class, so how could there be any transgressions which resulted in dismissal? Beuys refused to expel Angermann, and in doing so made, with poetic justice, what I regard as his single, lasting, though totally unintentional contribution to art.

What Angermann was trying to do, instinctively rather than through a thought-out agenda, was to find the edge, the limit of Beuys. He sensed, even then, that art has to have an edge. Everything does, for without edges everything is imperceptible. It was only later that he developed his philosophy of contrasts which now suffuses his art and his life, a theory slowly elaborated and honed during years of looking and painting. He is fond of quoting Wittgenstein: "If everything was red, nothing would be red." If we were eternally alive, we wouldn't be alive. In his gloriously funny painting *Fountain of Youth 1* (1991, p. 143) old, grey crocks of humanity creep and crawl into a pool, sink in and re-emerge, pink and thin-limbed, with perky penises and breasts, bounding with joy, leaping and yelling: "Now for fun and sex forever!" Angermann is the nearest thing we've got nowadays to Hieronymus Bosch. He has the rare, keen gift of being able to see us as we are, the ability to express the mad, raw energy that rushes through our lives, our ludicrous, insistent drive for food and sex, the magnetic, electric force that we all know is crucial to our existence, but which is somehow less than life itself, not life in its fullness. For life as we experience it cannot be life unless there is something to contrast it with. And that something is death. So, uproariously, in *From Time Immemorial* (1979, p. 61), a volcano erupts, chemical juices drip from the sky, tree ferns grope upwards, and two dinosaurs, happily fucking. That was in the beginning … we all know the feeling and have to laugh. That's what we are and what's driven us to where we are, and what we'll probably end up as – putrefied liquid, or as the British artist David Kemp calls it, dinosaur juice. And how is this raw energy conveyed in paint? Through the contrast of black and white, petrol and spirit, shadows and the glint of eyes and teeth. Colour would have added a different dimension, a rainbow hint of knowing where we're going, the more circumspect love of life that springs from fear of death. That

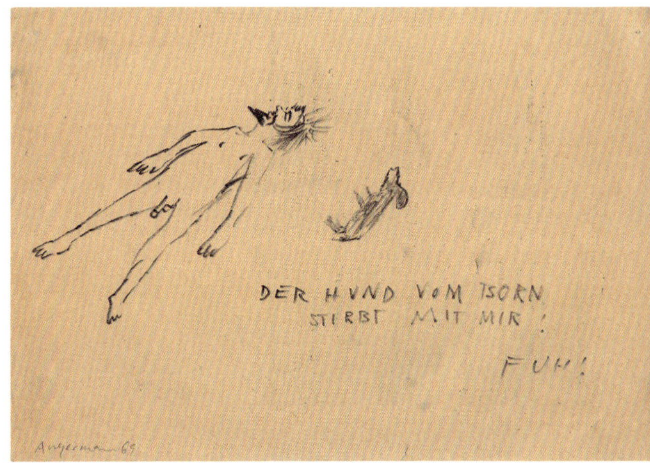

Solipsismus / Solipsism, 1969, Bleistift auf Papier / pencil on paper

was to be the later field of Angermann's work. In this early picture, we are given a dose of crude oil, with ungainly beasts hilarious in the ludicrousness of having to get on with it, but a cruelly true picture for all that, a work not only of the comic book but of art.

weiterzuleben. Dafür aber ein grausam wahres Bild, nicht bloß ein
Comic, sondern ein Kunstwerk.

Angermanns leuchtend klare Schwarzweiß-Welt entstammt
einem völlig anderen Universum als der filzgraue Wohlfühl-Schleier
von Joseph Beuys. Erstere besteht aus Malerei auf Leinwand, die
andere aus Geschehnissen im wirklichen Leben. Doch welches ist
die Illusion, die Täuschung? Angermanns Malerei, so scheint es zunächst, handelt es sich bei ihr doch eindeutig um bildliche Illusion.
Aber die Täuschung endet an der Bildfläche. Sie steht abgesondert
in einer Welt für sich. Sie lässt uns sie annehmen oder abweisen,
lässt uns völlige Freiheit, tief durchzuatmen und zu lachen oder uns
ohne Weiteres abzuwenden, wenn wir wollen. Sie fordert nichts.
Wenn es uns gefällt und wir es zulassen, kann sie uns einen erbau-
lichen Kick geben, gerade so viel wir wollen, nicht wie irgendwer

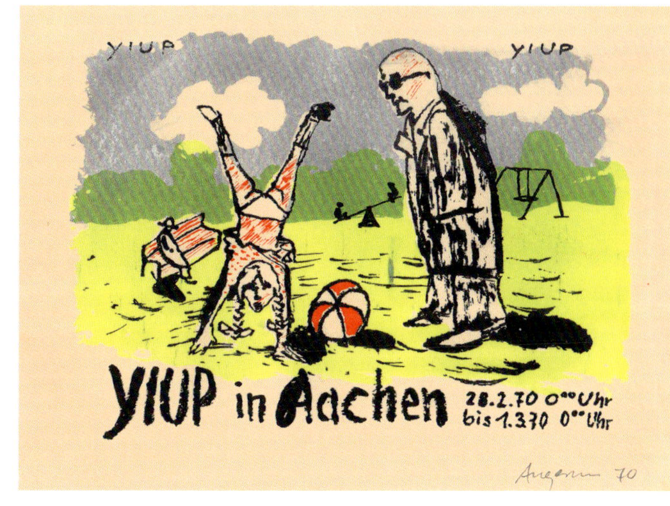

YIUP in Aachen, 1970, Plakat / poster Peter Angermann

sonst es für richtig halten möchte, schon gar nicht Angermann selbst. Keine Strippen hängen
an diesem Bild, uns in diese oder jene Richtung zu bugsieren. Es verbreitet keinerlei klebrige
Moralin-Spinnfädchen. Die Malerei ist Leben hinter Glas, mehr nicht. *It is a work of art, apart.*

Dagegen genau ging Beuys an, denn Kunst hatte Teil des Lebens zu sein. Reißt die
Schranken zwischen beidem nieder! Auf die Barrikaden! Jeder Mensch ist ein Künstler
(obwohl natürlich manche mehr Künstler sind als andere und daher zu Recht höhere Preise
nehmen). Wenn aber alles Kunst ist, was man tut, etwa Nägelschneiden oder Kartoffelschälen,
was ist dann keine Kunst? Und wenn jeder ein Künstler ist, bedeutet es rein gar nichts, ein
Künstler zu sein. Denn wenn alles rot ist, ist nichts rot. Und wenn alles Kunst ist, ist nichts
Kunst. Das war es, was Beuys lehrte und wirkte: den Tod der Kunst. Das war die eigentliche
Täuschung: Die Kunst aufzulösen in grauer Beliebigkeit– daher das durchgängige Grau.
Grauer Filz, grauer Hut; eigentlich eine simple und offensichtliche ästhetische Strategie:
abgerundeter Geschmack. Jeder Künstler weiß, wie man etwas geschmacklich abrundet: Man
braucht nur ein wenig von derselben Farbe der Umgebung beimischen, und schon stimmt alles
zusammen, sind alle Härten, jeder schärfere Kontrast aufgelöst. Graue Wichtigtuerei: der
völlige Gegensatz zu Angermanns Kunst zurückhaltender Brillanz.[1]

Angermanns Kunst ist Anti-Geschmack. Eine bemerkenswerte Werk-Runde –
„Runde" ist besser als „Gruppe", weil es die Kampfsituation anklingen lässt, und Angermann
kämpfte ständig in dieser Lebensphase – malte er auf etwa gleich große, quadratische
Tapetenstucke aus einem Musterbuch. Die Tapetenmuster selbst sind Miniaturfenster zu
geschmackvollen Interieurs, das völlige Gegenteil, sollte man meinen, einer Grundlage für
Kunst. Doch Angermanns Malerei bricht durch diese gediegene Oberfläche wie übermütiges,
beißend scharfes Graffiti. Er experimentierte damals mit Drogen, und das zeigt sich vor allem
in Bildern, die durch ihre Absurdität faszinieren, etwa einem feurigen Himmelskörper, der
von Saturn begleitet in einem Klinkermuster schwimmt, oder einem sabbernden Voyeur, der
durch ein vasenförmiges Schlüsselloch auf eine dralle strippende Blondine stiert. Andere,

Angermann's brilliantly clear, black-and-white world exists in a totally different universe from the grey felt, feel-good haze of Joseph Beuys. The former consists of painting on canvas; the other of happenings in real life. But which is the illusion, the deception? Angermann's painting at first seems to fit the bill. It is clearly a pictorial illusion. But the deception stops at the picture plane. It stands detached, in a different world from our own. It lets us take it or leave it, leaves us totally free to be ourselves, to breathe deeply and laugh or turn away if we want to, no questions asked. It makes no demands. If we would like to and we let it, it can give us a kick to go on living, but exactly as we want to, not as anyone, least of all Angermann, tells us to. No strings trail down from this picture to pull us in this direction or that. It emits no little sticky gossamers of *should*. The painting is life held up behind a glass; that is all. It is a work of art, apart.

That was precisely what Beuys railed against, for art had to be part of life. Break down the barriers between them! To the barricades! Everyone was an artist (though some, of course, were more artists than others, and so could legitimately charge higher prices). But if everything you do, like clipping your nails or peeling potatoes, is a work of art, then what is not a work of art? And if everyone is an artist, it means nothing to be an artist. For if everything is red, nothing is red. And if everything is art, nothing is art. That was what Beuys taught and wrought: the death of art. That was the real illusion: dissolving art in grey arbitrariness. That's why everything in it was grey. Grey felt, grey hat. In the end it was a simple and obvious aesthetic strategy: it was tasteful. Every artist knows how to make something tasteful: all you do is add a little bit of one colour to its neighbour and, like magic, everything tones in, slipping free from any containing edge, or any inherent contrast. Grey splurge: the very antithesis of Angermann's art, which is about contained brilliance.[1]

Angermann's art is *anti-taste*. A remarkable bout of work – "bout" is a better word than "group", because it suggests a round in a fight, and Angermann was fighting all the time at this stage in his life – was produced on similar-sized square slabs of wallpapers torn from a book of samples. The wallpaper patterns themselves are miniature windows on to good-taste interiors, the very opposite, one would have thought, of a foundation for art. But Angermann's paintings blast through this surface politeness, as hilarious, poignant and trenchant graffiti. He was experimenting with stimulants at the time, and this shows most in images that fascinate by being absurd, such as a cosmic fireball, complete with attendant Saturn swimming in a fake brick pattern, or peeping tom salivating as he peers through a flowerpot design at a buxom blonde stripping. Others, more sober, take their cue from the design – an imitation wood-grain, seen horizontally, becomes a desert complete with pyramids and jolly italic camels. Joseph Beuys himself appears, or at least his felt hat and, under it, his all-seeing ear, bathed in a sea of daisies – let a million flowers bloom!

Angermann was instinctively alert to the sameness in Beuys's court of four hundred followers: the uniformity of his acolytes, the seeping of grey dictatorship. All of his students used to model a head and shoulders; no one knew quite why – it was a ritual. All the heads turned out rather similar: thin and lean, serious and bald, a little less than life-size. The YIUP

nüchternere, lassen sich mehr vom Design leiten – eine Bretterwandimitation gerät in horizontaler Sicht zur kompletten Wüste mit Pyramiden und lustig stilisierten Kamelen. Joseph Beuys selbst erscheint, oder zumindest sein Filzhut, und darunter sein allsehendes Ohr, in einem Meer von Gänseblümchen – lasst Millionen Blumen blühen!

Angermann spürte es instinktiv in Beuys' Hof von vierhundert Gefolgsleuten: die Uniformität der Jünger, die Beize grauer Diktatur. All seine Studenten formten irgendwann mal eine Büste, keiner wusste recht warum, es war ein Ritual. Alle diese Köpfe fielen ziemlich ähnlich aus: mager, ernst und kahlköpfig, knapp lebensgroß. Nur die YIUP-Gruppe machte den ihren riesig und rund, mit kräftiger Haartolle, feisten Backen und einem breiten glücklichen Lächeln. Er saß halslos auf der Unterlage, wie geköpft. Und sie machten ihn aus Gips, einem für diesen Zweck verpönten Material. Lehm und Wachs waren erwünscht, sie sind geschmeidig, während Gips, einmal geformt, nicht mehr nachgibt. Zuletzt bohrte Angermann noch ein Loch für einen Feuerwerkskörper hinein, und fertig war der „Knallkopf". Das hieß, sein Verstand war kurz vor dem Explodieren. Aber er flog immer noch nicht raus.

Später hatte er dann doch mal einen kleinen Erfolg. Beuys kam zufällig vorbei, als er mit Milan Kunc zusammen einen der ironischen Siebdrucke vom Stapel ließ, gestattete einen seltenen Blick hinter seine gleichmacherische Maske und kommentierte: „Solche Bilder sollte man verbieten!" Erfreut über wenigstens diese Reaktion, zitierten sie das bei jeder Gelegenheit, doch es brachte sie letztlich auch nicht weiter: Ihr Kampf gegen diese neue, heimtückische Orthodoxie konnte nur ins Leere gehen. Wie die ostdeutschen Kommunisten immer über den Westen sagten: Was nützt die Redefreiheit, wenn dir sowieso niemand zuhört? So ließ sich auch das kapitalistische Establishment unter dem fröhlichen Motto *anything goes* die Possen der sogenannten Avantgarde gefallen, und Beuys' Hinterlassenschaften wechselten in den frühen 1980ern für Millionen die Besitzer, als seine Werke als bestmögliche Investition in moderne Kunst den Wall-Street-Index anführten.

Ein gegen Ende von Angermanns Studium entstandenes Selbstporträt zeigt seine ganze Frustration. Auf sich selbst hinabschauend wie von der Zimmerdecke (seine gewagten Spiele mit der Perspektive, die für seine Kunst so bezeichnend werden sollten, stammen ursprünglich von Comicstrips), hat er sich in bösem Grün gemalt, mit Verachtung speienden Augen. Ein winziger Fuß deutet zur Staffelei hin, während sein Pinsel in eine Leinwand sticht, bemalt mit irgendwelchen abstrakten Mustern, einem verrenkten Malewitsch. Umgeben ist er von den abgelegten traditionellen Kunstmotiven: einem Tisch mit lächerlich pingelig gemaltem kleinen Stillleben darauf (das zu malen ihm größten Spaß machte, wie er später bemerkte), dahinter auf dem Sofa ein reichlich vage gehaltenes Aktmodell und rechts hinter einem niedrigen halbrunden Gitterfenster eine ferne Landschaft, die sich alle Mühe gibt, attraktiv zu sein. Es war sein Abschied von der Kunst, ein Manifest des Rückzugs, der Selbstentfernung, da niemand sonst bereit war, ihn zu entfernen. Er verließ die Akademie und verließ die Kunst, nahm Gelegenheitsjobs an und begeisterte sich für Comics, besonders für die von Robert Crumb, und fing an, seine eigenen zu entwickeln. Diese zeigten etwa die Figur des gehorsamen Wurms Lothar, der zur Schule ging und, obwohl ohne Arme, seine Büchertasche unter den

group alone made theirs huge and round, with thick lumps of hair, plump cheeks and a big, happy smile. It was cut off at the neck as if it had been severed by a guillotine. And they made it in plaster, a medium that was outlawed for this purpose. Clay and wax were favoured – they could slip and run, whereas plaster, once set, was intractable and hard. As a finishing touch, Angermann drilled a hole in its head and inserted a firework. No longer a brainteaser, but a head-banger. He was saying that his mind was now about to explode. But still he couldn't get sacked.

Later he did have one small success. Beuys happened by chance to drift into the silk-screen studio when he and Milan Kunc were reeling off one of their posters. With a rare slip of his egalitarian mask, he commented: "Art like this should be forbidden." Delighted at last to get a reaction, they plastered his quote over everything, but still it got them nowhere: there was no fighting the new, insidious orthodoxy. As the East German communists used to say of the West, what's the point of having free speech if no one cares what you say? So the capitalist establishment slipped, as ever, through the antics of the so-called avant-garde, under the cheery cover of "anything goes", and Beuys's leavings changed hands for millions in the early 1980s, when his works topped the Wall Street index as the best investment to be had in modern art.

A self-portrait from the close of Angermann's student career indicates his intense frustration. Peering down on himself, as if from a high corner in the room (his daring games with perspective, which were to become such a feature of his art, derived originally from comic strips), he has painted himself an evil green, his eyes almost spitting in bottled-up fury. One diminutive foot points at the easel while his brush stabs at a canvas on which is painted a random scatter of abstract shapes, a dislocated Malevich. Around him are the abandoned subjects of art: a table with a ludicrously fiddly little still life (which he realised later he had quite enjoyed painting), behind it a rather vague nude posing on a sofa, and at the back to the right, through a low, semicircular barred window, a distant landscape doing its best to be attractive. It was his good-bye to art; a manifesto of self-removal, since no one was prepared to remove him. He left college and left art, took odd jobs, and became fascinated with comic strips, particularly those of Robert Crumb, and started to develop his own. These featured the character of a very obedient worm, Lothar, who went to school, and though he had no arms, carried his satchel under the empty flap of his jacket sleeve. He drew hundreds of these figures, painting some much later. Painting, he knew, was crucial to his being, but how could he begin again? He was a painter, he knew. He had been born to it somehow. He *had* to find a way of becoming one – it was his life; but how? What could he paint? And, just as importantly, for whom? Could a painter exist in modern times? Radical and fresh in everything, Angermann's new art was hatched among other people. Other people are essential to Angermann. He is a modern Epicurean.

Though virtually none of the writings of the famous Ancient Greek philosopher remain, we know from his followers that Epicurus taught that everything is made up of atoms and emptiness, that everything is changing and that no one can escape death. Suffering, therefore, is an intrinsic aspect of enjoyment. We cannot avoid it, but we can alleviate it, by leading a life that brings us pleasure, eating and drinking well (but not to excess, which brings pain) among

leer baumelnden Ärmeln seines Mantels trug. Er zeichnete Hunderte dieser Figuren, einige malte er später. Malen, das wusste er, war für ihn wesentlich, aber wie konnte er wieder damit beginnen? Er war ein Maler, das wusste er. Er war irgendwie dafür geboren. Er *musste* wieder einen Weg dahin finden – es war sein Leben –, aber wie? Was konnte er malen? Und, ebenso wichtig, für wen? Konnte man heutzutage überhaupt als Maler existieren? In jeder Hinsicht radikal und frisch, wurde Angermanns Kunst in Gemeinschaft und Auseinandersetzung mit anderen ausgebrütet. Andere Leute sind wesentlich für Angermann. Er ist ein moderner Epikuräer.

Obwohl offenbar keine Schriften des berühmten altgriechischen Philosophen erhalten sind, wissen wir von seinen Nachfolgern, dass Epikur lehrte, alles bestehe aus Atomen und Leere, alles sei im Wandel begriffen, und niemand könne dem Tod entrinnen. Leiden ist demnach ein dem Genuss innewohnender Aspekt. Wir können es nicht umgehen, doch wir können es mildern, indem wir ein Leben führen, das uns Freude bringt, durch gutes Essen und Trinken (doch nicht unmäßig, das bringt Schmerzen) mit guten Freunden in reizender Umgebung. Er lehrte seine Philosophie durch sein Beispiel, in seinem Garten. Über den Eingang schrieb er die Worte: „Fremder, Du tust gut daran, hier einzukehren, denn unser höchstes Gut ist die Freude". Jeder war willkommen, einschließlich Frauen und Sklaven (die damals weitgehend gleich behandelt wurden), denn Epikur war einer der ersten wahren Verfechter der Gleichberechtigung auf der Welt. Diese Worte könnten auch wieder über das Tor geschrieben werden, hinter dem Angermann mit seiner Frau Renate lebt, seiner wachsenden Familie und den Haustieren, ein ständiges Kommen und Gehen durch verschiedene Türen. Im Garten nach Süden hin hat er einen kleinen Schwimmteich für alle angelegt, mit eigenem Sandstrand, wo die nächsten Generationen Sandburgen bauen, sitzen und träumen können. Eine große Schlange kommt jeden Sommer zu Besuch, die überzähligen Frösche zu verschlingen. Das Haus ist Teil einer früheren Kaserne, gebaut 1938, und auf einer Außenwand befindet sich noch immer das Relief eines Adlers mit einem Wappen in den Klauen, das Angermann in eine Packung Wellensittichfutter „Trill Knabberspaß" umgestaltet hat. Der Adler hebt jetzt ab im Auftrag, kleinen Vögeln beizustehen.

Angermann lernte mit fünfzehn Saxophon spielen; er liebt es, mit Freunden zu improvisieren, und hat von Zeit zu Zeit in Bands gespielt. 1994 gründete er Die Offizielle Polkakapelle, die in der Gegend auftrat, bis 2000 ein Mitspieler starb. Anders als die meisten modernen Künstler ist er sehr an seinen Zuhörern und an einer Antwort auf ihre Reaktionen interessiert. Er wusste, dass die neue Kunst, die er anstrebte, sozial zu sein hatte, weder ein Egotrip im Treibhaus, eine Show, die sich in der Botschaft erschöpft: „Schau mich an, schau mich an, schau mich an!", noch ein peinliches aufgeblasenes Hadern im selbst auferlegten Kerker. Die neue Malerei, die Angermann machen wollte, sollte freundlich und nach außen gewandt sein, in keiner Weise egozentrisch. Aber konnte Malerei gesellschaftlich sein? Oder gar gesellig, gemütlich? Durfte sie schön, vielleicht sogar lustig sein? Durfte sie bewegend und herzerwärmend sein? Menschlich? Durfte sie ganz einfach normal sein? Aus diesen Fragen erwuchs kein fester Plan, kein Aktionsprogramm, kein Manifest – nichts dermaßen Ernstes und

good friends in a delightful environment. He taught his philosophy by example, in his garden. Over its entrance he inscribed the words: "Stranger, you do well to enter, for here our highest good is pleasure". Everyone was welcome, including women and slaves (who were at the time treated in much the same way), for Epicurus was one of the world's first true egalitarians. These words could justly be re-inscribed over the gateway to Angermann's home, where he lives with his wife, Renate, his extending family and their pets, forever coming and going through different doors. In the garden to the south he has built a little lake for everyone to swim in, with its own sandy beach for coming generations to build castles in, to sit and dream on. A large snake visits regularly in summer to gobble up any surplus frogs. The house forms part of what was originally a barracks, built in 1938, and on one exterior wall there is a relief of an eagle, its claws gripping a little plaque which Angermann has repainted as a packet of budgie seed. The eagle now has lift off in a mission to succour little birds.

Angermann learnt to play the saxophone at fifteen; he loves improvising with friends and has played sporadically in bands since his teens. In 1994 he formed Die Offizielle Polkakapelle (The Official Polka Band), which performed gigs around the district until 2000, when one player died. Unlike most modern artists, he's interested in his audiences and in responding to their reactions. He knew that the new art he was groping towards had to be social, neither an ego trip in a hothouse, a flourish saying nothing more than "Look at me, look at me, look at me!", nor an anguished, self-aggrandizing scratching in a self-imposed dungeon. The new paintings Angermann wanted to make needed to be friendly and outward-going, not egoistical at all. But could painting be social? Or even sociable? Could it be enjoyable, even fun? Could it be moving and heart-warming? Could it be human? Could it be, quite simply, normal? These questions weren't a set agenda, a programme for future action, a manifesto – nothing so serious or boring. They were just feelings, an extension of a way of living and enjoying, the spume from a natural flow. That's how painting began again for Angermann, as spontaneous and refreshing as laughter in good company.

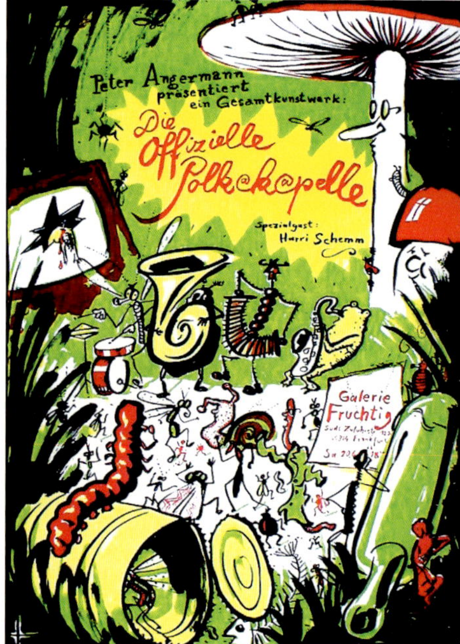

Die Offizielle Polkakapelle, 1998, Plakat / Poster
Peter Angermann

Angermann began creating art again in 1973, a year and a half after he'd finished at the academy, but while he was still living in Düsseldorf. He started drawing simply what he liked, the sights around him, dashing off about a hundred drawings in vibrantly coloured felt-tip pens: Dufy meeting up with Disney in the mountains. It's extraordinary how these predict his later work – cartoon versions of his later landscapes, already brilliant in their light, like the first spillover of a dam about to burst. With new friends, in particular Milan Kunc, he worked up roomier, dreamier, improvised "Brainstormings", groping towards the "art of the future" on big paper sheets. His first big canvas was *Crime Scene* (1973, p. 47), a red landscape with mountainous breasts and an abrupt T-junction right in the middle. The road to the left is signposted "Da" (here), the one to the right "Dort" (there). The two words combined are a pun on the painting's German title "Tatort". With typical, searing simplicity, Angermann has created *the* image of the dead end of art, which is neither here nor there, nor going anywhere. There is no road ahead, only a wander off into the wilderness. And

Langweiliges. Es waren einfach Gefühle, eine Erweiterung der Art zu leben und zu genießen, der Schaum des natürlichen Stroms. Genau so kam Angermann wieder zur Malerei zurück, so spontan und herzerfrischend wie Gelächter in guter Gesellschaft.

Angermann fing 1973 wieder mit der Kunst an, anderthalb Jahre nach Ende seines Studiums, er lebte noch immer in Düsseldorf. Er fing an, einfach das zu zeichnen, was er mochte, was er um sich herum sah, warf um die hundert vibrierend farbige Filzstiftzeichnungen hin: Dufy trifft Disney in den Bergen. Es ist merkwürdig, wie diese seine spätere Arbeit vorwegnehmen – Cartoon-Versionen seiner späteren Landschaften, bereits strahlend in ihrem Licht, wie das erste Überschwappen an einem kurz vor dem Bersten stehenden Damm. Mit neuen Freunden, besonders mit Milan Kunc, machte er nun weiter ausholende, traumartigere, improvisierte „Brainstormings" und tastete sich auf großen Packpapierbahnen zur „Kunst der Zukunft" vor. Seine erste große Leinwand war *Tatort* (1973, S. 47), eine rote Landschaft mit bergigen Brüsten und einer schroffen T-Abzweigung in der Mitte. Die Straße nach links ist mit „Da" ausgeschildert, die nach rechts mit „Dort". Beides zusammen bildet ein fränkisches Wortspiel mit „Tatort". Mit seiner typischen treffsicheren Einfachheit hat Angermann *das* Bild von der Sackgasse der Kunst geschaffen, die weder nach da noch nach dort noch sonst wohin führt. Es gibt keine Straße geradeaus, nur eine Wanderung hinaus in die Wildnis. Und diese Abzweigung ist ein Tatort: der Ort des Mordes an der Kunst in unserer Zeit. Die Leiche liegt irgendwo im Gebüsch. Das ist eine außerordentlich kurze und bündige Feststellung, ein persönliches Manifest der Marschrichtung oder besser der Abwesenheit einer solchen. Hier gibt Angermann auf, sich leiten zu lassen. Die Kunst ist überall um uns herum, gleich nebenan. Über dem Gras auf der linken Seite flattert ein Schmetterling. Es ist ein gelber, ein Zitronenfalter, der erste, der im Frühling unterwegs ist nach der Überwinterung, seine Flügel noch bedeckt mit Eiskristallen, tiefgefroren, doch lebendig; derjenige Schmetterling, dem die Wissenschaftler den Trick des *antifreeze* abgeguckt haben … nicht dass Angermann davon gewusst haben wird, als er es malte. Er mochte einfach die Farbe, aber wenn Künstler eine profunde Einsicht haben, stimmt eben alles.

Sein nächstes Bild, wieder ein Wortspiel, war *Schwarzenbach* (1974, S. 49). Das Motiv, wie es wohl aussähe, wenn das makellos hübsche, typisch bayrische Dorf ganz selbstverständlich nur von Schwarzen bewohnt wäre, die sich's sichtlich gut gehen lassen, heckte er mit seinen Freunden in der Kneipe aus. Es war eine Idee, die allein durch Malerei völlig realisiert werden konnte, denn der Verfremdungseffekt war rein visuell. Schwarze Gesichter, die aus den schnieken Fenstern der Weißen gucken, schwarze Familien, die auf den makellosen Rasenflächen der Weißen spielen. Das Durchspielen und Umkehren alter Ängste in Bildern, nicht in Worten. Angermann hat immer Gefühle und Ideen mitteilen wollen, die nicht in Worten auszudrücken, die aber nichtsdestoweniger erhellend sind. Und es war stets persönlich. Auf den Anger seines imaginären afrikanischen Schwarzenbach setzte er den nierenförmigen Teich, den er später in seinem Garten anlegen sollte. Kunst wurde für Angermann ein kreatives Kontinuum.

Als Nächstes kam ein Bild mit Fröschen, *Großes Froschbild* (1974, S. 51), ein glückliches Pärchen auf einem Seerosenblatt genießt die Regentropfen, Prinz und Prinzessin mit baumeln-

this dead-end junction is the scene of a crime: the murder of art in our time. The body lies somewhere in the bushes. This is an extraordinarily concise statement; a personal manifesto of direction, or rather lack of direction. Here Angermann gives up being directed. Art is everywhere, all around, off to the side. Above the grass on the left a butterfly flits. It's a yellow one, a brimstone, the first to fly in spring, after hibernating through the winter, its wings covered in ice crystals, deep-frozen, yet still alive; the butterfly that gave scientists the clue to antifreeze … not that Angermann knew any of this when he painted it. He just liked the colour, but when artists have a profound insight, everything fits.

His next painting, again playing with the meaning of words, was *Schwarzenbach* (1974, p. 49). The picture hatched in his mind over a meal in a typical, immaculately neat Bavarian village (whose name means "black brook"), when he and a couple of friends were toying with the idea of what it would look like if it were inhabited by black Africans enjoying themselves hugely. It was an idea that could only be fully realised in painting, for the flip in expectation was purely visual. Black faces looking out of white men's prim windows. Black families playing on white men's pristine lawns. Old fears rehearsed and reversed in images, not texts. Angermann has always sought to express feelings and ideas that can't be expressed in words but which are nevertheless enlightening. And it was always personal. In the centre of this imaginary African Schwarzenbach he put the kidney-shaped pool he was later to build in his garden. Art for Angermann was becoming a creative continuum.

Next came a painting of frogs, *Large Frog Painting* (1974, p. 51), a happy couple on a lily pad enjoying the raindrops, prince and princess, their pudenda dangling, both wearing crowns since they'd kissed each other. The pun here is purely visual – the famous stop-action photograph of the effect of a drop falling into water, splashing back up to make a droplet coronet. Rain is fantastic for making love in, as generations of frogs before them have known, and dinosaurs before them, back to the beginning of time. *Magpie Painting* (1974, p. 53) is a pessimistic picture of the world sinking into a sea of junk, while thieving magpies fly off with glinting treasures, a ring, a nappy pin, a string of pearls that fall back as bubbles – sparkling, evanescent hopes – as the sides of the world, towering skyscrapers all around, cave in. At the bottom President Nixon, struggling at the time of painting to keep afloat in Watergate, surfaces briefly for a gasp of air before submerging forever beneath a rising tide of something putrid and bright orange … all of the joy, wit and penetrating insight is already here, fresh and stark. But still, despite these triumphant successes, Angermann didn't want his painting to be a solitary activity. He wanted painting to be normal.

Group NORMAL began as an informal painting collective of Angermann and two Czech artists, Milan Kunc and Jan Knap. All were by different means feeling their way out of the hollow orthodoxy of Minimalist and Conceptual art. The group lasted from 1979 to 1981. While continuing to pursue their own paths independently, the three artists came together to paint. They were like a rock group, working on a picture, improvising before the public – art as a jam session. Had anyone ever before tried to do such a thing? They got engagements to "perform" at art fairs and in galleries, in Paris, New York and Berlin. It was

den Geschlechtsorganen, die beide Krönchen tragen, seit sie sich geküsst haben. Der Witz ist hier rein visuell – das bekannte Kurzbelichtungsfoto eines ins Wasser fallenden Tropfens, der beim Aufklatschen ein Tropfenkrönchen formt. Im Regen lässt sich fantastisch Liebe machen, wie Generationen von Fröschen vor ihnen wussten, und davor schon Dinosaurier, seit Anbeginn der Zeit. *Elsternbild* (1974, S. 53) ist ein pessimistisches Bild von der Welt, die in einem Meer von Müll versinkt, während diebische Elstern mit glitzernden Schätzen davonfliegen, einem Ring, einer Sicherheitsnadel, einer zerreißenden Perlenkette – funkelnde, vergängliche Hoffnung –, während die Flanken der Welt, aufragende Wolkenkratzer, in sich zusammenstürzen. Unten Präsident Nixon, wie er sich damals im Watergate-Sumpf abstrampelte, wie er kurz auftaucht, um Luft zu schnappen, um dann für immer in einer Flut von etwas Fauligem, hell Orangenem unterzugehen … all der Witz und die durchdringende Einsicht ist hier schon vorzufinden, frisch und kraftvoll. Doch trotz dieser triumphalen Erfolge wollte Angermann seine Malerei nicht als einsame Übung sehen. Er wollte Malerei als Normalität.

Die Gruppe NORMAL begann als loses Malerkollektiv, bestehend aus Angermann und zwei tschechischen Künstlern, Milan Kunc und Jan Knap. Alle erahnten sie auf unterschiedliche Weise ihren Weg aus der hohlen Orthodoxie des Minimalismus und der Konzeptkunst. Als Gruppe arbeiteten sie von 1979 bis 1981. Während sie sonst unabhängig ihrem jeweils eigenen Pfad folgten, trafen sich die drei Künstler immer wieder zum Malen. Sie waren wie eine Rockgruppe, arbeiteten an einem Bild, improvisierten in öffentlichen Malaktionen – Kunst als eine Jamsession. Hat je zuvor jemand so etwas versucht? Sie wurden engagiert, um in Paris, New York und Berlin auf Kunstmessen, bei Ausstellungen und in Galerien aufzutreten. Es war ganz wie YIUP, aber eher mit einer kreativen statt einer krawalligen Agenda. Die Ergebnisse waren wild, dynamisch und laut. Es gab ein großes Bild, auf dem Tiere in einer Fabrik am Fließband schufteten, mit gequält guckendem Tiger und Fluppen paffendem Frosch. Ein anderes, in Paris bei der Biennale des Jeunes gemaltes, zeigt eine Prozession von Herzen, die den Boulevard hinuntermarschieren, ein paar davon bellen ins Megafon, eines eine aufgeputzte Nutte, ein anderes ein Kriegskrüppel im Rollstuhl (Schatten von Otto Dix), während in einer Ecke, betrunken und versehrt, ein sinkendes blaues Herz drohend eine Krücke schwingt, all das unter dem weinenden Auge eines gebeugten Eiffelturms – ein Bild vom Ende der Straße der Liebe oder wenigstens der pariserisch-romantischen Sorte?

1980 wurde die Gruppe NORMAL eingeladen, an der *Times Square Show* in New York teilzunehmen, die von der Kunstorganisation Colab in einem leeren Busdepot und ehemaligen Massagesalon organisiert wurde. Über hundert Künstler wirkten mit, darunter einige, die später sehr bekannt werden sollten, wie Keith Haring und Basquiat. Man gab sich hyperaktuell, provokativ und avantgardistisch. Die Gruppe NORMAL vertrat natürlich eine gegenteilige Position und malte auf die Wände eines Raums gemeinschaftlich eine ländliche Idylle – eine hingestreckte Landschaft mit Bäumen, Vögeln und kleinen Wigwams, mit einer blauen Kette pyramidenförmiger Hügel entlang dem fernen Horizont. Ein Mädchen mit Schürze und Zöpfen füttert ein Wickelkind, während noch der Storch, der es vielleicht gerade gebracht hat, im Schwimmteich planscht. Ein hübscher Kinderwagen steht herum. Spielzeugenten dekorieren

like YIUP all over again, but with a creative rather than a knocking agenda. The results were messy, dynamic and loud. There was a big painting of animals working at a factory conveyor belt, the tiger looking pained, the frog puffing on a fag. Another, made in Paris on the occasion of the Biennale des Jeunes, shows a procession of hearts marching down a boulevard, some bawling into megaphones, one a painted tart, another a war cripple in a wheelchair (shades of Otto Dix), while in a corner a blue heart sinks, drunk and crippled, brandishing a crutch, all under the bent eye of a weeping Tour Eiffel – an image of the end of the road for love, or at least the Parisian romantic sort?

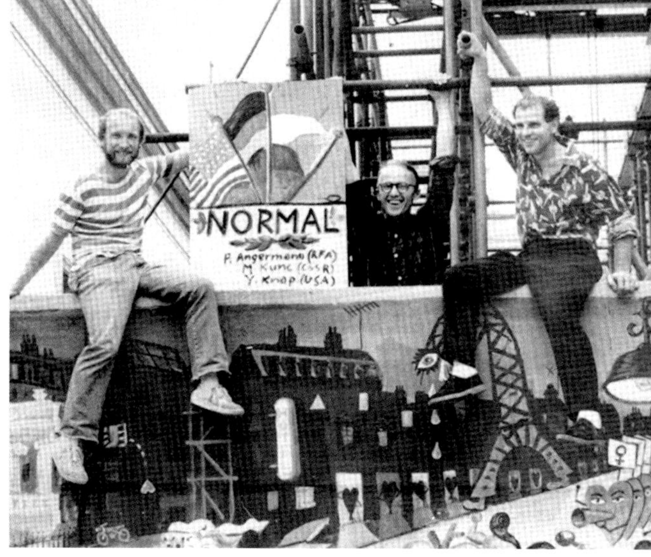

Gruppe / Group NORMAL in Paris, 1980

In 1980, group NORMAL was invited to participate in the *Times Square Show* in New York, organised by the art organisation Colab in an empty bus depot and massage parlour. Over a hundred artists took part, including a few who subsequently became famous, such as Keith Haring and Basquiat. The tone was cutting-edge, provocative and avant-garde. Group NORMAL, naturally, took a contrary line and painted together a country idyll on the walls of one room – a sweeping landscape with trees and birds and little wig-wams, with blue pyramidal hills ranged along the distant horizon. A girl wearing a pinny and a pigtail nurses a baby in swaddling clothes, while the stork that perhaps brought him paddles in the swimming pool. A pretty pram stands idly by. Toy-farm ducks with grass wedges on their feet decorate the grass. The church roof is emblazoned with the sign of McDonald's Golden Arches, perhaps a note of irony, though not entirely because the halloed baby is about to be fed a burger, if the bird eyeing it doesn't get it first.

In Cologne NORMAL painted a big, mad, open-air party. Beetles, bugs and worms dance and play and sing on the grass under arching sprays of plantains, dandelions and Canterbury bells, while in the background a nuclear bomb explodes. A red-eyed frog looks a little startled, while a giant blackbird pokes his head over the grasses and wonders which insect to have for his last meal, before the coming holocaust. It is funny and horrific; everyone partying as if there was no tomorrow, when there is no tomorrow. Sometimes the artists worked in pairs. Jan Knap, a noble soul quietly restoring Catholic content to painting, worked with Angermann on a contemporary version of the *Flight into Egypt* (1981, p. 68). Mary and Jesus sit on a tartan blanket. She's taken off her white trainers and placed them neatly on the grass. Joseph kneels to the right of them, pouring coffee out of a flask. The donkey nibbles clover flowers. On the sloping hillside behind them, a tractor fells logs above the road. How can such a painting be so full of bliss? But it is. At other times each of them worked alone, but you often feel, at least with Angermann, that his pictures sprang naturally from collective thought. These works might be the expressions of individuals, but they are still normal, just part of life, but separate and apart from it, beyond the bounds of Beuys.

den Rasen. Das Kirchendach schmücken die goldenen Bögen des McDonald's-Emblems, eine ironische Note vielleicht, oder auch wieder nicht, soll doch das Baby einen Burger kriegen, falls ihn nicht der lauernde Vogel vorher wegschnappt.

In Köln malte NORMAL eine große verrückte Freiluftparty. Käfer, Insekten und Würmer tanzen, spielen und singen im Gras unter gebogenen Wegerichhalmen, Löwenzahn und Glockenblumen, während im Hintergrund eine Atombombe explodiert. Ein rotäugiger Frosch schaut ein wenig erschrocken, während eine riesige Amsel ihren Kopf über die Gräser reckt und sich ein Insekt für ihre letzte Mahlzeit vor dem Holocaust aussucht. Es ist lustig und schrecklich zugleich; alles feiert, als gäbe es kein Morgen, und es gibt kein Morgen. Manchmal arbeiteten die Künstler paarweise. Jan Knap, ein Feingeist, der ruhig und gefasst der Malerei katholische Inhalte zurückbringt, arbeitete mit Angermann an einer zeitgemäßen Version der *Flucht nach Ägypten* (1981, S. 68). Maria und Jesus sitzen auf einer Tartandecke. Sie hat ihre weißen Turnschuhe ausgezogen und ordentlich im Gras platziert. Joseph kniet rechts von ihnen und gießt Kaffee aus einer Thermosflasche. Der Esel nascht Klee, am Hang hinter ihnen ein Traktor beim Baumfällen oberhalb der Straße. Wie kann ein derartiges Bild so voller Glückseligkeit sein? Und es ist es doch. Dann arbeitete mal wieder jeder allein für sich, aber man spürt oft, zumindest bei Angermann, dass seine Bilder ganz natürlich dem Gemeinschaftsgedanken entsprangen. Auch wenn diese Werke Ausdruck von Individuen sind, sind sie doch stets normal und aus dem Leben gegriffen, jedoch davon abgesondert, frei von den Beuys'schen Fesseln.

Was diese drei Künstler entdeckt hatten, gemeinsam wie auch einzeln, war damals Neuland für die Malerei: Es ging einfach darum, Einblicke aufzuzeigen, die es so nicht gibt, die man nicht fotografieren kann, die erst geschaffen werden mussten, Einblicke voller Bedeutung für uns. Das war immer die Aufgabe der Malerei gewesen, und Angermann und die Gruppe NORMAL machten es wieder so. Malerei allein war schon ein hinreichend radikaler Schritt, obwohl wir uns heute kaum mehr vorzustellen vermögen, wie arg die grundlegende menschliche Fertigkeit, die Pinsel zu schwingen, damals verpönt war. Während der 1960er und 1970er Jahre fand ein Wust von Vorurteilen zusammen, um das Handwerk der Malerei und aller anderen Formen visueller Kreativität auszurotten. Ich habe das im Einzelnen in meinem Buch *The Eclipse of Art* analysiert und brauche es hier nicht zu wiederholen. Es mag genügen festzustellen, dass in den 1970ern für einen Mann Mut dazugehörte, mit einem phallusförmigen Stock voller farbigem Samen über eine rein weiße, jungfräuliche Leinwand zu streichen, besonders in aller Öffentlichkeit. Angermann war solch kleinliche Schüchternheit fremd: Malen war für ihn ein Handwerk wie Kochen, und es interessierte ihn, weil es das einfachste, schnellste, billigste und wirkungsvollste Verfahren war, die Bilder zu schaffen, die er wollte. Und es machte Spaß. Er nahm den Pinsel in die Hand und brachte sich geradewegs und aufs Neue bei, wie gemalt wird. Auf diese Weise gewann er nicht nur die Sprache der Malerei zurück, sondern auch seine Themen, die verpönten Abteilungen aus seinem grünen Selbstporträt. Er konnte jetzt alles malen, was er wollte. Warum denn nicht? So einfach es sich anhörte, es war eine

What these three artists had discovered, together and individually, was a new terrain for painting: its job was simply to create sights that don't exist, which couldn't be photographed, which had to be created, sights that are full of meaning for us. This had always been the role of painting, and Angermann and group NORMAL made it so again. Painting was in itself a radical enough step, hard though it may be for us today to imagine the stigma that had been attached to the basic human skill of wielding brushes. During the 1960s and 1970s a complex confluence of prejudices combined to eradicate the craft of painting and all other forms of visual creativity. I have analysed them in some detail in my book *The Eclipse of Art* and need not rehearse them here. Suffice it to say that in the 1970s it required courage for a man to stroke a phallic-shaped stick loaded with coloured semen over a pure white virgin canvas, especially in public. Angermann was having none of this self-defeating nonsense: painting was a craft like cooking, and it interested him because it was the simplest, quickest, cheapest and most effective way of creating the images he wanted. And it was fun to do. Picking up his brush, he straightforwardly taught himself how to paint again. In doing so, he not only reclaimed the language of painting but also reclaimed its subject matter, the outlawed sections of his self-portrait in green. He could paint whatever he wanted to. Why not? It sounded simple enough, but it was a slow and brave journey across frontiers marked "Out of Bounds", the red and white tape that separated off the scene of the crime.

The first breakthrough was finding how to express sentiment without sentimentality. It took great courage, hard as it might now be to imagine, to paint *Bear Picture 1* in 1976 (p. 57). Two teddy bears cuddling, cheek to furry cheek, gazing at the sunset! Such a painting is possible nowadays because it would be considered kitsch. But Angermann, even then, was ahead of now. The truly radical thing about this painting, its extraordinary breakthrough, is that it is *not* kitsch; it's genuinely felt. Peter and Renate had only recently got together; this is a painting of an early camping trip. It is, quite simply and ecstatically, a painting of new love, when the world is lit up with a glowing light and feels, everywhere, one degree warmer; when the sun is no longer a distant, irrelevant, on-going nuclear explosion, but seems nearer and larger as it reaches out to touch the teddy bears' hearts, which are rising out of the top of their heads, in their exhilaration, as shaggy pairs of ears. This sounds over the top, hopelessly embarrassing even, when stated in words, but, bizarrely, it isn't when it's created in paint.

We have to smile; we all know the feeling. It's genuine and normal. What's wrong with being cuddly? The two bikes are kissing too, wheel to wheel in harmony. Everything is animated when you're in love. Why not teddy bears? We loved them as children and we can love them again. When he started this painting, Angermann was breaking through barriers. You can feel

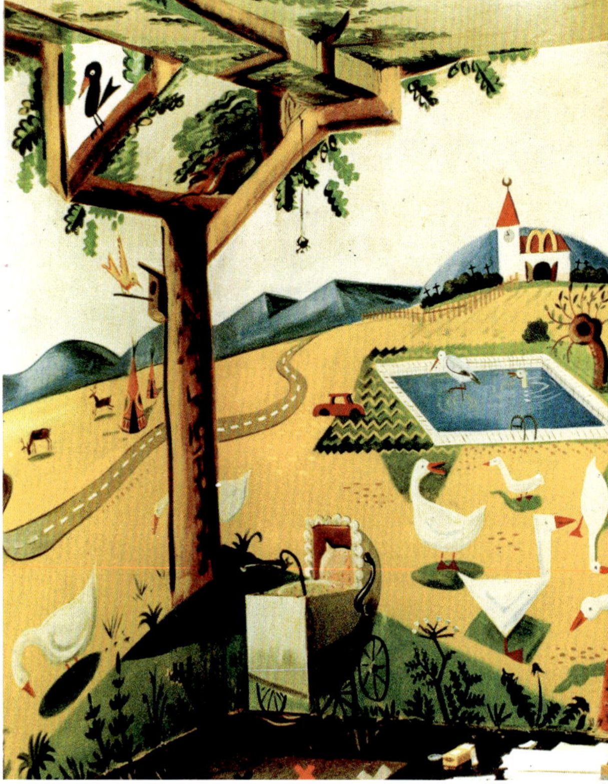

Times Square Show, 1980, 41 Street 7th Avenue, New York, mit / with Milan Kunc und / and Jan Knap, Latexfarbe auf Wand / latex paint on wall (zerstört / destroyed)

langsame und tapfere Reise über die Grenze ins Sperrgebiet, über das rot-weiße Flatterband, welches den Tatort abriegelte.

Der erste Durchbruch bestand darin herauszufinden, wie man Gefühl ohne Sentimentalität ausdrücken kann. Es brauchte 1976 großen Mut, *Bärenbild 1* (S. 57) zu malen, aus heutiger Sicht schwer vorstellbar. Zwei kuschelnde Teddybären, Wange an flauschiger Wange, die in den Sonnenuntergang starren! Solch ein Bild ist heutzutage möglich, weil man es als Kitsch sehen würde. Aber Angermann war schon damals weiter. Das wahrhaft Radikale an

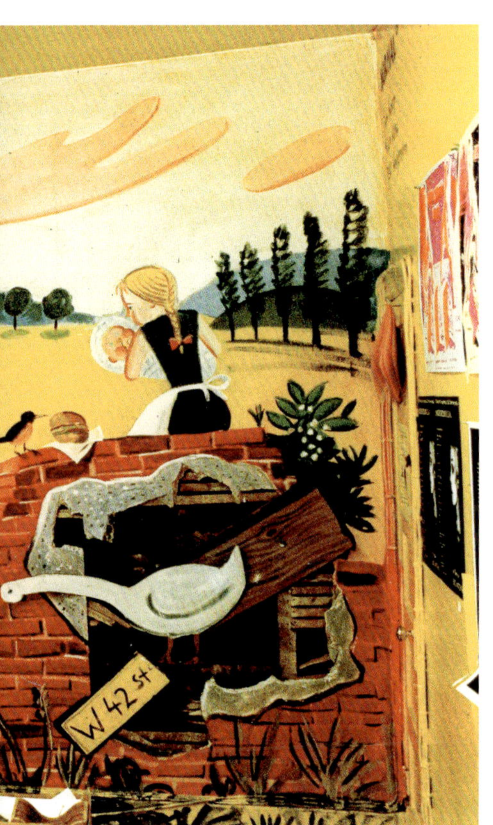

diesem Bild, sein außerordentlicher Durchbruch besteht darin, dass es eben kein Kitsch ist; es ist echt erlebt. Peter und Renate waren frisch liiert; es ist ein Bild eines frühen Campingausflugs. Es ist, so einfach wie ekstatisch, das Bild neuer Liebe, wenn die Welt in mildes Licht getaucht ist und sich überall ein Grad wärmer anfühlt; wenn die Sonne nicht nur mehr eine ferne, bedeutungslose, anhaltende Kernexplosion ist, sondern groß und nah die Herzen der Teddybären berührt, die ihnen vor Heiterkeit als struppige Ohrenpaare aus den Köpfen wachsen. Das ist nun wirklich nicht mehr feierlich, hoffnungslos peinlich sogar, wenn in Worte gefasst, doch bizarrerweise nicht in gemalter Form.

Wir müssen lächeln; wir alle kennen das Gefühl. Es ist echt und normal. Was ist falsch daran zu kuscheln? Die zwei Fahrräder küssen sich auch, Rad zu Rad in Harmonie. Wenn man verliebt ist, ist alles beseelt. Warum nicht Teddybären? Wir haben sie als Kinder geliebt und können sie immer noch lieben. Als er dieses Bild begann, durchbrach Angermann Grenzen. Das ist an dem scharfen Nachdruck der Pinselstriche zu spüren. Doch während der Arbeit begann dieser Kraftakt weniger wichtig zu werden als die Entdeckung des echten Gefühls. Er war kein Zyniker, der mit dem Kitsch spielte, sondern ein wahrer Narr, der tatsächlich an das glaubte, was er tat! Angermann hat inzwischen etwa sechzig Teddybärenbilder geschaffen. Alle sind autobiografisch, schildern sein Familienleben. Jemand sollte eine Ausstellung mit ihnen machen: Es wäre eine Offenbarung. Das neueste ist eine Großelternszene, wieder der Künstler und Renate, zwei Teddys auf einer Bank, Rotwein trinkend, den Enkeln vor dem Zubettgehen beim Spielen zusehend, wobei abermals die rote Sonne untergeht. Es ist ein schönes Resümee. Wir alle kennen das Gefühl.

Der nächste Durchbruch war vielleicht noch wichtiger. Eines Tages im Jahr 1987 hing Angermann mit Peter Hammer, einem Künstlerfreund, herum, und sie überlegten, was sie wieder wirklich Schräges anstellen könnten. Angermann spürte, dass es da noch immer Krusten zu knacken gab. Und dann geschah es: Warum nicht rausgehen und *en plein air* malen, im Freien? Niemand außer Amateuren tat das noch. Also zogen sie los mit einer Flasche Wein und hatten zu ihrem Erstaunen eine wirklich gute Zeit. Von da an war Angermann darauf

it in the incisive vigour of the brushstrokes. But as he worked, he began to get interested not so much in the act of cutting through as in the genuine sentiment he was uncovering. He wasn't a cynic, playing at kitsch, but a real idiot who actually believed in what he was doing! Angermann has now done about sixty teddy-bear paintings. They are all autobiographical, about his family life. Someone ought to mount an exhibition of them: it would be a revelation. The most recent is a grandparent scene, the artist and Renate again, two teddies sitting on a bench, drinking red wine, watching the grandchildren play before their bedtime, as the red sun goes down. It is a beautiful summation. We all know the feeling.

The next breakthrough was, perhaps, even more crucial. One day in 1987 Angermann was sitting with Peter Hammer, an artist friend, discussing what they could do that day that would be really daring. Angermann still sensed there were barriers to be broken. And then it occurred to them: why not go out and paint *en plein air*, in the open? No one, apart from amateurs, did that any more. So they kitted themselves out, took a bottle of wine, and much to their surprise had a really enjoyable time. From that moment on Angermann was hooked. It was like learning to paint again or, even more significantly, learning to see again. He began trying to paint what things actually looked like – the dowdy greens of trees, the precise colour of a cloud, the tint of the earth. This was much more interesting and much more difficult than he could ever have imagined. Like many of us today in our post-Darwin, wonder-less world, Angermann had, up until then, taken for granted most of what he could see in everyday life. He hadn't really looked around him. (I have examined the causes of this globally belittling condition in my book *The Art of Wonder: A History of Seeing*.) Then he began to look, and what he saw was a revelation. The world he lived in became beautiful for him again. And so he entered a different, and welcome, kind of incarceration. No longer smothered under Beuys's blanket greyness, he was waking up every day to a shower of contrasts, a glorious sphere of colour. His world was a beautiful prison. Why should he leave it? Everything was there – or, rather, here.

He began painting landscapes whenever he wasn't teaching, or working on a big, imaginative canvas in his studio, or just idling about. Laziness is the vital empty half of creativity; it cushions artists from doing anything just because others say they ought to and gives them the breathing space to do what really interests them. Cycling around the neighbourhood, with his easel, paints and canvas, neatly packed in a specially made case, he looked for a place he'd like to be for three hours or so. The final motif came later, chosen when he had settled down and allowed what he could see to begin to speak to him – for as he is now ready to admit, one can, in fact, paint anything. These canvases, of which there are now several hundred, slowly became lighter and brighter and easier as he worked. They had started out greenish-grey, very naturalistic, but gradually he learned to let the sunshine in. His colours grew stronger and subtler, less buried under their representational skin. Nothing was colourless anymore. Of course many artists before him had seen hidden hues, above all the Impressionists and Post-Impressionists. But Angermann discovered his own particular palette for himself. Green he came to see

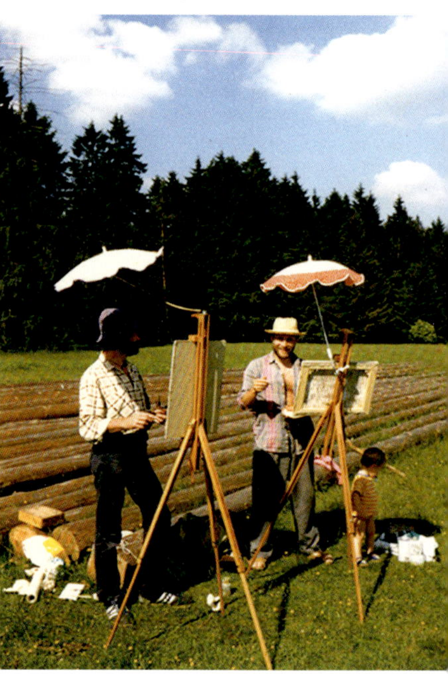

Das erste Pleinair-Bild / The first plein-air painting, 1987. Von links / From left: Peter Hammer, Peter Angermann, Max Angermann

abgefahren. Es war wie neu malen zu lernen, mehr noch, wie neu sehen zu lernen. Er fing
mit dem Versuch an, die Dinge zu malen, wie sie wirklich aussahen – das gedämpfte Grün
der Bäume, die genaue Farbe einer Wolke, den Ton der Erde. Das war viel interessanter und
schwieriger, als er je geglaubt hätte. Wie viele von uns in unserer postdarwinistischen und
entzauberten Welt hatte Angermann bis dahin das meiste für bare Münze genommen, was er
in seiner alltäglichen Umgebung sah. Er hatte nicht richtig geschaut. (Ich habe die Gründe für
diese weltweit festzustellende Verkümmerung in meinem Buch *The Art of Wonder: A History
of Seeing* untersucht). Damals begann er zu schauen, und was er sah, war eine Offenbarung.
Die Welt, in der er lebte, wurde wieder schön für ihn. Und so begab er sich in eine andere und
willkommene Gefangenschaft. Nicht länger unter dem Beuys'schen Grau verschüttet, erwachte
er jeden Tag in einem Schauer von Kontrasten, in einer prächtigen Farbensphäre. Seine Welt
war ein schönes Gefängnis. Warum sollte er es verlassen? Alles war dort – oder besser, da.

Er begann Landschaften zu malen, wann immer er nicht gerade lehrte oder an einer
großen thematischen Leinwand arbeitete oder einfach nur faulenzte. Faulheit ist die vitale leere
Hälfte der Kreativität. Sie bewahrt Künstler davor, etwas nur zu tun, weil andere es von ihnen
erwarten, und lässt ihnen Luft, zu machen, was sie wirklich interessiert. Durch die Umgebung
radelnd, Staffelei, Farben und Leinwand in einem extra angefertigten Kasten säuberlich verstaut,
suchte er nach einem Platz, wo sich's zwei, drei Stunden gut aushalten ließ. Das endgültige Motiv
kam später, nachdem er sich niedergelassen und die Dinge zu sich sprechen gelassen hatte – denn,
wie er inzwischen bereit ist zuzugeben, man kann tatsächlich alles malen. Diese Leinwände,
von denen es inzwischen mehrere Hundert gibt, wurden allmählich heller und leuchtender und
leichter. Zuerst waren sie grünlich-grau, sehr naturalistisch, doch nach und nach lernte er, den
Sonnenschein hereinzulassen. Seine Farben wurden stärker und subtiler, weniger unter ihrer
abbildenden Oberfläche verborgen. Nichts war mehr farblos. Natürlich hatten viele Künstler vor
ihm versteckte Töne gesehen, allen voran die Impressionisten und Postimpressionisten. Aber
Angermann entdeckte seine ureigene besondere Palette. Grün erwies sich als gefährlich. Er fing
an, seine Pleinair-Leinwände blassgelb, blassblau oder rosa vorzutönen. Der sanfte Rötel des
örtlichen Bodens wurde ihm bewusst. Er bemerkte, dass er von einem Pigment umgeben war,
und begann damit zu malen, verrieb es mit Weiß zu einem lieblichen, feinen, leicht lilafarbenen
Rotbraun. Sein zunehmend sicherer Umgang mit Farbe machte ihn mehr und mehr zu einem
Meister im Lichtmalen. Die eben angeschalteten Straßenlampen im tiefsten Winter, wenn alles
mit Schnee bedeckt ist; der Glanz eines hellen Frühlingstages, wenn sich die Bäume kräftig vor
den Ackerhängen abheben und helle Pfützen klare himmelblaue Löcher in den zerfurchten Weg
schneiden; das Licht der Nacht, wenn Scheinwerferkegel über eine Autobahnbrücke kriechen,
während der Rest der Welt in stiller Finsternis versinkt. All das sind Bilder realer Erlebnisse,
und sie sagen Dinge, die nicht in Worten gesagt werden können. Auch sind sie in zunehmender
Einfachheit und Knappheit ausgedrückt, da Angermann die Dinge immer klarer sieht und immer
ökonomischer umzusetzen versteht.

Betrachtet man diese Bilder aus der Nähe, die kleinen, vor Ort gemalten wie auch die
großen Atelierbilder, dann fällt auf, aus wie wenig Strichen sie bestehen, wie ihr Farbaufwand

as dangerous. He began to prime his plein-air canvases with a pale yellow, pale blue, or pink. The gentle red ochre of the local earth, *Rötel*, seeped into his consciousness. He realised he was living surrounded by a pigment and began to paint with it, grinding it with white, to produce a lovely, subtle, slightly lilac reddish brown. As his grasp of tone and colour grew more confident, he became more and more adept at painting light, the street lamps just triggered into lighting up in deep midwinter, when everything is covered with snow; the brilliance of a bright spring day, when the trees stand out stark against the sloping fields and luminous pools of skylight cut clear holes into the rutted path at your feet; the light of night, as headlights sear across a viaduct, while the rest of the world is sunk in quiet dark. All these are paintings of real experiences and say things that cannot be said in words. And they are expressed with increasing simplicity and brevity, as Angermann continues to see things more clearly and knows how to put them down more economically.

When you look closely at these pictures, both the small ones painted on site and the large ones worked up later in his studio, it is remarkable how few strokes they are composed of, how reduced to essentials is their range of colour. The flat brushstrokes dragged up in *Camillo* (2007, p. 170) are enough to evoke grass clumps sticking through the snow blanket. One scintillating long sweep of mid-blue in *Forst* (2005, p. 166) is all that's needed to capture a sky-reflecting road running up a neat Bavarian hillside. Angermann, typically self-effacing, claims that it is laziness that makes him find the simplest way to do things. Of course it's not that at all: it requires deep thought and great skill to reduce all the elements so that the paint can do the work. The British painter Roger Hilton once said that it's not what you put in but what you leave out that matters. This is what abstraction really means; as Angermann quipped during our conversation: "It's the abstraction that is missing in abstract art" – a remark that deserves to go down in history. David Hockney, of course, has the same instinct to simplify. He didn't begin painting until he'd found a simple way of expressing what he wanted to: slanting rain, light under water, reflections on glass. But in comparison with Angermann's, Hockney's marks remain devices, two-dimensional signs, essentially graphic. Hockney can draw like an angel, but Angermann paints like one. Looking at his work, you know again what painting is, with a rich, endlessly subtle artistic language of its own, rediscovered by an artist who had the humility and the guts simply to look around him, pick up his brushes, and paint.

The result is beauty, another breakthrough of Angermann's and another major rediscovery in art. Who would have thought beauty could be radical? But it was and still is. Genuine beauty, that is, not kitsch trinkets decorating sordidness – just normal, healthy, vigorous, sexy beauty, like cherry blossom in sunshine in spring. Could anyone ever paint such a thing again? Angermann did in *May (Walberla)* in 1990 (p. 133), just for the sheer joy of it, without a streak of cynicism. He even added a green-roofed, beaming Franconian church. Who could see beauty in a motorway, a row of plastic-covered hay bales, an Ikea store? Angermann has. What could be further away from the grim, introspective, self-important, tight-lipped, mean, cold-hearted, calculating and calculated thin dribbles of grey matter exuded in those places called "contemporary art venues"? Angermann has shown again that art, real art – created, wordless pictures – can live outside this

aufs Wesentliche reduziert ist. Die flachen, hochgezogenen Pinselstriche in *Camillo* (2007, S. 170) reichen aus, um Grasbüschel heraufzubeschwören, die durch die Schneedecke stechen. Ein schillernder, langer Schwung mittleren Blaus ist in *Forst* (2005, S. 166) alles, was es braucht, um eine den Himmel reflektierende Landstraße einzufangen, die sich einen hübschen bayerischen Hang hinaufzieht. In seiner typischen Bescheidenheit behauptet Angermann, es sei Faulheit, die ihm den einfachsten Weg weise. Dem ist natürlich überhaupt nicht so: Es erfordert tiefes Denken und großes Geschick, all die Elemente so zu reduzieren, dass die Farbe die Arbeit tun kann. Der britische Maler Roger Hilton sagte einmal, es komme nicht drauf an, was man dazugibt, sondern was man weglässt. Das ist es, was Abstraktion wirklich bedeutet, wie Angermann während unserer Unterhaltung spöttelte: „Es ist die Abstraktion, die ich in der abstrakten Kunst vermisse" – eine Anmerkung, die es verdient, in die Geschichte einzugehen. David Hockney natürlich hat denselben Instinkt zur Vereinfachung. Er fing nicht zu malen an, bevor er nicht eine einfache Ausdrucksweise seiner Vorstellungen gefunden hatte: schräger Regen, Licht unter Wasser, Spiegelungen auf Glas. Aber verglichen mit Angermann bleiben Hockneys Markierungen Kunstgriffe, zweidimensionale Zeichen, im Wesentlichen grafisch. Hockney kann zeichnen wie ein Engel, aber Angermann malt wie einer. Wenn man sein Werk betrachtet, weiß man wieder, was Malerei ist, eine reiche, unendlich subtile eigene künstlerische Sprache, wiederentdeckt von einem Künstler, der die Demut und den Mumm hatte, sich einfach umzusehen, die Pinsel zu nehmen und loszulegen.

Das Ergebnis ist Schönheit, ein weiterer Durchbruch Angermanns und eine weitere bedeutende Wiederentdeckung in der Kunst. Wer hätte gedacht, dass Schönheit radikal sein könnte? Doch das war sie und ist es noch immer. Echte Schönheit, also nicht kitschiger Zierrat – einfach normale, gesunde, kraftvolle, sexy Schönheit, wie die Kirschblüte in der Frühlingssonne. Hätte je wieder jemand solch ein Motiv malen können? Angermann tat es 1990 in *Mai (Walberla)* (S. 133) aus schierer Freude, ohne einen Funken Zynismus. Nicht einmal die in grüner Patina erstrahlende fränkische Kirche durfte fehlen. Wer könnte Schönheit in einer Autobahn sehen, in einer Reihe plastikverpackter Grasballen, in einer Ikea-Filiale? Angermann eben. Was könnte jenem verbissenen, in sich gekehrten, selbstfixierten, schmallippigen, schäbigen, kaltherzigen, berechnenden und berechneten dünnen Getröpfel grauen Zeugs ferner sein, wie es an jenen Veranstaltungsorten sogenannter Gegenwartskunst abgesondert wird? Angermann hat wieder gezeigt, dass Kunst, wirkliche Kunst – geschaffene, wortlose Bilder – außerhalb dieses Gefängnisses der Selbstbespiegelung leben, tief atmen, singen kann und sich an alle wendet. Wie weit ist er gekommen seit Düsseldorf, als er grün und geduckt war, als er angewidert auf die suprematistischen Abstraktionen auf seiner Leinwand blickte, in einiger Entfernung umgeben von den verratenen Kunstgenüssen: Früchte, Frauen, frische Luft. Jetzt dominiert diese Umgebung; seine Kunst gibt ihm den Atem zurück.

Er hat ein Bild von dieser Umkehrung der Rollen gemalt, *Landschaft mit Blindem Fleck* (1999, S. 160), sein Abschied vom vergangenen, umnachteten Jahrhundert. Sein alter Lehrer und Gegner Joseph Beuys geht durch eine herrliche, dahinfließende, mit Kirchen bestückte, rapsgelb gestreifte bayerische Landschaft, wie in van Goghs Porträt seiner selbst auf dem Weg

self-reflecting prison, breathe deeply and sing and appeal to anyone. How far he has come from Düsseldorf, when he was green and huddled, looking daggers at the suprematist abstractions on his canvas, surrounded, at a distance, by the abandoned delights of art: fruit, females and fresh air. Now the outside dominates; his art draws its breath in his life.

He has painted a picture of this reversal of the roles of art, *Landscape with Blind Spot* (1999, p. 160), his good-bye to the last, benighted century. His old tutor and adversary, Joseph Beuys, walks through a glorious, rolling, church-studded, yellow-rape-strewn Bavarian landscape, like van Gogh's portrait of himself going out to paint. But Beuys in this painting is a gap in the centre, a bit of reddish-brown underpaint, edged up to but not touched by Angermann's brushes, except when he first laid it in as a foundation. Beuys is a vacancy, an absence, a blind-spot in an ocean of shining light and colour. In this painting, Angermann has finally done what he did his damnedest to do at college: he has found the edge of Beuys, isolated his manipulative misery with joy and love and light and colour, as pure white corpuscles cluster round a foreign body in the blood, or penicillin surrounds and consumes a corrupting influence. That is what Angermann has done for art, and us. But Angermann isn't angry; he is kind. It is a most en-dearing trait. He argues, with the wisdom of hindsight, that without Beuys he would never have accomplished what he has done. He sees the non-art of Beuys as a necessary contrast to what he is now about – a basis, a reddish-brown underpaint, for him to paint against. But as ever, I am not so generous. Why should Angermann have spent all those years digging himself out of a hole? We are grateful that he did, but what a waste of time and talent! Had he been a student of Picasso or Matisse, he could have been even further on today. His green anguish might not have been necessary, or if it had been, it would have been even greener. But *Landscape with Blind Spot* is not just about Beuys and the hollow, dead branch of modernism he represents; it's about the experiment of modern art as a whole. This picture reminds me, as so many of Angermann's plein-air works do, of the paintings which Gabriele Münter and Wassily Kandinsky created during a brief period before World War I when they lived and worked together in Murnau – glorious songs of colour and love, before Kandinsky moved away and set his mind on self-conscious, abstract construction. *Landscape with Blind Spot* is a talisman**,** a new beginning for painting, not just forty but a hundred years on.

Angermann cannot stop thinking. Seeing for him is a springboard for contemplation. He is a natural philosopher, seeking as he lives to come to a closer understanding of what life is. And he feels most intensely alive when he is looking, engaged and active, painting something. His paintings are not only of what he sees but of what he thinks he sees. Our whole world, as he understands better than many, is a mental construction, a fiction that only makes sense from our perspective. Shift a bit in time and space and everything would look different. He does this repeatedly in his landscape painting. That is why he doesn't need (and is indeed reluc-tant) to move far. Angermann's agile mind is always leaping, somersaulting, looking at things afresh. These are springs of joy, the sudden alertness of interest. This is the rolling movement in his work, the flying feeling, skiing, spinning round, the dynamism of an active mind. From time to time he tries to get close to what these brain-flips are, these moments of inspiration,

zum Malen. Aber Beuys ist in diesem Bild eine Lücke im Zentrum, ein wenig rotbraune Unter-
malung, ausgespart und nicht von Angermanns Pinseln berührt, außer bei der Grundierung.
Beuys ist Leere, eine Abwesenheit, ein blinder Fleck in einem strahlenden Meer aus Licht und
Farbe. In diesem Bild ist Angermann endlich das gelungen, worum er sich an der Akademie
mit allen Mitteln bemüht hatte: die Kante von Beuys zu finden, dessen Gängelei in Freude,
Liebe, Licht und Farbe einzukapseln, so wie die weißen Blutkörperchen sich um einen Fremd-
körper im Blut zusammenballen oder Penizillin einen schädlichen Eindringling umhüllt und
auffrisst. Das ist es, was Angermann für die Kunst getan hat, und für uns. Aber Angermann ist
nicht wütend; er ist freundlich. Es ist ein höchst liebenswerter Zug. Im Nachhinein behauptet
er, ohne Beuys hätte er das alles nie geschafft. Er sieht in der Nicht-Kunst von Beuys den
notwendigen Kontrast dazu, worum es ihm jetzt geht – eine Grundlage, eine rotbraune Unter-
malung, gegen die er anmalen kann. Aber auch hier bin ich wieder weniger großzügig. Warum
hätte Angermann all die Jahre damit zubringen müssen, sich freizuschaufeln? Wir sind froh,
dass er es tat, doch welche Vergeudung von Zeit und Talent! Wäre er Student von Picasso oder
Matisse gewesen, könnte er heute sogar noch weiter sein. Seine grüne Wut war womöglich
gar nicht nötig oder wäre, falls doch, vielleicht noch grüner gewesen. Aber bei *Landschaft mit
Blindem Fleck* geht es nicht nur um Beuys und den hohlen toten Ast des Modernismus, den
er vertritt; es geht um das Experiment der modernen Kunst insgesamt. Dieses Bild wie auch
viele von Angermanns Pleinair-Arbeiten erinnern mich an die Bilder, die Gabriele Münter
und Wassily Kandinsky während einer kurzen Periode vor dem Ersten Weltkrieg schufen,
als sie zusammen in Murnau lebten und arbeiteten – großartige Lieder aus Farbe und Liebe,
bevor Kandinsky sich abwandte und sich im Abstrakten befangener Konstruktion widmete.
Landschaft mit Blindem Fleck ist ein Glücksbringer, ein Neuanfang für die Malerei, nicht nur
für vierzig, sondern für die nächsten hundert Jahre.

Angermann kann das Denken nicht lassen. Sehen ist für ihn ein Sprungbrett in
die Kontemplation. Er ist ein Naturphilosoph auf der Suche nach einem immer besseren
Verständnis dessen, was das Leben ausmacht. Und am intensivsten fühlt er das Leben beim
engagierten und aktiven Schauen, während er malt. In seinen Bildern geht es nicht nur darum,
was er sieht, sondern auch, was er zu sehen denkt. Wie ihm klarer ist als vielen, ist unsere
ganze Welt eine geistige Konstruktion, eine Fiktion, die nur aus unserer Perspektive Sinn
macht. Man verschiebe nur ein wenig Zeit und Raum, und alles sieht anders aus. Er tut das
ständig bei seiner Landschaftsmalerei. Deshalb braucht er auch nicht (was ihm tatsächlich
widerstrebt) weit zu fahren. Angermanns agiler Geist springt sowieso dauernd, schlägt
Purzelbäume, sieht die Dinge mit neuen Sinnen. Es sind dies Quellen der Freude, Augenblicke
plötzlich erweckten Interesses. Es ist dieses Rollende in seinem Werk, das Gefühl des Fliegens,
Skifahrens, Herumwirbelns, die Dynamik eines aktiven Geistes. Von Zeit zu Zeit sucht
er diesen Hirnkapriolen auf die Schliche zu kommen, diesen Momenten der Inspiration,
Höhenflügen der Fantasie, wie immer man sie nennen mag. Er hat sie oft. Seine Wandmosaike
für die U-Bahnstation Hohe Marter in Nürnberg (1985) sind ein frühes Beispiel. Er wollte
eigentlich nicht unbedingt den Zuschlag, nahm aber am Wettbewerb teil, weil er das Geld

flights of imagination, call them what you will. He has them often. His mosaic murals for the Hohe Marter subway station in Nuremberg (1985) are an early example. He didn't really want the commission but entered the competition because he needed the money. While he was half-heartedly working up a design, a friend asked him which station it was for. Angermann suddenly had a revelation. Of course, the station was right under the telecommunications tower! The tower flipped over in his mind and lay stretched along the platform, shooting into sunlight as a train came in on one side; lit up and towering into the night as another train went off in the opposite direction on the other; then, when you left the station, there the real tower would be, shooting up into the sky. Suddenly he was interested, won the competition, and had his design carried out in ceramic tiles. It's still exciting in its powerful simplicity and symmetry (and would be more so if it were better lit) – an early manifestation of Angermann's acrobatic thought. This dynamism of perspective springs in part from Angermann's love of comic strips, and is yet another attribute of visual art that he has reclaimed for painting. With typically cheerful cheek he has, of course, played with it, tossed it around, turned it upside down and inside out, and had it for dinner, with a glass of red wine tipping at a dangerous angle.

There is a serious philosophical aspect to all this playfulness, a vein of thinking about the nature of perception that has not yet, I think, fully worked its way into and through his art. This perspective punning isn't just postmodern, post-Renaissance, macro/microcosmic gamesmanship, but a genuine attempt to get close to the feeling which a great many people have that our world is spinning out

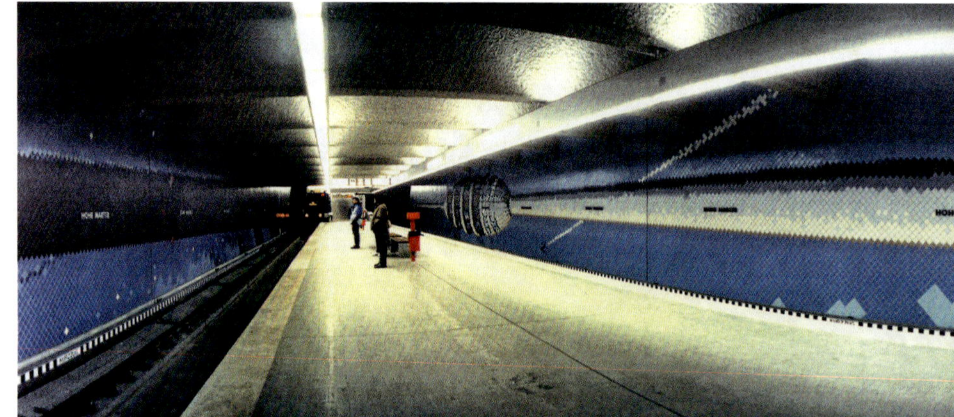

U-Bahnhof Hohe Marter in Nürnberg / Subway station Hohe Marter in Nuremberg, 1986, Keramik / ceramics, beide Seiten je / both sides each 6 x 97 m

of control. Like a conjuror drawing cards, endless silk ribbon, and finally a startled rabbit out of his hat, Angermann has, in a deceptively offhand manner, produced many images that, in time, are likely to become icons of our age. What better projection is there of our perilous belief in material advance than *Tower of Babylon 1* (1989, p. 125)? What could express the tipping point of global warming more subtly and at the same time starkly than *Slate 2* (1991, p. 140)? Who can imagine a creepier, more terrifying portrayal of artificial intelligence multiplying itself *ad infinitum* than *Artificial Intelligence 2* (2001, p. 163)? The painting really is a fractal, reflecting recursive cybernetic structures. "Look, no hands!" the kid calls as he pedals his bike, before the tumble and the grazed knee. A world with only heads and no hands? Who does the work – some invisible, brainless underclass? No wonder the bosses are grinning. Is this the world we want to build? It has only one dimension, the same endlessly diminishing or expanding leer. And on a quotidian level, who has caught more perfectly than Angermann, in *Standing Traffic 2* (1992, p. 145), the feeling of helplessness of the individual stuck in a traffic jam, which extends

brauchte. Während er halbherzig an einem Entwurf arbeitete, fragte ihn ein Freund, um welche Station es denn gehe. Da hatte Angermann eine Erleuchtung. Natürlich, die Station lag direkt unterhalb des Fernsehturms! Vor seinem inneren Auge kippte der Turm und lag ausgestreckt entlang dem Bahnsteig, stach ins Tageslicht, wo der Zug von der einen Seite hereinkam; ragte beleuchtet in die Nacht, wo auf der anderen Seite ein anderer Zug in der Gegenrichtung verschwand; dann, beim Verlassen des Bahnhofs, sähe man dort den echten Turm aufragen. Da erst interessierte ihn die Sache wirklich, er gewann den Wettbewerb und ließ seinen Entwurf als Computermosaik in Keramikfliesen ausführen. Er ist nach wie vor aufregend in seiner Einfachheit und Symmetrie (und wäre das noch mehr bei besserer Beleuchtung) – eine frühe Manifestation von Angermanns akrobatischer Denkweise. Diese perspektivische Dynamik entstammt wohl Angermanns Liebe zum Comicstrip und ist eine weitere bildnerische Möglichkeit, die er für die Malerei in Anspruch genommen hat. Mit typischer heiterer Frechheit natürlich hat er damit gespielt, sie gebeutelt, oben nach unten und

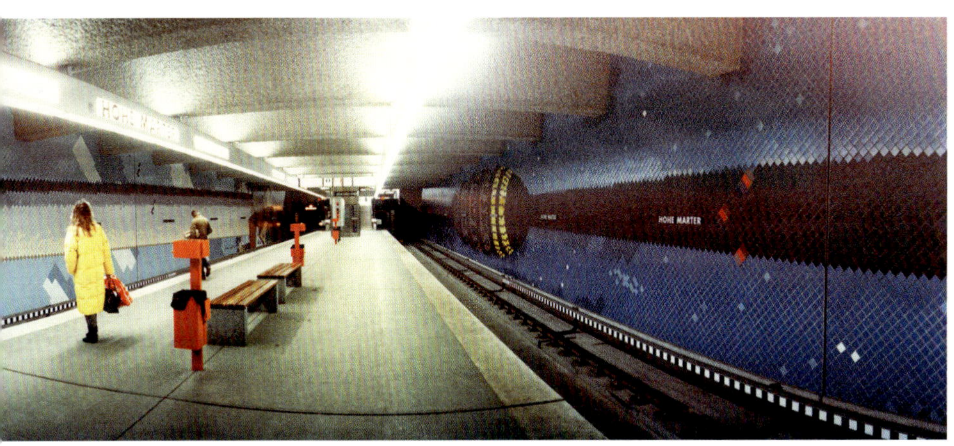

innen nach außen gekehrt, und sie sich zur Brust genommen, mit einem gewagt balancierten Glas Rotwein.

All diese Verspieltheit hat einen ernsthaften philosophischen Aspekt und verrät einen Hang, über die Natur der Wahrnehmung nachzudenken, der, wie ich glaube, noch nicht vollständig seine Kunst durchdringt. Dieses Herumspielen an der Perspektive ist nicht nur postmodern, post-Renaissance, makro/mikrokosmische Trickserei, sondern ein echter Versuch, dem weit verbreiteten Gefühl auf die Spur zu kommen, dass unsere Welt außer Kontrolle gerät. Wie ein Zauberkünstler Karten, endlose Seidenbänder und schließlich ein verdattertes Kaninchen aus dem Hut zieht, hat Angermann mit scheinbarer Lässigkeit zahlreiche Bilder produziert, die das Zeug haben, sich einmal als Ikonen unseres Zeitalters zu erweisen. Was könnte unseren gefährlichen Glauben an das materielle Wachstum besser vorführen als *Turmbau zu Babel 1* (1989, S. 125)? Was könnte das Kippen globaler Erwärmung subtiler und zugleich lapidarer veranschaulichen als *Schiefer 2* (1991, S. 140)? Wer kann sich ein gruseligeres, furchteinflößenderes Porträt der sich *ad infinitum* fortpflanzenden künstlichen Intelligenz vorstellen als *Artificial Intelligence 2* (2001, S. 163)? Das Bild ist wirklich selbst ein Fraktal und verweist so auf rekursive kybernetische Strukturen. „Guck, freihändig!", ruft das radelnde Kind kurz vor dem Sturz und dem aufgeschürften Knie. Eine Welt nur mit Köpfen und ohne Hände? Wer verrichtet die Arbeit – irgendeine unsichtbare, hirnlose Unterklasse? Kein Wunder, dass die Bosse feixen. Ist das die Welt, die wir bauen

to a feeling of helplessness in the face of the whole world? By the simple device of reversing the perspective, he shrinks the people in the foreground to nothing, while the trucks behind them loom to a gargantuan size.

His career would be extraordinary if that was all there is. But there is more, and I'm confident there will be more to come. Ever subtler, even more profound and even more original works are emerging from his fertile, thoughtful, sensitive and endlessly resourceful mind. And what is extraordinary about them is that they are beginning to combine his years of experience of painting *en plein air* with his simple love of the present and of being here and his deep feelings and concern about where we, as a species living on this planet, are heading. The wholeness of his life is gathering momentum and finding forceful expression. I'll mention just two paintings among several. *Deaf in Bischofsheim* (2007, p. 199) could at first sight be a plein-air picture. The pink road receding straight into and through a purple shade is perfect Angermann, as are the high blob clouds and people running. But you notice at once a disquieting expression on the cyclist's face. Then your eye is drawn to the ditch on the right. You can't believe what you are seeing in this sunlit, ordinary suburban scene. Two drunken thugs are clubbing a woman to death, blood spurting everywhere. A kid in a hood crouches to watch, while two other lads brandish cans at passers-by and yell to invite them to join the party. The murder took place in a little German town earlier that summer, right by a public promenade. Angermann read about it in the paper. What is amazing about this painting is that he has seen it so clearly – murder in the broad daylight he now knows how to paint. I know of no other artist, except Goya, who can paint evil in such ordinary light. And the handling, as ever, is deadly in its dexterity. The briefest brushstrokes express the kicks, laughs and screams of the gang and their victim.

But your eye keeps returning to the cyclist's face, his little staring blue pin-point eyes, his look of knowing and not wanting to know, hearing and not wanting to hear, worry and uncertainty, not knowing what to do, thinking it can't be this bad, perhaps they're just having fun, hoping it will go away, as he goes away, his spindly legs still turning. In a stroke of inspiration, possibly only half-conscious, Angermann has painted the bicycle's shadow not across the ground – which would have given it stability – but close up to it, as if the man were cycling as near as he could to a pink wall, for safety's sake. The wobble of the wheels and this wavering shadow make his whole, top-heavy balance more precarious. By these simple means Angermann expresses what is going on in the cyclist's mind, his fear and incapacity and clinging to normality. Normal. What a distance his art has journeyed from that of the group. It is still the same in its freshness, directness and eagerness of spirit, but now it is so sophisticatedly simple that it can encompass the whole of human experience, the impotent abutting of love of life and fear of death. Who else today could have painted such a scene? Who else would have even thought of doing so? Perhaps the Scottish painter Peter Howson, but he would have focussed on the thuggery – much easier prey than the complex feelings of the passer-by. Angermann resists any hint of moral self-righteousness, any tub-thumping muscularity. He has included something of himself in the face of the cyclist: he always tends to, when he paints anyone in the

wollen? Mit nur einer Dimension, einer Kaskade immergleichen, unentwegt wuchernden Glubschens. Und wer hat auf eher alltäglicher Ebene das Gefühl hilflos im Stau steckender Individuen genauer getroffen als Angermann in *Stehender Verkehr 2* (1992, S. 145), ein Gefühl der Hilflosigkeit gegenüber der Welt insgesamt? Durch den simplen Einfall, die Perspektive umzukehren, schrumpft er die Leute im Vordergrund zum Nichts, während die LKWs hinten sich in immenser Größe auftürmen.

Seine Karriere wäre schon außergewöhnlich, wenn das alles wäre. Aber da ist noch mehr, und ich bin zuversichtlich, dass Weiteres nachkommen wird. Immer feiner ausgefeilte, noch tiefer schürfende, ja originellere Werke entspringen seinem fruchtbaren, nachdenklichen, feinfühligen und unerschöpflichen Geist. Und sie fangen ungewöhnlicherweise an, seine jahrelange Pleinair-Erfahrung mit seiner einfachen Liebe zur Gegenwart, zum Dasein zu verbinden, auch mit seinen tiefen Gefühlen und seinen Sorgen, wohin wir als Spezies auf diesem Planeten wohl treiben. Sein gesamtes Leben gewinnt an Fahrt und findet kraftvollen Ausdruck. Ich möchte nur zwei Bilder unter mehreren erwähnen. *Taub in Bischofsheim* (2007, S. 199) könnte auf den ersten Blick ein Pleinair-Bild sein. Die rosa Straße, die schnurstracks in violetten Schatten verschwindet, ist, wie die hohen Wolkentupfer und die rennenden Leute, Angermann in Vollendung. Aber man bemerkt sofort einen beunruhigenden Ausdruck im Gesicht des Radfahrers. Dann zieht es den Blick auf den Graben rechts. Man möchte nicht glauben, was man in dieser sonnigen, alltäglichen Stadtrandszene sieht. Zwei betrunkene Rowdys schlagen eine Frau tot, alles ist blutbeschmiert. Einer mit Kapuze sieht kauernd zu, während zwei andere den Passanten zuprosten und brüllend zur Party einladen. Der Mord geschah in jenem Frühsommer in einer deutschen Kleinstadt, direkt neben einem Spazierweg. Angermann las es in der Zeitung. Das Erstaunliche an diesem Bild ist, dass er es so klar gesehen hat – Mord am helllichten Tag, er weiß jetzt, wie das gemalt wird. Ich kenne keinen anderen Künstler außer Goya, der das Böse in solch einem gewöhnlichen Licht malen kann. Und die Ausführung ist, wie gehabt, von tödlicher Geschicklichkeit. Die knappsten Pinselstriche drücken die Schläge, Lacher und Schreie der Bande und ihres Opfers aus.

Aber der Blick kehrt zum Gesicht des Radfahrers zurück, zu seinen stieren, blauen Stecknadelkopf-Äuglein, seinem Wissen und Nichtwissenwollen, Hören und Nichthörenwollen, seiner Sorge und Unsicherheit, nicht zu wissen, was zu tun ist, so schlimm wird's ja nicht sein, vielleicht ist alles nur Spaß, es möge verschwinden, wie er selbst verschwindet, unentwegt und dünnbeinig die Pedale tretend. In einem Geistesblitz, vielleicht nur halbbewusst, hat Angermann den Schatten des Fahrrads nicht quer über den Boden gelegt – was Stabilität gegeben hätte – sondern dicht aufwärts, als ob der Mann sicherheitshalber so nah es geht an einer rosa Wand entlangfahren würde. Das Beben der Räder und dieser wankende Schatten machen die ganze kopflastige Balance nur noch heikler. Mit solch einfachen Mitteln zeigt Angermann, was in dem Radler vor sich geht, seine Furcht und Unfähigkeit und sein Sichklammern an die Normalität. Normal. Wie hat sich seine Malerei von der der Gruppe entfernt. Gleich geblieben in ihrer Frische, Unmittelbarkeit und Neugier, ist sie doch jetzt so raffiniert einfach, dass sie die ganze menschliche Erfahrung umfassen

wrong. The cyclist and the thugs are part of all of us. In its humble, mundane way, there is here a greater healing too, for Germany's horrific Nazi past.

Angermann's most extraordinary painting to date is *Behind, Far Away…* (2008, p. 205). This is a painting not of the light out there, but of the light in his mind. All his paintings are, of course, exactly that; indeed all paintings are – mind glows, projections of what artists think they see, flares of their luminous understanding, searchlights on the scenes before them and in their imaginations. The more clearly they see, the more brightly their pictures shine. That's what painting is: the play of contrasts within the shimmering sphere of the mind's eye. And few artists today, if any, see more clearly than Angermann. *Behind, Far Away…* is a painting of an intense revelation, a moment, experienced by most people at some time during their lives, when you seem to be looking down at yourself and your surroundings from above, an out-of-body, momentary sensation of heightened self-consciousness. His paintings suggest that Angermann has had such revelations often, from his green self-portrait on. They inform his interest in shifts of perspective and inspire his most telling works. *Behind, Far Away…* is such a painting, on a monumental scale. It is, on one level, the simplest, most common domestic scene in the world: a family, Angermann's own, watching television. The blue eyes of the cyclist in *Deaf in Bischofheim* are looking straight at us again, but this time not shrinking or shaded with doubt. In *Behind, Far Away…* the family's eyes, even the baby's, are wide open, goggle-eyed, gazing, wondering, not sure how to respond to what they are seeing, but going on staring nevertheless from the comfort of their living room, each blue eye as innocent of what is happening in front of it as the blue sky is of everything man does under it. For that is the perspectival flip, the moment of heightened awareness that this painting is about: Angermann has painted himself and his family not only as if he were watching them all watching television but at the same time as if he were seeing what they are seeing on the screen in their minds. Inside, outside, near and far, here and there; it is a complex game with words, but one that painting can handle with supreme ease. Velázquez did it in *Las Meninas*.

Seeing *Las Meninas* in the Prado in Madrid is an extraordinary experience, which is difficult to imagine via a reproduction. You feel as though you're looking not at a painting, but through a huge window into the room next door, watching Velázquez painting a portrait of the King and Queen of Spain (you can see them mirrored in the back), with the Infanta and her entourage standing beside him, looking at her parents being painted. Then suddenly the sensation flips. It has something to do with the life-sized scale of the picture. You don't feel you're behind a glass, peering through a one-way mirror at a private scene. You feel that you're standing in the room with Velázquez and that he's painting *you*. The light in the painting embraces you; the extraordinary intensity and sensitivity of Velázquez's vision, the breadth and gentleness of his brushstrokes, his all-encompassing humanity, are for these memorable moments the air you breathe. *Behind, Far Away…* is the only painting I can think of that even begins to approach *Las Meninas* in modern times, embracing you with a terrifyingly thinner, more rigidly tragic strain of air.

kann, die ohnmächtige Anlehnung der Liebe zum Leben an die Todesangst. Wer sonst heute hätte solch eine Szene malen können? Wem sonst wäre das überhaupt in den Sinn gekommen? Vielleicht dem schottischen Maler Peter Howson, doch der hätte sich auf das Verbrechen konzentriert – eine viel leichtere Beute als die komplexen Gefühle des Passanten. Angermann widersteht jedem Hauch moralischer Selbstgerechtigkeit, jedweder daumensenkenden Kraftmeierei. Er hat dem Gesicht des Radlers Züge von sich selbst gegeben: wie oft, wenn er jemanden in negativer Rolle malt. Der Radler und die Mörder sind Teil von uns allen. Auf bescheidene und nüchterne Art wirkt das auch sehr heilsam mit Blick auf Deutschlands schreckliche Nazivergangenheit.

Das außergewöhnlichste unter Angermanns neueren Bildern ist *Hinten, fern…* (2008, S. 205). Es ist kein Bild des äußeren, physikalischen, sondern des inneren Lichts. Natürlich gilt genau das für all seine Bilder; Bilder überhaupt sind geistiges Leuchten, Projektionen davon, was Künstler zu sehen denken, das Aufflackern ihrer Erleuchtung, Suchscheinwerfer auf ihr Umfeld und ihre Vorstellung. Je klarer sie sehen, desto heller strahlen ihre Bilder. Das ist es, was Malerei ausmacht: das Spiel der Kontraste innerhalb der schimmernden Sphäre des geistigen Auges. Und nur wenige heutige Künstler, wenn überhaupt, sehen klarer als Angermann. *Hinten, fern…* ist eine Offenbarung, jener Augenblick, den die meisten aus ihrem eigenen Leben kennen, wenn man scheinbar wie von oben auf sich und seine Umgebung herabblickt, in einem plötzlichen Gefühl des Außersichseins, der gesteigerten Selbstwahrnehmung. Seine Bilder lassen vermuten, dass Angermann solche Offenbarungen öfters hatte seit seinem grünen Selbstporträt. Sie entsprechen seinem Interesse für Perspektivverschiebungen und inspirieren seine aussagekräftigsten Werke. *Hinten, fern…* ist davon ein monumentales Exemplar. In gewisser Hinsicht ist es die einfachste, alltäglichste häusliche Szene der Welt: eine Familie, Angermanns eigene, beim Fernsehen. Da gucken uns wieder die blauen Augen des Radfahrers in *Taub in Bischofsheim* geradewegs an, doch diesmal nicht verzagt und zweifelnd. In *Hinten, fern…* sind die Augen der Familie, sogar die des Babys, weit geöffnet, glotzend, stierend, verwundert, nicht recht wissend, was von all dem zu halten sei, nichtsdestoweniger weiterhin aus der Geborgenheit ihres Wohnzimmers hervorstarrend, jedes blaue Augenpaar an dem, was vor ihm geschieht, ebenso unschuldig wie der blaue Himmel an allem, was unter ihm getan wird. Denn das ist der perspektivische Salto, der Moment gesteigerten Gewahrwerdens, um den es in diesem Bild geht: Angermann hat sich und seine Familie nicht nur so gemalt, als sähe er sie alle fernsehen, sondern zugleich so, als sähe er, was sie vor Augen haben. Innen, außen, nah und fern, hier und dort; mit Worten ein kompliziertes Spiel, welches Malerei jedoch mit überlegener Leichtigkeit bewältigen kann. Wie Velázquez in *Las Meninas*.

Las Meninas im Prado in Madrid zu sehen ist eine außerordentliche Erfahrung, die man sich anhand einer Reproduktion kaum vorstellen kann. Es ist, als ob man nicht auf ein Bild blickte, sondern durch ein riesiges Fenster in den Nebenraum, wo man Velázquez an einem Porträt des Königs und der Königin von Spanien arbeiten sieht (sie sind im Hintergrund gespiegelt), neben sich die Infantin und ihre Entourage, die zusieht, wie ihre Eltern gemalt werden. Dann kippt plötzlich die Situation. Das hat etwas mit der Lebensgröße des Bildes

The conceit is the same, except that the picture surface is not a mirror but a television screen. The rainbow ball at the top left – incidentally, beautifully painted – is the TV-channel logo, hovering on the pixel surface. What's happened is that the image on the screen has taken over the whole room. The floor recedes into the desert, the wooden boards fade into sand. Beyond the ball of knitting wool there are pools of blood. The whole has a cartoon feel, as befits something that is not really real. That bloody splat in the centre – can we actually be watching a real man's head exploding? Yes, we are, but still we go on looking, as bombs go off and black smoke pours from buildings and men line up to be shot, in an evocation, in cryptic strokes, of Goya's *The Third of May*. And yet, despite the horror, you can look at the painting closely. Each mark is meant, each shape tells, all executed with consummate simplicity. Angermann took a series of photos, as he sometimes does, of this painting as it formed on the canvas. The sureness of each stage – essentially a mere twelve of them – is extraordinary: each sweeping, overall and to the point, no fussing, no going back, hardly any corrections until, near the end, he suddenly gives Renate a bigger behind, and adds a ball of wool, and someone popping their head up behind the sofa as if playing hide-and-seek. The people appear first on the bare canvas, as the briefest zigzag red gestures, but after that their basic positions, so clearly envisaged from the beginning, never alter. The black smoke and splat appear early, the startled blue eyes near the end, along with the remote control. You have the feeling, watching this picture emerge, layer by layer from the clearing mists of Angermann's mind, that he is half-tempted to switch the whole scene off, but can't. That is what makes him the great artist he is: he cannot avoid seeing what he can see.

Angermann hardly ever leaves his home and immediate environment. Why should he? He lives on the top of the world. We all do on ours. There's too much of interest to keep him in his locality, as there is for all of us, wherever we are, if we're honest. In this concentration on being local in an increasingly global world he is, as in so many things, radical. He is an artist of the future who, by his work, by living and concentrating on his vicinity, is helping to make the world richer and fuller again for all of us, rather than smaller and emptier. This is what we all need: a bigger world for us all to live in. Angermann is fond of telling visitors that his house stands on a ridge that is the watershed between two great river systems – the Danube running north, which then bends round and takes its course to the south and east, and the Rhine running south, which then bends north and west. He lives, he says – by accident, not design – at

Entstehungsprozess von *Hinten, fern…*
Developing process of *Behind, Far Away.*
2008 (12 Phasen / 12 stages)

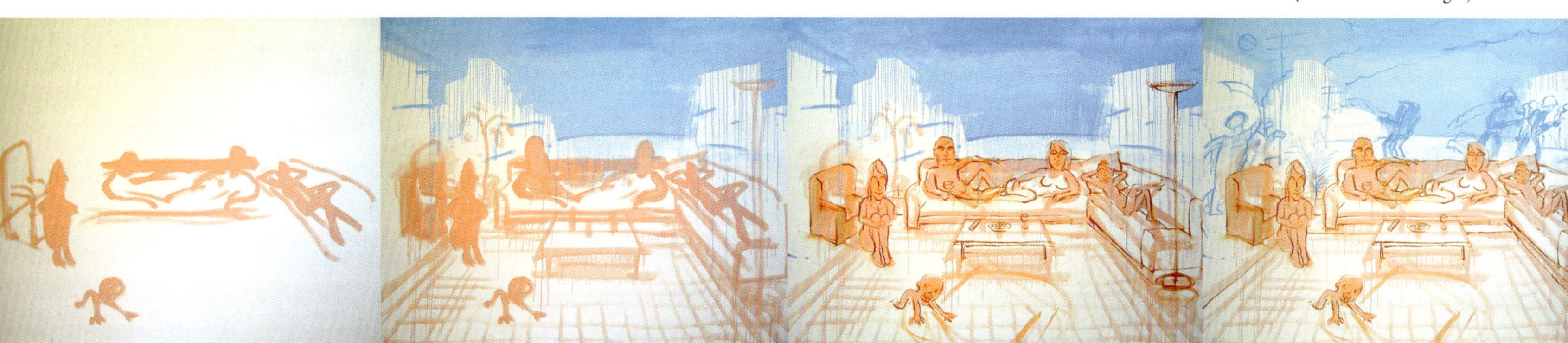

zu tun. Man hat nicht das Gefühl, durch einen halbdurchlässigen Spiegel auf eine private
Szene zu gucken. Man hat das Gefühl, bei Velázquez im Raum zu stehen und selber von ihm
gemalt zu werden. Das Licht in dem Raum umfängt einen; die außergewöhnliche Intensität
und Empfindsamkeit von Velázquez' Vision, die Breite und Sanftheit seiner Pinselstriche,
seine allumfassende Menschlichkeit, bilden in diesen denkwürdigen Momenten die Luft, die
man atmet. *Hinten, fern…* ist das einzige mir bekannte Bild, das in heutiger Zeit *Las Meninas*
wenigstens ansatzweise nahekommt, indem es einen mit erschreckend dünnerem, unerbittlich
tragischerem Luftzug umfängt.

Das Konzept ist dasselbe, außer dass die Bildoberfläche hier kein Spiegel, sondern der
Bildschirm ist. Der Regenbogenball links oben – nebenbei bemerkt wunderschön gemalt – ist
das auf der Pixelebene gleitende Senderlogo. Was passiert ist: Das Bild auf dem Schirm hat den
ganzen Raum eingenommen. Der Fußboden geht in die Wüste über, das Parkett verschwindet
im Sand. Unter dem Wollknäuel sind Blutlachen. Das Ganze hat eine cartoonartige Anmutung,
als handele es sich um etwas nicht wirklich Reales. Dieser blutige Klecks in der Mitte – sollten
wir tatsächlich den Kopf eines echten Menschen explodieren sehen? Ja, so ist es, aber wir schauen
immer noch hin, wie Bomben hochgehen und schwarzer Rauch aus Gebäuden quillt und
Menschen reihenweise erschossen werden, eine finstere Beschwörung von Goyas *Erschießung der
Aufständischen*. Und doch kann man, dem Horror zum Trotz, das Bild aus der Nähe anschauen.
Jedes Zeichen ist gewollt, jede Form spricht, alles ist mit vollendeter Einfachheit ausgeführt.
Angermann hat, wie er es gelegentlich tut, die Entstehung dieses Bildes auf der Leinwand in einer
Reihe von Fotos festgehalten. Die Sicherheit eines jeden Stadiums – im Wesentlichen sind es
zwölf – ist außergewöhnlich: alles schwungvoll, überall und auf den Punkt gebracht, keine Um-
stände, kein Schritt zurück, kaum Korrekturen, bis er gegen Ende Renate plötzlich ein größeres
Hinterteil gibt, ein Wollknäuel hinzufügt und einen Kopf hinterm Sofa auftauchen lässt wie
beim Versteckspielen. Die Leute erscheinen als Erstes auf der leeren Leinwand, als knappste rosa
Zickzackgesten, doch von da an bleibt ihre Grundposition in ihrer Klarheit unverändert. Der
schwarze Rauch und der Blutklecks erscheinen früh, die erschreckten blauen Augen gegen Ende,
zusammen mit der Fernbedienung. Man meint, wenn man dieses Bild Schicht für Schicht aus
den sich lichtenden Nebeln in Angermanns Geist auftauchen sieht, er sei fast versucht, die ganze
Szene abzuschalten, kann aber doch nicht. Das ist es, was ihn zu dem großen Künstler macht,
der er ist: Er kann nicht vermeiden zu sehen, was er sieht.

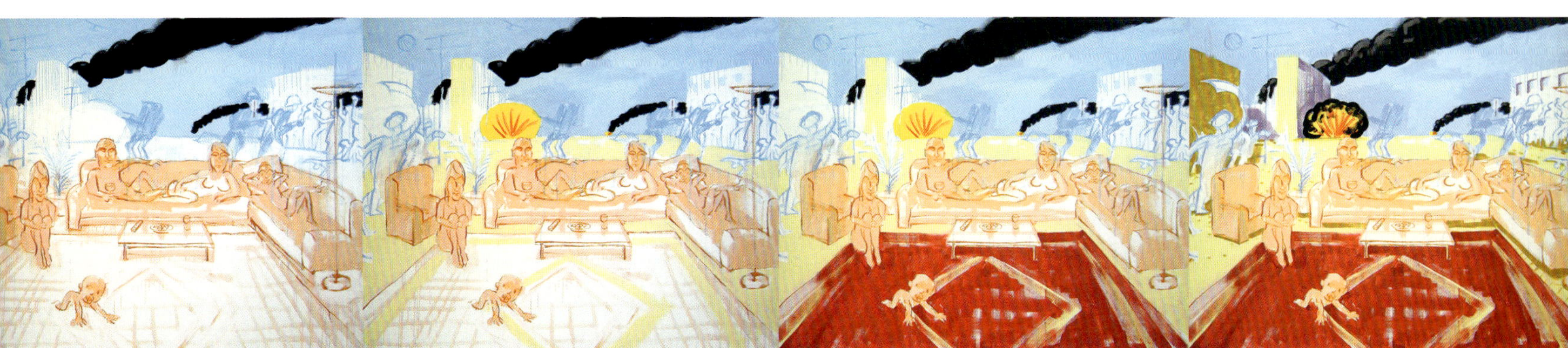

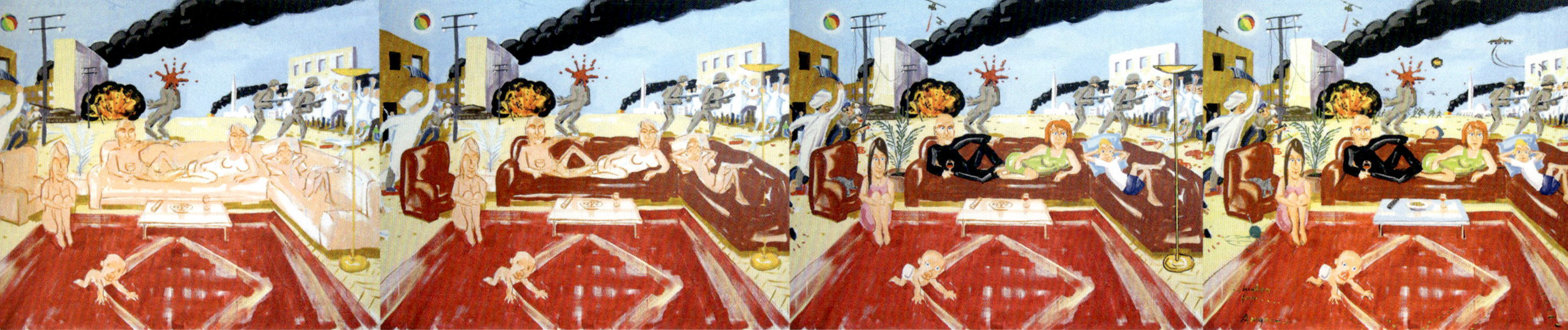

the pivot of the heart of Europe. Why go anywhere else? And if he is accused of escaping into the country (not that he would say there is anything wrong in that), just to the south of where he lives lies one of the main NATO training grounds. As opposition built up against Saddam Hussein, Angermann saw and heard a mini-war rehearse in his backyard. There were shell bursts behind his sofa, as in *Behind, Far Away….*

I've tried to tell briefly the story of the personal genius, the spirit, that has led Peter Angermann to where he is. But is Angermann also a "genius" in the more usual modern sense? It's not for us to say. People in the future will sort out for themselves who they think are the art-changing colossi of our time. There's nothing we can do to influence their opinion, and their judgement anyway will be skewed by what they then want out of art, which won't be exactly the same as what we want. Gainsaying the future is a mug's game, but one played often by art dealers, critics and art curators in museums. All we can do is to decide clearly what art *we* want – what art gives *us* the most. This might seem selfish, but it is the only honest stance. We have to be like the little boy in the Emperor's Court and tell plainly what we see. And if we see something we really like, it is our duty to shout it from the rooftops, so that everyone else can come and see it too! Art has to be a personal response; it can't be anything more. Thoughts added to it, in screeds in contemporary art magazines and on art-gallery walls, are wishful thoughts or self-inflating pomposity or, simply, bullshit. Art has to speak for itself. If it doesn't do so directly, the chances are it isn't there.

Angermann's great achievement is to show that painting isn't an outmoded means of expression but a living language for today. In his hands, painting is capable of communicating the joy of being here when we look around us now. His plein-air paintings aren't romantic, sweet visions of a world that was, but expressions of unsentimental visual delight in the world as it is. That would be victory enough, but there's much more to his achievement. Step by step, slowly and methodically, Angermann has re-conquered the whole alphabet of painting as a language of feeling. He's re-invigorated the tradition handed down from Rembrandt, Goya and Picasso, and enabled the art of painting to be, once more, both popular and profound. He's demonstrated by doing it – there's no other way to show it – that painting is once again capable of laying bare our subtlest yet most common emotions, such as the feelings aroused by watching a war on TV. And in doing so he's demonstrated, through sheer technical brilliance, that this most omnipresent yet

Angermann verlässt kaum je sein Zuhause und die nähere Umgebung. Warum sollte
er? Er lebt auf dem Gipfel der Welt. So wie wir alle. Es gibt für ihn zu viel Interessantes, was
ihn am Ort hält, so wie bei uns allen, wo auch immer wir sein mögen, machen wir uns nichts
vor! In dieser Konzentration auf Sesshaftigkeit in einer zunehmend globalen Welt ist er, wie in
so vielen Dingen, radikal. Er ist ein Künstler der Zukunft, der durch seine Arbeit, sein Leben
und die Konzentration auf seine Nachbarschaft die Welt wieder reicher und voller für uns alle
zu machen hilft, statt kleiner und leerer. Genau das brauchen wir: eine größere Welt, um alle
darin zu leben. Es macht Angermann Spaß, den Besuchern zu erzählen, dass sein Haus genau
auf der großen Europäischen Wasserscheide steht – dem Einzugsbecken der Donau nach
Norden, das bald nach Südosten abbiegt, und des Rheins nach Süden hin und anschließend
nach Nordwest. Er lebt, sagt er – zufällig, nicht geplant – an der Herzklappe Europas. Wozu
woanders hingehen? Und wirft man ihm Flucht aufs Land vor (nicht dass er daran etwas
verkehrt fände), südlich seiner Bleibe liegt einer der wichtigsten NATO-Truppenübungsplätze.
Als man gegen Saddam Hussein mobil machte, sah und hörte Angermann einen Minikrieg in
seinem Hinterhof. Granaten platzten hinter seinem Sofa, wie in *Hinten, fern…*.

Ich habe versucht, kurz die Geschichte des persönlichen Genies zu erzählen, des Geistes,
der Peter Angermann dahin geführt hat, wo er ist. Aber ist Angermann auch ein „Genie" im
gebräuchlicheren modernen Sinn? Es ist nicht an uns, das zu sagen. In der Zukunft werden
die Menschen selbst herausfinden, wen aus unserer Zeit sie für künstlerisch bahnbrechend
erachten. Wir haben keinerlei Einfluss auf ihre Meinung, und ihr Urteil wird ohnehin davon
abhängen, was sie einmal von der Kunst erwarten werden – wohl kaum genau dasselbe wie wir.
Sich die Zukunft zurechtzubiegen ist ein dämliches Spiel, aber eines, das von Kunsthändlern,
Kritikern und Museumskuratoren oft gespielt wird. Alles, was wir tun können, ist klar zu
entscheiden, was *wir* erwarten – was *uns* Kunst in erster Linie bedeutet. Das mag egoistisch erscheinen, aber es ist die einzig ehrliche Haltung. Wir müssen wie der kleine Junge in *Des Kaisers
neue Kleider* sein, und geradeheraus sagen, was wir sehen. Und wenn wir etwas sehen, das wir
wirklich mögen, ist es unsere Pflicht, das von den Dächern zu rufen, damit jeder kommen und
es auch sehen kann! Kunst hat eine persönliche Antwort zu sein, weiter nichts. Nachgereichte
Gedanken in langen Reden, in zeitgenössischen Kunstmagazinen und an Galeriewänden sind
Wunschdenken oder aufgeblasene Wichtigtuerei oder einfach Bullshit. Kunst muss für sich
selbst sprechen. Tut sie das nicht unmittelbar, steckt womöglich auch nichts dahinter.

Angermanns große Leistung ist zu zeigen, dass Malerei kein veraltetes Ausdrucksmittel
ist, sondern eine lebendige Sprache für die heutige Zeit. In seinen Händen kann Malerei die
Freude vermitteln, da zu sein und zu schauen. Seine Pleinair-Bilder sind keine romantischen,
süßen Visionen einer vergangenen Welt, sondern Ausdruck unsentimentaler visueller Freude
an der Welt, wie sie ist. Das allein wäre ein hinreichender Sieg, doch die Leistung ist noch viel
größer. Schritt für Schritt, langsam und methodisch, hat Angermann das gesamte Alphabet
der Malerei als eine Sprache des Gefühls zurückerobert. Er hat die Tradition wiederbelebt, wie
sie von Rembrandt, Goya und Picasso überliefert ist, und die Malerei noch einmal in die Lage
versetzt, populär und profund zugleich zu sein. Er belegt durch seine Arbeit – anders ist es

elusive of all modern visual sensations, the pixel brilliance of the television screen itself, can be conjured up vividly in that quaint old medium of paint on canvas.

And, in one of his latest paintings, *Streetview 2* (2011), the painter, as a Texan cowboy, rides in, brushes at the ready, and captures on his canvas the brilliant, fictive baubles of the omnipresent Google eyes that now map our world. Nothing, once again, is outside painting's domain! That's the trump card Angermann has played in the game of endless possibilities that is the art of painting.

[1] A fuller critique of Beuys is contained in my book *The Eclipse of Art* (Munich, 2003) and my e-pamphlet *Con Art – Why You Should Sell Your Damien Hirsts While You Can* (Amazon/Kindle 2011).

nicht möglich –, dass Malerei wieder imstande ist, unsere subtilsten und doch gewöhnlichsten Gefühle offenzulegen, wie etwa die beim Krieg im Fernsehen. Und dabei zeigt sich, und zwar durch schiere technische Brillanz, dass die allgegenwärtigste und doch am wenigsten fassbare aller modernen visuellen Sensationen, nämlich der Pixelglanz des Bildschirms selbst, in jenem wunderlichen alten Medium Farbe auf Leinwand derart lebendig heraufbeschworen werden kann!

Und in einem seiner letzten Bilder, *Streetview 2* (2011), reitet der Maler wie ein texanischer Cowboy herein, die Pinsel bereit, und fängt auf seiner Leinwand die leuchtenden, imaginären Blasen der allgegenwärtigen Google-Augen ein, die jetzt unsere Welt kartografieren. Und noch einmal: Nichts liegt außer Reichweite der Malerei! Das ist Angermanns Trumpfkarte im Spiel unbegrenzter Möglichkeiten, das wir die Kunst der Malerei nennen.

[1] Eine umfassendere Kritik von Beuys' Werk findet sich in meinem Buch *The Eclipse of Art*, München 2003, und meinem e-pamphlet *Con Art – Why You Should Sell Your Damien Hirsts While You Can*, Amazon/Kindle 2011.

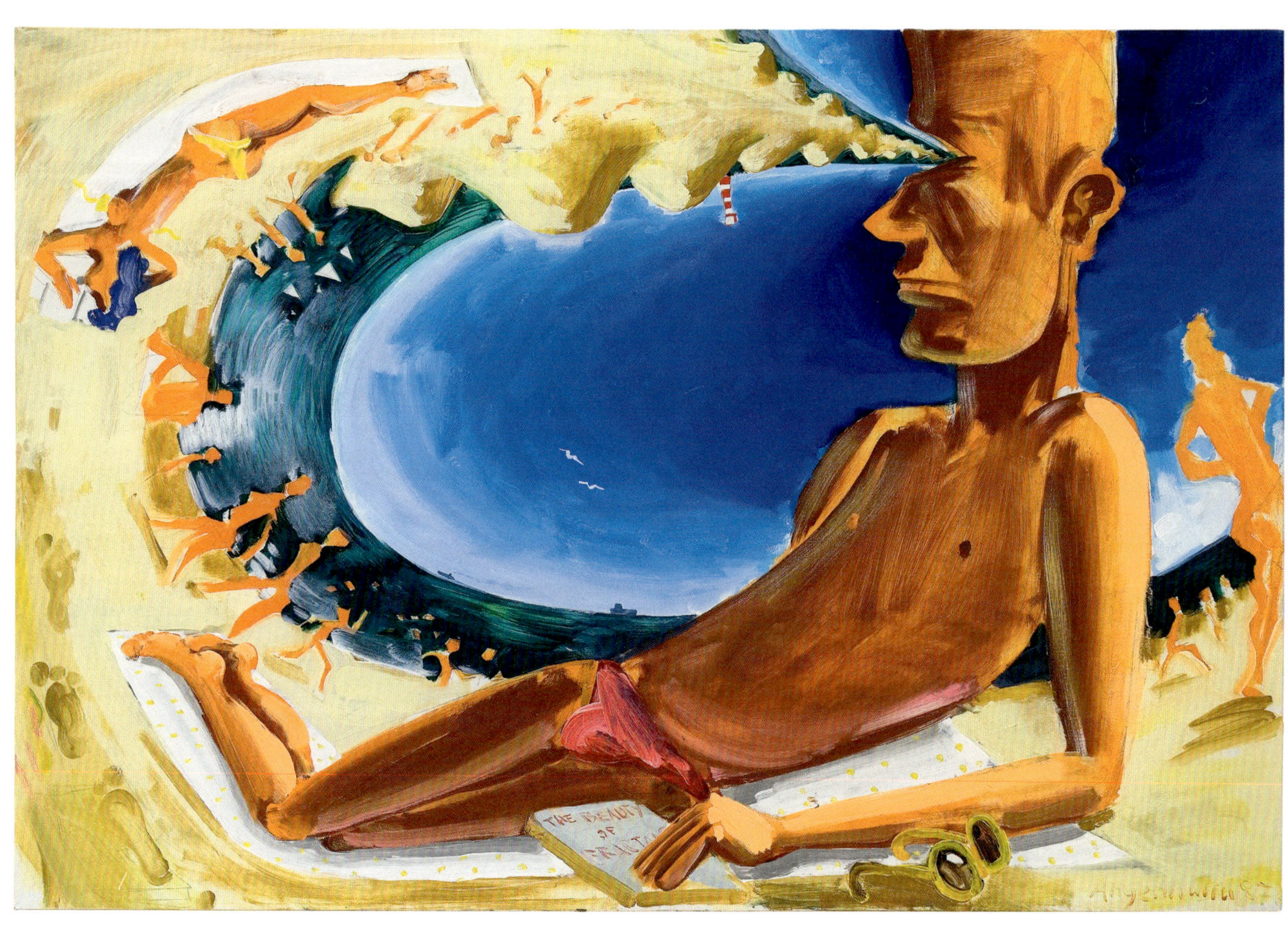

Selbst als Kleinsche Flasche / Self as Klein Bottle, 1987

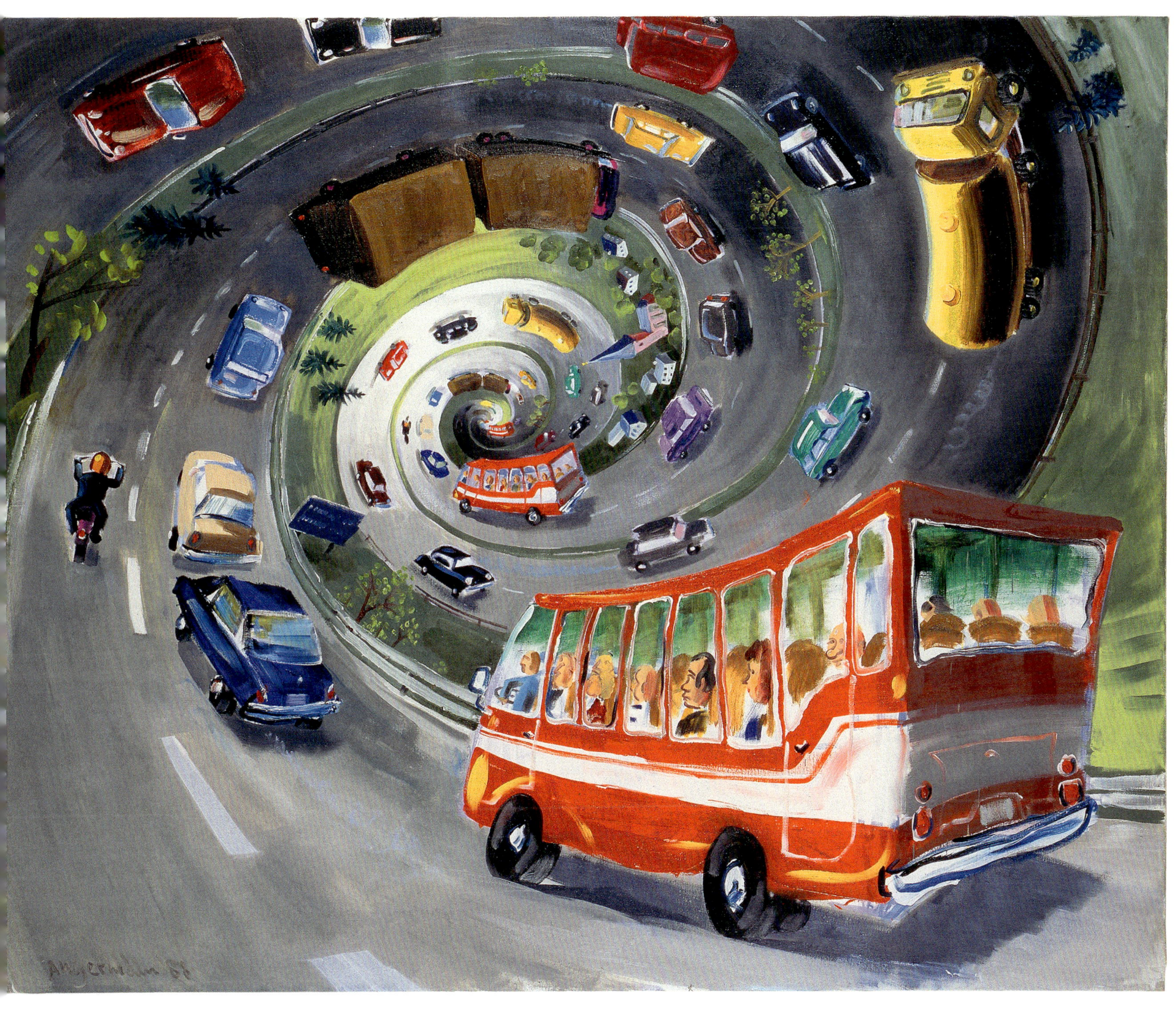

Spirale 1 / Spiral 1, 1988

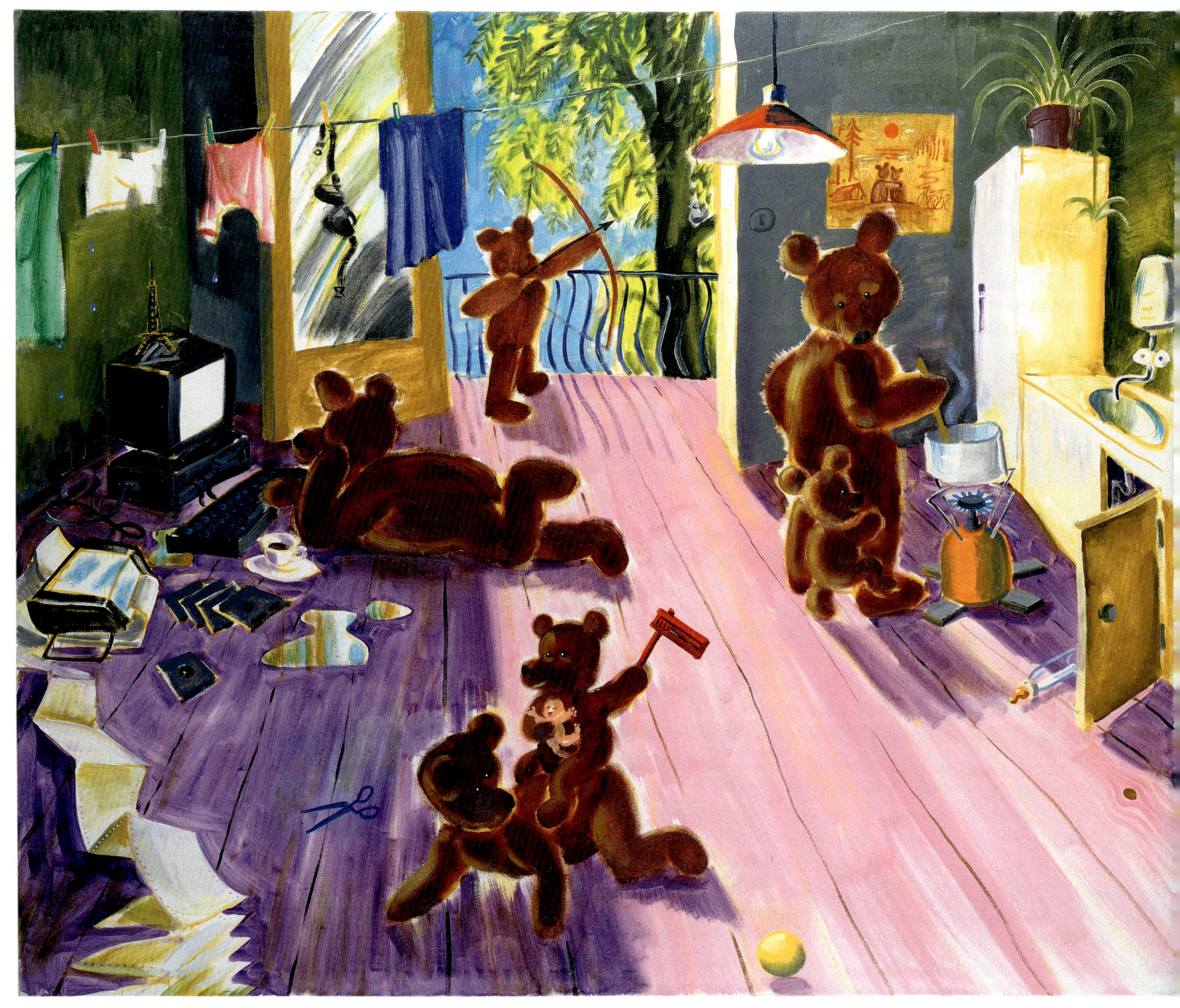

Bären daheim / Bears at Home, 1988

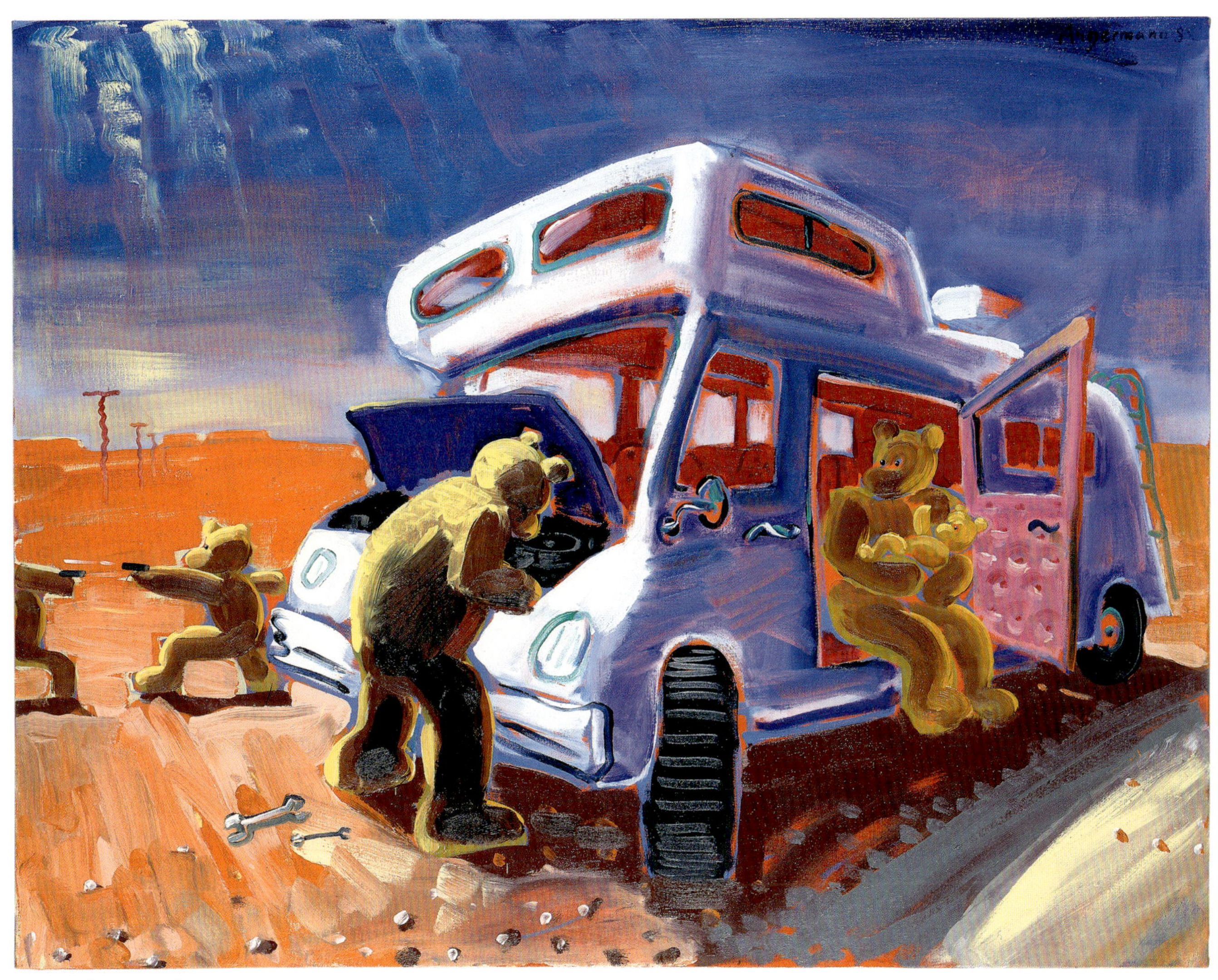

Yermo, 1988

121

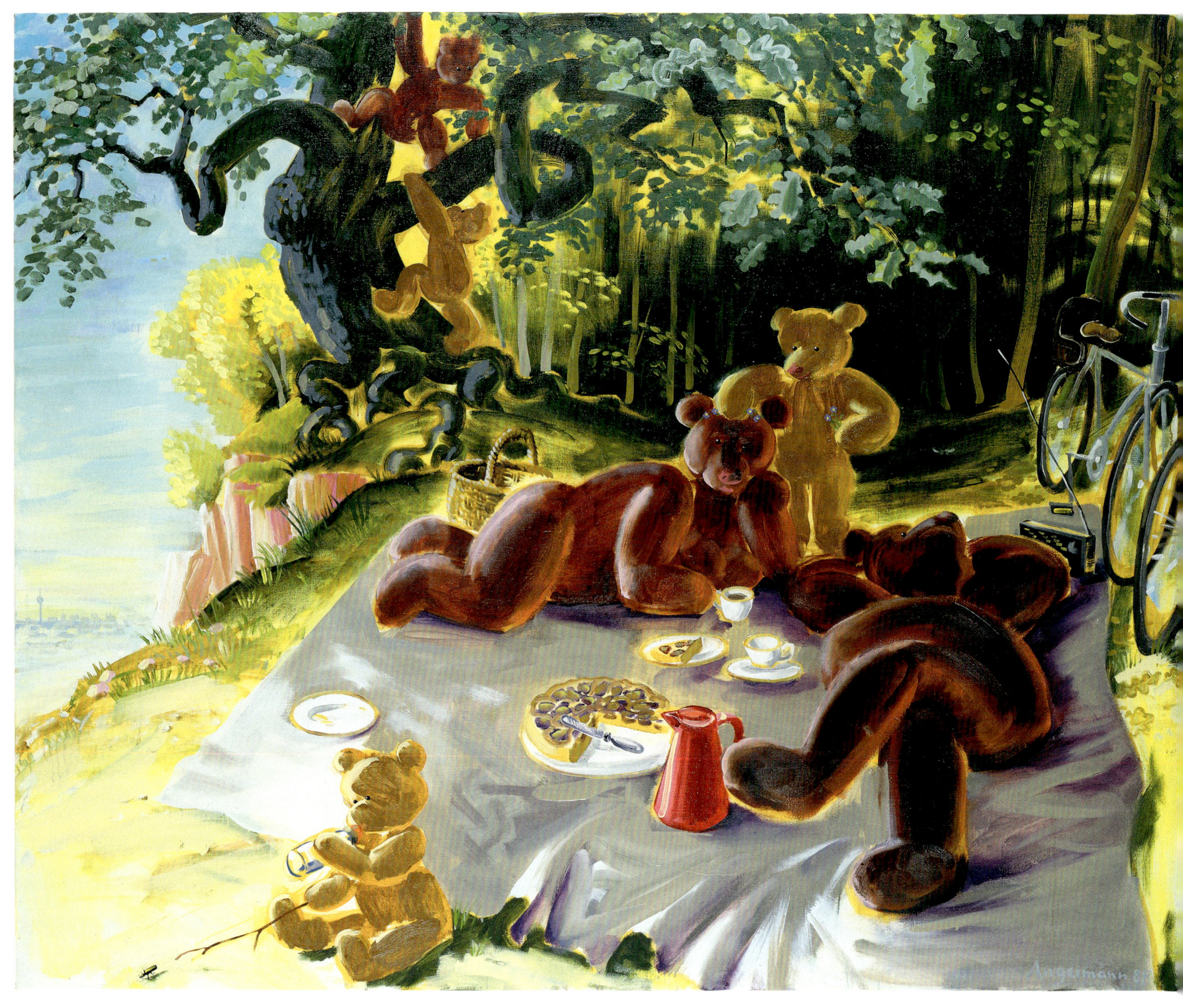

Bärenpicknick / Bears' Picnic, 1988

122

Turmbau zu Babel 1 / Tower of Babylon 1, 1989

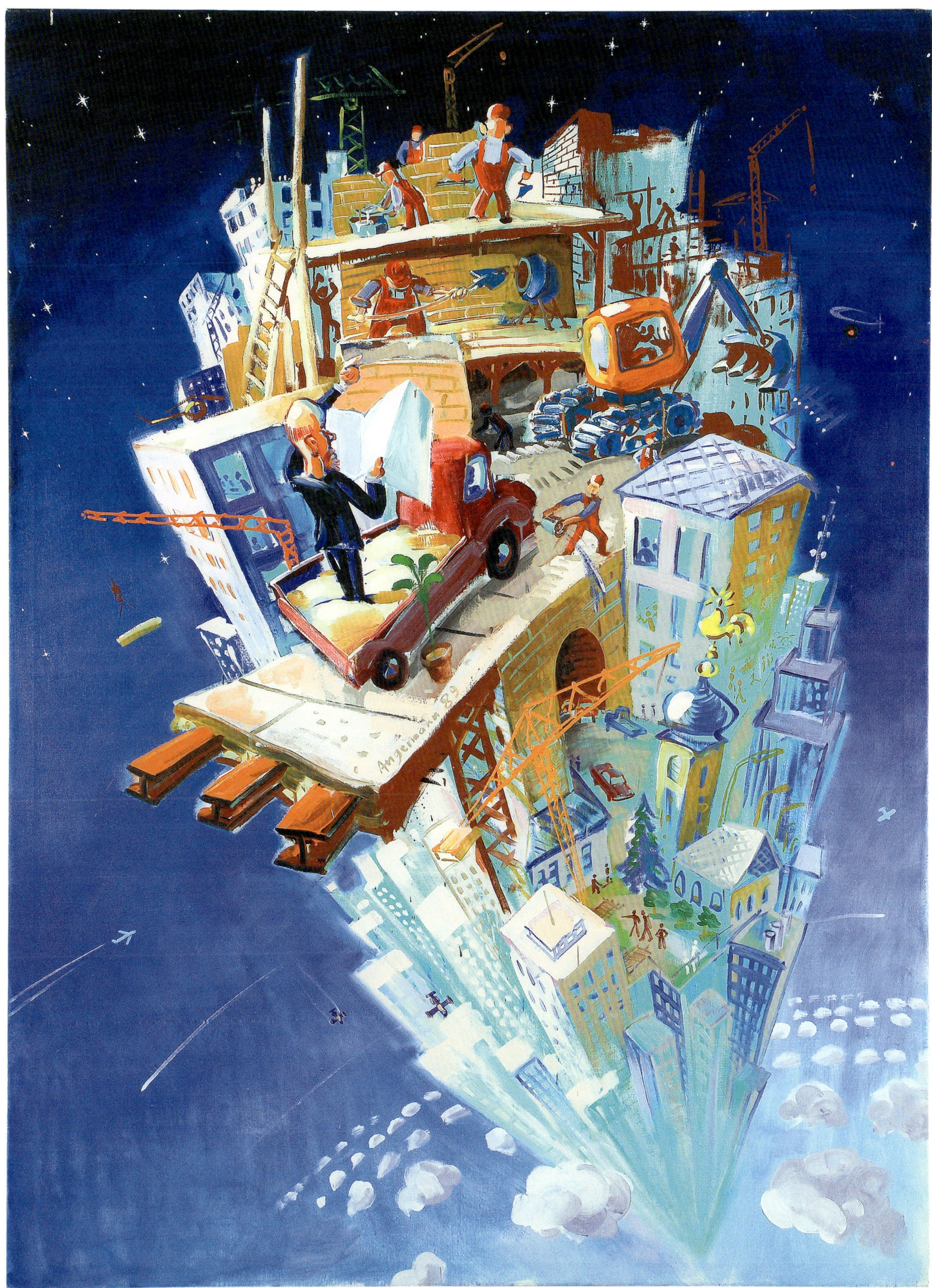

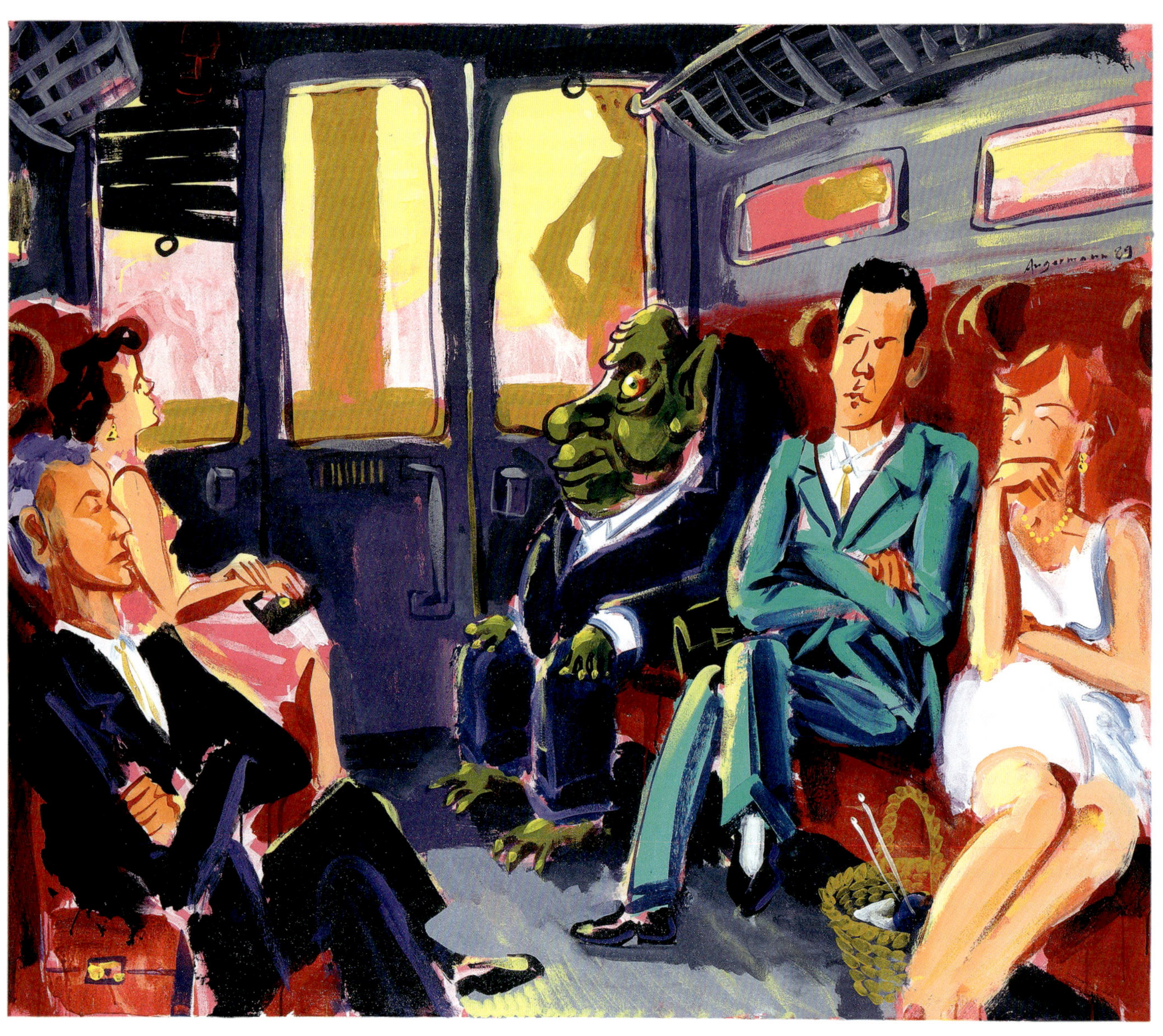

Abteil / Train Compartment, 1989

126

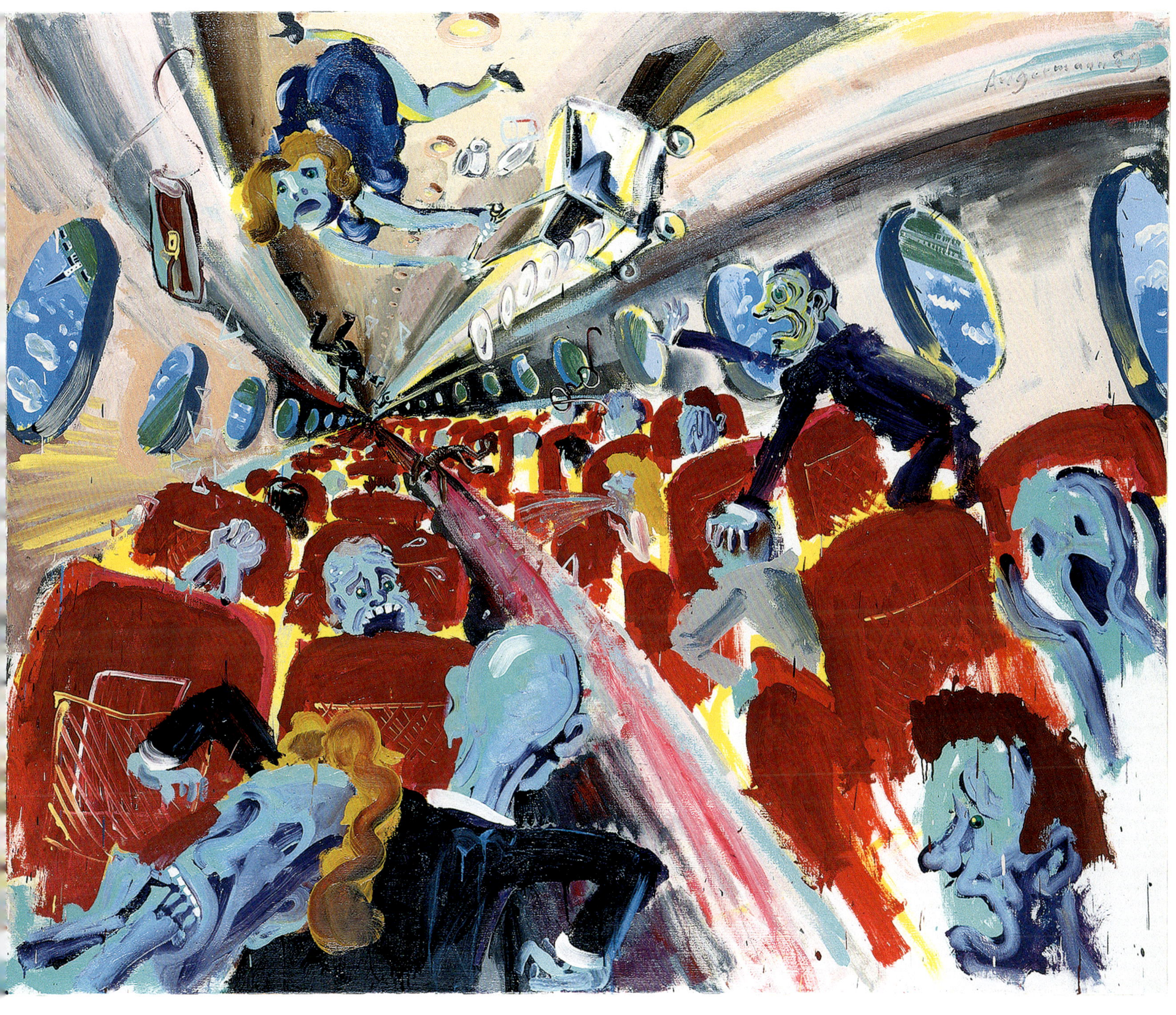

Absturz / Crash, 1989

127

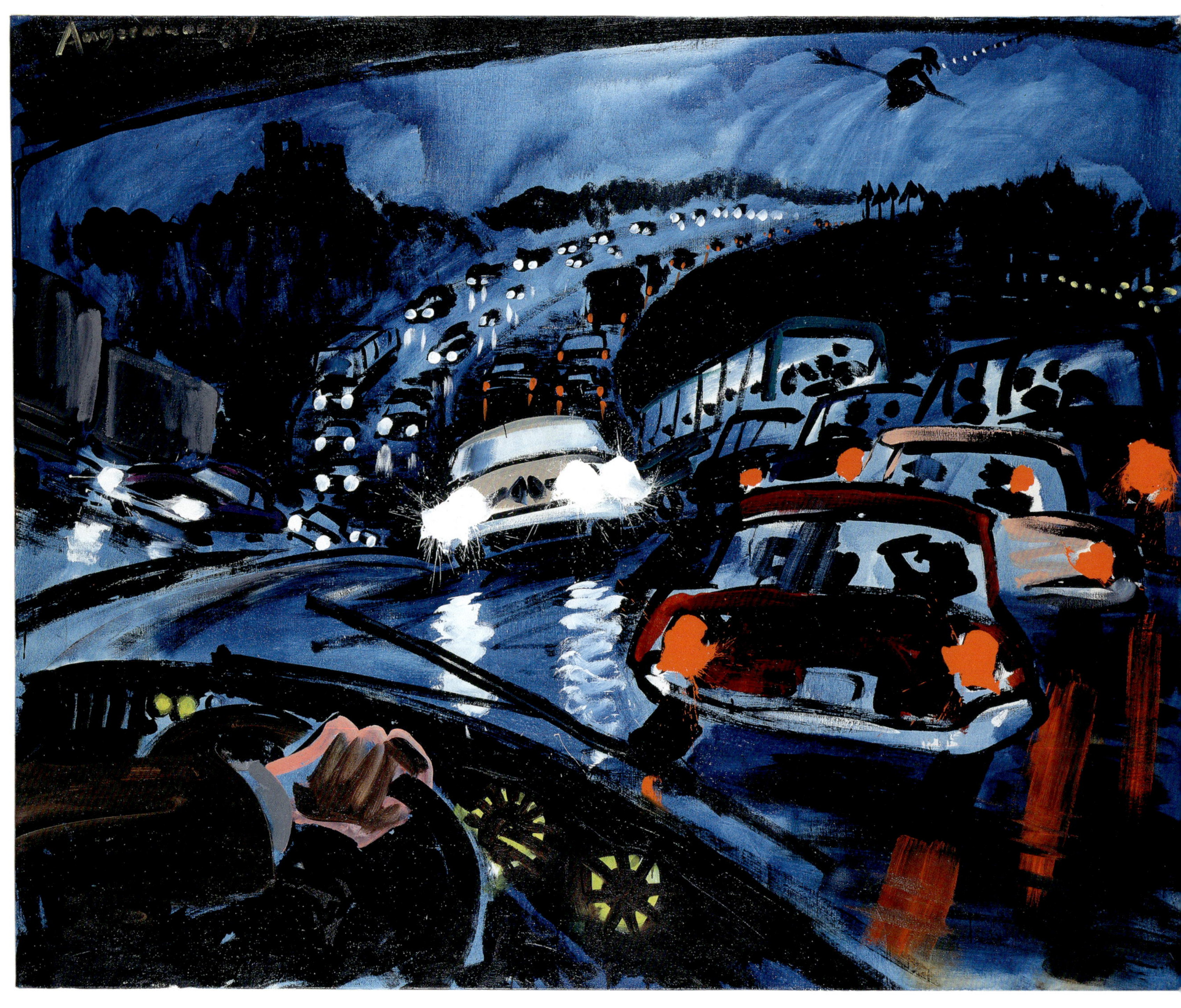

Geisterfahrer / Ghost Driver, 1989

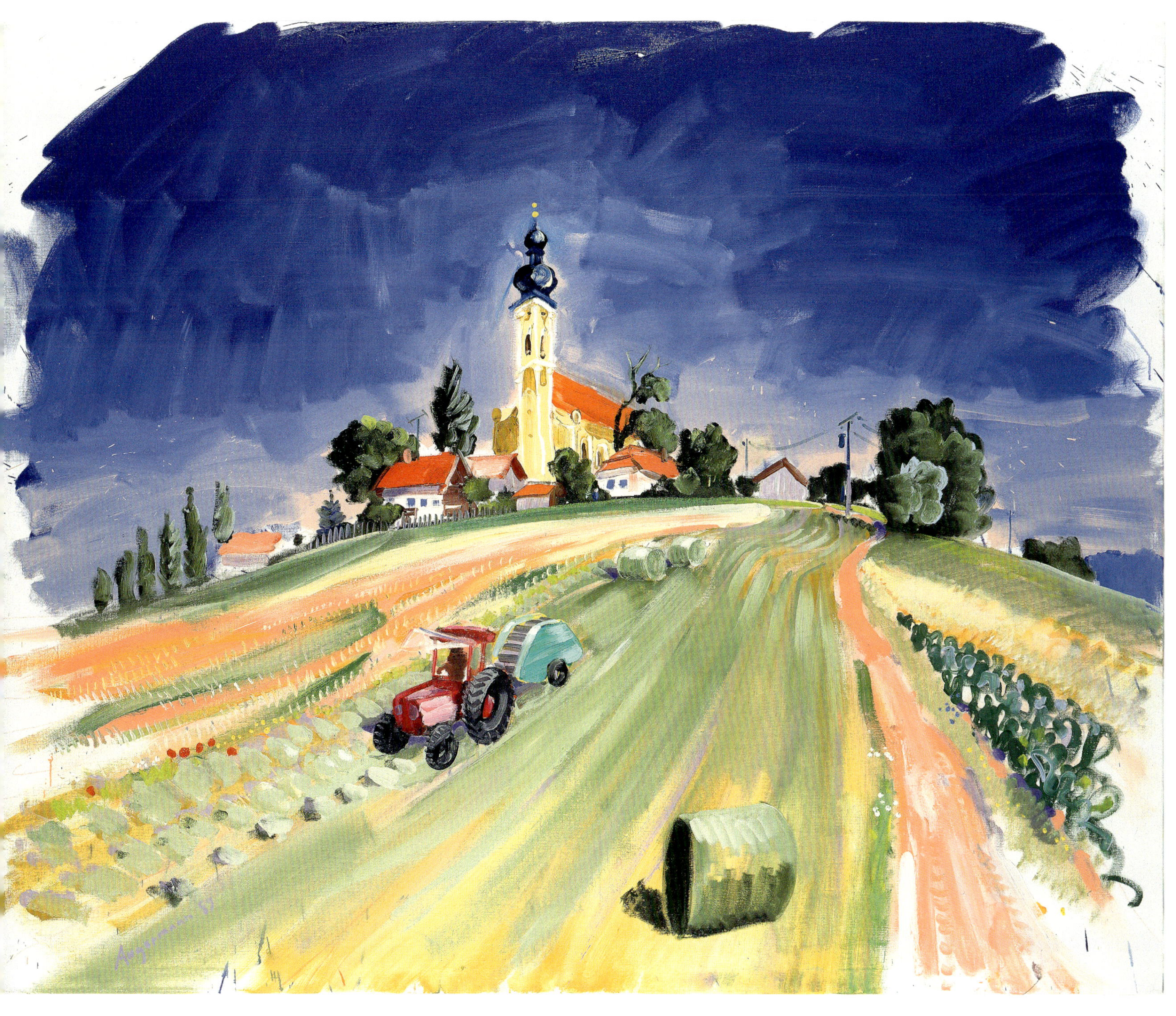

August 1, 1989

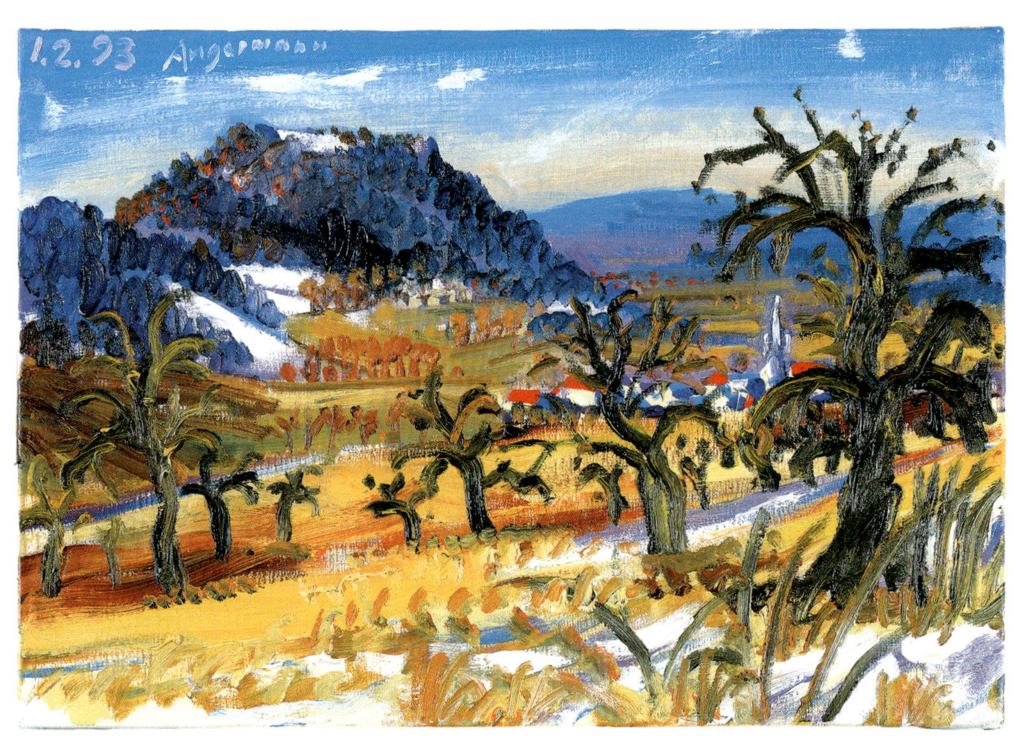

Februar (Walberla) / February (Walberla), 1993

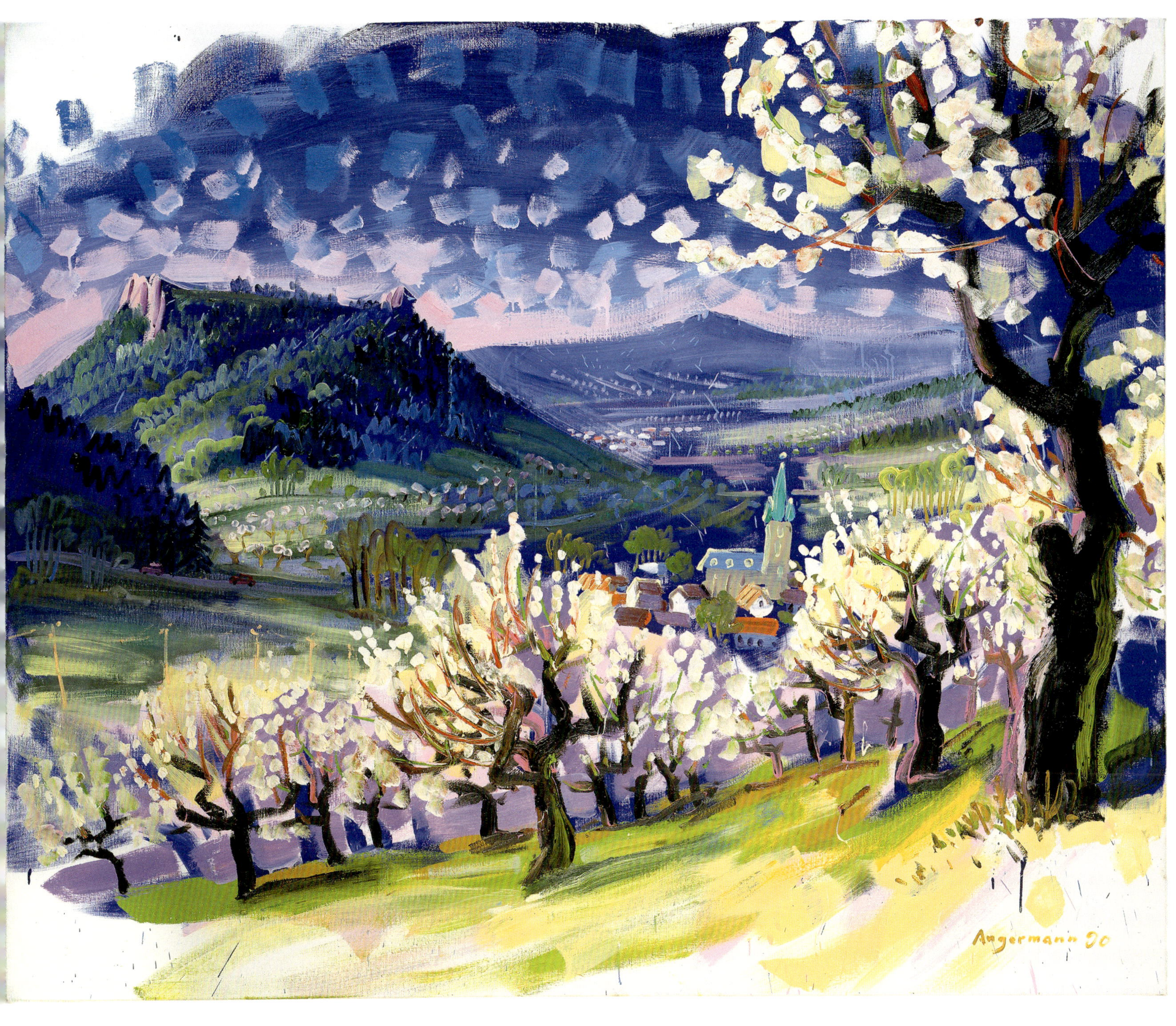

Mai (Walberla) / May (Walberla), 1990

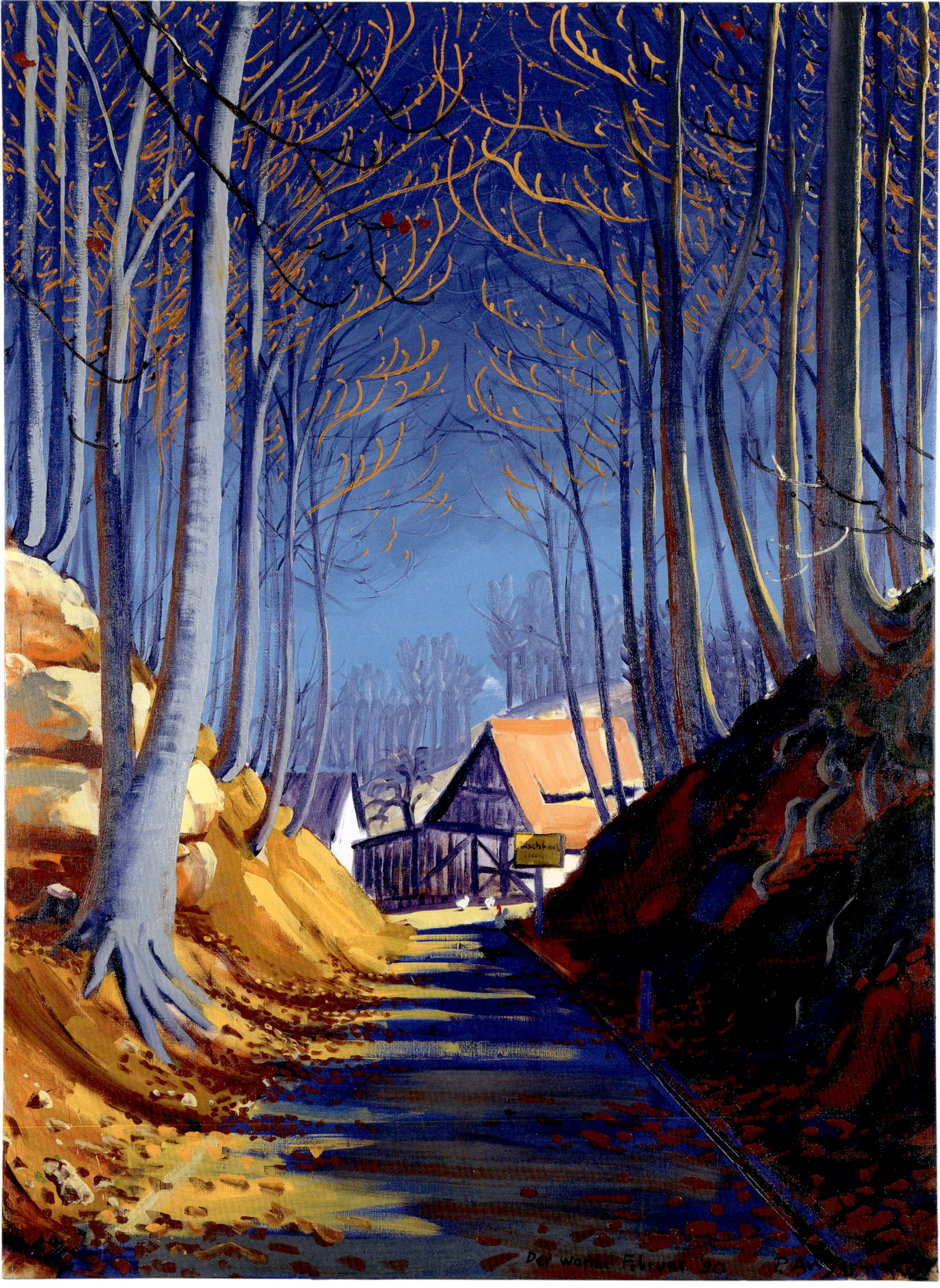
Der warme Februar 90

Der warme Februar 1990 / The Warm February 1990, 1990

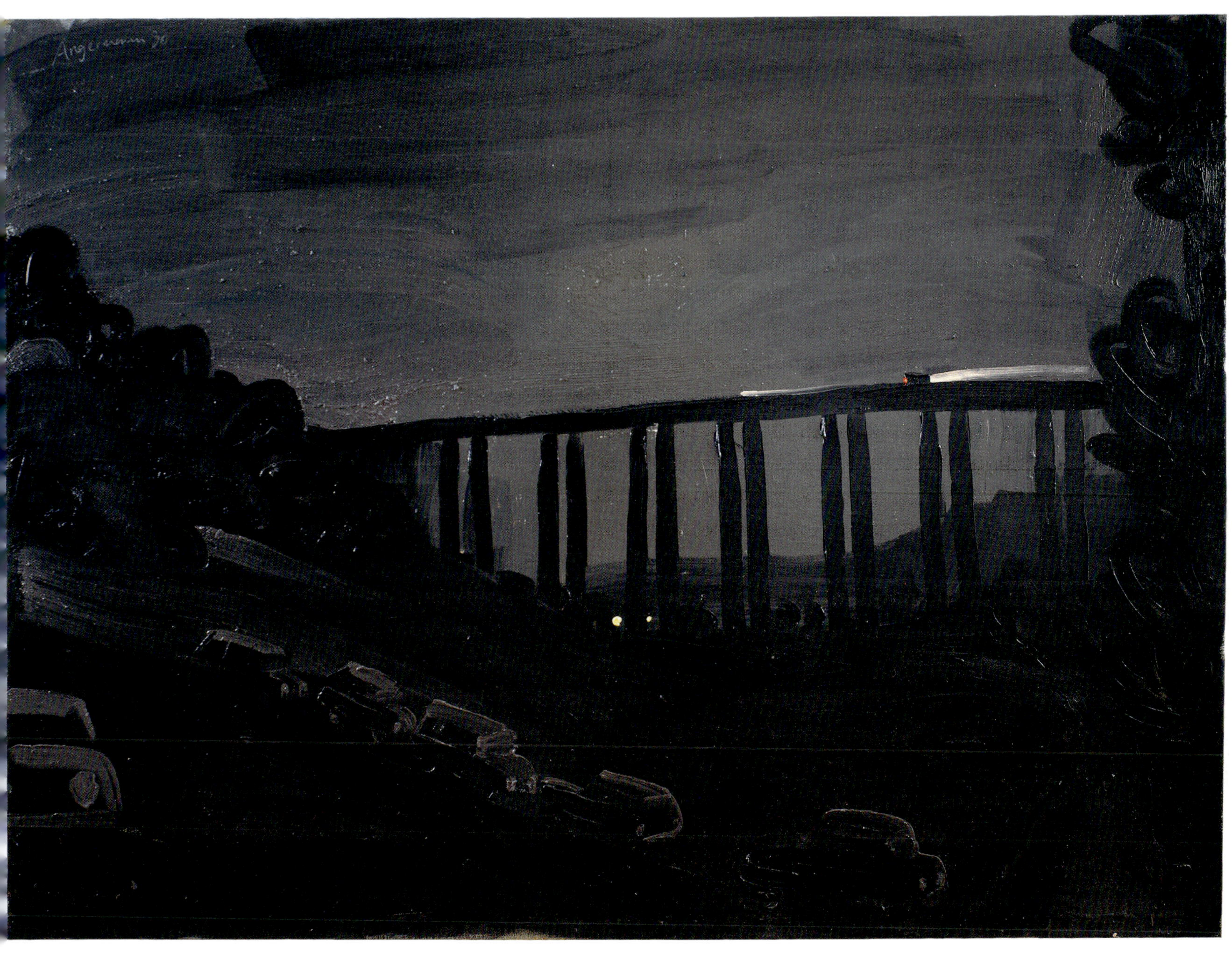

Nocturno / Nocturne, 1990

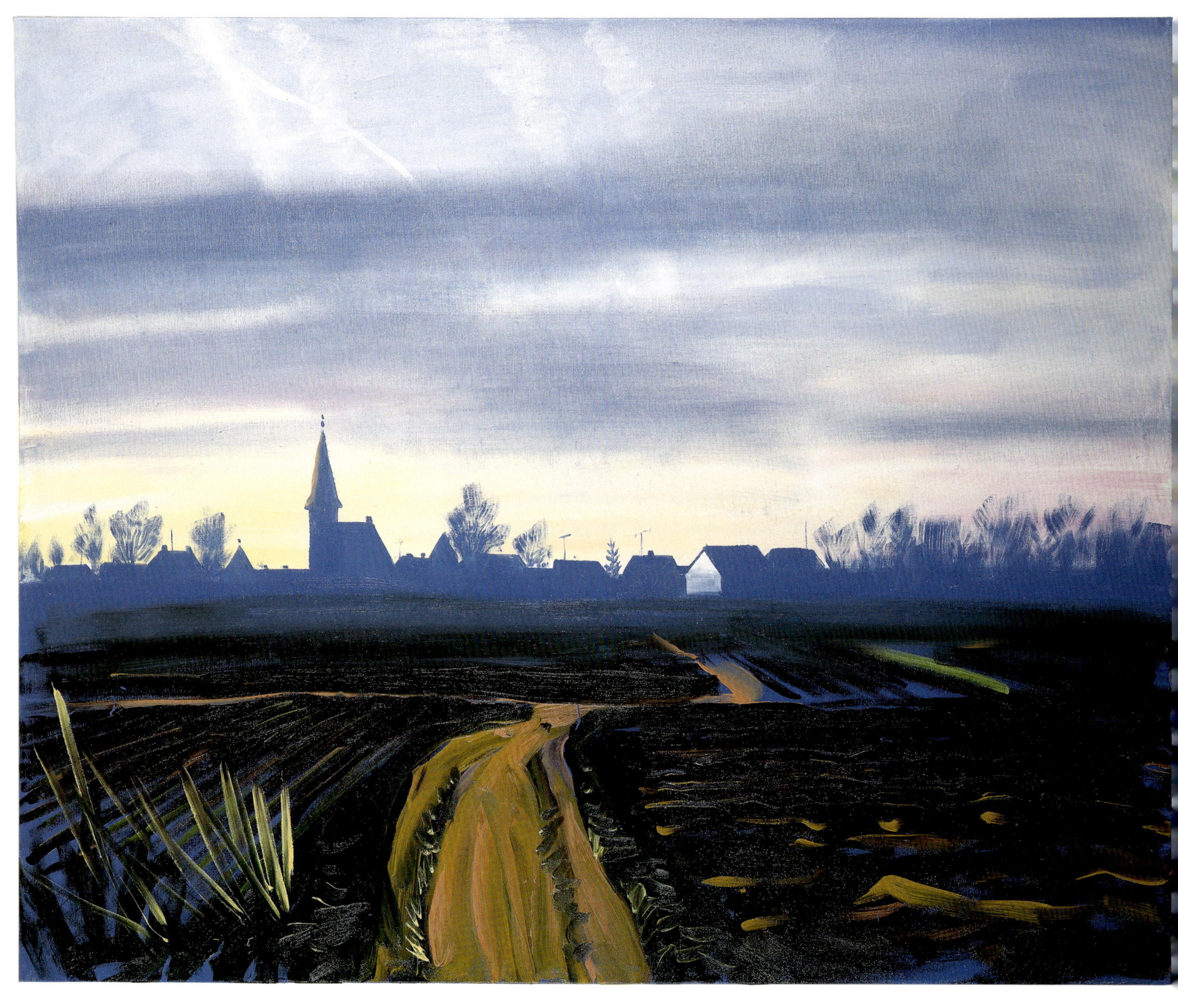

Dezember 1 / December 1, 1990

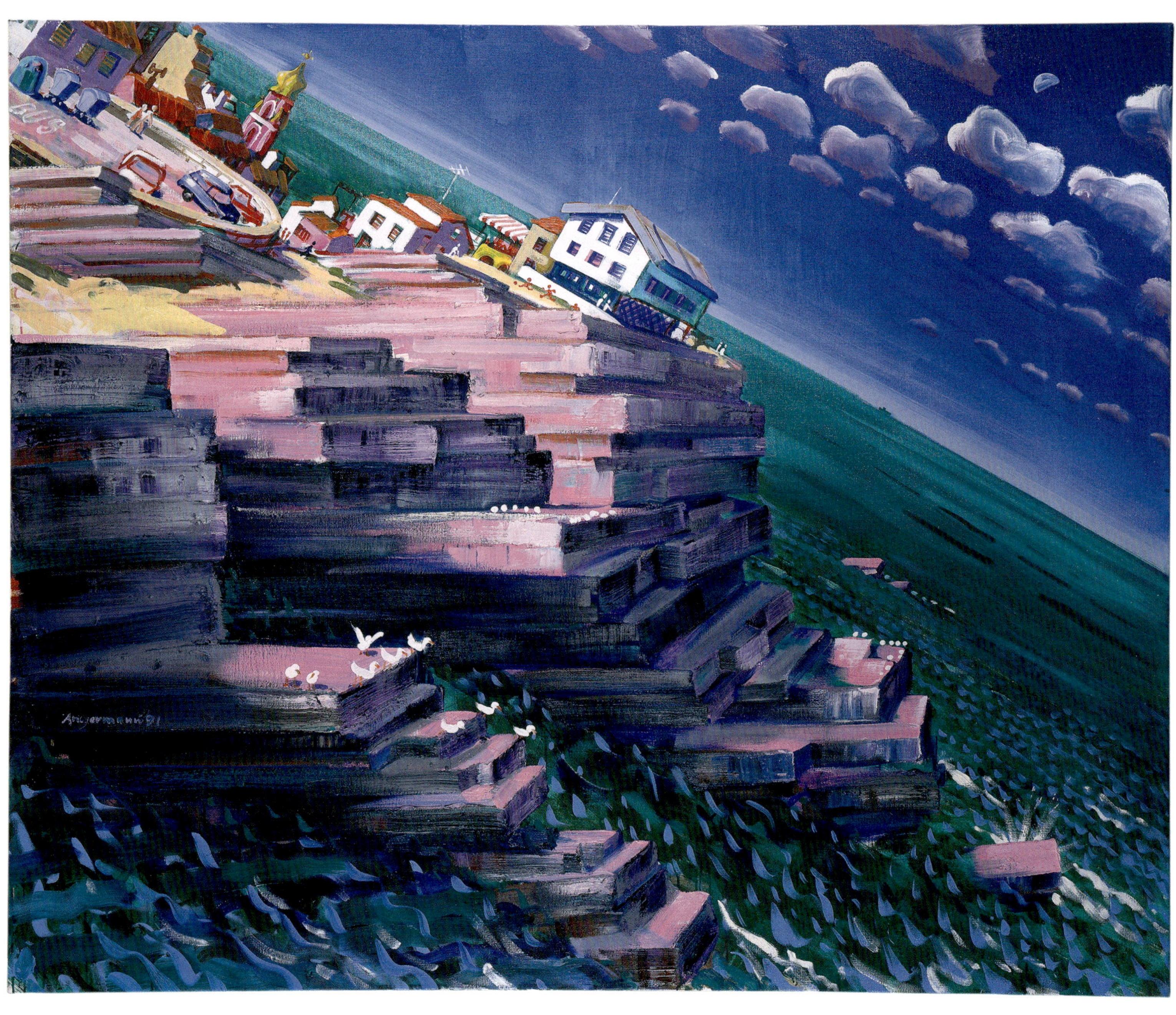

Schiefer 2 / Slate 2, 1991

140

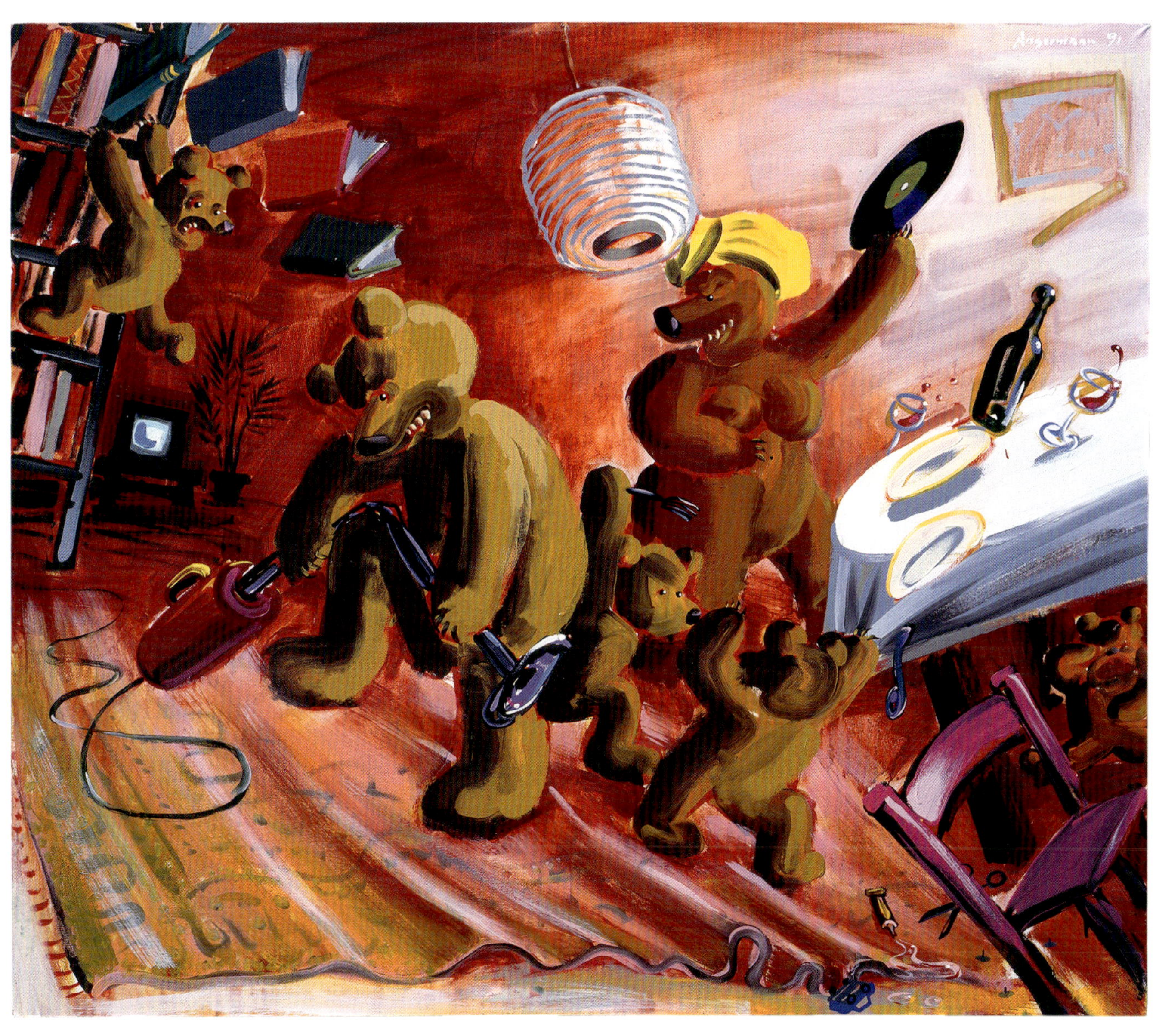

Familienkrach 1 / Family Row 1, 1991

141

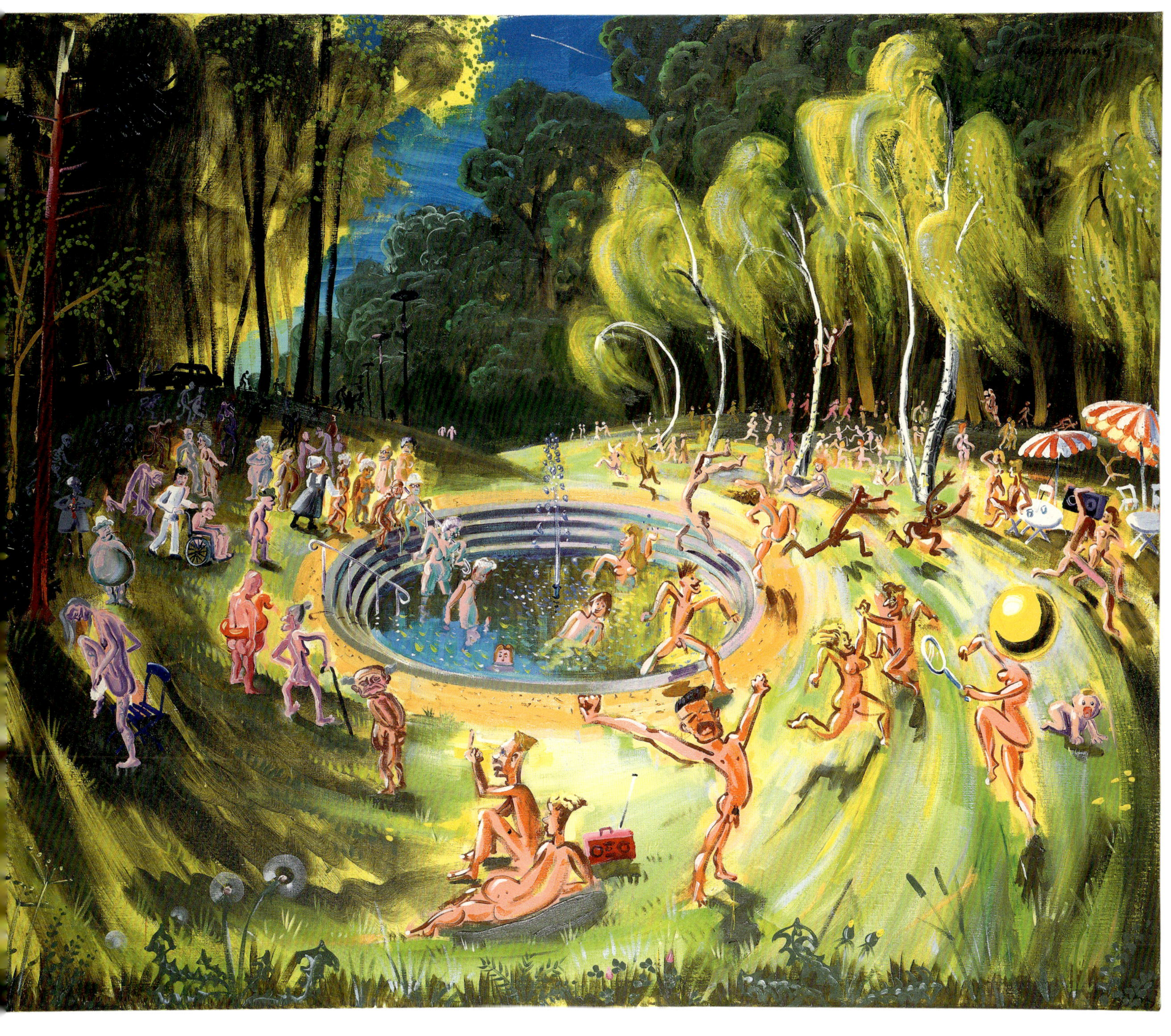

Jungbrunnen 1 / Fountain of Youth 1, 1991

143

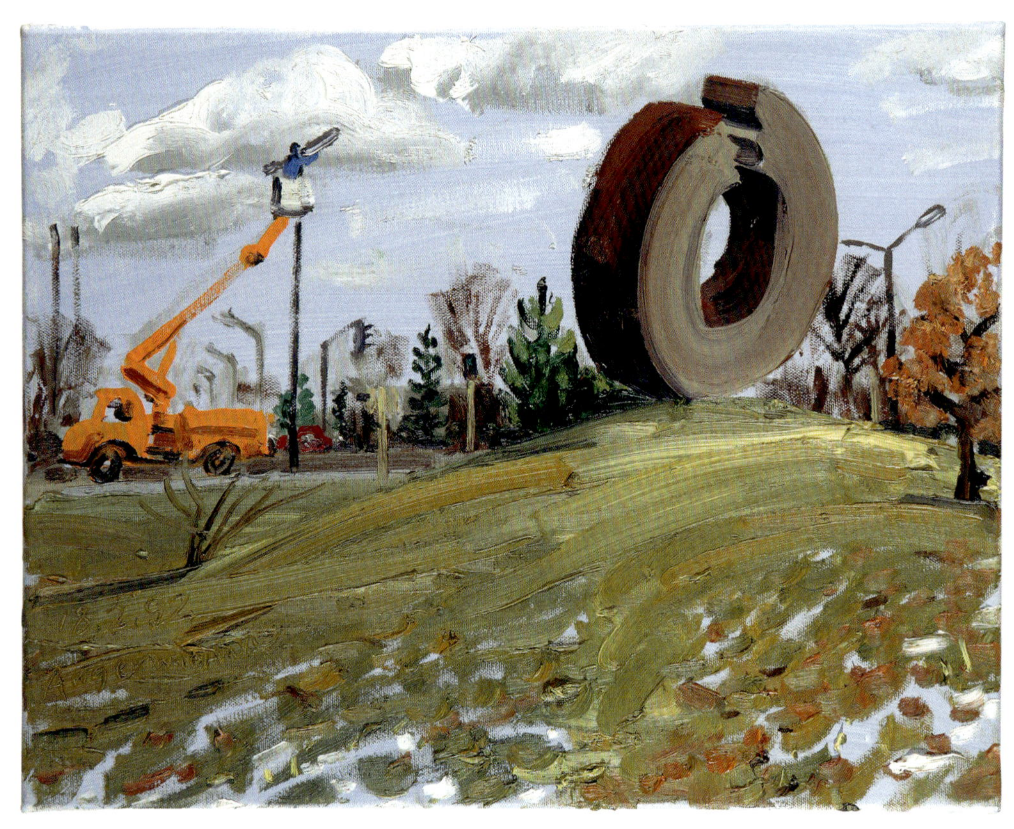

Stahlplastik / Steel Sculpture, 1992

Stehender Verkehr 2 /
Standing Traffic 2, 1992

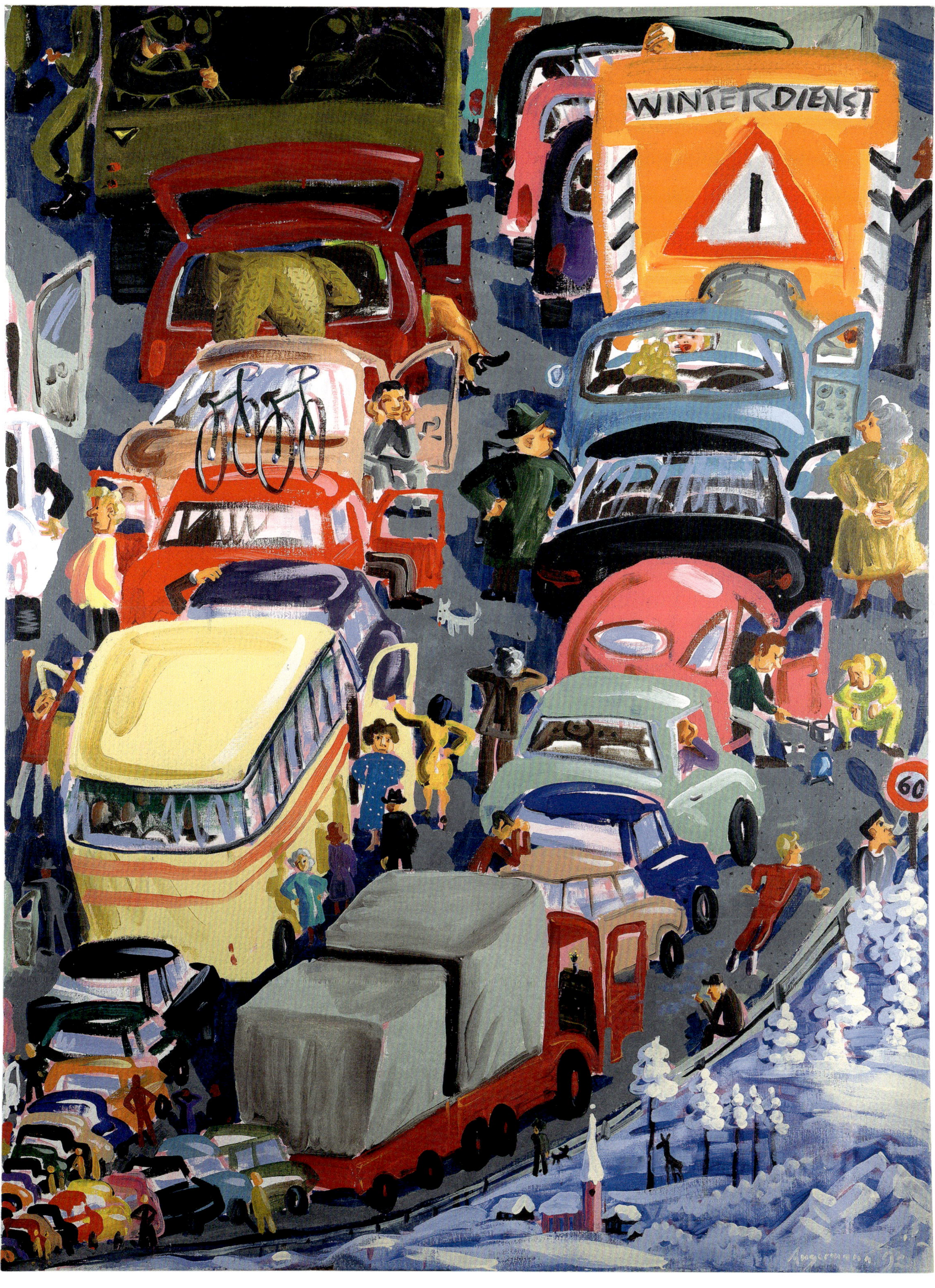

WINTERDIENST
60

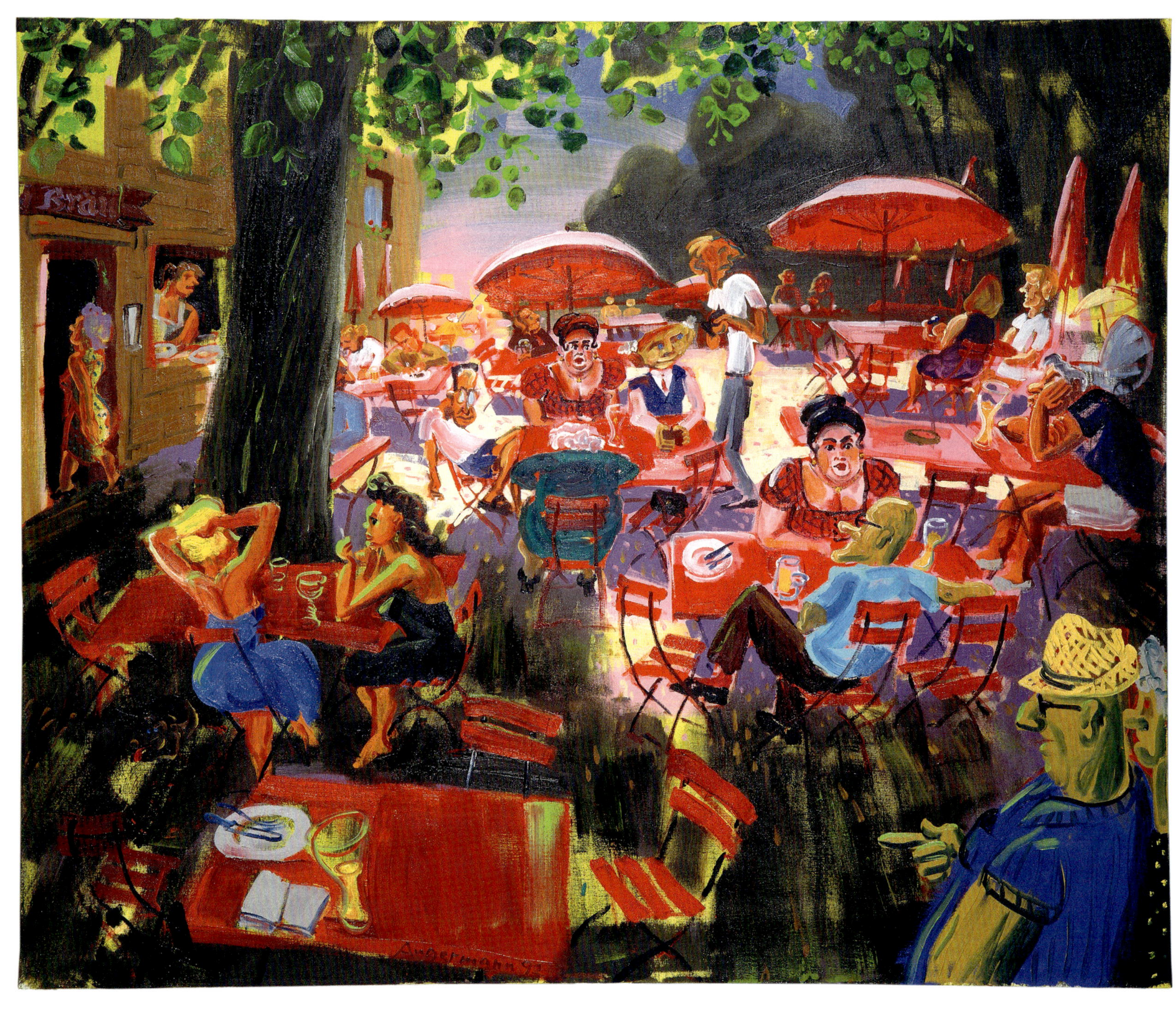

Juli (Biergarten) / July (Beer Garden), 1992

146

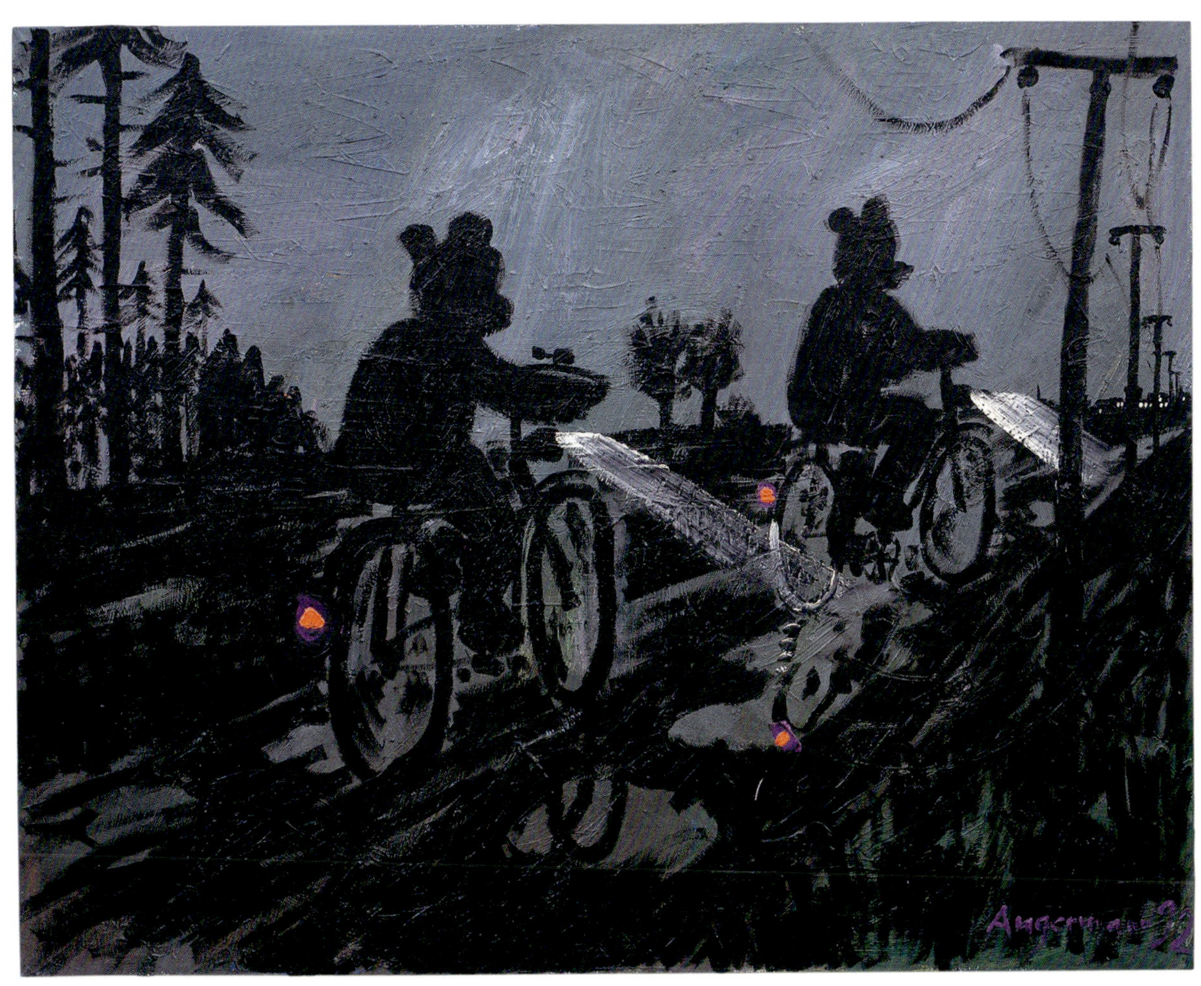

Heimweg 1 / Way Home 1, 1992

147

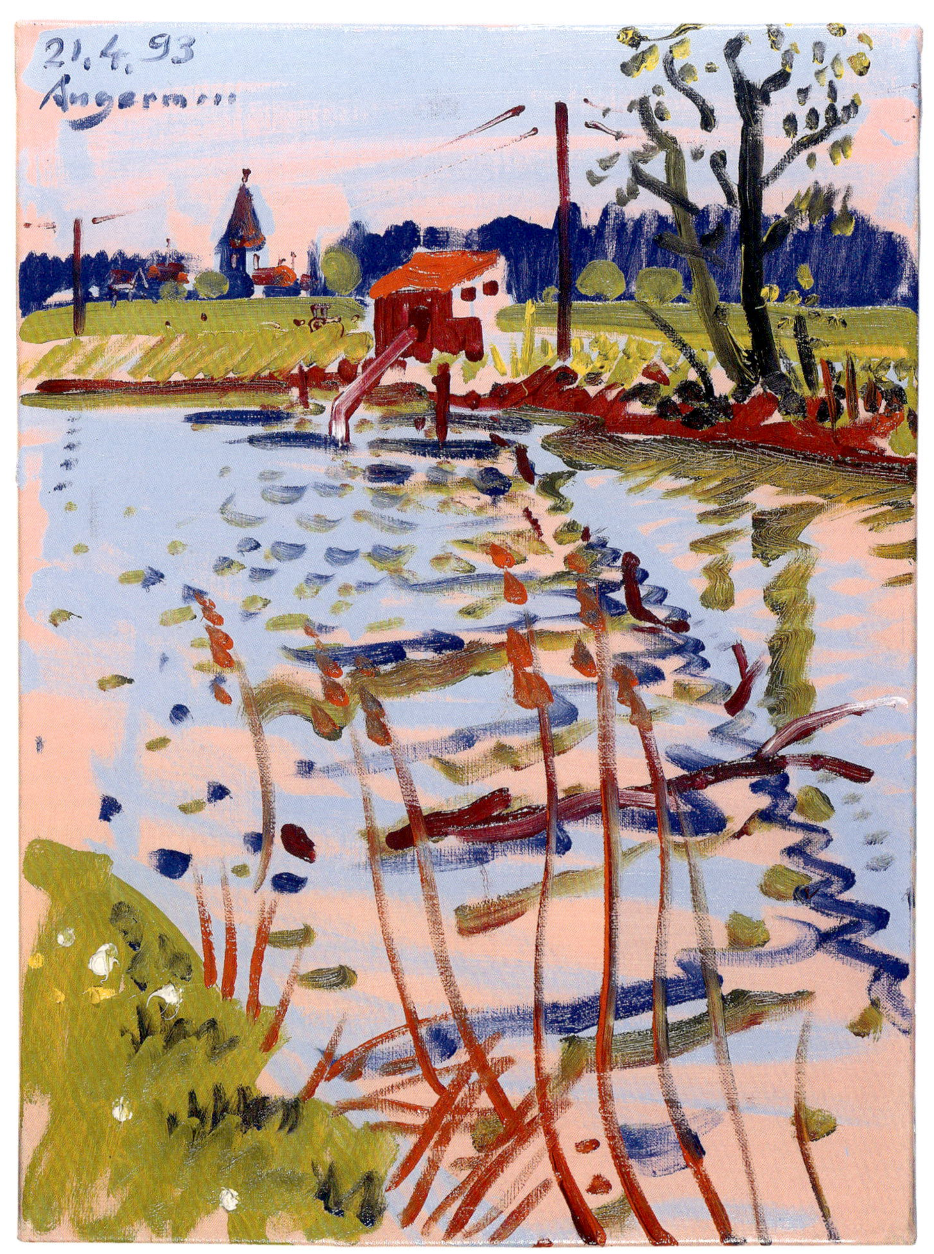

Regnitz 2, 1993

148

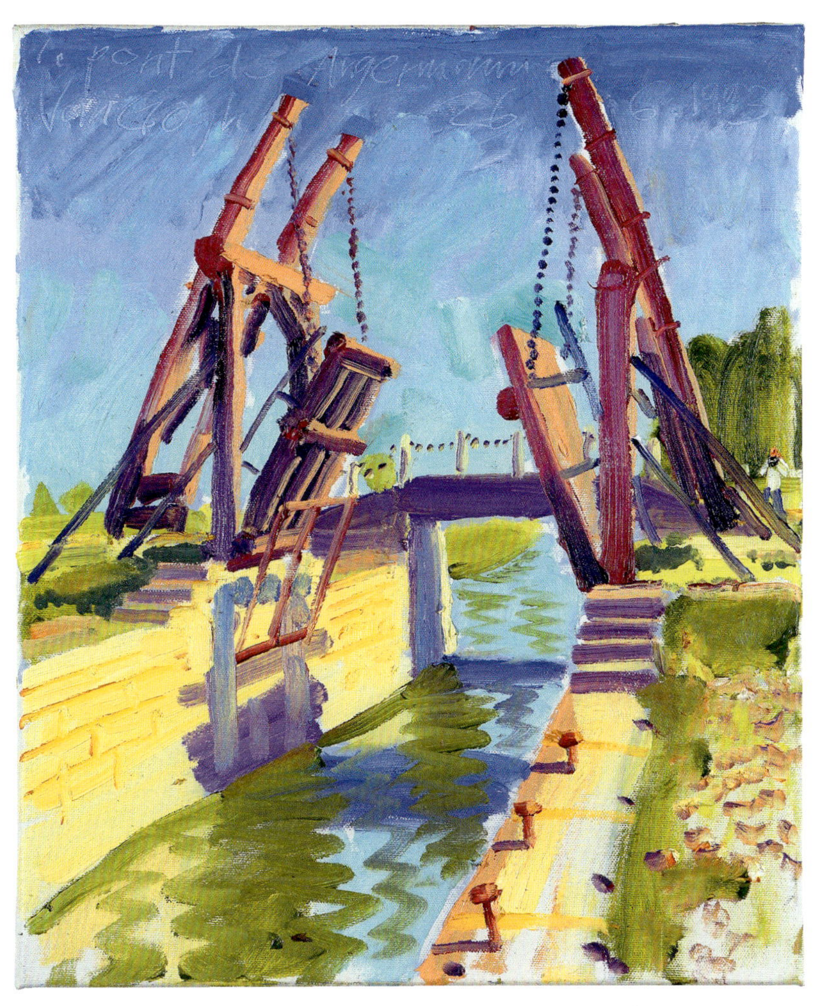

Zwei Brücken bei Arles / Two Bridges near Arles, 1993

149

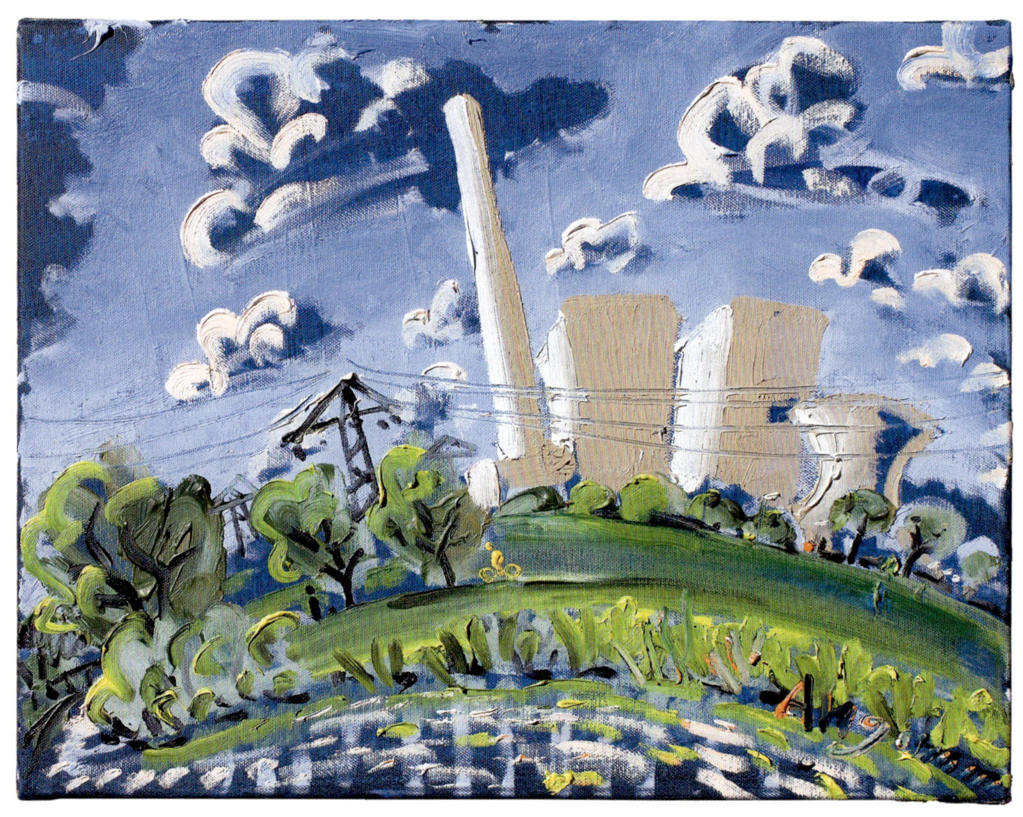

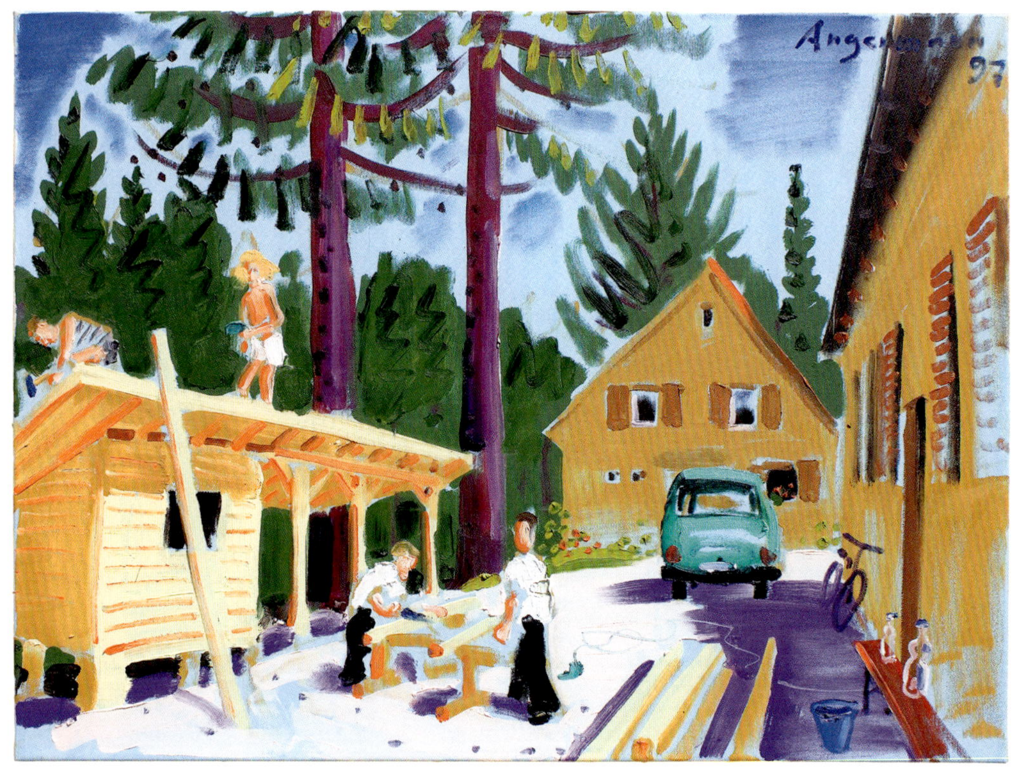

△ *Kraftwerk Frauenaurach / Frauenaurach Power Station*, 1994

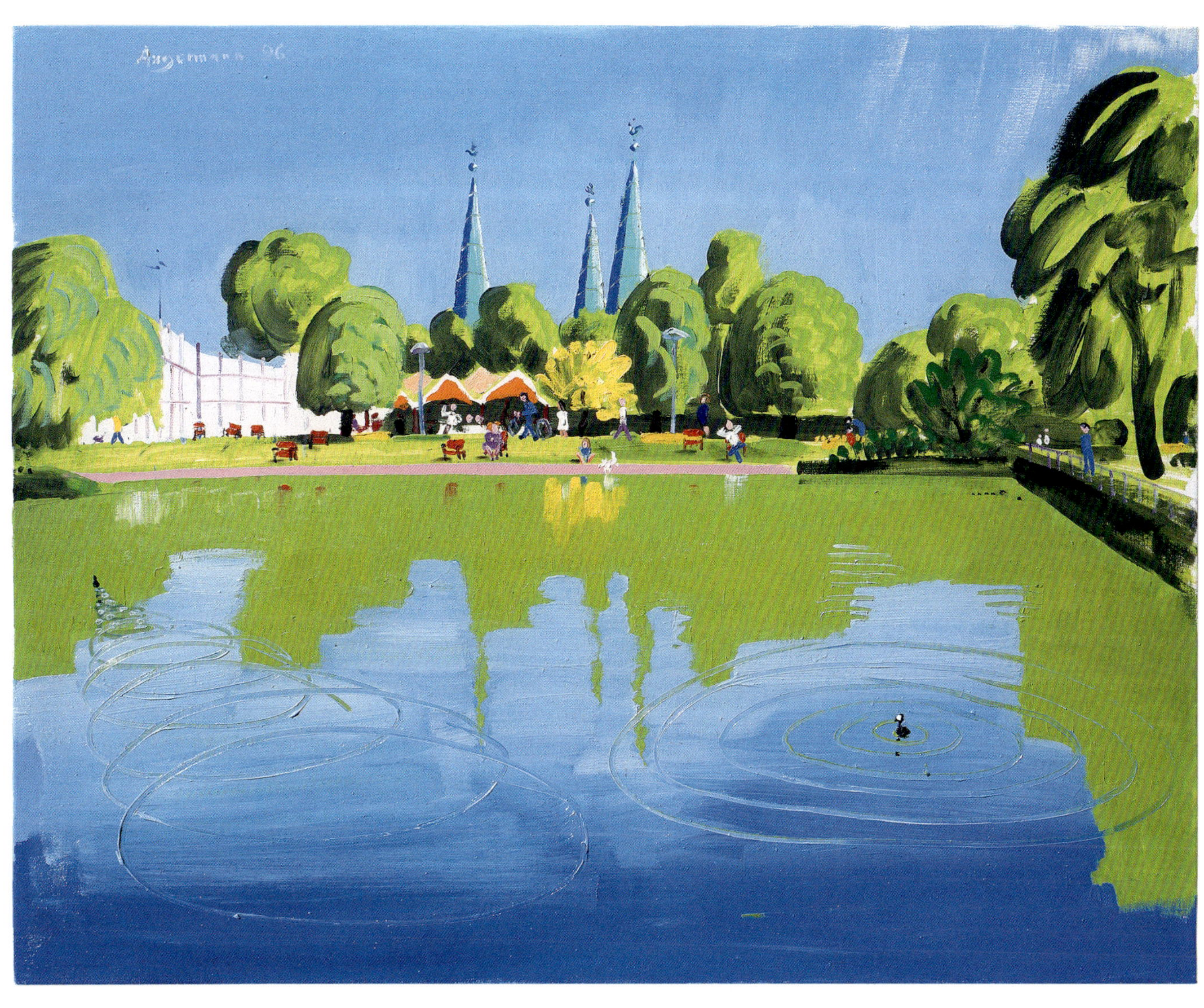

Der Bau des Hühnerstalls / The Construction
of the Chicken Coop, 1997

Stadtpark Nürnberg 2 / Municipal Park
Nuremberg 2, 1996

151

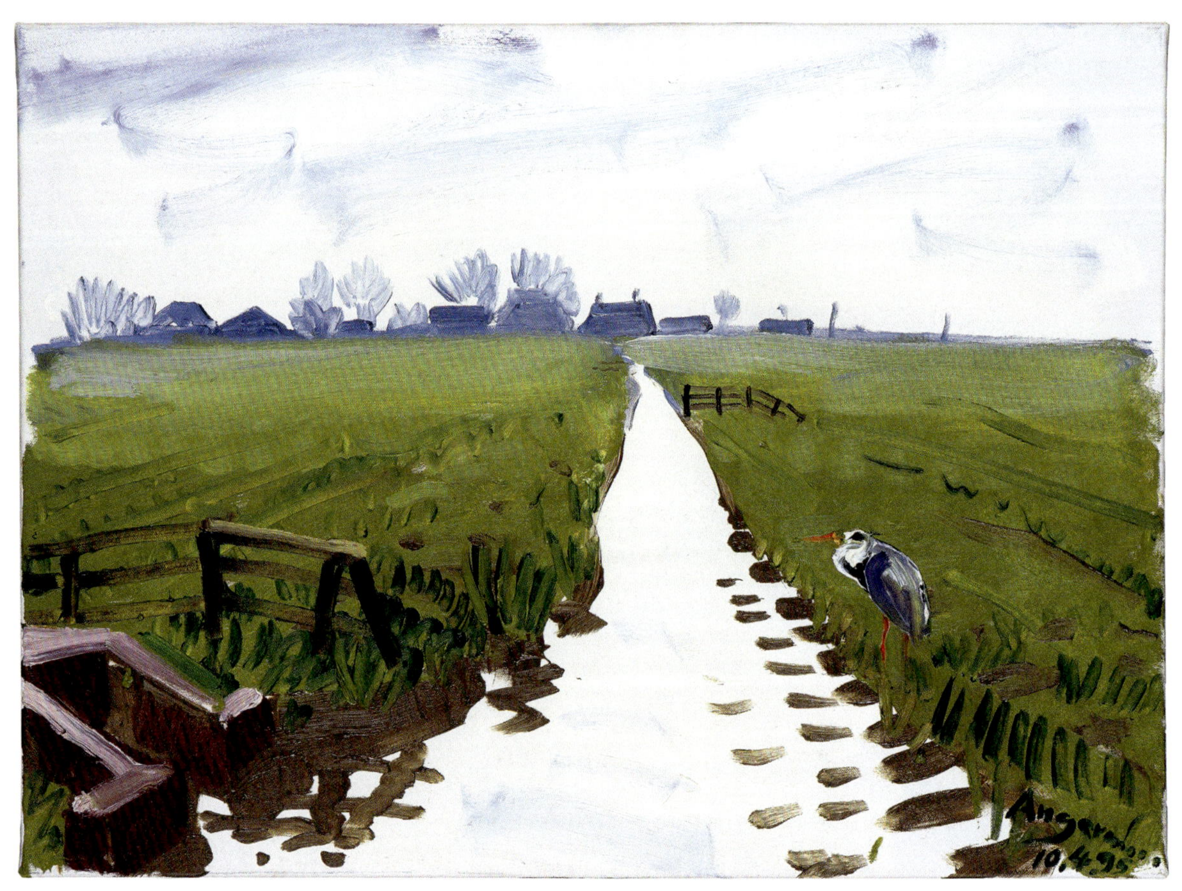

Reiher / Heron, 1995

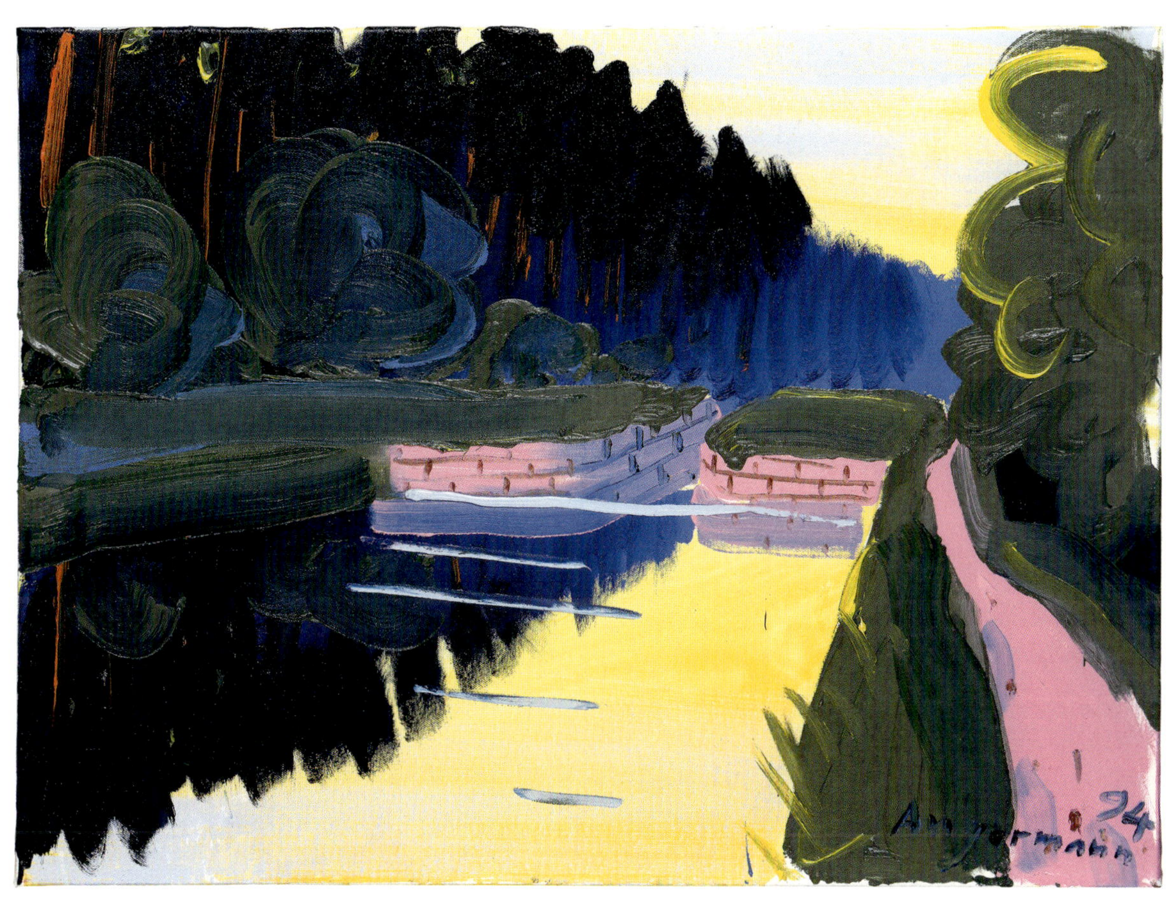

Am alten Kanal 4 / By the Old Canal 4, 1994

153

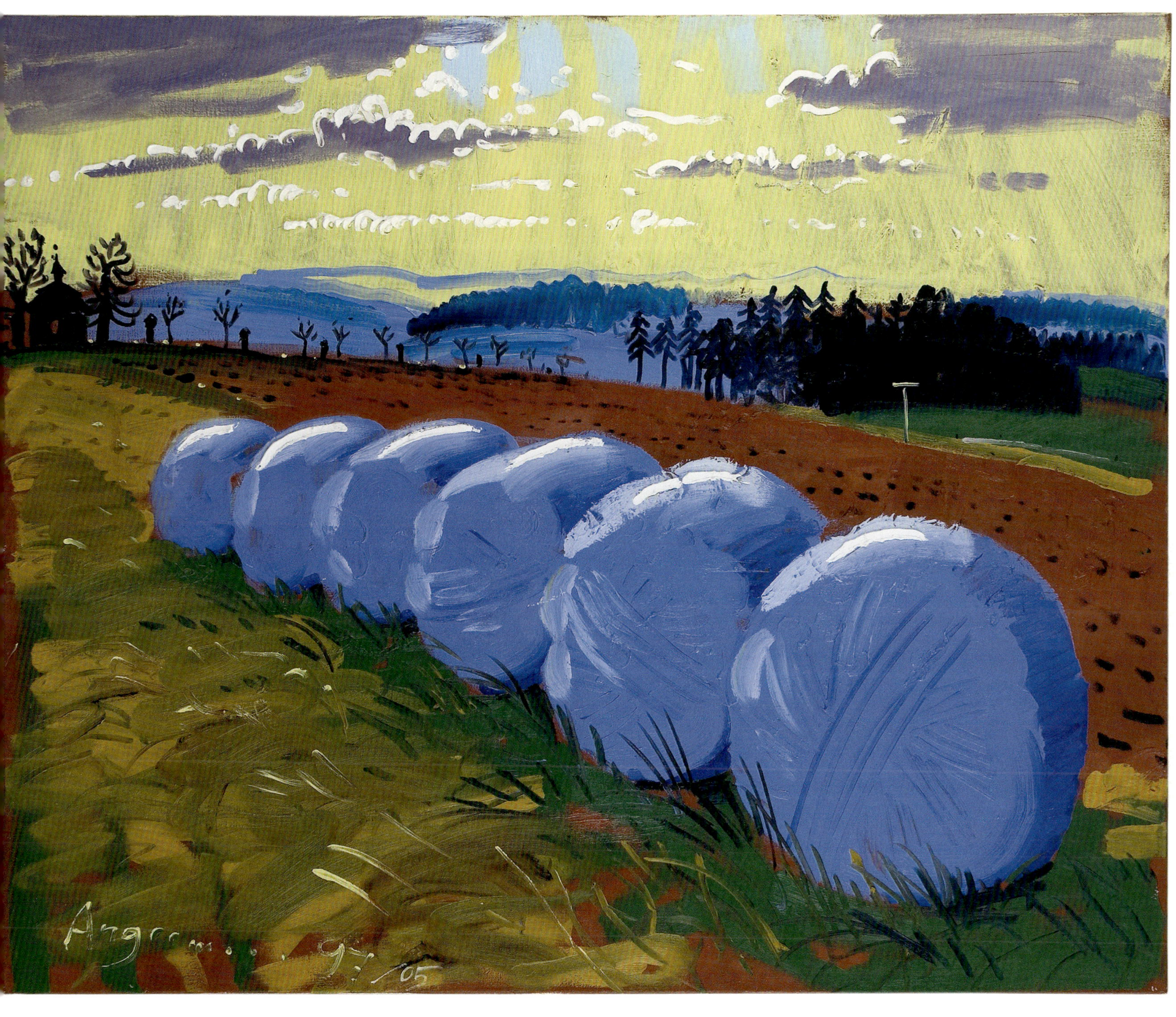

Sechs Wullis im Gegenlicht / Six Backlit Haylages, 1997

155

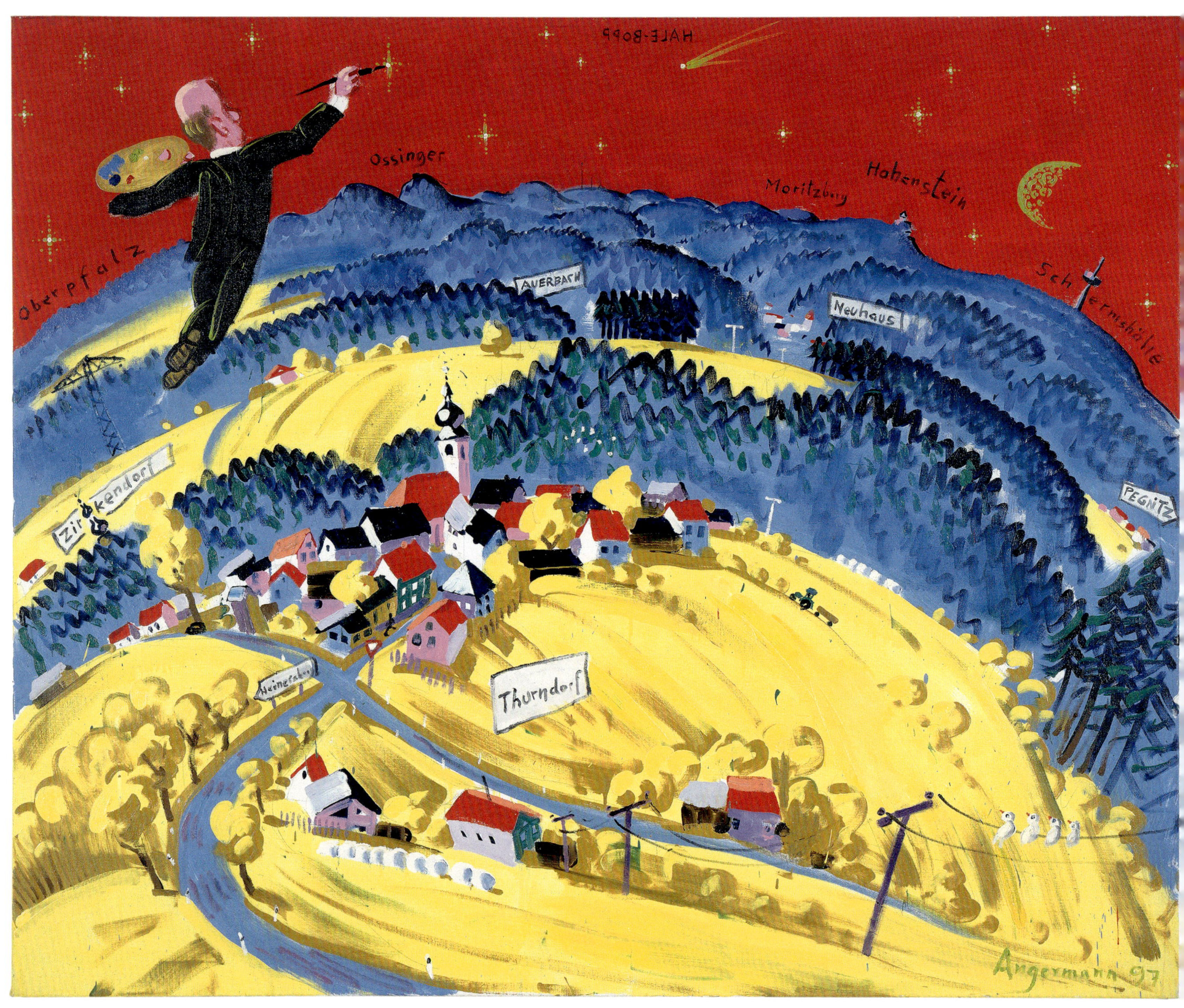

Weltbild / World Picture, 1997

156

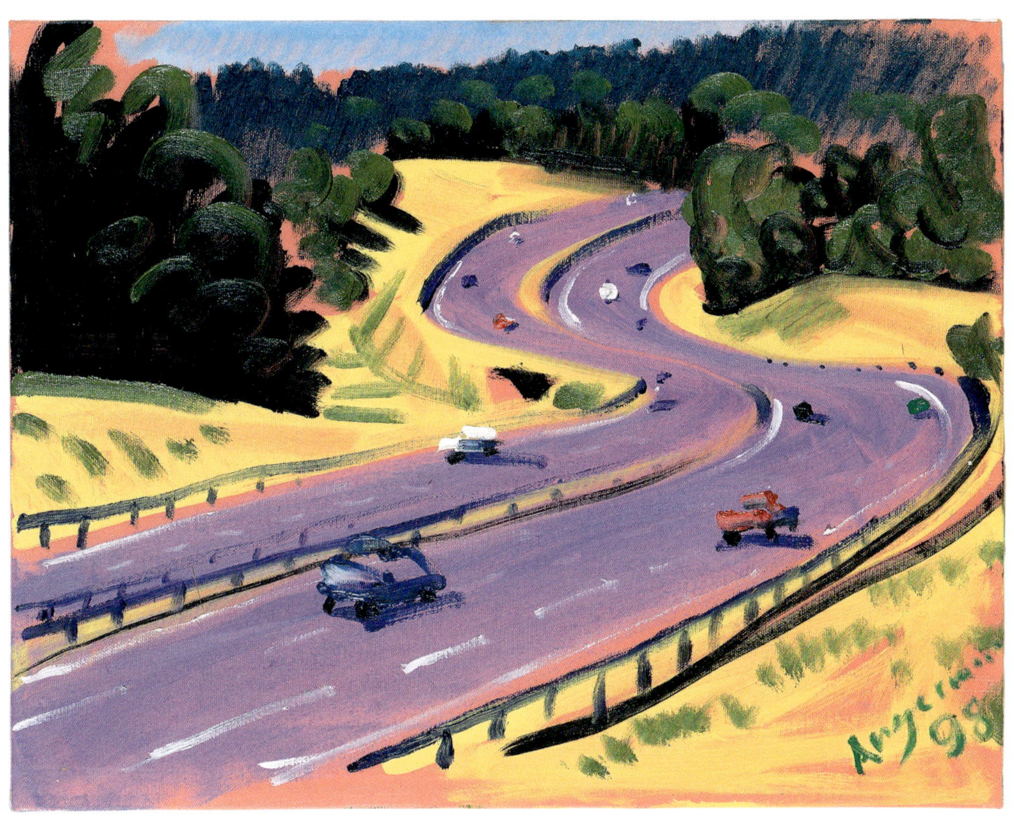

A9, 1998

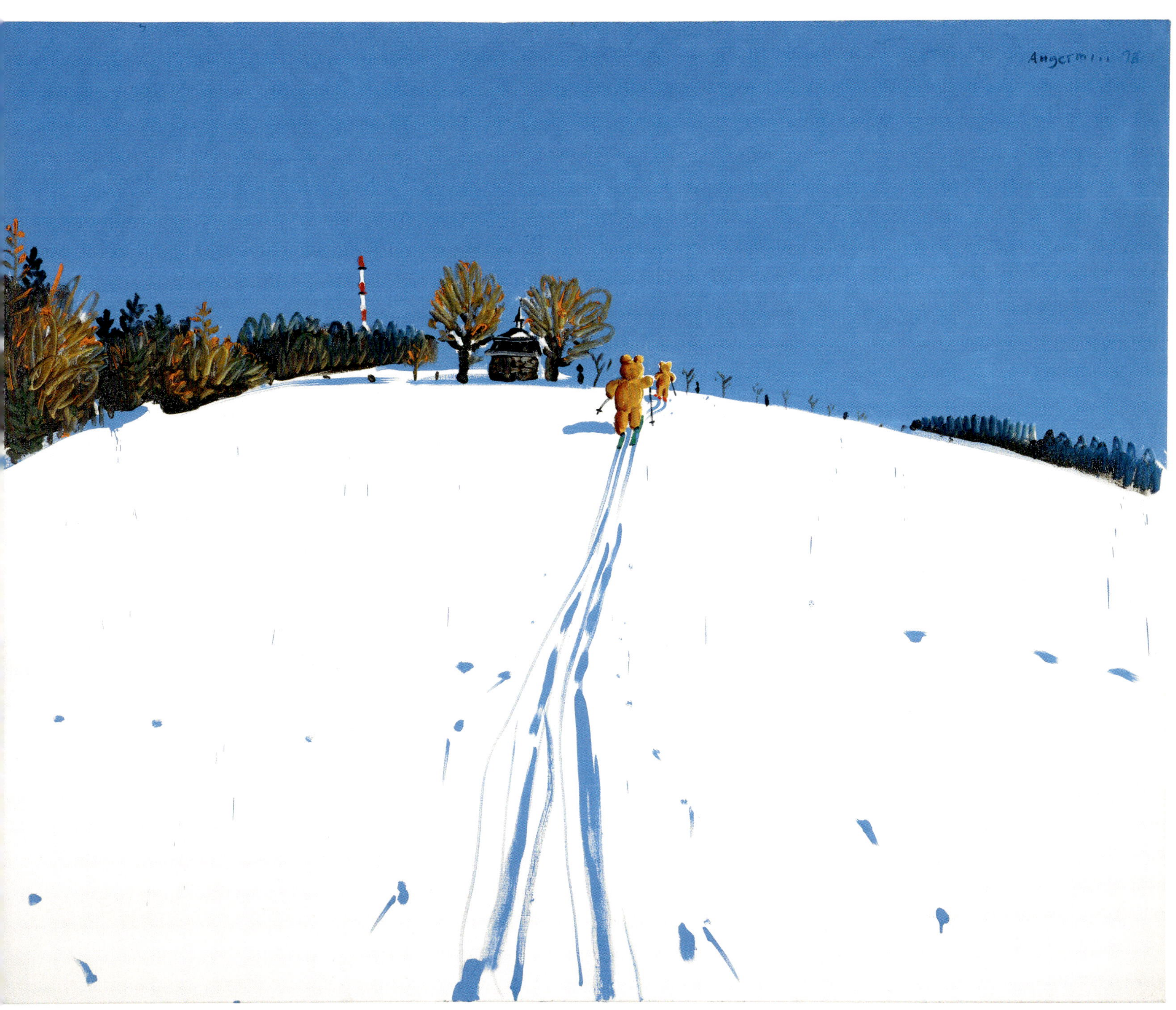

Zwei Skifahrer im Bärenkostüm / Two Skiers in Bear Outfits, 1998

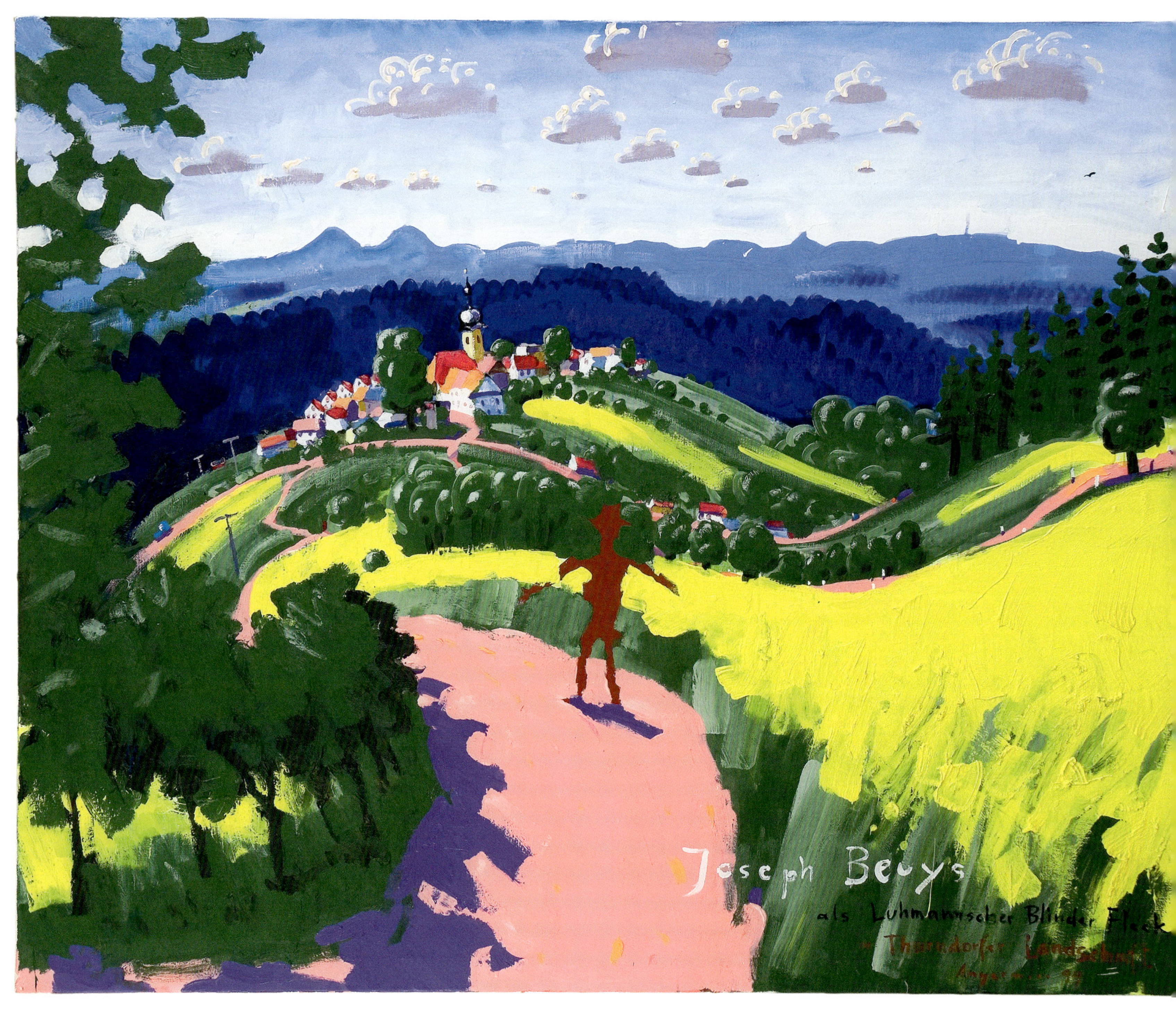

Landschaft mit Blindem Fleck / Landscape with Blind Spot, 1999

160

Artificial Intelligence 2, 2001

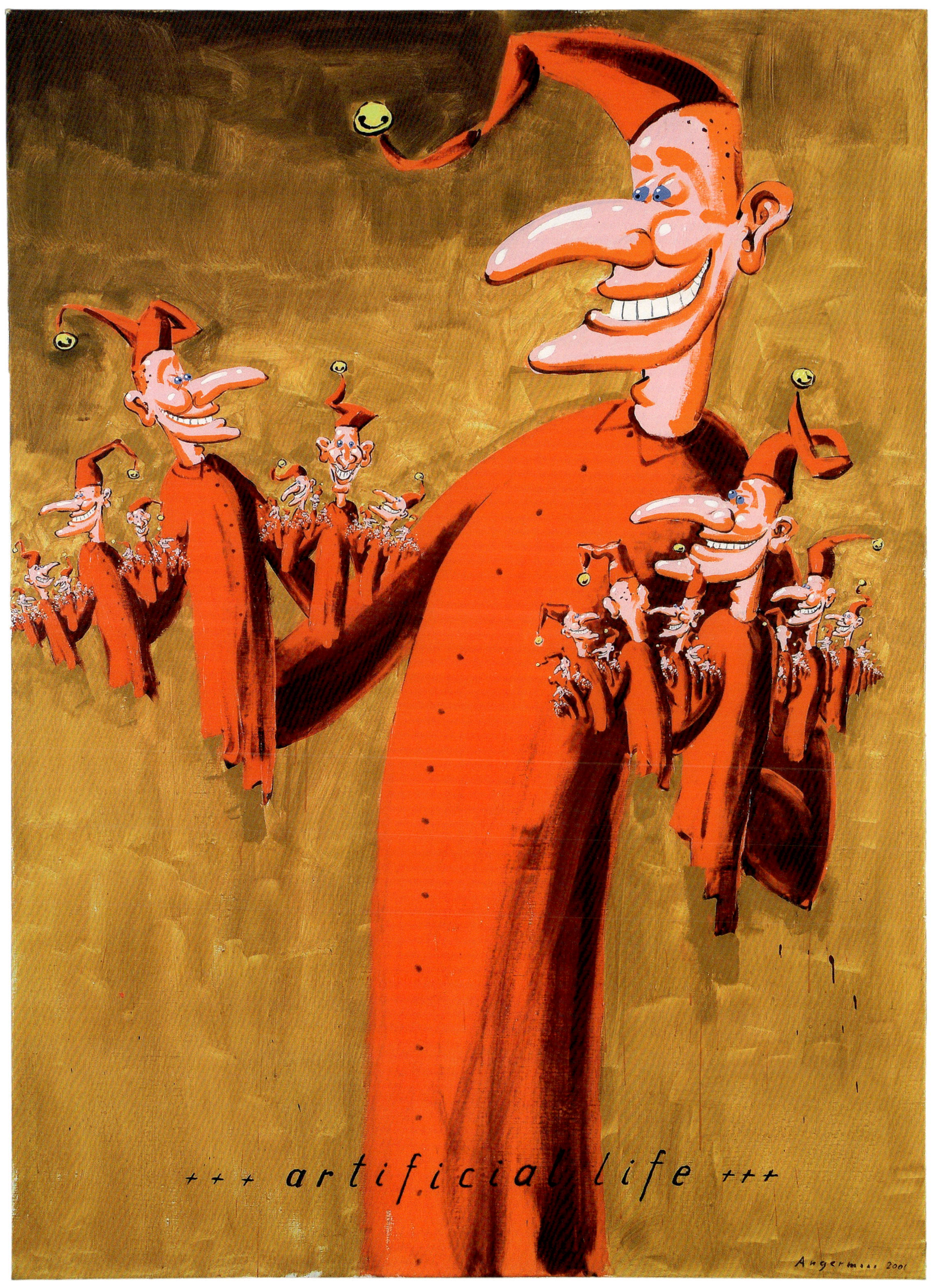

+++ artificial life +++
Angerm... 2001

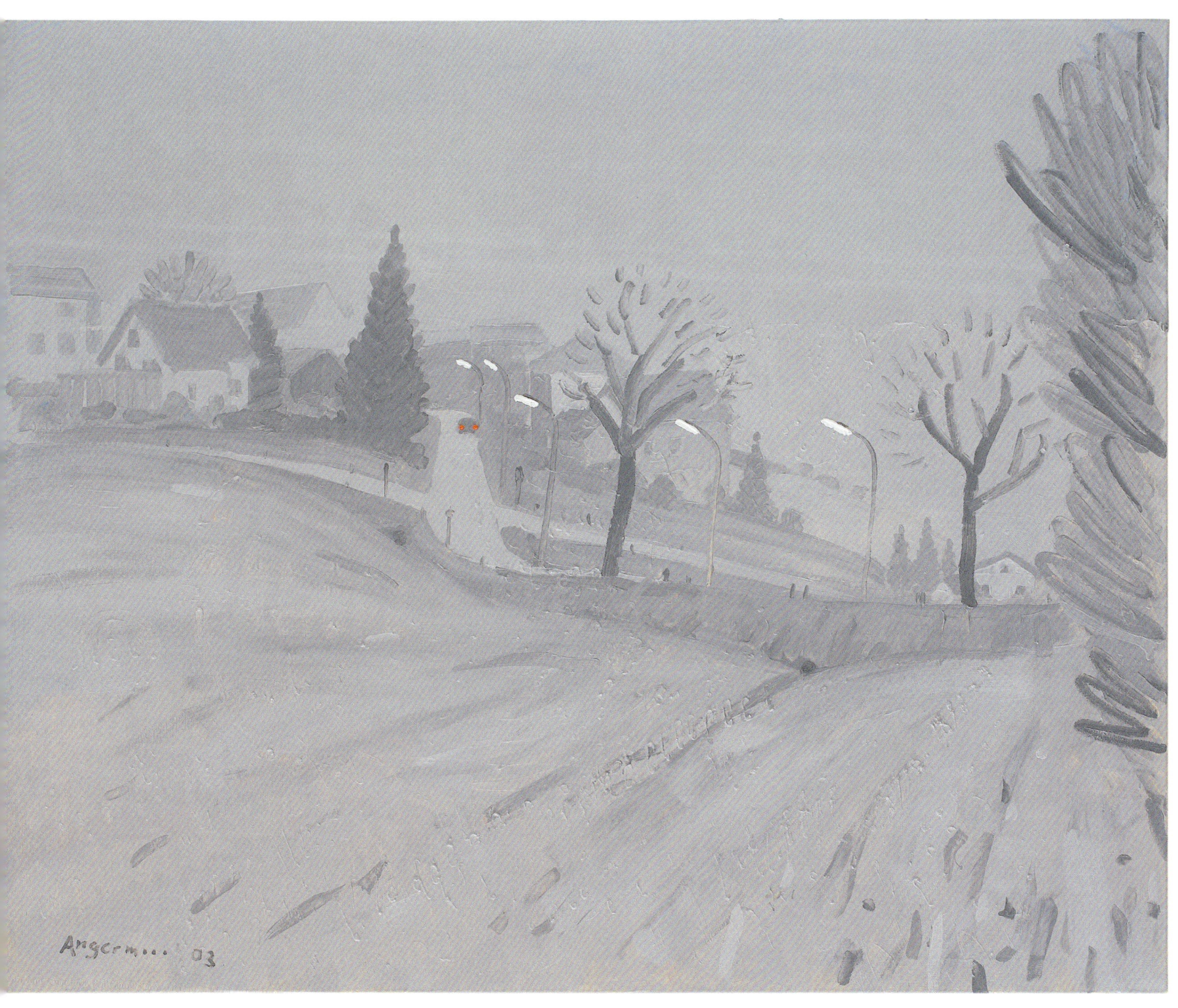

Nebel / Mist, 2003

165

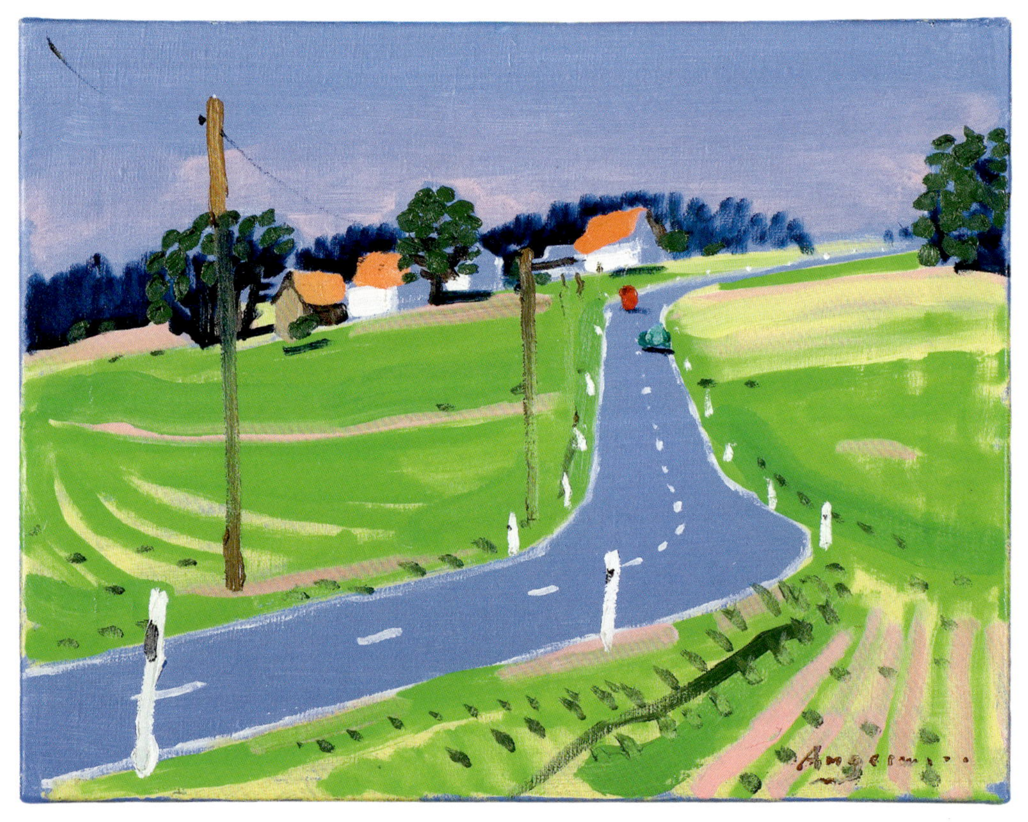

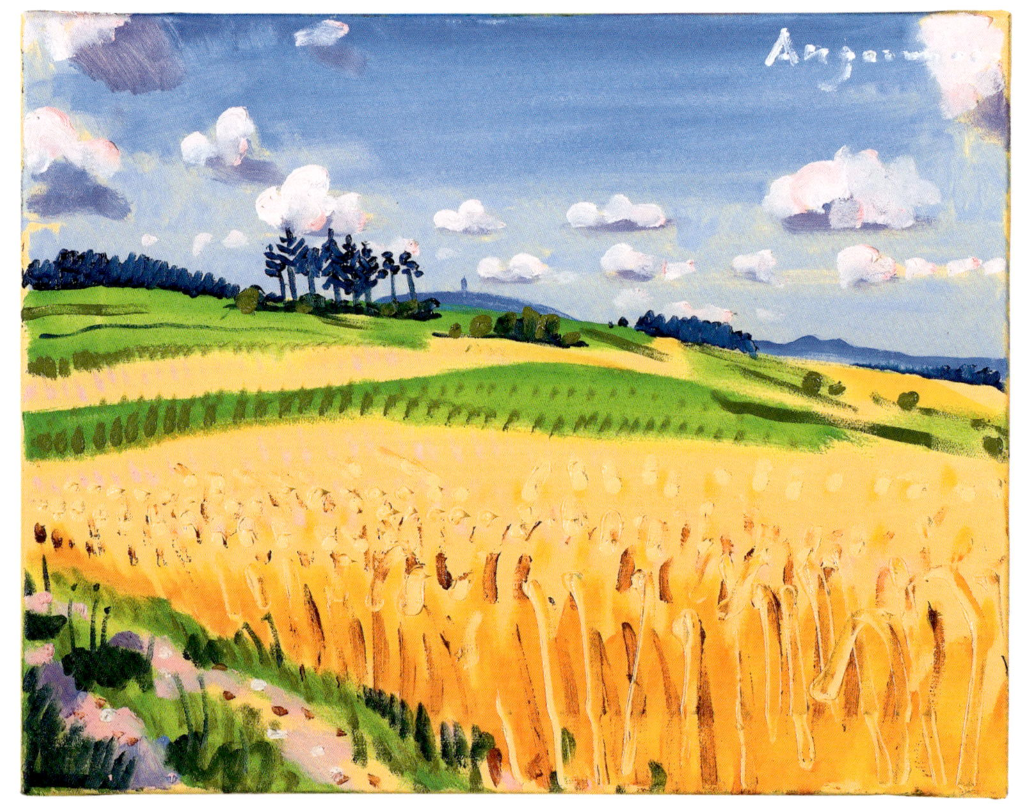

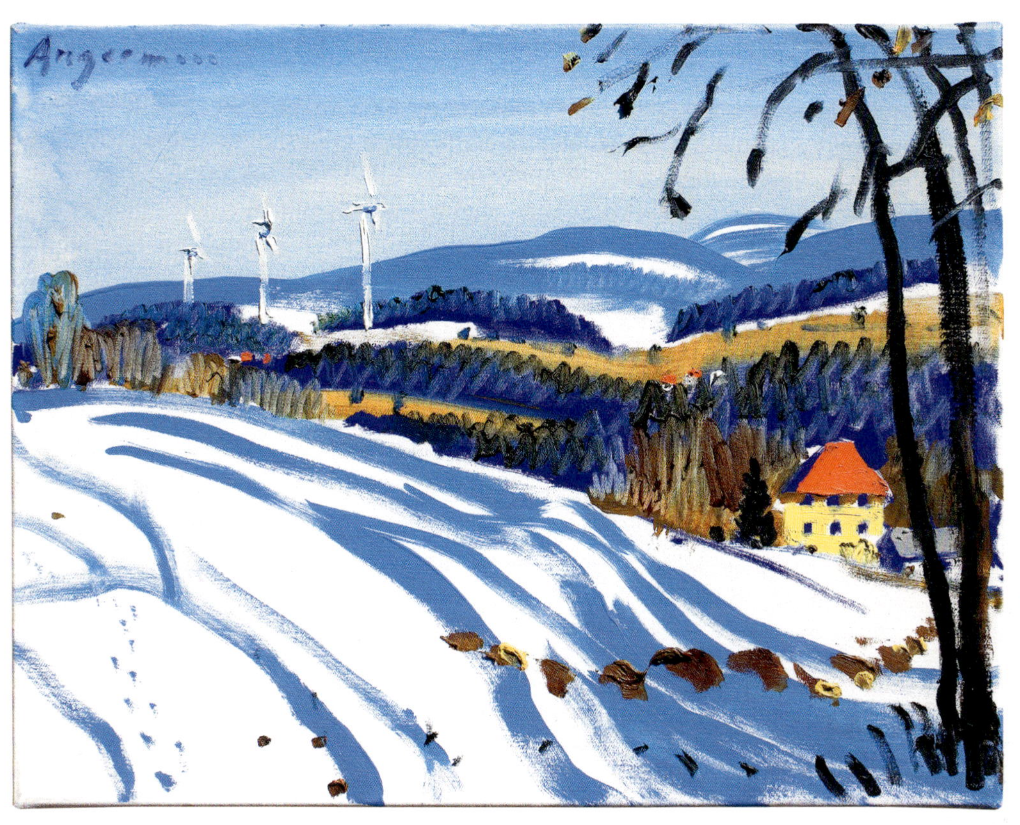

Forst, 2005

Zirkenhain, 2005

Drei Windrotoren / Three Wind Rotors, 2004

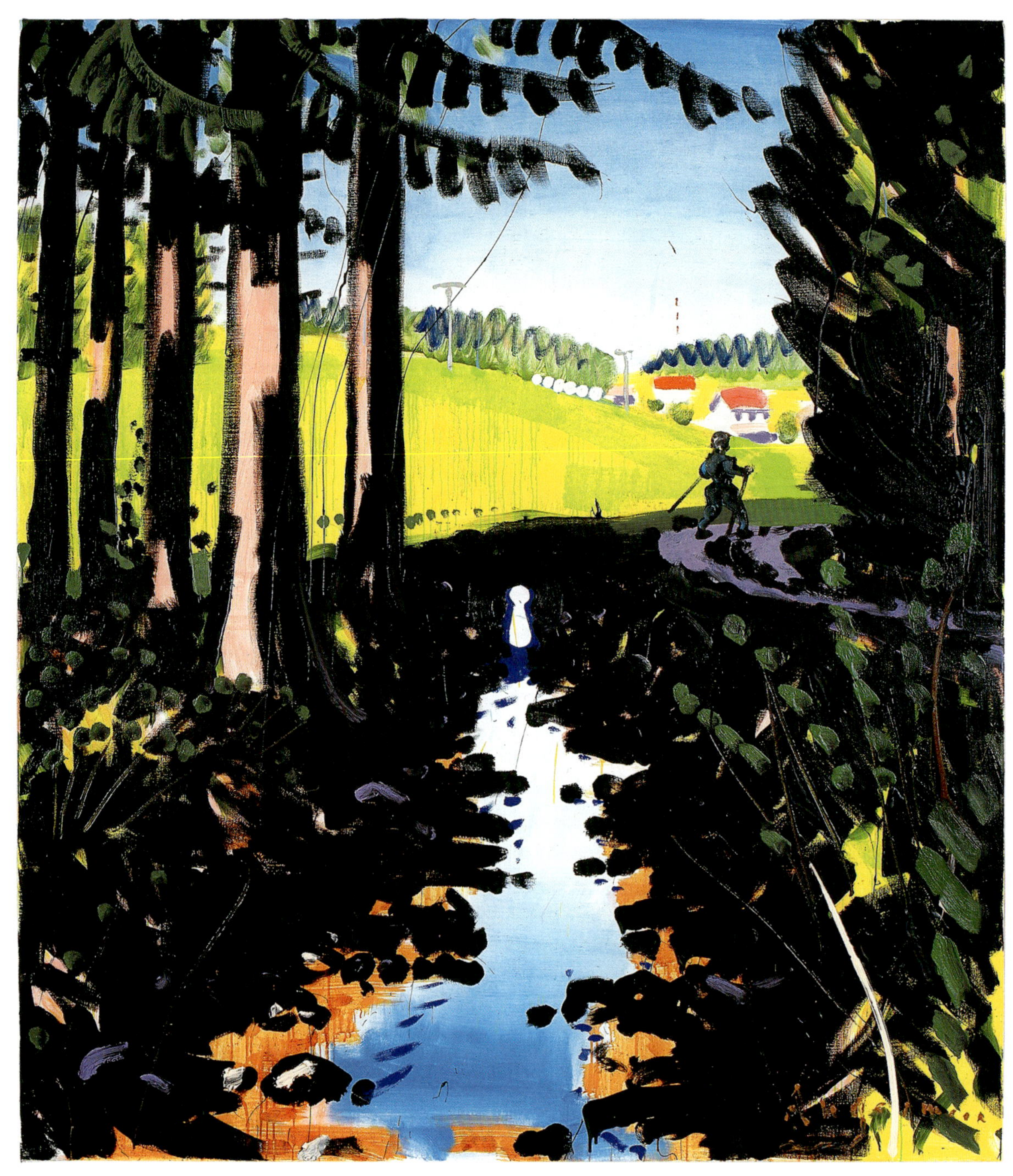

Höll 2, 2006

168

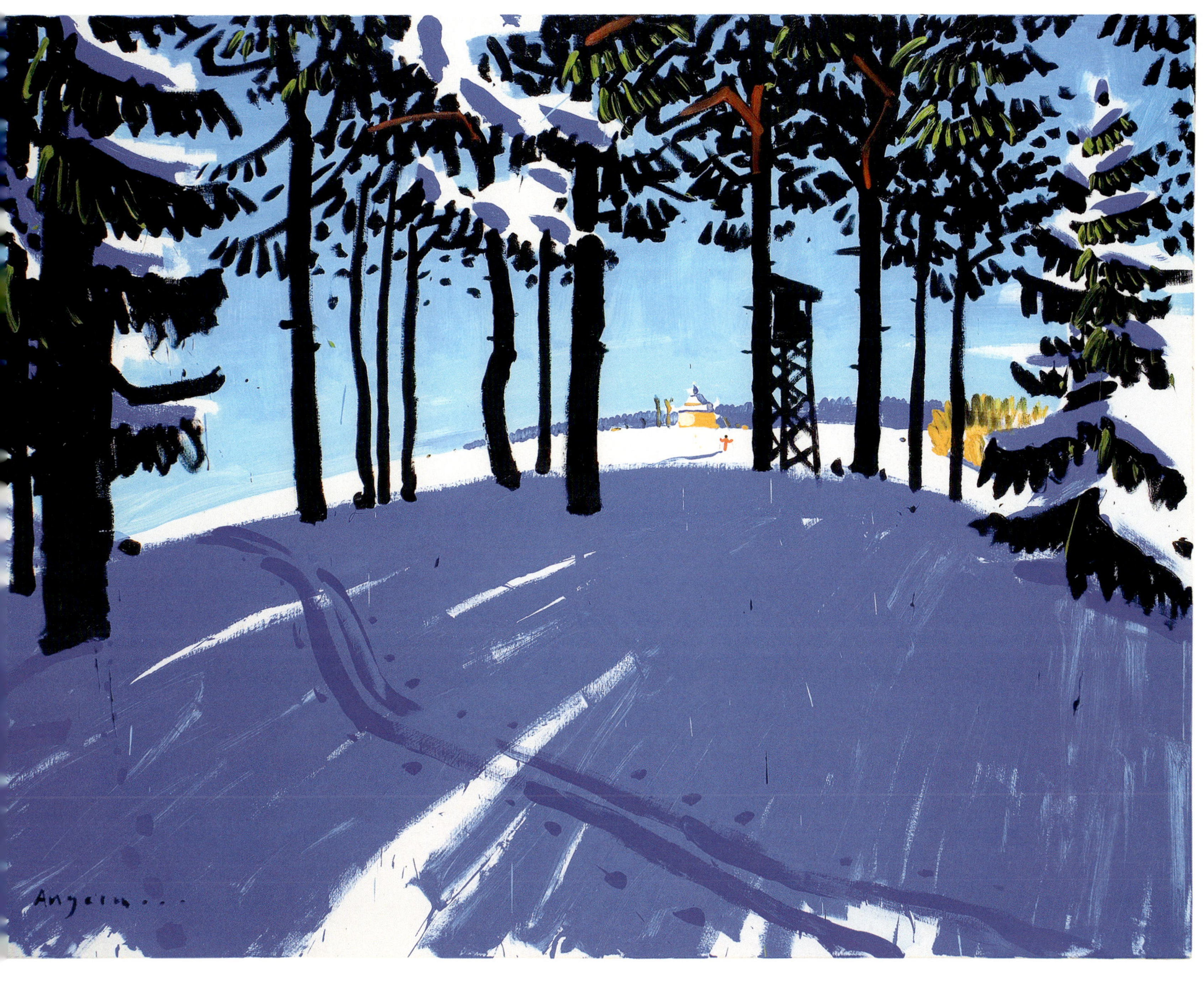

Waldrand 2 / Forest Edge 2, 2006

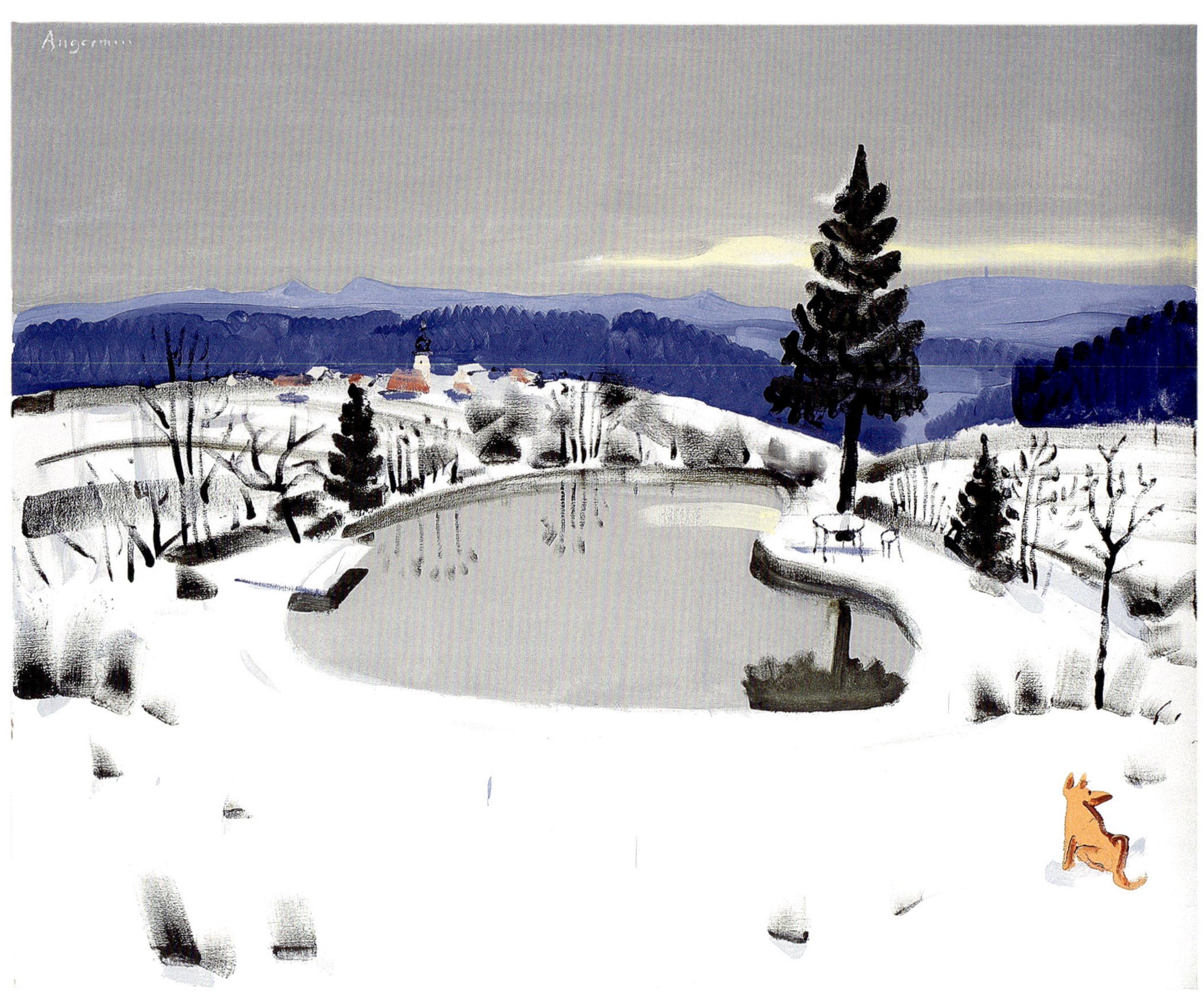

Camillo, 2007

"Art for the people, and against the art pussies!"

Peter Angermann interviewed by his former master-class student Matthias Egersdörfer

Matthias Egersdörfer: When did you reach the point where you said to yourself:
"I'm going to be an artist"?

Peter Angermann: When I was eleven and about to do my entrance exams
for junior high school, my parents were afraid I might fail and sent me to be coached
by an older pupil at the high school, Gunther le Maire. With that I came in contact
with an utterly different world. The le Maires had a house full of books and musical
instruments, interesting pictures on the walls, and obviously all in daily use. I went into
ecstasies.

For a long time I'd derived a lot of pleasure from
painting, and time and again I impressed my friends and
teachers with what I did. So now Gunther – he also painted
and quite resolutely so, with oils and turps, and did woodcuts
and linocuts – wanted to see my paintings, so I took them
along to my next lesson, which was then over before it
started. Everything revolved from that moment on solely
around painting. He showed me art books on the Impressionists, the Expressionists, on Cézanne, Munch, Klee and
Picasso, everything they had there in their house, and that
was a lot, and I soaked it all up like a sponge. I was knocked
for six. He plied me with real oil paints, let me paint, took me
seriously and I was almost bursting with pride and suddenly
I belonged somehow or other to this fascinating world of
painting.

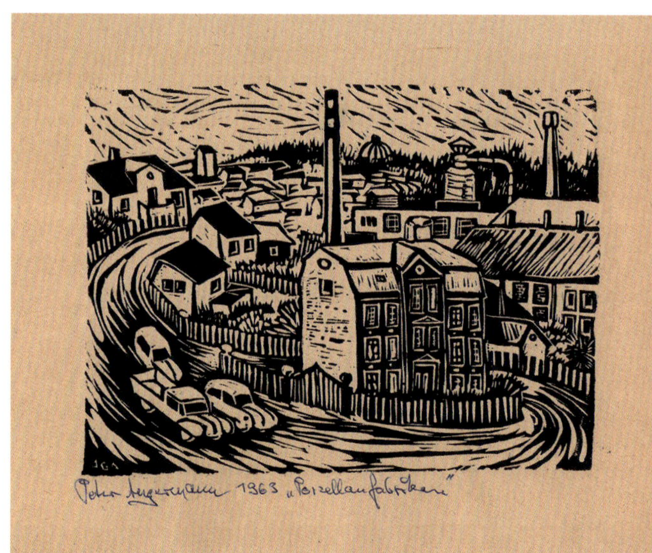

Selb, 1962, Linolschnitt / linocut

M.E.: And when did the point arrive where you no longer saw it as a hobby but as a real
way to make a living?

P.A.: I didn't take it seriously as a job for a long time, in keeping with the way my parents saw it. Apart from which, I didn't want to hear anything about that subject right
then. "The serious side of life", that's the kind of thing my parents would say, tiresome
and inhibiting. I couldn't care less about earning my crust by the sweat of my brow.
What I was more interested in was the life of an artist, with all the consequences, with
failure absolutely included if it wasn't to be avoided. Van Gogh for instance was a shining example to me. I'd read his biography and knew all about his misery and despair.
And yet being like that seemed like something to aspire to, such a magnificent artist,
whatever the cost. Obviously I would have preferred to establish myself and master life

„Kunst fürs Volk und gegen die Art Pussies!"

Peter Angermann im Gespräch mit seinem ehemaligen Meisterschüler Matthias Egersdörfer

Matthias Egersdörfer: Wann gab es für dich den Punkt, wo du gesagt hast:
„Ich werde Künstler"?

Peter Angermann: Als ich elf Jahre alt war und die Aufnahmeprüfung fürs Gymnasium
bevorstand, hatten meine Eltern Angst, ich könnte versagen, und schickten mich zu
Nachhilfestunden zu einem älteren Gymnasiasten, Gunther le Maire. Damit kam ich
in Berührung mit einer völlig neuen Welt. Die le Maires hatten das Haus voller Bücher,
Musikinstrumente, interessante Bildern an den Wänden, und all das offensichtlich in
alltäglichem Gebrauch. Ich war begeistert.

Ich selbst hatte schon lange großen Spaß am Malen gehabt und auch immer wieder mal Freunde oder Lehrer damit beeindruckt. Nun wollte Gunther, der selbst malte,
und zwar richtig entschieden, mit Öl und Terpentin, und der Linol- und Holzschnitte
druckte, meine Bilder sehen, und ich brachte sie das nächste Mal mit in die Nachhilfe-
stunde – die damit gestorben war. Stattdessen drehte es sich von da an nur noch um
Malerei. Er zeigte mir Kunstbände über die Impressionisten, die Expressionisten, über
Cézanne, Munch, Klee und Picasso, alles, was die so im Haus hatten, und das war eine
Menge, und ich saugte es auf wie ein Schwamm. Ich bin total darauf abgefahren. Er
drückte mir veritable Ölfarben in die Hand, ließ mich malen, nahm mich ernst, und ich
platzte fast vor Stolz, und plötzlich gehörte ich irgendwie dazu zu dieser faszinierenden
Welt der Malerei.

M.E.: Und wann war dann der Punkt, wo du das nicht mehr nur als Hobby gesehen
hast, sondern als richtigen Broterwerb?

P.A.: Als Beruf habe ich das noch lange Zeit nicht ernst genommen, entsprechend der
Sichtweise meiner Eltern. Davon abgesehen: Von dem Thema wollte ich damals auch
gar nichts hören. „Der Ernst des Lebens", das waren Sprüche der Alten, lästig und
hemmend. Der Broterwerb im Schweiße meines Angesichts war mir wurscht. Worum
es mir eher ging: die Existenz als Künstler mit allen Konsequenzen, Scheitern aus-
drücklich inbegriffen, wenn's nicht anders geht. Für mich war zum Beispiel van Gogh
ein leuchtendes Vorbild. Ich hatte seine Biografie gelesen und wusste von seinem Elend
und seiner Verzweiflung. Trotzdem schien es mir erstrebenswert, so jemand zu sein, so
ein grandioser Künstler, koste es, was es wolle. Natürlich wäre es mir lieber gewesen,
mich durchzusetzen und das Leben zu meistern wie Picasso, doch so recht wagte ich
das nicht zu hoffen. Van Goghs Schicksal schien mir die realistischere Aussicht.

like Picasso did, but I didn't really dare to hope for that. Van Gogh's fate seemed to be a
more realistic prospect.

M.E.: So your parents really had to fear that if everything went wrong, God forbid,
their boy would become an artist?

P.A.: They saw me anyhow as in constant danger. Evidently I was a bit of a strange child
with a mind of my own, who had what for them were cracked ideas and often behaved
in an odd and embarrassing manner. Somehow my parents were quick to expect the
worst for me, it seems. And when your parents see the worst for you, that's a good
reason to start looking round for another way to lead your life.

M.E.: So van Gogh was sort of the negative model, according to the motto: if it all turns
out for the worst I'll end up in the gutter. But even that'll enable me to break out of this
narrow world.

P.A.: That's right. I took up painting with banners raised high and didn't give a toss for
the losses. Although I did always have this other weakness, which was my passion for
natural sciences, that would rise from its slumbers every year or two and force my painting into the background for a while. In the older days these two fields of interest seemed
mutually exclusive. It took a long time until I saw the connections. Before that I felt that
the one was blocking the other.

M.E.: And when had things progressed to the point that you didn't actively embrace the
natural sciences but art instead?

P.A.: My parents of course would have preferred me to study physics or maths after
leaving school. I was normally very good in these subjects, but my marks were extremely
erratic throughout my schooldays, depending on how I got on with the various teachers.
Things stayed on a more even keel in art, and right from the outset I had a fantastic
teacher, Mr Lorenz, who held great store in me and gave me real encouragement. At any
rate, when it came to school finals my marks in physics were so bad that any hopes of a
course that suited my parents' taste were dispelled forever. I really managed to scupper
that one.

M.E.: All that remained for you was art.

P.A.: So then I studied from 1966 to 1968 at the Academy of Fine Arts in Nuremberg
in the class run by Gerhard Wendland. My idols were the Expressionists, the painters
from the Brücke and Blauer Reiter, whom I emulated, and soon a bit of Informel
as well, at any rate painting with a pronounced use of materials. As a proud artist
I was quite certain as to what made a good picture: strong gestures, spontaneous,
self-enamoured. A daring use of colour, sophisticated composition … in other words:
soon I was completely stuck. Then a ray of light appeared on the horizon: a poster

M.E.: Also die Eltern hatten ernsthaft zu befürchten, wenn's schief läuft, um Gottes willen, dann wird der Bub ein Künstler?

P.A.: Die haben mich sowieso immer in Gefahr gesehen. Offenbar war ich ein etwas seltsames Kind mit eigenem Kopf, mit in ihren Augen verschrobenen Vorstellungen und oft auffälligem und peinlichem Benehmen. Irgendwie haben meine Eltern schon früh ziemlich schwarz für mich gesehen, glaube ich. Und wenn die Eltern schwarzsehen für einen, dann ist das ein starker Grund, sich bald nach alternativen Lebensweisen umzusehen.

M.E.: Dann war sozusagen van Gogh das negative Vorbild nach dem Motto: Im schlimmsten Fall geht's halt in die Gosse. Aber auch das ermöglicht mir, aus dieser engen Welt auszubrechen.

P.A.: So ist es. Ich bin mit wehenden Fahnen und ohne Rücksicht auf Verluste in die Malerei eingestiegen. Allerdings hatte ich immer noch ein zweites großes Faible, und das war meine Begeisterung für die Naturwissenschaften, die alle ein, zwei Jahre neu erwachte und dann die Malerei für eine Weile in den Hintergrund drängte. Früher schienen sich diese beiden Interessensgebiete gegenseitig auszuschließen. Es dauerte lange, bis ich den Zusammenhang erkannte. Vorher kam es mir eher so vor, als würde das eine das andere blockieren.

M.E.: Und wann hat sich das Bahn gebrochen, dass du nicht in den Naturwissenschaften aktiv werden würdest, sondern in der Kunst?

P.A.: Die Eltern hätten natürlich lieber gesehen, dass ich nach dem Abitur Physik oder Mathematik studiere. In diesen Fächern war ich normalerweise recht gut, hatte aber während meiner ganzen Schulzeit extrem schwankende Noten, je nach dem, wie ich mit dem jeweiligen Lehrer klar kam. In der Kunst lief es etwas gleichmäßiger, und da hatte ich gleich am Anfang einen fantastischen Lehrer, Studienrat Lorenz, der große Stücke auf mich hielt und der mich entschieden förderte. Beim Abitur jedenfalls war ich dann in Physik wieder dermaßen schlecht, dass ein Studium nach dem Geschmack meiner Eltern in weite Ferne rückte. Das hatte ich sozusagen erfolgreich sabotiert.

M.E.: Da blieb dir nur die Kunst.

P.A.: Ich studierte dann von 1966 bis 1968 an der Akademie der Bildenden Künste in Nürnberg in der Klasse von Gerhard Wendland. Meine Idole waren die Expressionisten, die Maler von Brücke und Blauem Reiter, denen ich nacheiferte, bald auch ein bisschen Informel, jedenfalls Malerei mit entschiedenem Materialeinsatz. Ich war mir als stolzer Künstler natürlich schon völlig darüber im Klaren, was ein gutes Bild ausmacht: kraftvoller Gestus, spontan und selbstverliebt. Kühnes Kolorit, raffinierte Komposition … mit anderen Worten: Ich steckte bald mitten in der Stagnation. Da erschien ein Lichtstrahl am Horizont: ein Plakat an den Litfaßsäulen Nürnbergs. Eine Ausstellung

on the advertising columns in Nuremberg. A Pop art exhibition at the American Institute with Roy Lichtenstein's whammy: *Sweet Dreams Baby*. I was electrified: so that's also possible! It was as if someone had torn open the window. The one caught a cold, the other a breath of spring air. "Is that still art?" some asked, while the others were totally knocked out. The students fell into two camps. Just picture it: to me as someone who had grown up in the vicinity of Duckburg (really!), this comic style was totally familiar to me and close to my heart, but up till then it had been damned by my parents and teachers and despised by the old know-alls, and suddenly it emerged as a vehicle for artistic expression; *the* visual language for my generation! High art had never experienced a thing like that before. Pictures like the "Big Abstract Paintings", where Roy Lichtenstein took Abstract Expressionism to the height of perfection while simultaneously deflating it! The way he coolly made this la-di-da insider art accessible again, so that it had something to say to everyone, that was truly amazing!

M.E.: So what you liked was this blow to the belly of "lofty art"?

P.A.: Yes! But not simply the aggression but also the attitude, flouting the visual conventions that had been instilled in us, countering them with something fresh and up-front. I for my part felt it was high time to chuck out all the unbending certainties, all this premature mastery. And I wasn't the only one back then.

M.E.: So you saw that your early pictures had got stuck, you wouldn't produce anything new in painting if you kept using hard and fast visual concepts to conjure up the Franconian countryside. And then this liberation that came with Pop art.

P.A.: Right. That led me among other things to the principle of clashing styles, which I cribbed above all from Rauschenberg. Traditional technique was cracking up. Suddenly I had unlimited resources at my disposal and could enrich good old painting with whole new worlds of imagery: not only from comics but also the language of advertising, collage, photography, image signals and all kinds of signs, regardless of whether abstract or representational. What impressed me the most was the stylistic freedom the American artists had. How much freer and more interesting it was than all that Informel stuff! What decided me was the way that stylistic homogeneity, which up till then I thought I was bound to in my old European way, the tight formal notions, the conceited signature styles, was gently swept aside and suddenly there was room again for inspiration. And precisely those voluptuous clashes of styles, juggling with different kinds of imagery, became the principle behind my work. All at once my ideas had a free passage. I learnt from Pop art that formal dislocations can be a means of expression. I discovered the thrill of heterogeneity, of diversity in the materials, of playing around with stock styles and even with different contents.

I called these pictures "Brainstormings" (*Brainstorming 1* and 5, 1968, pp. 36/37). I based my work on the principle used in advertising which, applied to the visual arts,

von Pop-Art im Amerikahaus mit Roy Lichtensteins Kinnhaken *Sweet Dreams Baby*. Ich war wie elektrisiert: Das also ist auch möglich! Es war, als würde jemand die Fenster aufreißen. Die einen kriegten Schnupfen, die anderen Frühlingsgefühle. „Ist denn das noch Kunst?" die einen und vollkommen aus dem Häuschen die anderen. Die Studentenschaft war gespalten. Man stelle sich vor: Die Bildsprache des Comics, mir, als einem, der in der Gegend von Entenhausen (tatsächlich!) aufgewachsen ist, bestens vertraut und ans Herz gewachsen, die bis dahin aber immer von Lehrern und Eltern verteufelt worden war, von den alten Bescheidwissern verachtet, brach sich plötzlich als künstlerische Ausdrucksmöglichkeit Bahn; die ureigenste Bildsprache meiner Generation! So etwas hatte es bis dahin in der Hochkunst nicht gegeben. Bilder wie die „Big Abstract Paintings", wo Roy Lichtenstein dann auch noch den abstrakten Expressionismus zu höchster Vollkommenheit führt und ihm zugleich die Luft rauslässt! Wie er diese verstiegene Insiderkunst ganz souverän wieder anschlussfähig macht, so dass sie jedem was sagt, das ist einfach großartig!

M.E.: Also, was dir so gefallen hat, war auch der Kinnhaken für diese „holde Kunst" sozusagen.

P.A.: Ja! Aber nicht einfach nur die Agressivität, sondern diese Haltung, sich über die eingeübte Sehkultur hinwegzusetzen, frisch und frech etwas dagegenzusetzen. Ich spürte ja an mir selber, dass es höchste Zeit war, die alten starren Gewissheiten, diese verfrühte Meisterschaft über den Haufen zu werfen. Und das ging damals nicht nur mir so.

M.E.: Deine früheren Bilder fandest du also festgefahren, es konnte nichts mehr passieren in der Malerei, wo du mit festen Bildkonzepten versucht hattest, die fränkische Landschaft heraufzubeschwören. Und dann dieser Befreiungsschlag der Pop-Art.

P.A.: Richtig. Das führte mich unter anderem zu dem Prinzip der Stilbrüche, das ich vor allem Rauschenberg abguckte. Die traditionelle Technik brach auf. Plötzlich konnte ich aus dem Vollen schöpfen und die gute alte Malerei um ganze Bildwelten bereichern: nicht nur den Comic, auch die Bildsprache der Werbung, die Collage, die Fotografie, Bildsignale und Zeichen aller Art, ob abstrakt oder gegenständlich. Am meisten beeindruckte mich wohl die stilistische Unbefangenheit der amerikanischen Künstler. Wie viel freier und interessanter war das als alles Informel! Für mich war entscheidend, dass die Homogenität des Stils, der ich mich bis dahin alteuropäisch verpflichtet meinte, die engen formalen Vorstellungen, die eitle Handschrift, mit aller Leichtigkeit beiseite gewischt war und die Inspiration plötzlich wieder Raum fand. Gerade der lustvolle Stilbruch, das Jonglieren mit den Bildsprachen, wurde Prinzip meiner Arbeit. Die Ideen hatten auf einmal freie Bahn. Von der Pop-Art lernte ich, dass formale Verwerfungen ein Ausdrucksmittel sein können. Ich entdeckte das Spannungsvolle des Heterogenen,

means not restricting yourself particularly as regards form
or content, nor in style or the means you choose. Instead I
took as wide a range of elements as possible, allowed the most
diverse kinds of imagery to bounce off one another, and noted
with excitement how blithely this fount bubbled away. It's
part of the concept of "Brainstorming" to work collectively,
so in the end I put on paint parties in my studio on Poppenreuther Strasse, a mixture of loft and attic with cardboard
partitions where, apart from me, five or six people from the
academy lived.

M.E.: Those were comrades-in-arms back then who were all on the
same wavelength.

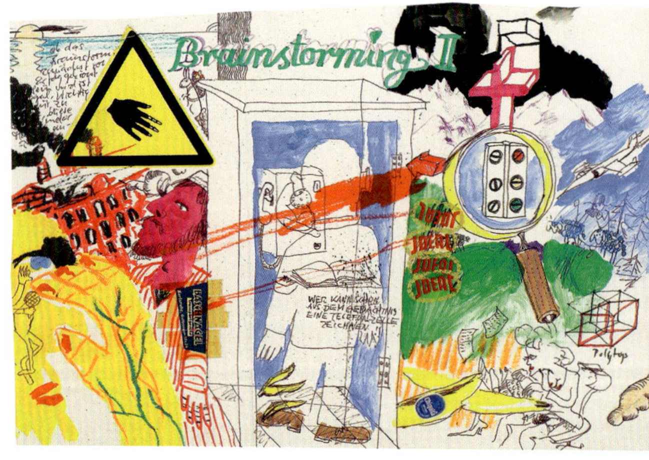

Brainstorming 2, 1968, Mischtechnik auf Papier / mixed media on paper

P.A.: Exactly. And most of them were art students. But there were also people from
outside, such as GIs. At that time the Yanks still had conscription, so there were people
there like us, not troopers at any rate. And they always had something to smoke on
them. All hell was let loose, and the painting orgies came about of their own accord.
The formats grew to wall size. Then a decal factory went bust on the floor below and we
inherited tons of decals, along with printing inks, paper and other materials, and in that
way the whole thing really blossomed. So it was only logical to put on events like that
in public. I decided to stage a big painting Happening with my friends on the station
forecourt and drag in the passers-by. Because the more there were and the more different they were, the more this burgeoning creativity we aimed at would proliferate.

M.E.: When was that?

P.A.: That was 1968.

M.E.: So you were totally a child of the times, when solid citizens were horrified at the
hippies who took drugs and sloshed away and disrupted normal life – the epitome of
the protest generation.

P.A.: Spot on! This rustling in the air had already made itself noticeable in the years before, this colourfulness that was still in hiding somewhere but now forcing itself out into
the light of day. It sounds like a cliché, and it is one for all I care, but I distinctly recall
the crocuses that March in 1968. They seemed to me to be different, more important,
more decisive than usual. And suddenly I wondered why the houses, the cars, people's
clothes were so grey and beige and drab, as they really were back then. And we were all
grabbed by this sense of a new start, like Huey, Dewey and Louie when they struck out
for freedom with their bundles of belongings on sticks over their shoulders. There was
no stopping it any more, and all I can say is: *Sgt. Pepper's Lonely Hearts Club Band*.

auch der Materialvielfalt, das Spiel mit stilistischen Versatzstücken und sogar mit Inhalten.

„Brainstormings“ nannte ich diese Art von Bildern (*Brainstorming 1* und *5*, 1968, S. 36/37). Das Prinzip aus der Werbewelt legte ich meiner Arbeit zugrunde, was auf die bildende Kunst übertragen bedeutet, sich weder formal noch inhaltlich, weder stilistisch noch in der Auswahl der Mittel besonders einzuschränken. Vielmehr bediente ich mich einer größtmöglichen Vielfalt von Elementen, ließ die unterschiedlichsten Bildwelten aufeinanderprallen und stellte begeistert fest, wie munter diese Quelle sprudelte. Es liegt in der Natur des Konzepts „Brainstorming“, im Kollektiv zu arbeiten, und so veranstaltete ich schließlich auch Malpartys in meinem Atelier in der Poppenreuther Straße, einer Mischung aus Dachboden und Loft, von Pappwänden unterteilt, wo außer mir noch fünf, sechs Leute aus der Akademie wohnten.

M.E.: Das waren alles Weggefährten, die genauso getickt haben zu der Zeit.

P.A.: Genau. Die meisten waren auch Kunststudenten. Es kamen aber auch Leute von außerhalb, zum Beispiel GIs. Damals hatten die Amis noch Wehrpflicht, und das waren Leute wie wir, keine Landsknechte jedenfalls. Die hatten auch immer was zu dampfen mit. Es war immer die Hölle los, und die Malorgien ergaben sich wie von selbst. Die Formate wuchsen auf Wandgröße. Ein Stockwerk unter uns ging dann noch eine Abziehbilderfabrik pleite, und wir erbten Unmengen unterschiedlichster Abziehbilder, aber auch Druckfarben, Papier und sonstiges Material, und damit konnte die Sache bestens gedeihen. Es war dann nur konsequent, solche Veranstaltungen in die Öffentlichkeit zu tragen. Ich beschloss, mit meinen Freunden ein großes Malhappening am Bahnhofsvorplatz zu veranstalten mit Einbeziehung der Passanten. Denn je mehr und je unterschiedlichere Leute mitwirkten, desto üppiger der angestrebte gestalterische Wildwuchs.

M.E.: Wann war das?

P.A.: Das war 1968.

M.E.: Na, da warst du ja absolut Kind der Zeit, wo dem Bürger vor diesen Hippies grauste, die Drogen nehmen und rumschmieren und das normale Leben stören – der Inbegriff eines Achtundsechzigers.

P.A.: Haargenau! Dieses Knistern in der Luft hatte sich ja schon die Jahre vorher bemerkbar gemacht, diese Farbigkeit, die noch irgendwo verborgen war und gewaltig ans Licht drängte. Es klingt wie ein Klischee, es ist eins meinetwegen, aber ich erinnere mich genau an die Krokusse in diesem März ’68. Die schienen mir anders, bedeutender, entschiedener als sonst. Und ich wunderte mich plötzlich, warum die Häuser, die Autos, die Klamotten so grau, beige, so fahl waren, wie sie tatsächlich damals noch waren. Und uns ergriff eine allgemeine Aufbruchstimmung wie Tick, Trick

So on that morning in June 1968 we went off with a broad roll of wrapping paper and a whole assortment of paint buckets, brushes, chalks, pencils and decals. We fixed a layer of wrapping paper on the advertising hoardings in front of the main station, set to and encouraged the passers-by to join in. A number of them allowed themselves to get caught up in our enthusiasm. But the euphoria was short-lived: the police turned up on the scene – and instead of wanting to paint with us they put a stop to it all.

Our frustration knew no bounds. We packed our things and moved off to the art school – first to get something to eat. And we sat around there with our materials and this stifled thirst for action and looked at the large, white, empty wall in the refectory …

M.E.: If I have understood you correctly: the story is that you were driven out of public space by the police and took the terror, as it were, back into the academy.

P.A.: But quite spontaneously and without planning it. And it is hardly a surprise that this great empty wall sucked up our bottled-up painting fever like a great big piece of blotting paper.

M.E.: So you really came straight from your defeat in public directly to the refectory wall in the academy?

P.A.: Yes, and after a brief moment of hesitation we let rip, like mad things! Before you knew it the entire wall was covered in this crude mixture of everything you could imagine. In the twinkle of an eye "Brainstorming" rampaged around the entire room, also spreading like ivy up the side walls and even over the ceiling, with a second, third and fourth layer creeping over this, getting ever denser and increasingly complicated in a simply breathtaking way.

M.E.: A number of others must have come and joined in.

P.A.: Yes, of course, and it carried on like that for the couple of days. An anarchic self-organising orgy of artistic creativity. The quality of the work was just as controversial as Roy Lichtenstein's *Sweet Dreams Baby*.

The whole thing escalated, there were threats of damage claims and rustication, which is not surprising. It was the hour of the student committees and politically motivated students, because it all fitted nicely with the student unrests, which had also just flared up elsewhere. They created connections with the outside world, with other academies and universities. The growing pressure from the academy authorities forced us to turn to the public and seek support from the art celebrities of the day and mount a public hearing in the refectory, to which we invited God and the world.

M.E.: A hearing at which to decide whether it was a public nuisance, simply scrawls and wilful damage, or art.

und Track, als sie, den Wanderstock mit ihren Siebensachen im Bündelchen über der Schulter, in die Freiheit aufbrachen. Da gab es kein Halten mehr und ich sag nur: *Sgt. Pepper's Lonely Hearts Club Band*.

An diesem Vormittag im Juni 1968 zogen wir also los, mit einer breiten Rolle Packpapier, allen möglichen Farbkübeln, Pinseln, Kreiden, Stiften, Abziehbildern. Wir befestigten eine Lage Packpapier auf den Werbetafeln vor dem Hauptbahnhof, legten los und animierten die Passanten mitzumachen. Einige ließen sich von unserer Begeisterung anstecken. Doch die Euphorie war nur von kurzer Dauer: Die Polizei erschien auf der Bildfläche – wollte nicht mitmalen, sondern stoppte die ganze Aktion.

Die Frustration war groß. Wir packten unser Zeug zusammen und verzogen uns Richtung Kunstakademie – erst mal was essen. Da hockten wir dann mit unserem abgewürgten Tatendrang und mit unserem Material und guckten auf die große, leere weiße Mensawand …

M.E.: Wenn ich das richtig verstanden habe: Die Geschichte ist also die, dass Ihr von der Polizei aus der Öffentlichkeit vertrieben wurdet und den Terror sozusagen zurück in die Akademie getragen habt.

P.A.: Aber völlig spontan und ungeplant. Ein Wunder war's nicht, dass diese große kahle Mensawand unsere aufgestaute Malwut aufsaugte wie ein riesiges Löschpapier.

M.E.: Ihr kamt also wirklich von Eurer Niederlage in der Öffentlichkeit direkt in die Akademie vor die Mensawand?

P.A.: Ja, und nach kurzem Zögern legten alle los, dass die Fetzen flogen! Die gesamte Mensawand war in kürzester Zeit mit einer kruden Mischung von allem Möglichen bedeckt. Im Nu überwucherte „Brainstorming" den Raum, breitete sich wie Efeu auch an den Seitenwänden und sogar an der Decke aus, kroch in einer zweiten, dritten und vierten Schicht über sich selbst hinweg, verdichtete und komplizierte sich in atemberaubender Weise.

M.E.: Da kamen dann beim Malen ja sicher noch welche dazu.

P.A.: Ja, klar, und die folgenden Tage ging das immer so weiter. Eine anarchistische selbstorganisierende Orgie künstlerischen Gestaltungswillens. Die Qualität des Werks war ebenso umstritten wie bei Roy Lichtensteins *Sweet Dreams Baby*.

Die Angelegenheit eskalierte, es wurde mit Schadensersatzforderungen und mit Rausschmiss gedroht, was ja auch weiter kein Wunder ist. Das war die Stunde der AStA-Leute und politisch motivierten Studenten, denn alles fügte sich gut in den Hintergrund der Studentenunruhen, wie sie anderswo auch gerade ausgebrochen waren. Sie stellten Verbindungen nach draußen her, zu den anderen Akademien und Hochschulen. Der wachsende Druck der Akademieleitung trieb uns an die Öffentlichkeit und

P.A.: The response was fantastic; professions of sympathy from all over the world. Hundertwasser expressed his solidarity in a two-page telegram that he sent us – which was a pricey business in those days – with tips about how we could carry on. Personal appearances at the hearing included the curator Manfred de la Motte and the artists HA Schult, Jürgen Claus, HAP Grieshaber and Joseph Beuys, who came in, eyed up the situation and immediately sat at the piano. The refectory was full to the gunnels and obviously the press was there as well.

M.E.: How did your opponents make their appearance?

P.A.: It was no joking matter for them, assuming they actually dared to show up. The most important of them, like the president, Wunibald Puchner, didn't even come. Which I can understand, because we were not at all interested in reaching an agreement. The future belonged to us alone! The whole thing served simply as a flight into the public in order to save our hides, which is what happened.

In order to liven things up we also organised a couple of white hens that fluttered around agitatedly between the people and underlined the importance of the occasion quite beautifully. In that way a great deal of fuss was kicked up and one repercussion in fact was that afterwards nobody could simply give us a hammering without identifying themselves as gormless reactionaries and without stirring up more unrest. They didn't want to pour oil on the flames, and so it all went smoothly.

Yet for me the artistic aspect counted more than the political one. I should emphasise that the situation at colleges was different before 1968 than it is now: things were simply undemocratic then and authoritarian. Questioning the often useless ideas we were confronted with was nothing short of taboo. We still had a struggle before us if we wanted to get our own say. So somehow we had to fight against this patronization, and the refectory wall painting provided us with the opportunity. Which means the artistic rebellion came before the political one, because politicisation only came once we had already seized our freedom. What was decisive is that we had taken hold of the academy, lustfully and impudently, but ultimately without damaging anything except a few egos. I mean, I think an art school has little reason to complain if creative desires break out in such a vital manner when the opportunity arises.

M.E.: Was it on this occasion that you first met Beuys?

Dienstag, 16. Juli 1968   NÜRN

Polizei für Prof. Puchner

Hüh

Heiße Diskussionen in der Kunstakademie

Die Mensawand in der Kunstakademie wird immer mehr zum Motor interessanter, verblüffender oder auch kurioser Aktionen und Reaktionen. Das Hearing der Studenten wurde gestern nachmittag fast zum Happening, als Professor Wunibald Puchner, der Vizepräsident der Akademie, Polizeischutz für sich beantragte, weil er sich bedroht fühlte.

Dabei hatten die jungen Revoluzzer, die sich die Köpfe heiß geredet hatten, nichts Böses im Sinn, als sie in einem geschlossenen Zug zum Haus des Vizepräsidenten zogen: „Wir wollten nur mit ihm sprechen." Puchner, später noch einmal zur Diskussion aufgefordert, aber: „Mit euch rede ich nicht."

Geredet wurde dafür um so mehr beim „Hearing" vor der Mensawand. „Konterrevolutionäre" hatten am frühen Morgen die Wand weiß getüncht, die grellen Farben schienen verwässert durch, das Gemälde erhielt einen eigenartigen Reiz: Die Aufforderung, weiter an der Wand herumzumalen, was am liebsten Professor Grieshaber und Professor Beuys gleich getan hätten.

Die Wand hat sich, seit sie besteht, ständig verändert. Sie ist für Professoren und Studenten, die morgens

Geistiger Vater der umstrittenen Mensawand: Kunststudent Peter Angermann.

Diskussio

in die Mer
sten Kaff
wieder ein
stern nach
sagt wurd

Mensawand-Hearing, Akademie der Bildenden Künste in Nürnberg / Refectory-wall hearing, Academy of Fine Arts in Nuremberg, *Nürnberger Zeitung*, 16. Juli 1968 / July 16, 1968

zwang uns, Rückhalt bei der damaligen Kunstprominenz zu holen und ein öffentliches Hearing in der Mensa zu veranstalten, zu dem wir Gott und die Welt einluden.

M.E.: Ein Hearing, in dem entschieden werden sollte, ob's sich um groben Unfug, Schmiererei und Sachbeschädigung handeln sollte oder um Kunst.

P.A.: Das Echo war toll; Sympathiebekundungen aus aller Welt. Hundertwasser schickte uns ein zwei Seiten langes Solidaritätstelegramm – damals ein teurer Spaß – mit Tipps, wie wir weiter verfahren könnten. Persönlich erschienen zu dem Hearing der Kurator Manfred de la Motte und die Künstler HA Schult, Jürgen Claus, HAP Grieshaber und Joseph Beuys, der reinkam, die Situation checkte und gleich auf dem Klavier Platz nahm. Die Mensa war rappelvoll, und natürlich war auch die Presse da.

M.E.: Wie sind die Gegner aufgetreten?

P.A.: Soweit die sich überhaupt dahin trauten, hatten sie nichts zu lachen. Die wichtigsten, wie der Präsident Wunibald Puchner, ließen sich gar nicht erst blicken. Was ich verstehen kann, denn es ging uns doch gar nicht um eine Einigung. Uns allein gehörte die Zukunft! Das ganze diente nur als Flucht an die Öffentlichkeit, um mit heiler Haut davonzukommen, was ja auch klappte.

Um das Kraut fett zu machen, hatten wir auch noch einige weiße Hühner besorgt, die aufgeregt zwischen den Leuten herumflatterten und sehr schön die Wichtigkeit des Ereignisses unterstrichen. So wurde mächtig viel Wind gemacht, und ein Effekt war immerhin, dass man uns danach nicht mehr ohne Weiteres in die Pfanne hauen konnte, ohne als dumpfer Reaktionär dazustehen und ohne die

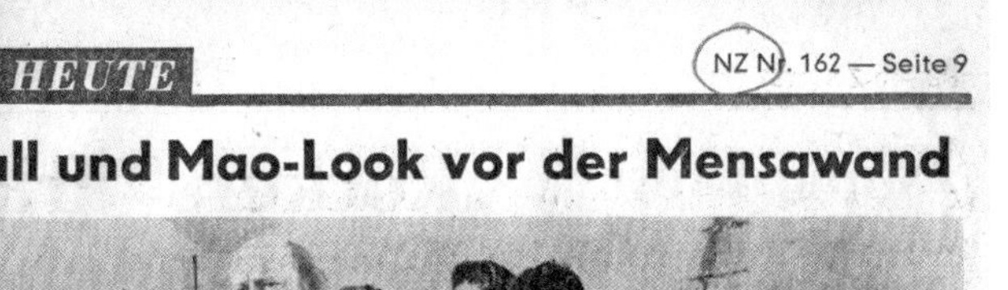

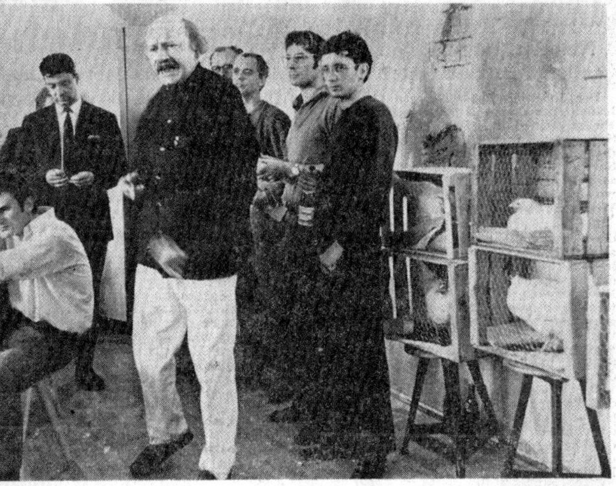

ühnerstall: Der bekannte Künstler Grieshaber erschien im Mao-Look und zersprang fast vor Temperament. Hinter ihm links Manfred de la Motte.

Unruhe noch mehr anzufachen. Man wollte kein Öl ins Feuer gießen, und so ging alles glimpflich ab.

Obwohl für mich mehr der künstlerische Aspekt zählte als der politische, muss ich betonen, dass die Situation an den Hochschulen vor 1968 sich von der heutigen unterschied: Es ging schlicht undemokratisch und autoritär zu. Die oft unbrauchbaren Vorstellungen, mit denen wir konfrontiert wurden, infrage zu stellen kam einem Tabubruch gleich. Das Mitspracherecht wollte erst noch erkämpft werden. Wir mussten uns damals irgendwie gegen diese Bevormundung wehren, und die Mensawandbemalung gab dazu den Anlass. Der künstlerische Aufstand kam also vor dem politischen, denn die Politisierung setzte ja erst ein, als wir uns die Freiheit bereits genommen hatten.

P.A.: That was my first encounter with him. Prior to that he had already been regarded as an insider tip by the few in our class who were in the know. I think Beuys was not only in Nuremberg for the hearing but also on account of an exhibition by the Deutscher Künstlerbund, which opened shortly after at the Künstlerhaus. I became involved with him again during the preparations for it, because I'd got a holiday job at the Künstlerhaus. I had the wonderful task of organising one or two hundredweight of margarine and a hundred air pumps for his installation – black enamelled pumps with those wooden handles you can unscrew. For the margarine I found something cheaper: vegetable shortening. I thought that would suffice for art. But Beuys complained, and I had to exchange it for real table margarine. He was satisfied with that, and me and another guy doing a holiday job there were allowed to witness an exclusive performance – for just the two of us – a non-public action as it were, or more correctly an installation, which he repeated the following autumn in Cologne with a lot less margarine under the title *Vacuum <–> Mass*. Beuys squatted on the floor and made large clods of margarine, about 20 cm in diameter. Then he stuck a pump into each finished clod, undid the cap at the top and removed the wooden handle complete with the piston and the washer, tossed them behind him and then threw the clod with the stem of the pump across the room at the large cast-iron radiator under the wall-to-wall window on the other side. With time a considerable pile of the stuff had built up. The wall and the parquet flooring were a total mess. Later, during the exhibition, the public got very worked up about this. Critical Nurembergers stuck toothpicks with newspaper clippings of starving Biafran children into the clods of margarine. And I was completely blown by it all.

M.E.: For you that was rather like the wall business in a nutshell. The "what is art?" question, as it were. That a decision was being made about you: are they simply rowdies, or what? You had achieved everything one could with an action at that time. You got pretty far.

P.A.: With that we had landed fully in the avant-garde. And soon I no longer restricted myself to painting but also played with other possibilities. I indulged in the extended concept of art.

M.E.: Beuys's margarine went a step further: away from some old Expressionistic line, away from wall painting, by creating a revolting mess and dispensing more or less with personal style.

P.A.: What Beuys presented there was the radical emancipation of art.

M.E.: In that moment when you saw all this with the clods, did you see it as the mastery of the field that you envisaged?

P.A.: Absolutely. And I must add that Beuys was an incredibly charismatic person. Already with the refectory wall business, when he at once found his place at the piano,

Entscheidend ist, wir hatten uns der Akademie bemächtigt, lustvoll und frech, aber letztlich ohne etwas anderes als Eitelkeiten zu verletzen. Ich meine, eine Kunstakademie hat eigentlich wenig Grund zur Klage, wenn sich dort zur passenden Gelegenheit künstlerischer Gestaltungswille auf derart vitale Weise Bahn bricht.

M.E.: Bei dieser Gelegenheit bist du Beuys zum ersten Mal begegnet?

P.A.: Das war mein erstes Zusammentreffen mit ihm. Er hatte schon vorher als Geheimtipp bei den paar Eingeweihten in der Klasse gegolten. Ich glaube, Beuys war nicht nur wegen des Hearings in Nürnberg, sondern auch wegen der Ausstellung des Deutschen Künstlerbundes, die kurz darauf im Künstlerhaus stattfand. Bei den Vorbereitungen dieser Ausstellung hatte ich dann wieder mit ihm zu tun, denn ich jobbte als Ferienarbeiter im Künstlerhaus. Ich hatte da die tolle Aufgabe, für seine Installation ein, zwei Zentner Margarine und hundert Luftpumpen zu besorgen und zwar die schwarz lackierten mit dem abschraubbaren Holzgriff. Als Margarine nahm ich was Billiges, Margarineschmalz. Ich dachte, für die Kunst tut's das allemal. Aber Beuys reklamierte, und ich musste das gegen richtige Frühstücksmargarine umtauschen. Damit war er dann zufrieden, und ich durfte zusammen mit einem anderen Ferienjobber einer exklusiven Veranstaltung – nur für uns beide – beiwohnen, sozusagen einer nicht-öffentlichen Aktion, richtiger einer Installation, welche er im folgenden Herbst in Köln unter dem Titel *Vakuum <–> Masse* und mit viel weniger Margarine wiederholte. Beuys kauerte auf dem Boden und formte große Klöße aus der Margarine, Durchmesser so knapp 20 cm. In jeden fertigen Kloß steckte er eine Luftpumpe, schraubte die obere Kappe ab, zog den Holzgriff mitsamt Stiel und Kolben ab, warf diesen hinter sich und warf den Kloß mit der Pumpenhülse längs durch den Raum an die gegenüberliegende Wand auf den großen gusseisernen Heizkörper unter dem wandfüllenden Fenster. Dort sammelte sich nach und nach ein beträchtlicher Haufen von dem Zeug an. Die Wand, das Parkett waren völlig versaut. Die Öffentlichkeit regte sich später, während der Ausstellung, enorm auf. Kritische Nürnberger steckten Zahnstocher mit aus der Zeitung ausgeschnittenen Biafra-Hungerkindern in die Margarineklöße. Und ich war vollkommen von den Socken.

M.E.: Das war für dich so was wie die Wandgeschichte auf den Punkt gebracht. Die Frage „Was ist Kunst?" sozusagen. Dass über Euch entschieden wird: Sind das nun Rabauken oder wie oder was? Ihr hattet ja alles erreicht, was man mit einer Aktion zu der Zeit erreichen konnte. Damit wart Ihr schon ziemlich weit.

P.A.: Damit waren wir voll im Avantgardismus angekommen. Und ich beschränkte mich bald nicht länger auf das Medium Malerei, sondern spielte auch mit anderen Möglichkeiten. Ich gönnte mir den erweiterten Kunstbegriff.

he struck me as impressive. Less from the stuff he said than from his blustering presence. Afterwards I asked him straight out whether he would take me into his class, and he said: I should turn up with a portfolio. It wasn't a problem getting accepted because Beuys took everyone who wanted to be with him. But later when I presented my portfolio in Düsseldorf I was really proud of course when he praised my work to the skies and I thought, it's just a matter of months now before I am world famous.

At first everything was also quite harmonious. The shattering objects and nested containers – boxes, bottles, sacks and barrels with structured and more or less correct tables of contents which I had done while still in Nuremberg – fitted the scene perfectly. I carried on here with this kind of fluxusy stuff: I cast milestones in concrete with some numbers or other on them and placed them along the roadside in the lower Rhineland, or a small cupboard with a glass door and closed with a padlock, and lying inside you could see the key, or all sorts of devious objects with light bulbs and devilish circuitry, sockets with plugs and four metres of abruptly severed wire … simply Conceptual stuff, of the sort that always distinguished the academic mainstream, the standard curator kitsch. One way or another these works had very often a revealing connection with denial, as for instance my designs for sight screens.

M.E.: That in fact was all in line with the professor's ideas. In that way you were the classic Beuys student.

P.A.: Which is why I absolutely had to go there. I felt at home. Naturally I continued to draw, but more conceptually. Such as – I'll have to describe that, but Conceptual art is in any case best when it's simply description! – such as a painting book for children. But instead of filling in the blank white spaces, like you're supposed to, I painted over the coloured areas with white. Ha ha.

M.E.: Were there others there who'd come along from Nuremberg?

P.A.: Yes, a number. 1968 saw a real exodus from the Nuremberg academy. Although we had warded off the worst after the refectory wall painting and the hearing, not many of us saw much of a future any more in Nuremberg. The majority went to Düsseldorf, such as the head of our student committee, Johannes Munker, and Günter Sieber. Others went to Munich or Berlin. So there I was in Düsseldorf, happy and full of hope with my totally naive expectation that if you're good, it's only a question of months before one is recognised and famous. And that I was good – Beuys in person had testified to that repeatedly, without any closer reason … until I couldn't hear it any more.

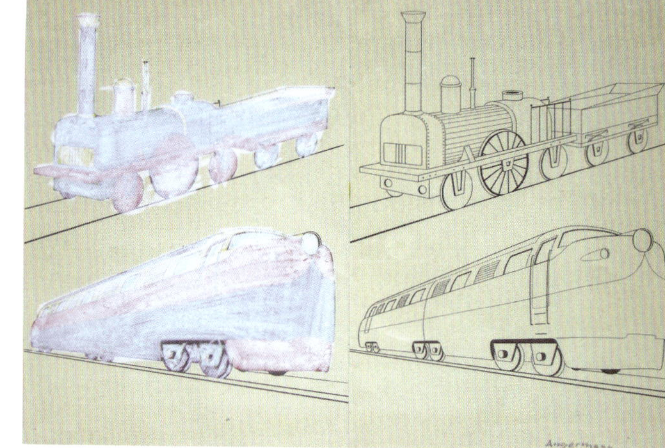

Aus „Malbuch" / From "Painting Book", 1969

M.E.: Was there any idea there about how one was supposed to get a career going?

M.E.: Die Margarine von Beuys war da noch ein Schritt weiter: weg
von irgendeinem expressionistischen Strich, weg von der Wandma-
lerei, eine große Sauerei anrichten und auf individuellen Stil mehr
oder weniger verzichten.

P.A.: Das war die radikale Emanzipation der Kunst, was
Beuys da vorführte.

M.E.: In dem Moment, als du das mit den Klößen gesehen hast, war
das für dich die Meisterschaft auf dem Gebiet, das dir vorschwebte?

P.A.: Unbedingt. Und dazu muss ich noch sagen, Beuys war
ein unglaublich charismatischer Typ. Schon bei dieser Mensa-
wandgeschichte, als er sofort seinen Platz auf dem Klavier
gefunden hat, kam er beeindruckend rüber. Weniger durch

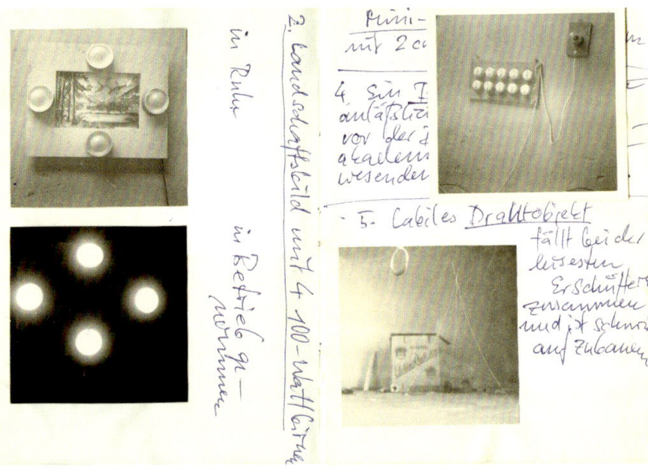

Fluxusobjekte / Fluxus Objects, 1968, Montage / montage, diverse Maße /
various dimensions

das Zeug, das er so von sich gab, als durch seine dröhnende Präsenz. Ich fragte ihn
danach auch direkt, ob er mich in seine Klasse aufnehmen würde, und er: Ich solle mal
mit einer Mappe anrücken. Ein Problem war es ja nicht, aufgenommen zu werden, denn
Beuys nahm alle auf, die zu ihm wollten. Aber als ich ihm dann später in Düsseldorf
meine Mappe vorlegte, war ich natürlich mächtig stolz, wie er meine Arbeit über den
grünen Klee lobte, und ich dachte, jetzt ist es nur noch eine Frage von Monaten, bis auch
ich weltberühmt bin.

Anfangs lief das auch alles ganz harmonisch. Die Zertrümmerungsobjekte und
verschachtelten Behälter – Schachteln, Flaschen, Säcke und Fässer mit gegliederten
und mehr oder weniger korrekten Inhaltsangaben – die ich noch in Nürnberg gemacht
hatte, passten hier voll in die Landschaft. Mit solchem fluxusartigen Zeug machte ich
hier weiter: Ich goss Kilometersteine aus Beton mit irgendwelchen Zahlen versehen
und platzierte sie an niederrheinischen Straßenrändern, oder ein Schränkchen
mit Glastür und mit Vorhängeschloss verschlossen, und im Inneren sah man den
Schlüssel liegen, oder tückische Objekte aller Art mit Glühbirnen und schikanösen
Schaltungen, Steckdosen mit Steckern und vier Metern abrupt gekapptem Kabel … halt
konzeptionelles Zeug, wie es nach wie vor den akademischen Mainstream ausmacht, den
üblichen Kuratorenkitsch. Sehr oft und bezeichnenderweise hatten diese Werke auf die
eine oder andere Art mit Verweigerung zu tun, meine Entwürfe von Sichtblenden etwa.

M.E.: Das war ja eigentlich alles im Sinne vom Professor. Damit warst du doch der
klassische Beuys-Student.

P.A.: Deshalb musste ich doch unbedingt dorthin. Da fühlte ich mich zu Hause.
Gezeichnet hab ich natürlich auch weiterhin, halt eher konzeptionell. Etwa – ich muss
das beschreiben, aber Konzeptkunst ist als schiere Beschreibung eh am besten! – ein
Malbuch für Kinder. Aber ich füllte nicht, wie's sich gehört, die weiß gelassene Seite
farbig, sondern übermalte die bunte mit Weiß. Haha.

P.A.: In my case none whatsoever! Quite unlike present-day students, the majority of us hadn't a clue about the art market and not even a distant interest. Career-mindedness was not simply regarded as dubious but actually as ridiculous and pathetic. Initially the 1968 generation genuinely thought that way, or that at least was the consensus. It was a cool basis that was as naive as it was wonderful. There were exceptions, of course. They were the first to become famous. But my naivety in this area was absolutely the norm. And so my breakthrough was slow to come, for all the enduring Beuysian praise. Slowly I got impatient and wanted to have it spelt out. So I also presented him with weak pieces at a crit, the kind you normally prefer to leave out. He liked them as well. So I had to turn out some real rubbish, arrant nonsense. Like a whole series of works on various sizes of paper, each with just one horizontal line on it. Obviously he registered that, but once again he liked it. In this way he studiously allowed me to get nowhere. To the vacuousness of the extended concept of art. In the moment when this man's colossal charisma became commonplace, the content he actually should have conveyed would have been all the more important. But there wasn't any teaching behind it in the time-honoured sense. And especially not for a painter like me.

M.E.: But couldn't you see how he made his money, apart that is from his wages as a professor? Didn't he explain it, or couldn't you see how?

P.A.: Obviously his success didn't simply come from his ability to smear margarine in the corner and amaze people like me. That wouldn't have been enough. No, what was more important over and beyond that was the way he really provoked the public, what the "elite" deem to be idiots. He was artistic arrogance personified in the way he mocked popular tastes and aesthetic habits. There was nothing actually unusual in that, because artists often like to try and play that tune, then as now. But Beuys was simply the best at it and kept on prodding his audience. Public opinion was at boiling point and he never missed a chance to place himself in the limelight. Thanks to his phenomenal presence of mind, he was quick to see his chances and exploit them. He was very clear about the effect he had on people. If you consider that to be art, he was really terrific.

M.E.: I can believe it. But for you he appeared the moment you were staging a rebellion. And then lo and behold: he knew better than you how to work a rebellion. So weren't you able then as a student to see how you could likewise earn your crust through rebellion? Or didn't that interest you in any way?

P.A.: Once again, and whether you believe it or not: that scarcely interested me. That as I said was the mood of the times. We were so naive and idealistic, and it also didn't seem to play any role for Beuys. Basically we were all just hippies, primal communistic romantics who were free of jealousy, free of greed and envy, or so we believed. And having a career didn't mean getting rich, at most as a side effect, but piling up fame and glory. And anyone who was less naive than that tried not to show it.

M.E.: Sind da noch weitere Leute mit hin von Nürnberg?

P.A.: Ja, einige. '68 gab es einen richtigen Auszug aus der Nürnberger Akademie. Nach dieser Mensawandbemalung und dem Hearing hatten wir zwar Schlimmeres abgewendet, aber so richtig sahen die wenigsten von uns da noch eine Zukunft. Die meisten gingen nach Düsseldorf, etwa unser AStA-Chef Johannes Munker oder Günter Sieber. Andere gingen nach München oder Berlin. Da war ich nun also in Düsseldorf, glücklich und hoffnungsvoll mit meinen völlig naiven Vorstellungen, dass, wenn man gut ist, es nur eine Frage von Monaten sei, bis man anerkannt und berühmt ist. Und dass ich gut war, hat mir Beuys höchstselbst und ohne nähere Begründung wiederholt bescheinigt, bis ich es nicht mehr hören konnte.

M.E.: Gab es da eine Vorstellung, wie es funktionieren soll mit der Karriere?

P.A.: Bei mir überhaupt nicht! Ganz anders als heutige Studenten hatten die meisten von uns keinen Schimmer vom Kunstmarkt und auch nur distanziertes Interesse. Karrieredenken war nicht nur suspekt, sondern es galt als lächerlich und erbärmlich. Anfangs tickten die Achtundsechziger tatsächlich so, jedenfalls war das der Konsens. Es war eine ebenso naive wie wunderbar coole Basis. Natürlich gab's Ausnahmen. Die wurden als Erste berühmt. Aber meine Naivität auf diesem Gebiet war absolut der Normalfall. Und so ließ der Durchbruch auf sich warten, trotz anhaltenden Beuys'schen Lobs. Ich wurde langsam ungeduldig und wollte es genauer wissen. So legte ich ihm zur Korrektur dann auch die schwachen Arbeiten vor, solche, die man normalerweise lieber aussortiert. Die fand er auch noch gut. Also musste ich gezielt Mist verzapfen, offensichtlichen Blödsinn. Etwa eine ganze Serie Papierarbeiten unterschiedlichsten Formats mit jeweils nur einer waagrechten Linie darauf. Das bemerkte er dann natürlich und fand auch das wieder gut. So ließ er mich gepflegt ins Leere laufen. In die Leere des erweiterten Kunstbegriffs. In dem Moment, wo das kolossale Charisma dieses Menschen alltäglich wurde, wäre das, was er inhaltlich zu bieten gehabt hätte, umso wichtiger geworden. Im althergebrachten Sinn einer Lehre war da aber nichts. Schon gar nicht für einen Maler wie mich.

M.E.: Aber konnte man nicht sehen, wie kommt der, abgesehen von seinem Professorengehalt, ans Geld ran? Hat er das nicht dargelegt, oder konnte man das nicht abgucken?

P.A.: Natürlich kam sein Erfolg nicht einfach daher, dass er so schön Margarine in die Ecke schmieren konnte und Leute wie mich damit beeindruckte. Das hätte nicht gereicht. Nein, wichtiger war, dass er darüber hinaus die Allgemeinheit, aus Sicht der „Elite" also die Deppen, ungeheuer provozierte. Er war die personifizierte künstlerische Arroganz, wie er jedweden gängigen Geschmacksmustern und ästhetischen Gewohnheiten spottete. Das war eigentlich nichts Ungewöhnliches, denn Künstler versuchen oft und gern und nach wie vor, auf diesem Klavier zu spielen. Aber Beuys

M.E.: Okay. But then I don't understand your point about being dissatisfied.

P.A.: I was unable to pile up fame and glory, despite Beuys's praise. He didn't really have anything to say to me. And once again my work was going round in circles. In form and content. Where was I to find a foothold in the extended concept of art? At first it's refreshing and a weight off of you when there are no more binding formal criteria to abide by. But the moment after that you see that it's all complete garbage. Because as ever, a concept is only as useful as it is precise and clearly delineated and not woolly. And at that point Beuys simply brought his own subjective taste to bear, which of course we are all free to do, and on top of that his sheer power of suggestion.

M.E.: So at some time or other you were at this point where you weren't making any headway and essentially were rebelling against the rebellion.

P.A.: You could put it like that. From then on it started to get interesting again. It was called the YIUP group: Robert Hartmann, Hans Rogalla, Hans Heiniger, Hans Henin and me. A bad boys club dominated by southern Germans. First off we were sick to the teeth with the sectarian feel to the Beuys class. We enjoyed mocking the guru with his disciples. For that we had only to turn the typical arrogance of the class in on itself. We annexed Room 13, a studio for the Beuys class, and taunted everyone and everything with brazen cheek. A fiendish delight, which immediately got out of hand and paradoxically earned us a great deal of unmerited respect. Because there's scarcely anyone who likes having the piss taken out of them more than the big shots of contemporary art. That's just what they want! And after all, the extended concept of art includes that!

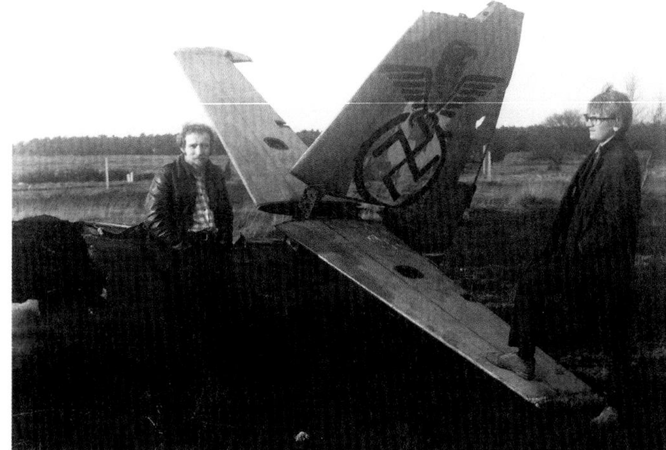

Abschuss, 1970, Peter Angermann mit / with Hans Rogalla

M.E.: The wicked inversion or mirroring of what Beuys was offering.

P.A.: Mostly our actions were in fact mean tricks, at best harmless pranks like climbing the east face of the academy in winter or purloining Beuys's hat. But our hallmarks were dirty deeds done with relish and an ostentatious display of malice.

M.E.: That went almost in the direction of terror.

P.A.: We were not far short of that. And it was luck alone that not only were we madcaps and totally unpredictable, but that the real hard-core politicos saw it exactly the same and didn't have any great interest in the academy. Otherwise it could have had fatal consequences, because we were quite ready to use violence back then.

konnte es halt am besten, und immer gab er dem Affen wieder Zucker. Die öffentliche
Meinung kochte hoch, und er ließ keine Gelegenheit aus, sich in Szene zu setzen. Mit
seiner sagenhaften Geistesgegenwart erkannte er schnell seine Chancen und nutzte sie
entsprechend. Er war sich sehr im Klaren über seine Wirkung. Wenn man das schon
für Kunst hält, war er wirklich toll.

M.E.: Das glaube ich. Aber für dich war er aufgetaucht in einem Moment, wo du Revolte machtest. Und dann siehst du: Der hat's noch besser drauf, wie Revolte funktioniert.
War es da für dich als Student nicht möglich zu sehen: Wie verdiene
auch ich mit der Revolte Kohle? Oder hat dich das überhaupt nicht
interessiert?

    P.A.: Noch mal, und ob du's nun glaubst oder nicht: Das
hat mich wirklich kaum interessiert. So war wie gesagt der
Zeitgeist. Wir waren derart naiv und idealistisch, und auch
für Beuys schien das keine Rolle zu spielen. Wir waren
eigentlich alle noch Hippies, urkommunistische Romantiker,
die keine Eifersucht kennen, keinen Neid und keine Habgier,
daran glaubten wir. Und Karriere machen hieß nicht, reich zu
werden, höchstens als Nebeneffekt, sondern es hieß, Ruhm
und Ehre auf sich zu häufen. Und wer weniger naiv war, ließ
sich das möglichst nicht anmerken.

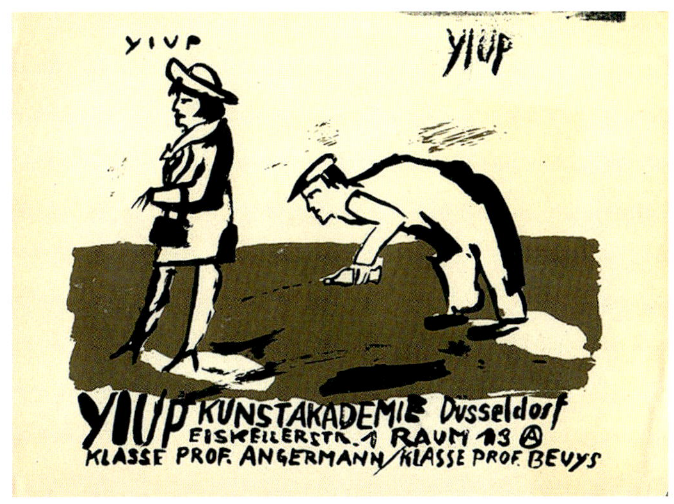

YIUP: Spritz! / YIUP: Splash!, 1970, Siebdruck auf Papier / silk screen on paper

M.E.: Okay. Aber diesen Punkt der Unzufriedenheit verstehe ich dann nicht.

    P.A.: Ruhm und Ehre mochten sich bei mir trotz Beuys' Lob nicht häufen. Er hatte
mir nicht wirklich was zu sagen. Und ich bin wieder auf der Stelle getreten mit meinen
Sachen. Inhaltlich und formal. Wo wäre da ein Ankerpunkt im erweiterten Kunstbegriff? Anfangs ist das erfrischend und entlastend, wenn eigentlich keine verbindlichen
formalen Kriterien mehr gelten. Aber im nächsten Moment zeigt sich, dass das völliger
Quatsch ist. Denn nach wie vor ist ein Begriff umso brauchbarer, je enger er gefasst ist,
je präziser und je weniger schwammig. Und Beuys setzte halt an diese Stelle einfach
seinen eigenen subjektiven Geschmack, was natürlich jedem frei steht, und dazu seine
pure Suggestivkraft.

M.E.: Dann bist du also irgendwann mal an dem Punkt, wo du nicht mehr weiter-
kommst, und rebellierst letztendlich gegen die Rebellion.

    P.A.: So kann man sagen. Von da an wurde es wieder interessanter. Das nannte sich
dann YIUP-Gruppe: Robert Hartmann, Hans Rogalla, Hans Heiniger, Hans Henin
und ich. Ein süddeutsch dominierter Böse-Buben-Club. Als Erstes ging uns das Sek-
tenhafte der Beuys-Klasse auf den Geist. Wir fanden Gefallen daran, den Guru und
seine Jünger vorzuführen. Dazu brauchten wir nur die klassentypische Arroganz nach

M.E.: Did the YIUP group allow you to rise up from your torpor and new developments to occur, or did it all just remain a cynical reaction?

P.A.: The result was a mixture of sobering up and isolation. We had bought ourselves respect at the price of our hope that art could be of some conceivable use today and still have some meaning. On the contrary: as was evident and experiments proved, it was the purest nonsense, just contemptuous deceptions and a vainglorious hoo-ha. I wondered: has everyone gone completely round the bend or something? Instead of smashing us in the gob they're cheering us on! We're dealing with a bunch of masochists! That was the bottom line at the end of my academic training in 1971.

M.E.: At which point you really had reached the end of the line.

P.A.: Absolutely. With that art was passé, done with, over and gone, so after college I turned my back on it completely. Concentrated once again on physics and epistemology, where I like to think I contributed a rather nice idea. I remained abstemious as an artist, and only Robert Crumb of all my contemporaries delivered what I still hoped for from art.

This complete rejection of art was necessary in order that almost two years later, in the middle of 1973, I could slip out of my cocoon, freshly in love, and start all over again. I listened to Led Zeppelin, had a stack of smooth, slippery DIN A1 sheets and a set of the cheapest felt-tip pens lying around, and mundane sentimentalities in my brain. This mixture soon took off and art had me back in its clutches.

Meeting Milan Kunc did the rest. Each of us discovered in the other's work precisely what was missing in his own. From my viewpoint: thanks to his background at the Prague academy he was doing something that was quite unthinkable for me, something that was completely sneered at by Western art at that time, something not even the YIUP group would think of: he opened himself up to beauty and decoration, without any compunction and without using irony as a pretext, without the slightest fears of pandering to kitsch. It was the pure opposite of what I would have thought of as promising. But I saw that not only had it an unexpected potential for provocation but that simultaneously it fulfilled the fading promises of Pop art as well as of the 1968 romanticists in quite a surprising way: painting could be approachable instead of being elitist in a West-art way. Art for the people, and against the art pussies (to use Dan Reeder's delightful expression)! A kind of premature GDR nostalgia.

He by turn was taken quite similarly by my aggressive pieces, and we at once started to work together like people possessed. We were convinced that we were creating nothing less than the art of the future! And this euphoria captivated others – the "Sohnstrasse scene", Martin Figuli, who egged us on, and Jan Knap – and developed years later into the group NORMAL, right in time for the New Fauves boom.

The formats got larger. At first only on wrapping paper, all manner of comedies and tragedies, stories and tripe. Then Martin Figuli felt that this cheap material was no

innen zu kehren. Wir annektierten den Raum 13, ein Atelier der Beuys-Klasse, und piesackten von dort aus maximal unverschämt alles und jeden. Es war ein höllisches Vergnügen, lief von Anfang an aus dem Ruder und brachte uns paradoxerweise eine Menge unverdienten Respekts ein. Kaum jemand lässt sich nämlich lieber verarschen als die zeitgenössische Kunstkaste. Die will das so! Und so was ist im erweiterten Kunstbegriff schließlich eh inbegriffen!

M.E.: Die bösartige Umkehrung oder Spiegelung dessen, was Beuys ja auch bot.

P.A.: Unsere Aktionen waren eigentlich meist Schweinereien, im besten Fall so harmlose Scherze wie die Akademie-Ostwandbesteigung im Winter oder die Beuyshut-Entwendung. Aber genussvoll inszenierte Gemeinheiten und ostentativ zur Schau gestellte Niedertracht waren unser Markenzeichen.

M.E.: Das ging ja fast schon in Richtung Terror.

P.A.: Da hätte nicht mehr viel gefehlt. Und es war nur ein Glück, dass wir einerseits viel zu unberechenbare Spinner waren und andererseits die richtig harte Politszene das ganz genau so sah und an der Kunstakademie gar kein großes Interesse hatte. Das hätte sonst auch fatal enden können, denn wir waren damals durchaus gewaltbereit.

M.E.: Hatte die Gruppe YIUP denn den Effekt, dass du wieder aus der Erstarrung rauskamst, dass eine Weiterentwicklung möglich wurde, oder blieb das nur ein zynischer Reflex?

P.A.: Das Ergebnis waren Ernüchterung und Einsamkeit. Wir hatten uns Respekt verschafft auf Kosten der Hoffnung, Kunst könnte heute zu irgendwas gut sein, könnte noch irgendeinen Sinn haben. Im Gegenteil: Offensichtlich und nunmehr experimentell bewiesen handelte es sich um reinen Unfug, um würdeloses Blendwerk und eitles Getue. Ich dachte mir: Sind die jetzt alle bescheuert um uns herum oder was? Statt uns aufs Maul zu hauen applaudieren sie uns auch noch! Wir haben es mit einer Horde Masochisten zu tun! Das war 1971 das Fazit meiner akademischen Ausbildung.

M.E.: Damit war ja wirklich ein Endpunkt erreicht.

P.A.: Absolut. Die Kunst war damit für mich passé, abgehakt, aus und vorbei, und ich wendete mich nach meinem Studium völlig von ihr ab. Ich widmete mich wieder der Physik und der Erkenntnistheorie, wo ich glaube, noch eine schöne Idee beizutragen zu haben. Künstlerisch blieb ich abstinent, und von den Zeitgenossen konnte nur Robert Crumb einlösen, was ich mir noch von Kunst versprach.

Diese völlige Abkehr von der Kunst war nötig, damit ich fast zwei Jahre später, Mitte 1973, frisch verliebt dem Kokon entschlüpfen und von Grund auf neu anfangen konnte. Ich hörte Led Zeppelin, hatte einen Stapel glitschig glatte DIN-A1-Bögen und

longer good enough and turned one of Jan Knap's canvases
round on its stretcher – one of the "Big Abstract Expressionist Paintings" à la de Kooning, but done in earth pigments
like the old masters – which he had left behind when he
emigrated to America. I painted *Crime Scene*[1] (1973, p. 47)
on it. I had found my thing.

M.E.: After the emptiness that engulfed you after Beuys, there were
two possibilities: on the one hand the possibility of terror, or as we
see – and I am putting this now in quotes – "the conservative direction": a return to painting and the abandonment of the extended
concept of art. But isn't it no less possible that you could have struck
success earlier on, while still on the road to this? That you caught
for instance the attention of a gallerist who said: "Your milestones!
They're fantastic!"?

P.A.: (Laughs) That's what I would have wished for back
then! Hard to tell what would have become of me. Perhaps I
would have become one of these mainstream nerds with my
black light bulbs and shattering objects. Thankfully I've been
spared that!

M.E.: But one can still say that you have remained faithful to the concept you all developed back then.

P.A.: One can. The artistic strategy pursued by NORMAL, undermining orthodox
avant-gardism by means of serious craftsmanship and conscious simplicity, continues
to be as productive as ever. And even if I am no longer particularly interested these days
in provocation: my anti-avant-garde defiance continues to lend me wing. I thank it for
instance for the wonderful rediscovery of en plein air painting! At first it was just a gag
which I indulged in with Peter Hammer in summer 1987. Setting up my field easel
like the housewives do on a painting course run by an adult-education centre. But it
soon turned out to be one of the most important steps in my career. Prior to that I had
scarcely a clue about paint. And now I have become more and more of a colourist, even if
that probably doesn't say much to people nowadays.

M.E.: What may happen, of course, is that the applause starts to come from the wrong
side. That people say: oooh, he's painting our church, our Bavarian skies …

P.A.: That's true, the danger of being taken up by the petty bourgeoisie cannot be
overlooked. Even if by a kind of petty bourgeoisie that you're more likely to find now in
an old folks' home. I can live with that. By contrast, the modern philistine knows what
one is supposed to have, what is hanging in the museums and what not, and he prefers

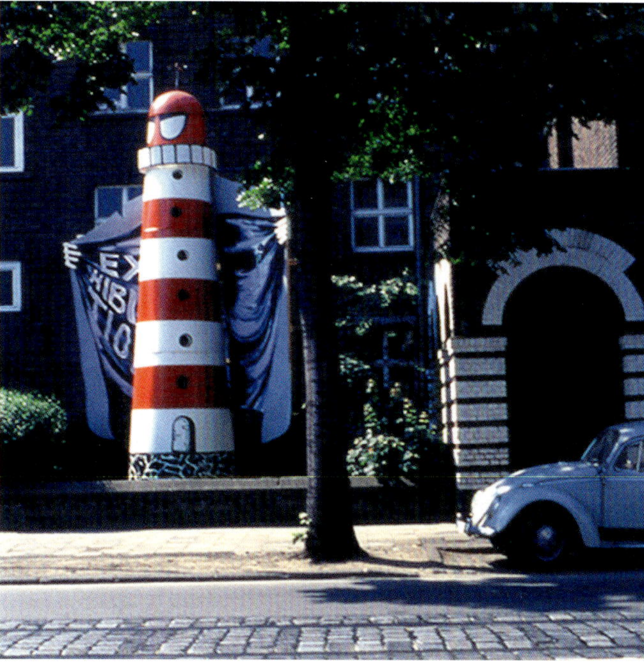

Display für / for *Exhibition*, Grafenberger Allee, Düsseldorf, 1978, Hartfaser,
Holz, Dispersion / hardboard, wood, dispersion, Höhe / height 7 m

einen Satz billigste Filzstifte rumliegen und alltägliche Sentimentalitäten im Kopf. Dieses Gemenge zündete, und die Kunst hatte mich wieder.

Das Zusammentreffen mit Milan Kunc tat dann ein Übriges. Wir fanden gegenseitig in der Arbeit des anderen genau das, was jeweils unserer eigenen Arbeit fehlte. Aus meiner Sicht: Er machte dank seiner Herkunft von der Prager Akademie etwas, was für mich völlig undenkbar schien, etwas in der Westkunst damals absolut Verpöntes, etwas, das selbst der YIUP-Gruppe nicht in den Sinn kam: Er ließ sich bedenkenlos und ohne Ironie vorzuschützen auf Schönheit und Dekoration ein, ohne die geringste Berührungsangst mit dem Kitsch. Es war das buchstäblich glatte Gegenteil dessen, was ich für vielversprechend gehalten hätte. Aber ich sah einerseits ein unerwartetes Provokationspotenzial darin und gleichzeitig die welkenden Versprechen der Pop-Art ebenso wie die der Achtundsechziger-Romantik auf überraschende Weise einlösbar: dass Malerei anschlussfähig sein darf statt westkunstmäßig elitär. Kunst fürs Volk und gegen die Art Pussies (Dan Reeders reizender Ausdruck)! Eine Art vorzeitige Ostalgie.

Ihm ging's umgekehrt mit meinen alten agressiven Sachen irgendwie ähnlich, und wir fingen sofort an, wie besessen zusammenzuarbeiten. Wir waren überzeugt, dass wir jetzt nichts Geringeres als die Kunst der Zukunft schufen! Und diese Euphorie riss noch andere mit: Die „Sohnstraßenszene", Martin Figuli, den Einheizer, und Jan Knap, und sie mündete Jahre später in die Gruppe NORMAL, rechtzeitig zum Neue-Wilde-Boom.

Die Formate wurden größer. Erst nur auf Packpapier, Kommödien und Tragödien aller Art, Geschichten und Blödsinn. Dann fand Martin Figuli dieses billige Material nicht mehr adäquat und spannte eine von Jan Knaps Leinwänden um, eines der „Big Abstract Expressionist Paintings" à la de Kooning, aber in altmeisterlichen Erdfarben, die der vor seiner Auswanderung nach Amerika zurückgelassen hatte. Ich malte darauf den *Tatort* (1973, S. 47). Ich hatte mein Ding gefunden.

M.E.: Nach dieser Leere, die bei dir nach Beuys auftauchte, hätte es also zwei Möglichkeiten gegeben: einmal die Möglichkeit des Terrors, oder eben, ich nenne es mal in Anführungsstrichen, „Die konservative Richtung": Man malt jetzt wieder und wendet sich von diesem erweiterten Kunstbegriff ab. Aber hätte es nicht auch sein können, dass schon früher, auf dem Weg dahin, sich plötzlich der Erfolg eingestellt hätte? Dass zum Beispiel ein Galerist auf dich aufmerksam geworden wäre und gesagt hätte: „Deine Kilometersteine, die sind ja großartig!"

P.A.: (Lacht) So hätte ich mir das ja damals gewünscht! Schwer zu sagen, was dann mit mir passiert wäre. Vielleicht wäre aus mir eben auch irgend so ein Mainstream-Fuzzi geworden mit meinen schwarzen Glühbirnen und Zertrümmerungsobjekten. Zum Glück ist mir das erspart geblieben!

cooler clichés. My plein-air paintings are not up his street. But the seemingly retrograde nature of my counter-position to avant-gardism can clearly lead to misunderstandings. My old YIUP friend Robert Hartmann coined a label for the group NORMAL that was as ingenious as it was perfidious: the "Neo-Nazarenes". The sky over Bavaria is nevertheless beautiful. And fortunately the art scene isn't quite the hopeless case it seemed to be at the end of my studies.

But the applause from the wrong side, however tiresome it may be, is no more of a hindrance to me than the knee-jerk reactions of the art know-alls. Ultimately their pig-headedness and instant flush of indignation at my presumptuousness have always inspired me and spurred me on.

M.E.: So one way or the other you need the art pussies?

P.A.: The art pussies have always been a nice source of friction for me.

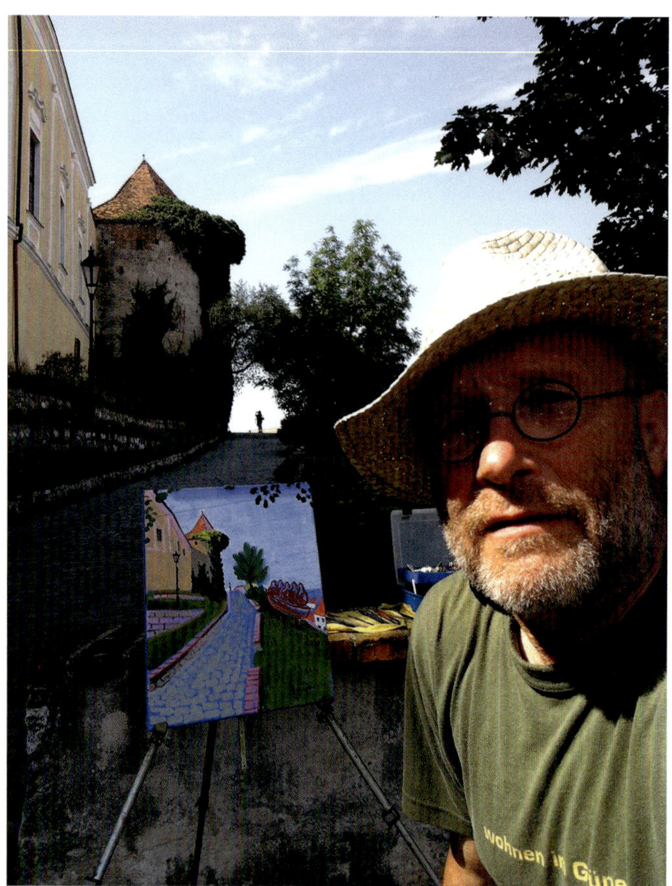

Peter Angermann vor / in front of *Mikulov 4*, 2012

---

¹ The German title, *Tatort*, alludes to a popular weekly series of criminal-investigation stories on German television.

M.E.: Man kann doch sagen, dass du diesem Konzept, das Ihr damals zusammen entwickelt habt, bis heute treu geblieben bist.

P.A.: Kann man. Die künstlerische Strategie von NORMAL, durch handwerklichen Ernst und selbstbewusste Einfalt den orthodoxen Avantgardismus zu unterlaufen, gibt bis heute unvermindert was her. Und auch wenn ich heute keinen besonderen Wert mehr darauf lege, zu provozieren: Mein anti-avantgardistischer Trotz wirkt nach wie vor beflügelnd auf meine Arbeit. Ihm verdanke ich zum Beispiel die wunderbare Wiederentdeckung der Pleinairmalerei! Das war zuerst ein Gag, den ich mir zusammen mit Peter Hammer im Sommer 1987 leistete. Sich mit der Feldstaffelei rauszustellen wie die Hausfrauen im Malkurs der Volkshochschule. Es erwies sich aber schnell als einer meiner wichtigsten Entwicklungsschritte. Ich hatte vorher kaum eine Ahnung von Farbe gehabt. Seither aber werde ich mehr und mehr zum Koloristen, auch wenn das gegenwärtig vielleicht wenigen was sagt.

M.E.: Was dabei natürlich passieren kann, ist der Applaus von der falschen Seite. Dass da Leute sagen: Mensch, der malt unsere Kirche, unseren bayerischen Himmel …

P.A.: Das stimmt schon, die Gefahr, vom Spießertum vereinnahmt zu werden, ist dabei nicht von der Hand zu weisen. Wenn auch von einer Art Spießertum, das man inzwischen eher im Altersheim antrifft. Damit kann ich leben. Der moderne Spießer dagegen weiß längst, was man heute so hat, was in den Museen hängt und was nicht, und er bevorzugt coolere Klischees. Meine Pleinair-Bilder sind nichts für ihn. Doch das vermeintlich Rückwärtsgewandte meiner Gegenposition zum Avantgardismus kann schon zu Missverständnissen führen. Mein alter YIUP-Freund Robert Hartmann prägte für die Gruppe NORMAL das gleichermaßen geniale wie perfide Label „Neonazarener". Der Himmel über Bayern ist trotzdem schön. Und glücklicherweise ist ja auch die Kunstszene kein so gänzlich hoffnungsloser Fall, wie es mir damals am Ende meines Studiums erschien.

Der Applaus von der falschen Seite aber, so lästig er sein kann, ist für mich so wenig ein ernsthaftes Hemmnis wie auf der anderen Seite die reflexartigen Vorurteile der Kunstbescheidwisser. Deren Borniertheit und prompte Erhitzung angesichts meiner Zumutungen hat mich schließlich immer wieder inspiriert und angestachelt.

M.E.: Dann brauchst du die Art Pussies auf irgendeine Weise ja schon?

P.A.: Die Art Pussies waren immer eine nette Reibfläche für mich.

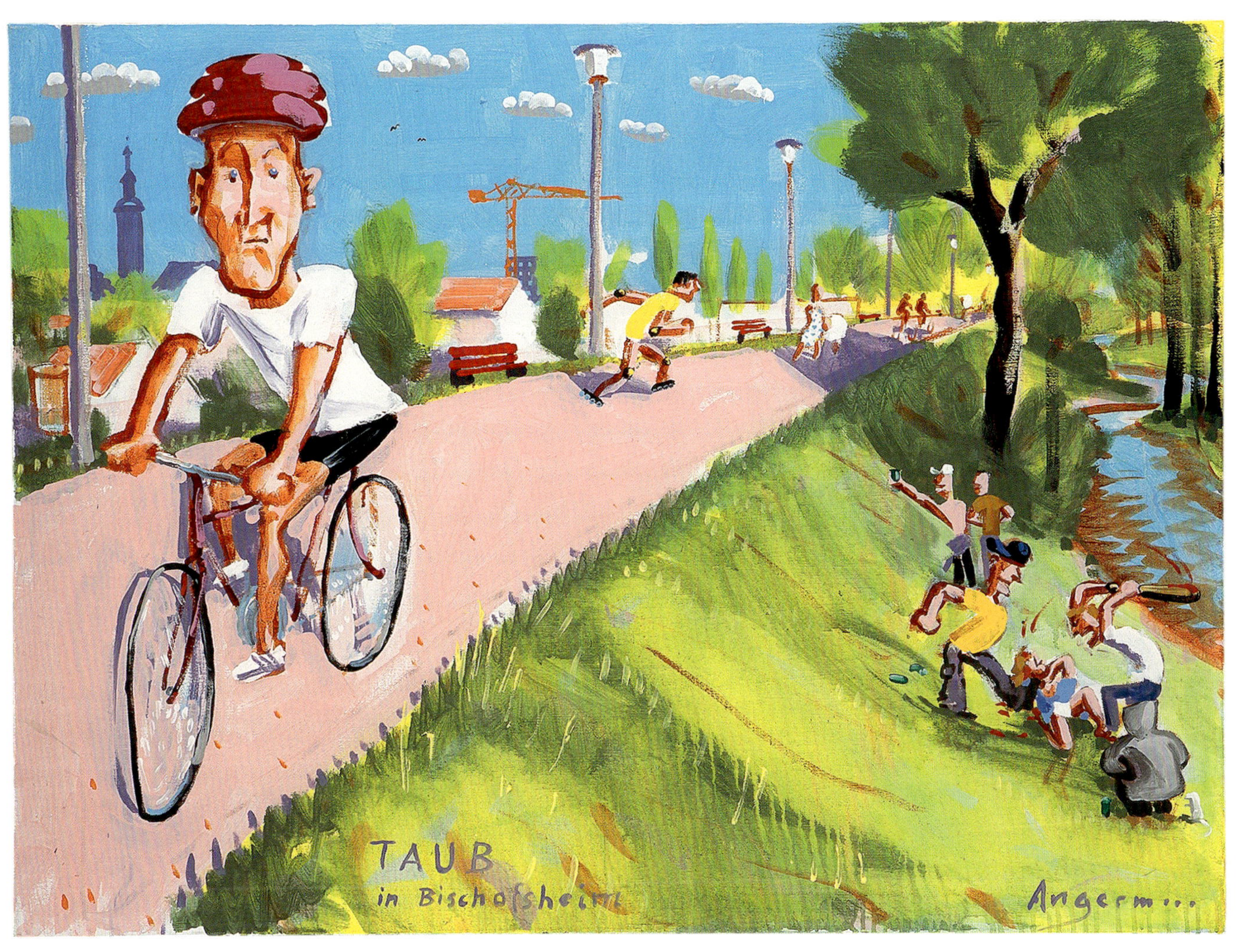

Taub in Bischofsheim / Deaf in Bischofsheim, 2007

199

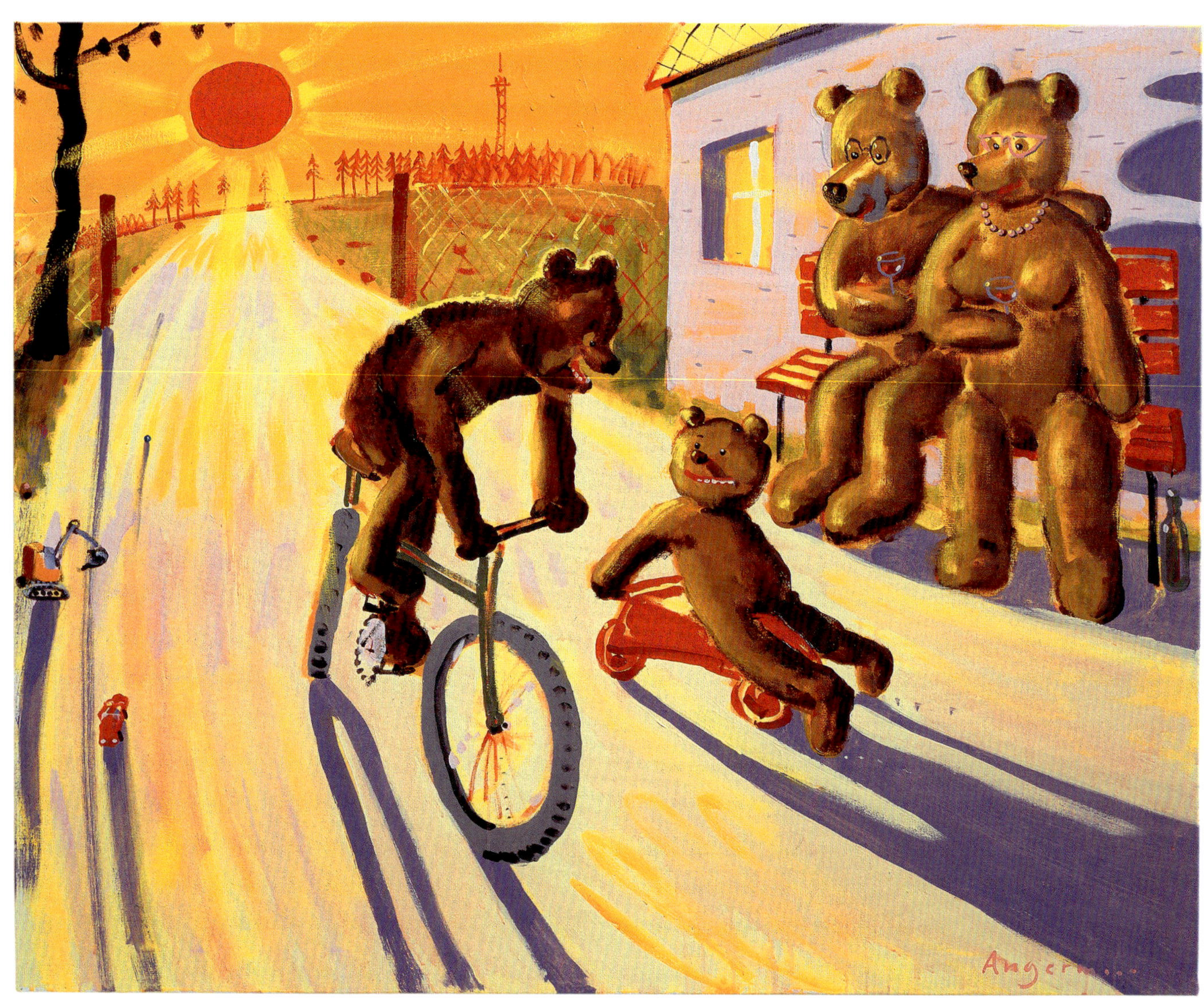

Großelternbild / Grandparents Picture, 2007

200

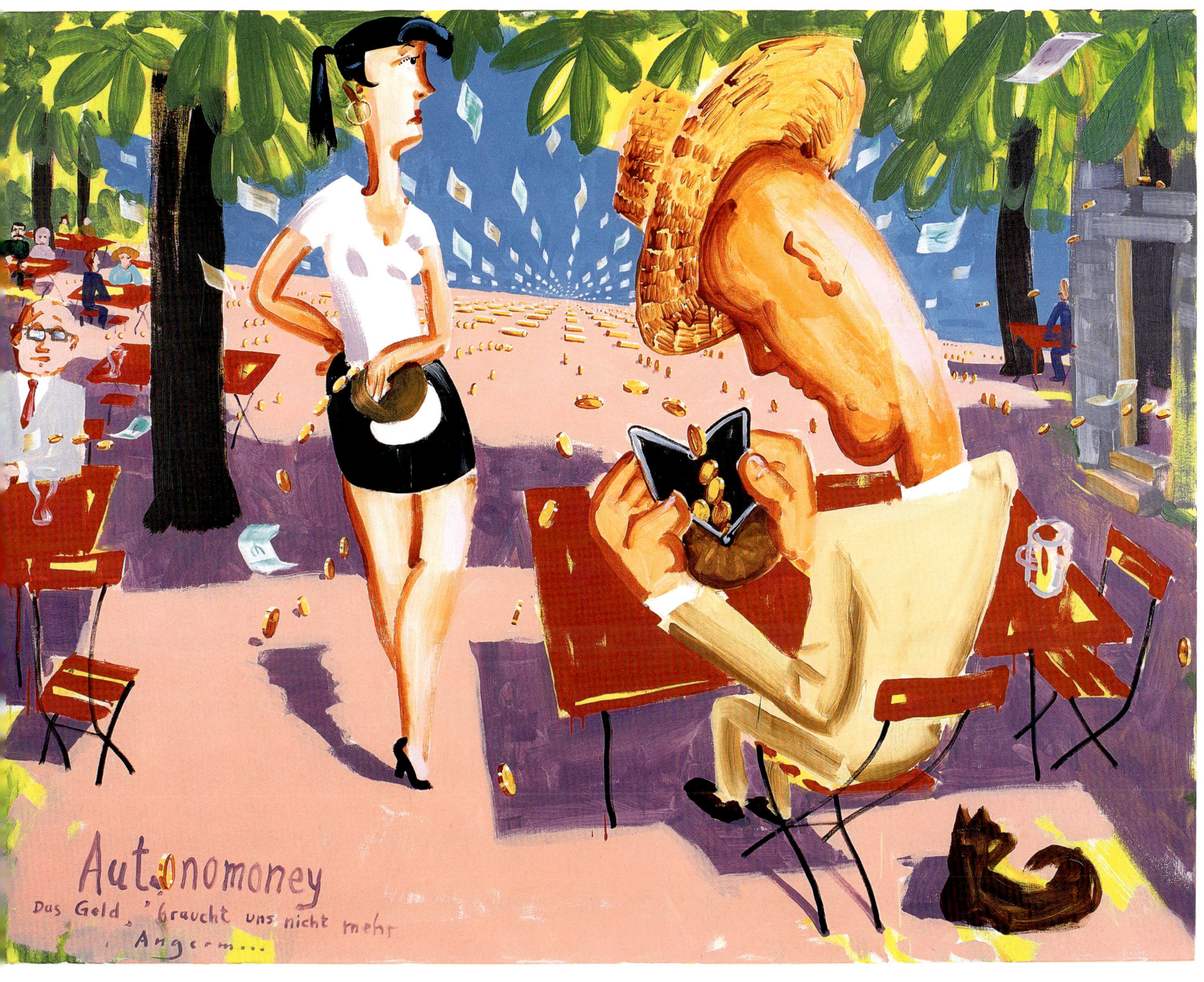

Autonomoney 2, 2007

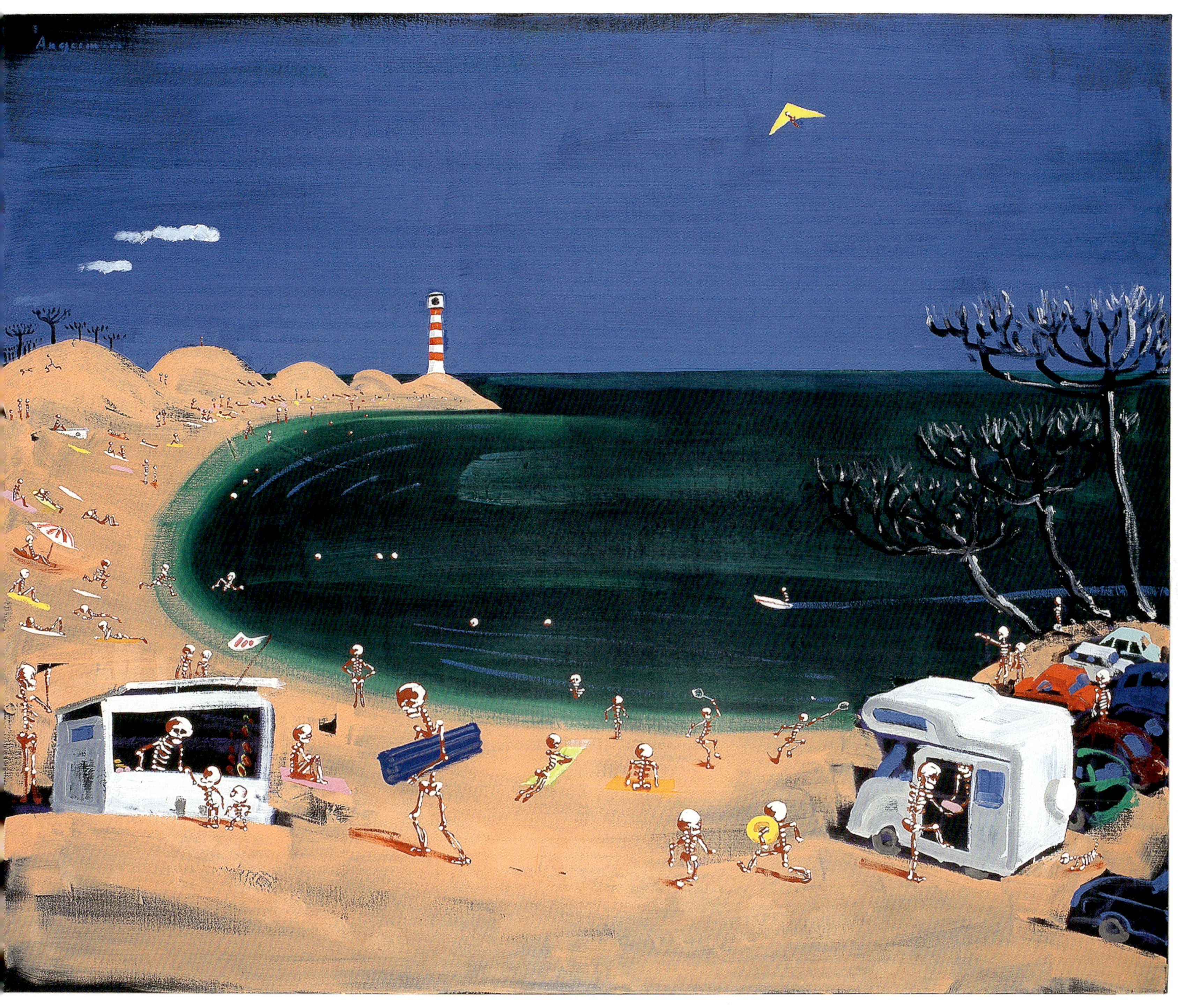

Urlaub für immer / Holiday for Ever, 2007

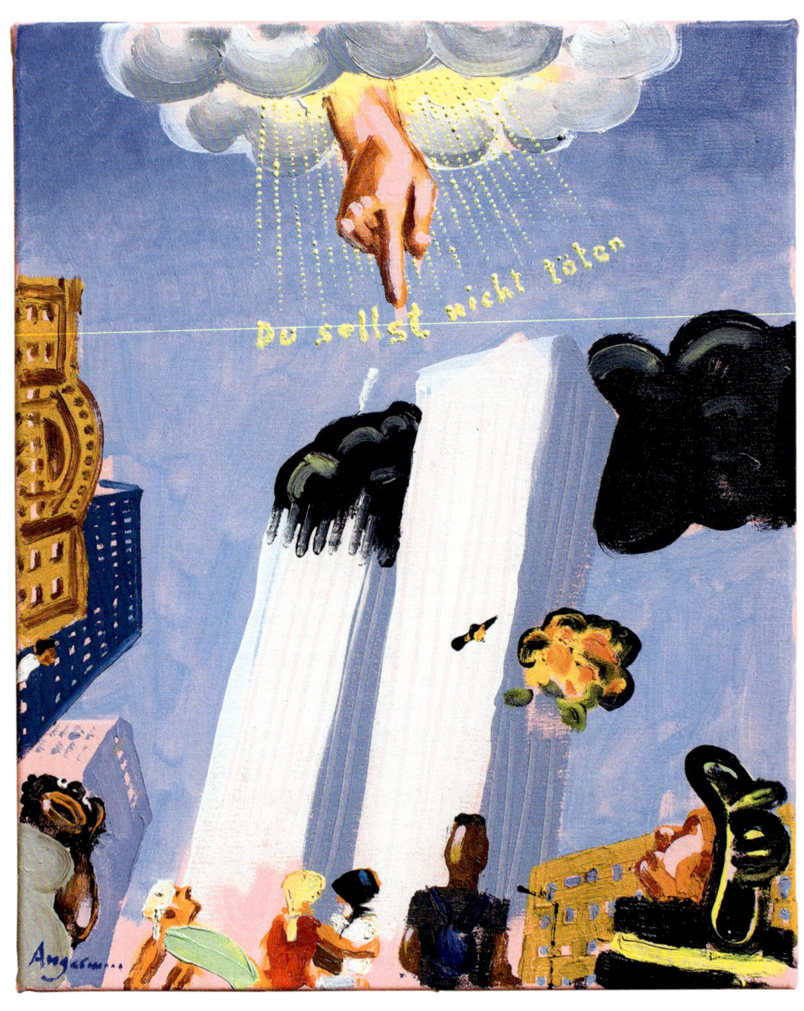

Fingerzeig / Pointer, 2001

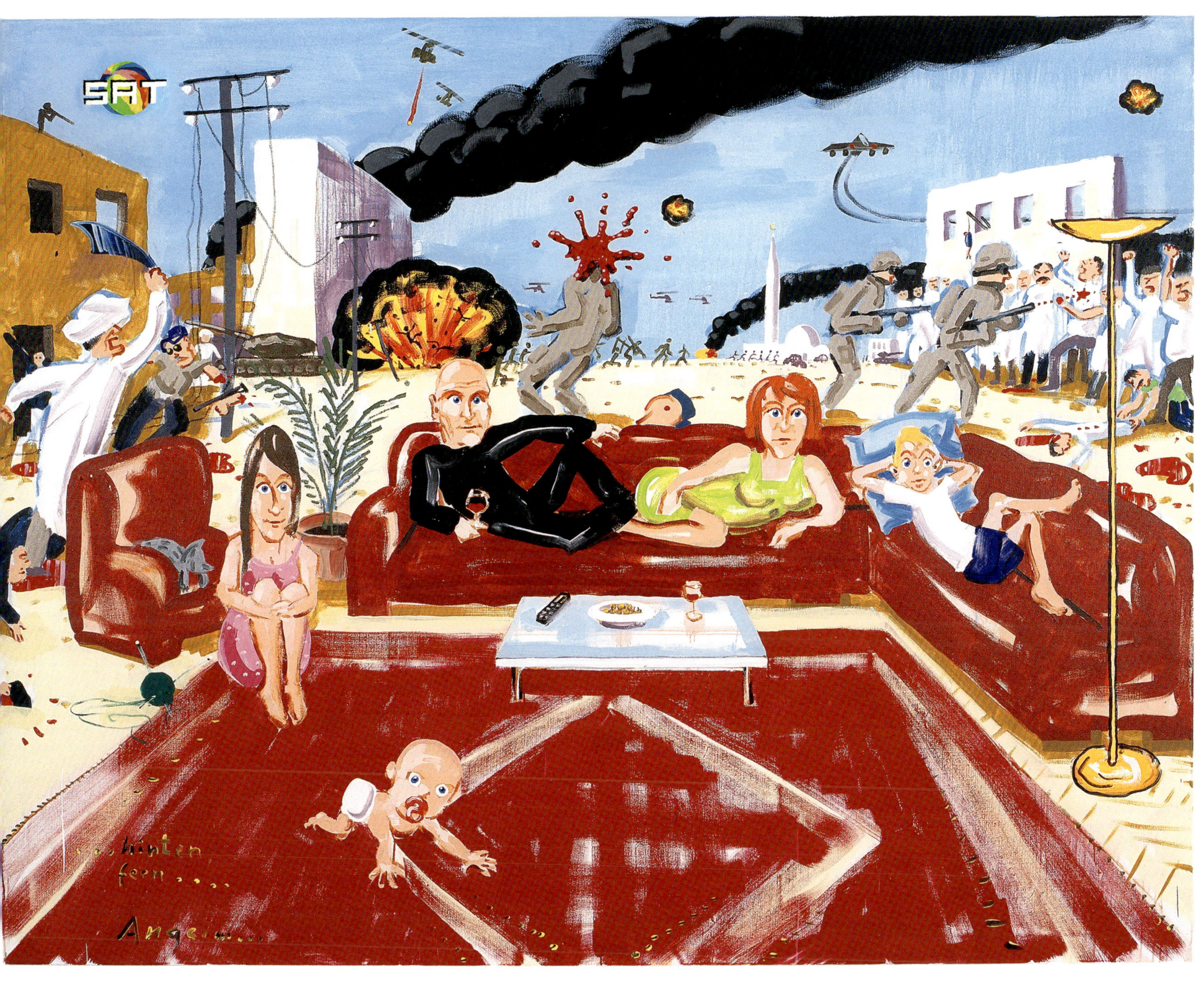

Hinten, fern… / Behind, Far Away…, 2008

205

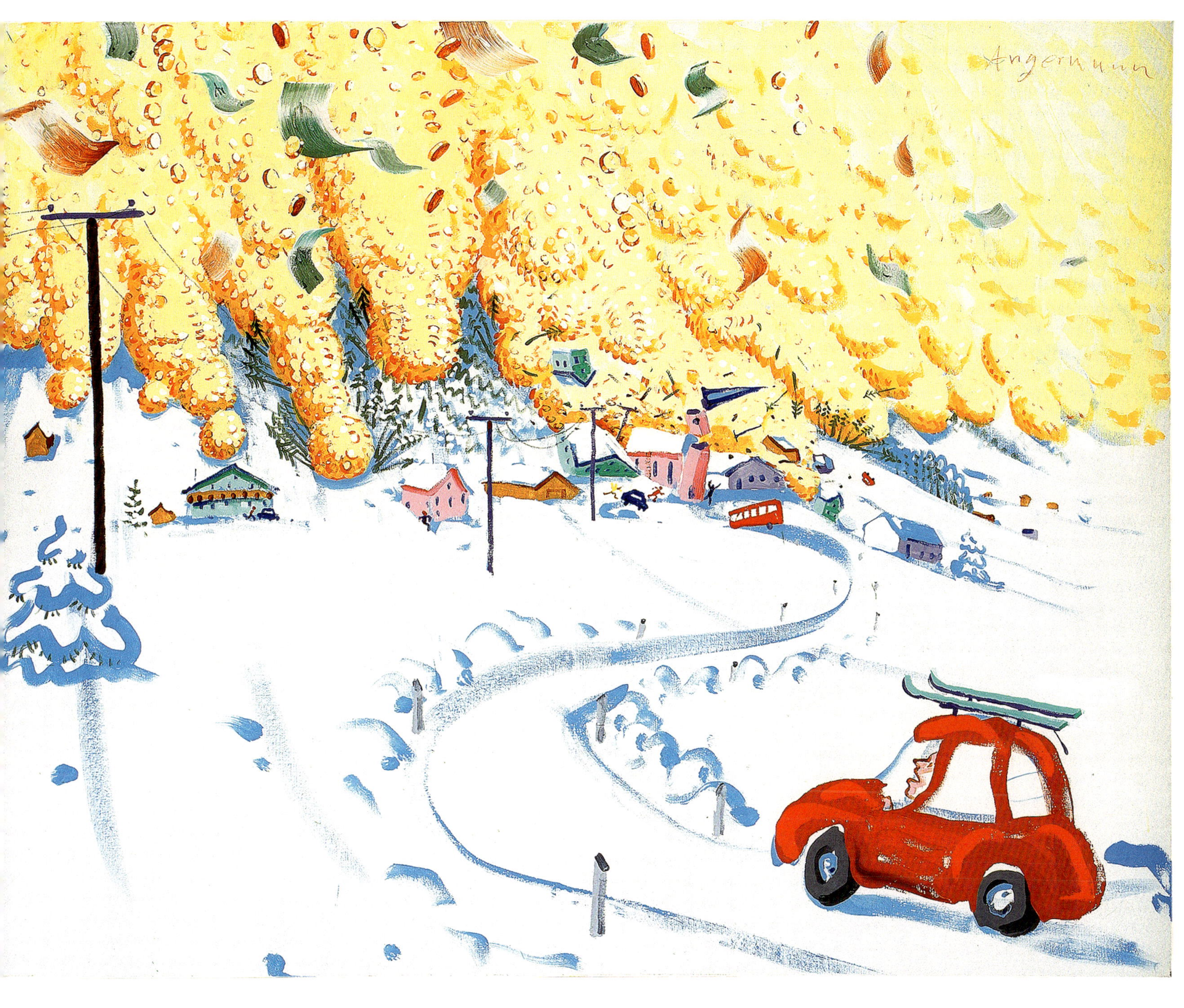

Lawine 2 (Das Große Geld) / Avalanche 2 (The Big Money), 2008

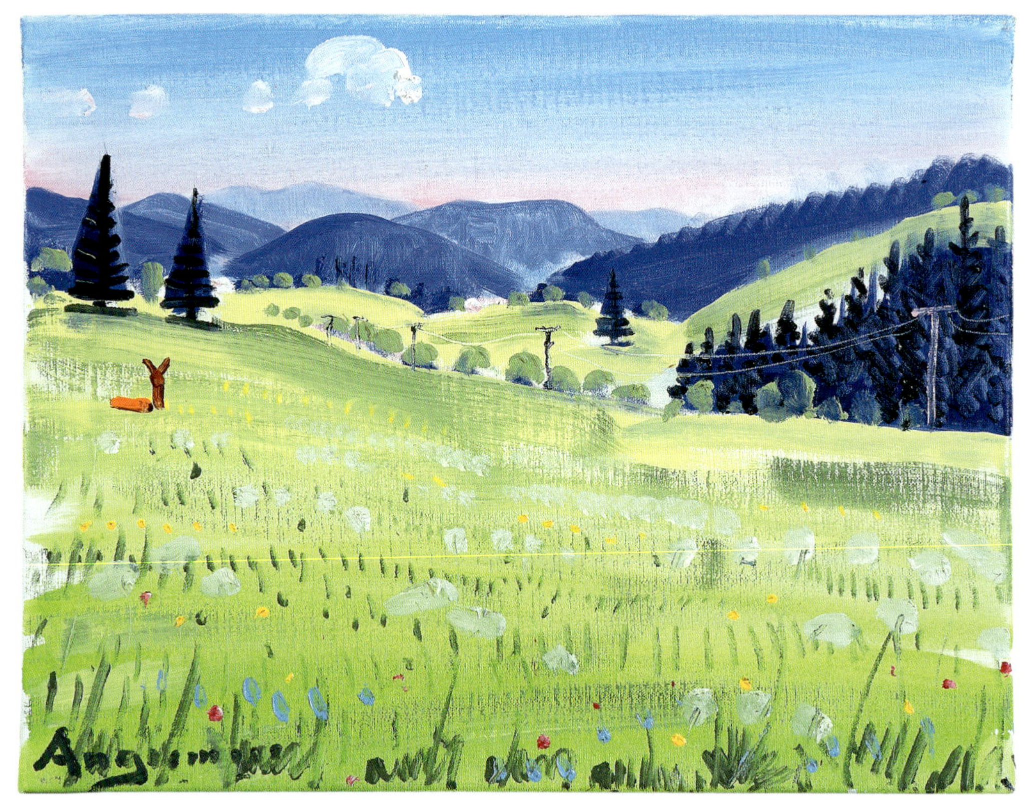

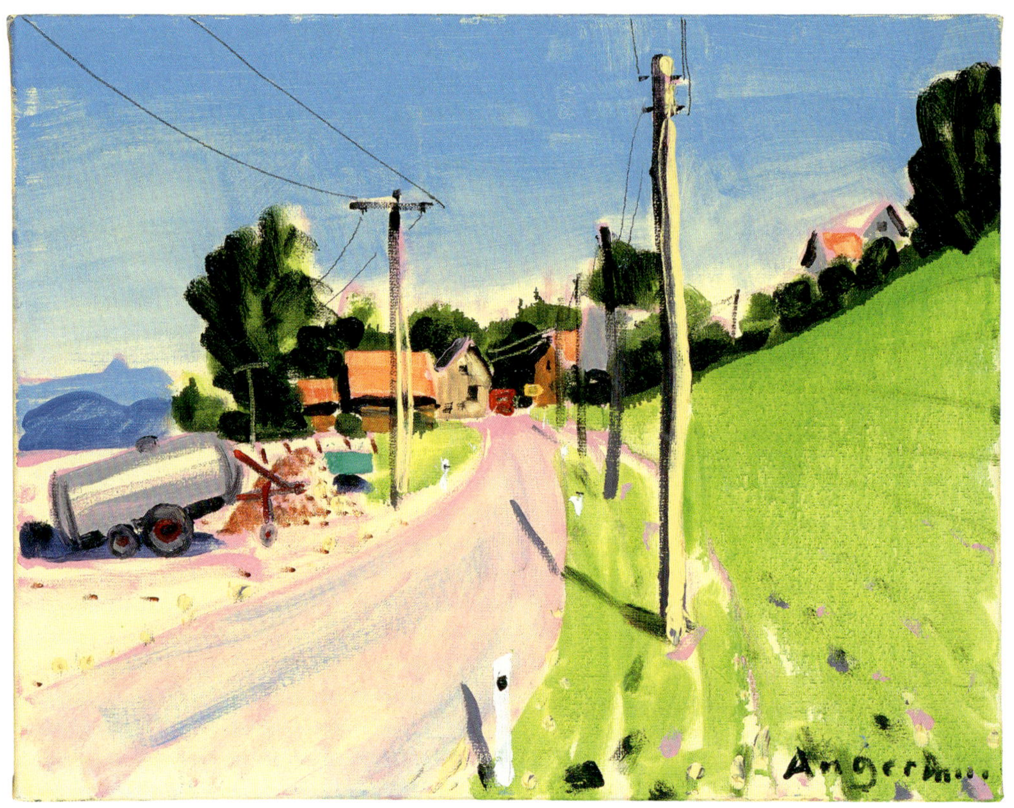

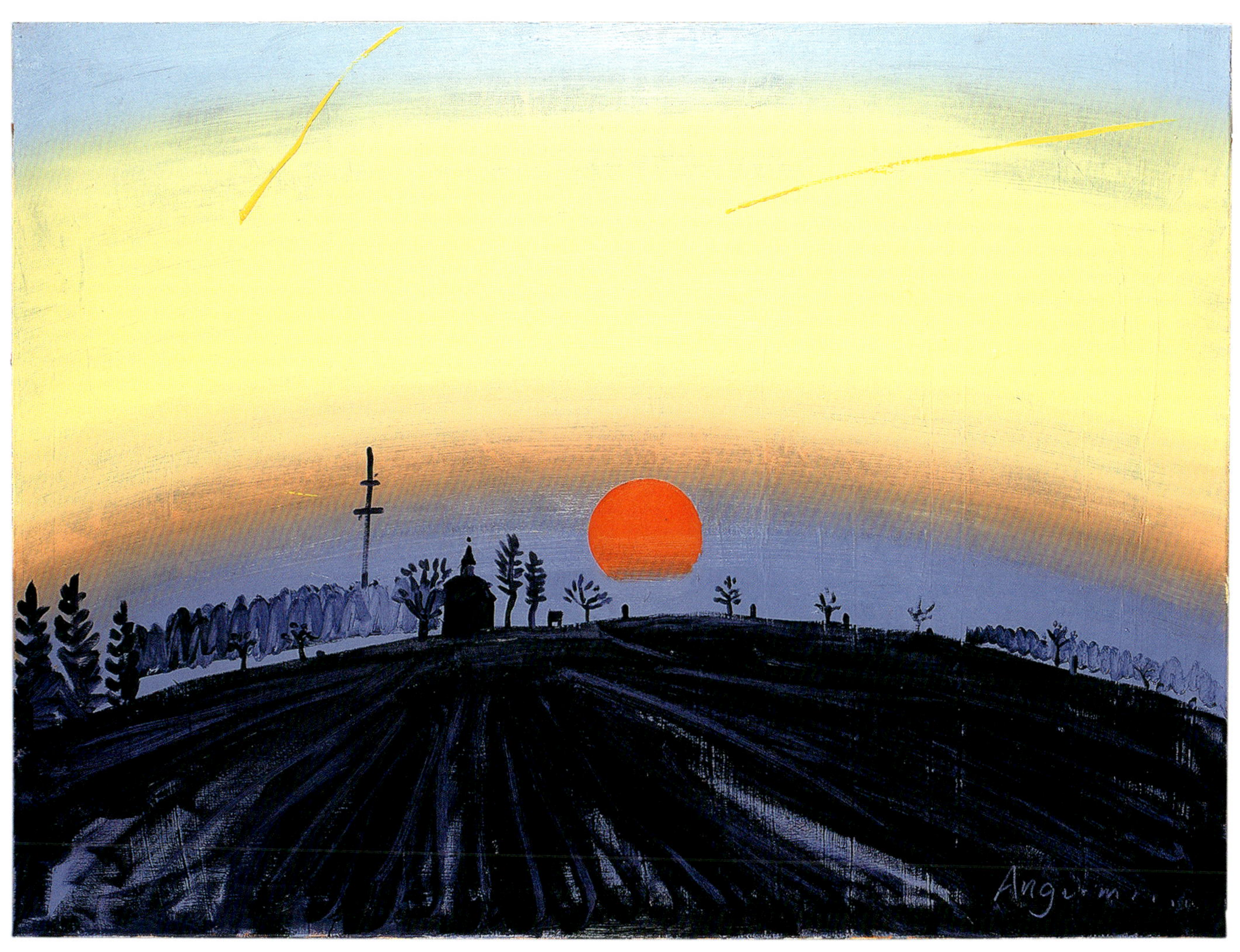

Nové Hutě, 2008

Gößmannsreuth, 2008

Sonnenaufgang / Sunrise, 2008

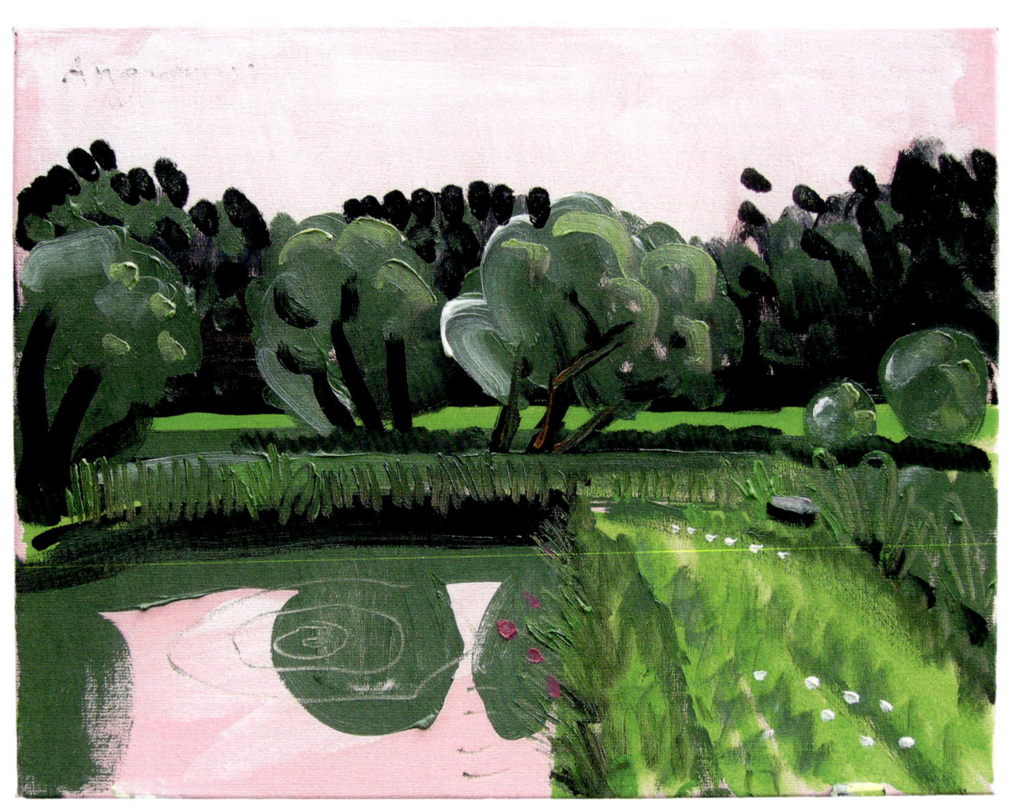

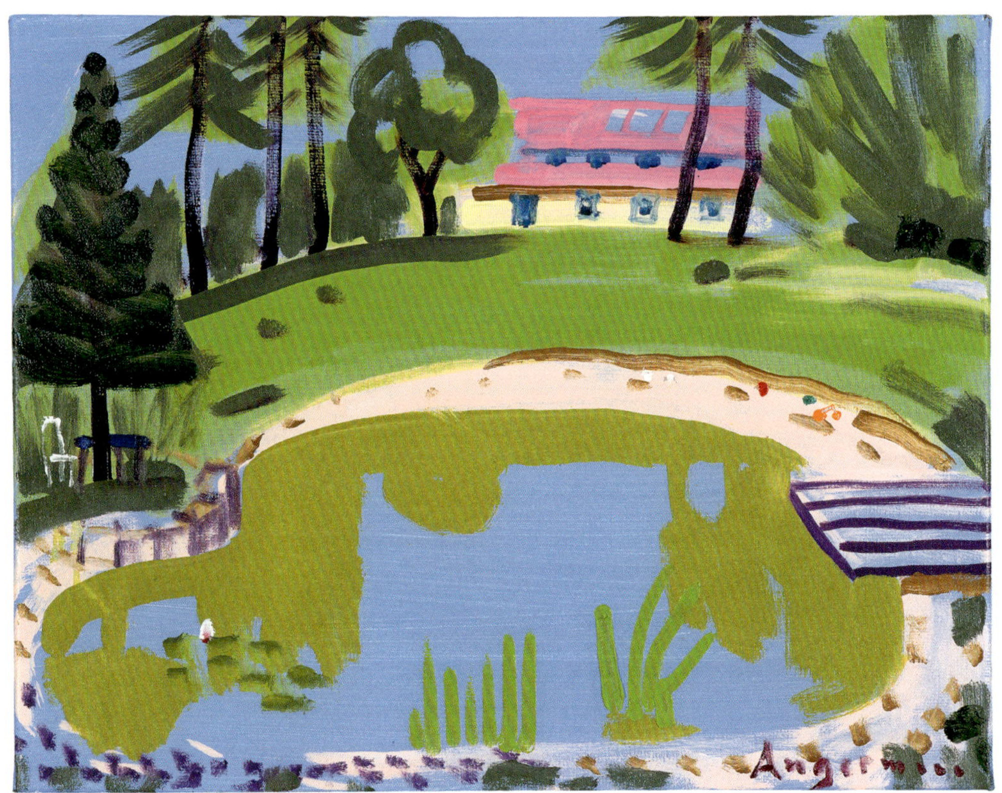

Rotmaintal, 2009

Malerwinkel 2 / Painter's Nook 2, 2009

210

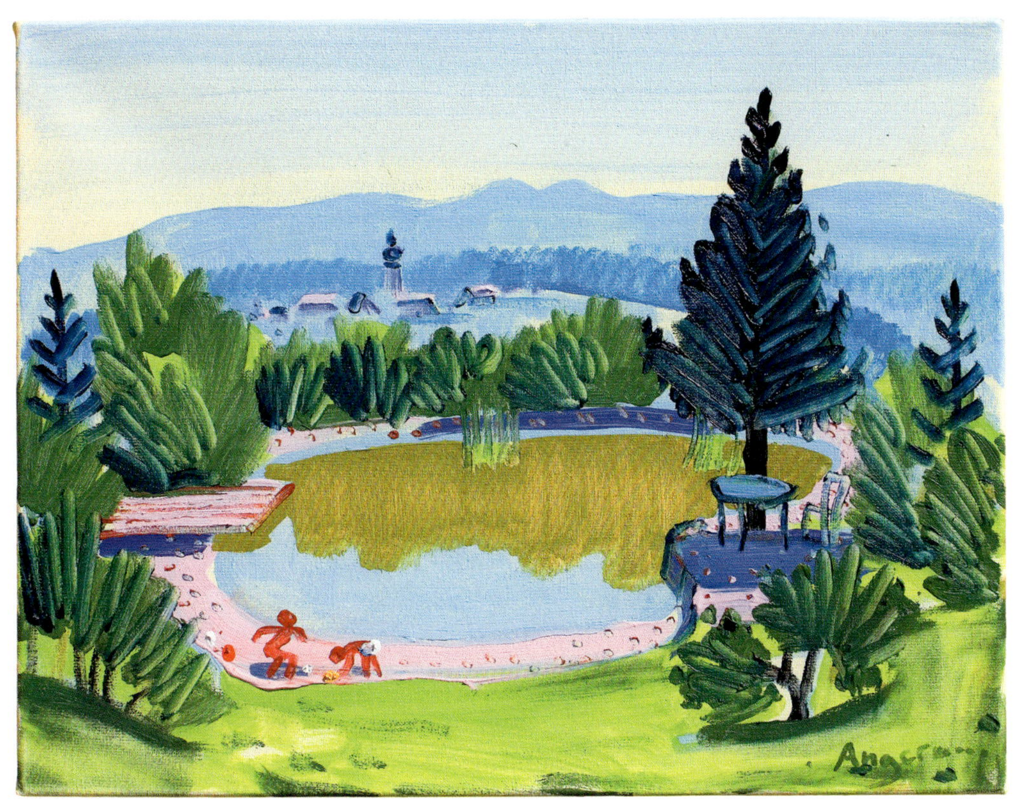

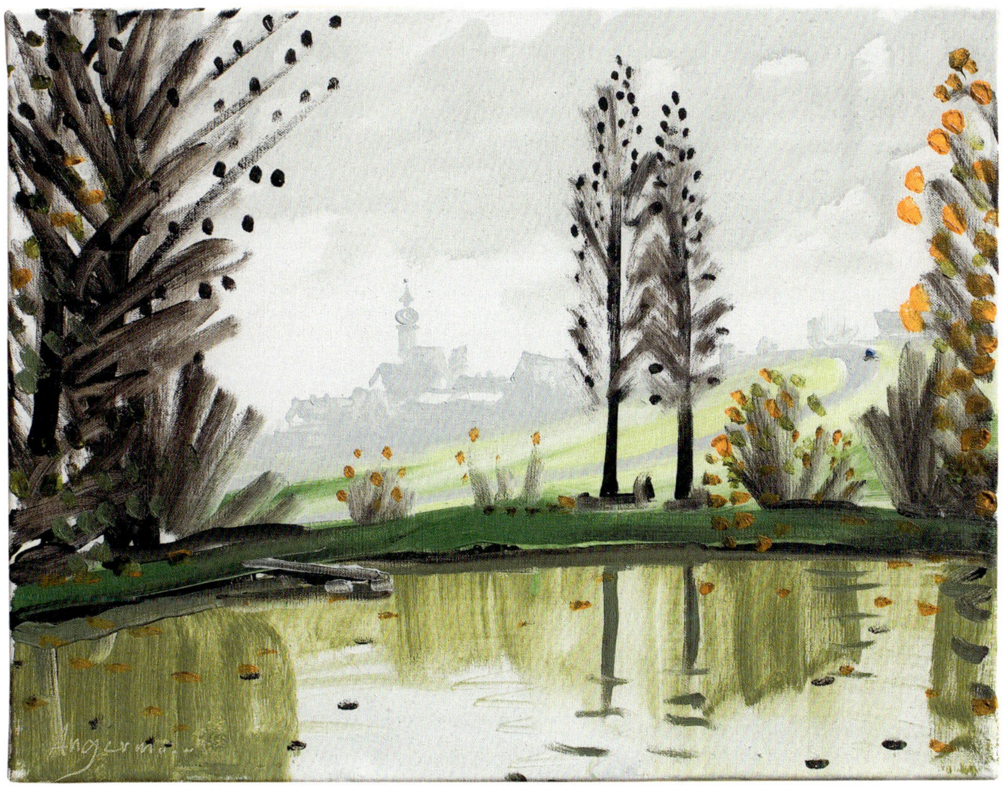

Jurameer 2 / Jurassic Sea 2, 2009

Sehnerweiher im Herbst / Sehnerweiher in Autumn, 2009

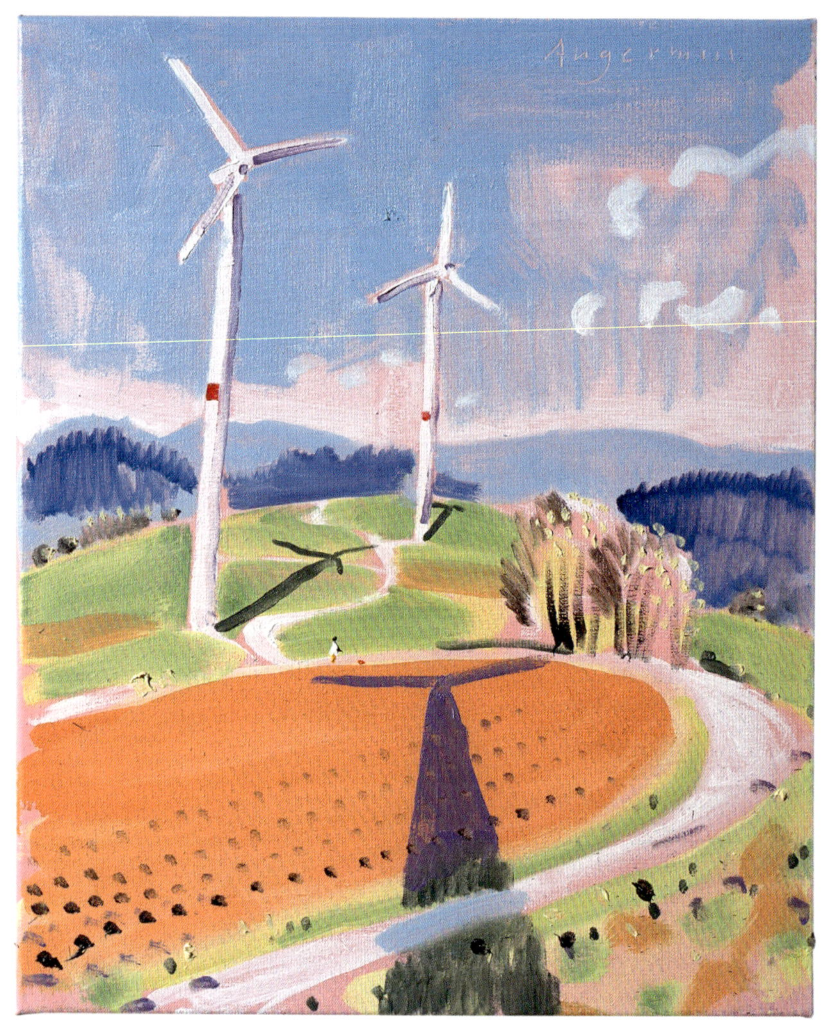

Windmühlenschatten / Windmill Shadows, 2009

Eiche am Deutes / Oak Tree on Deutes Hill, 2010

Frisch geteert / Freshly Tarred, 2010

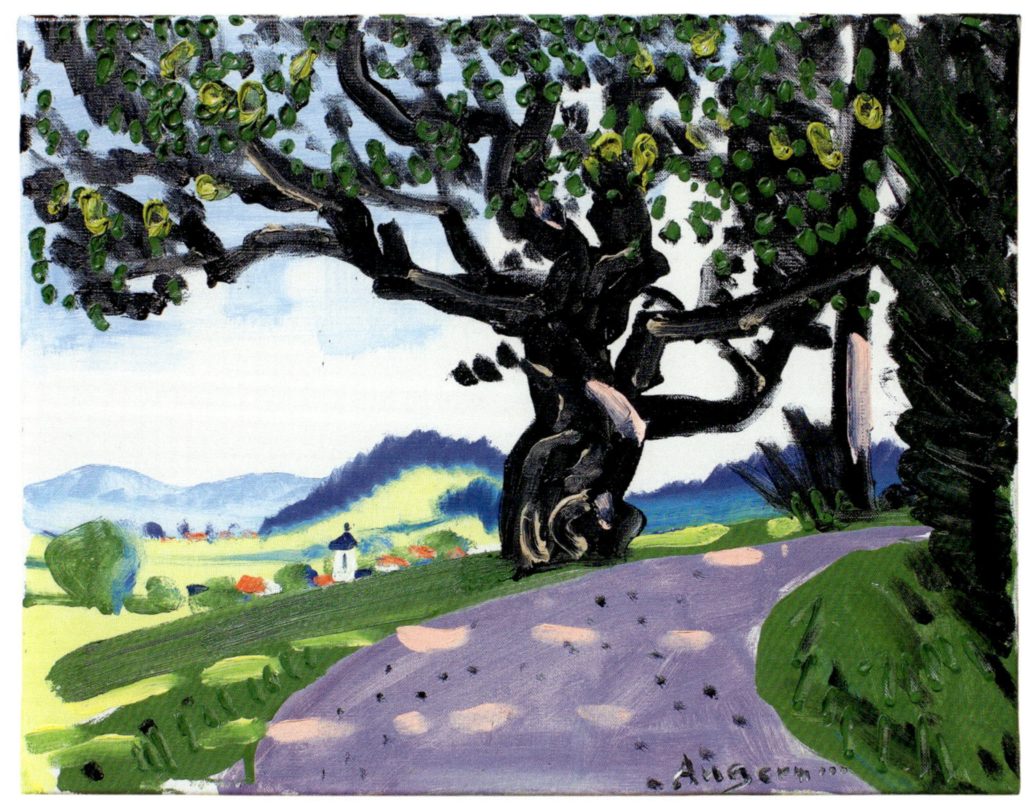

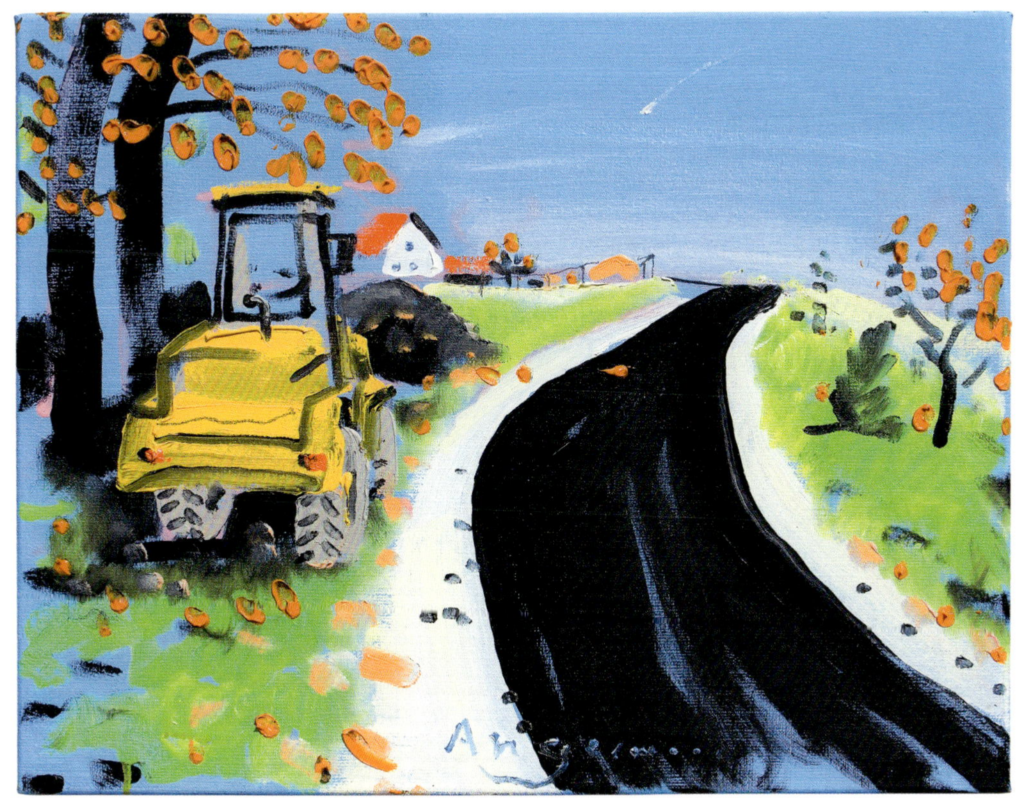

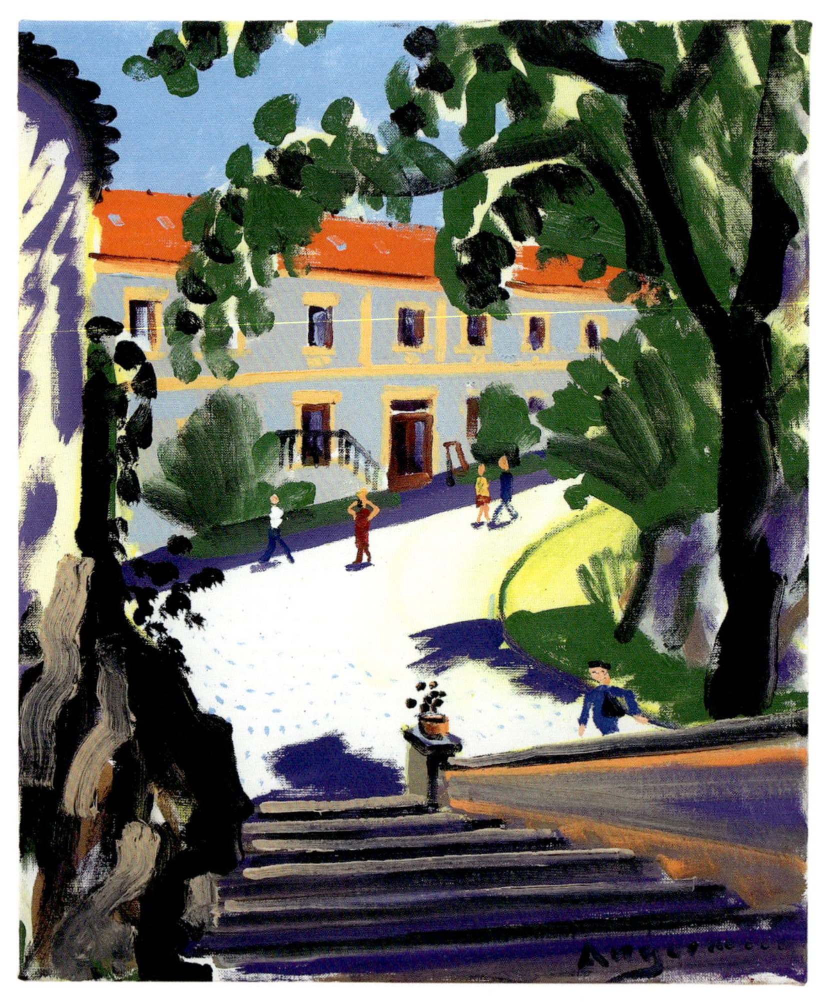

Mikulov 1, 2012

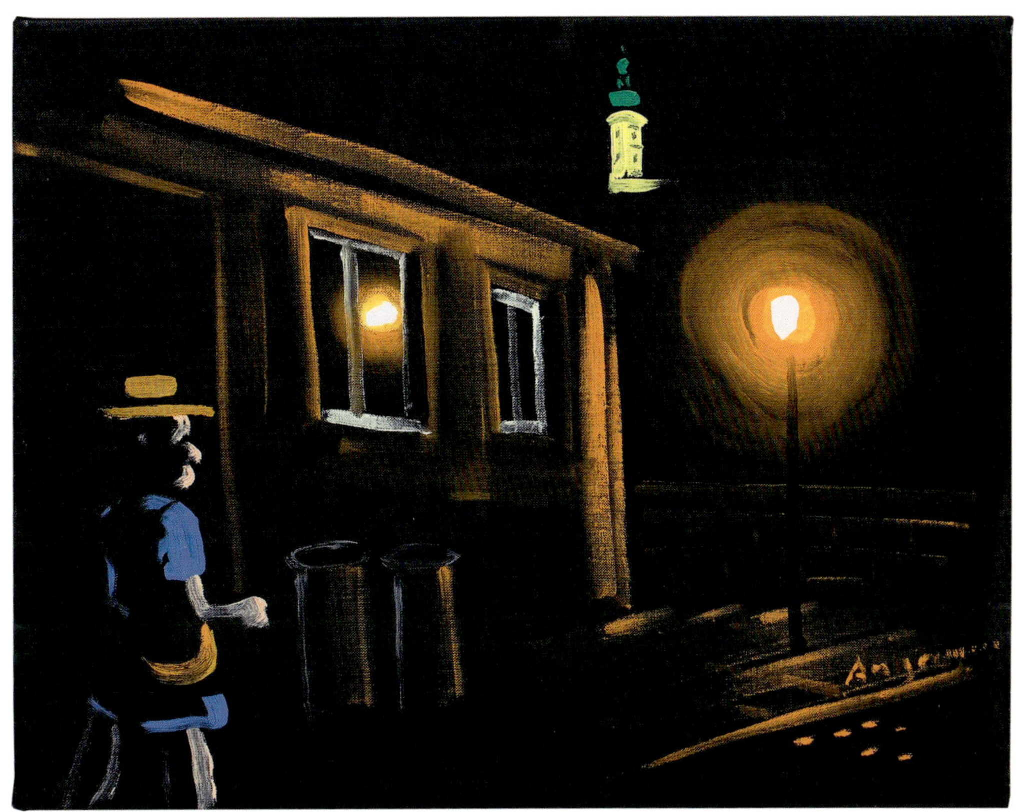

Noc, 2012

215

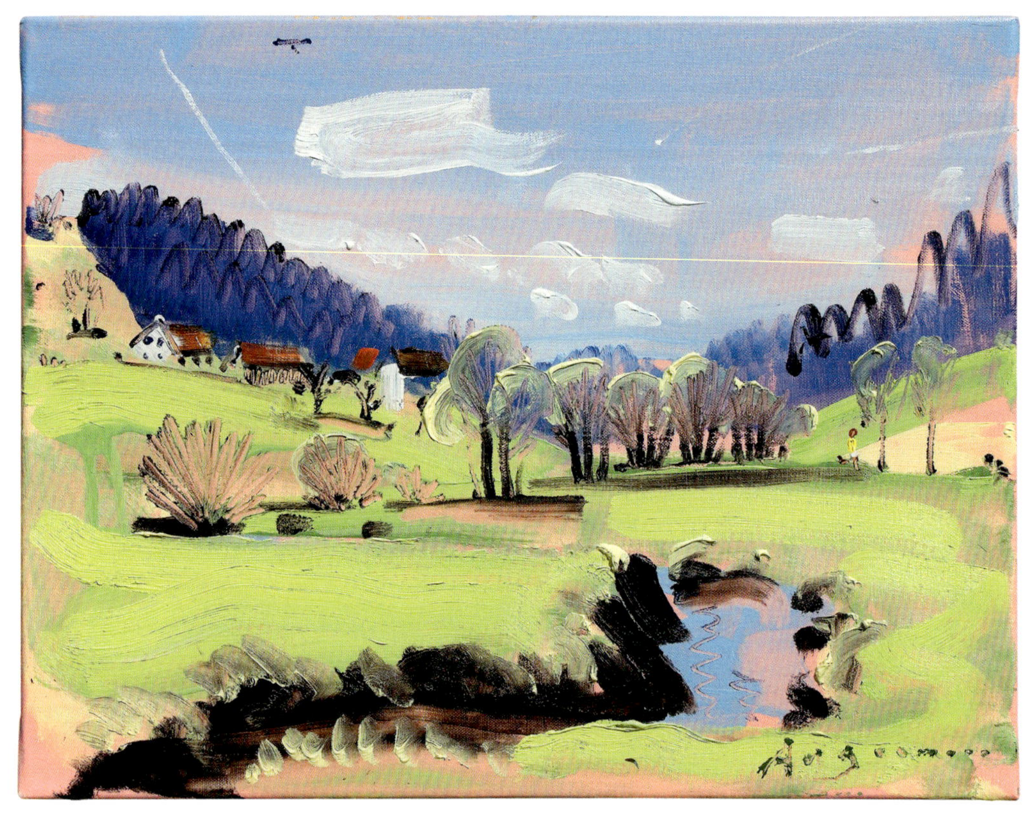

Streit, 2012

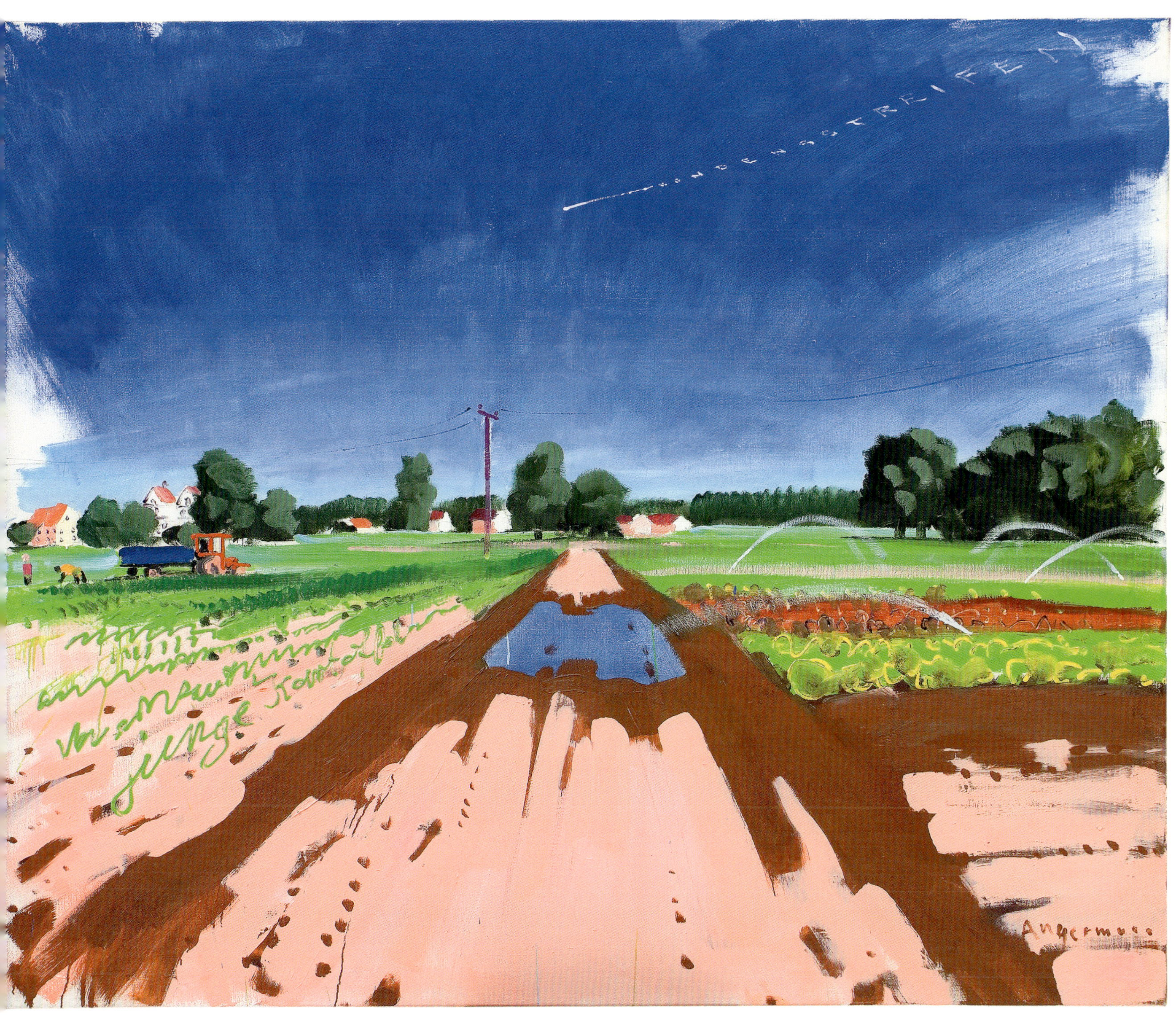

Kondensstreifen / Vapour Trails, 2013

217

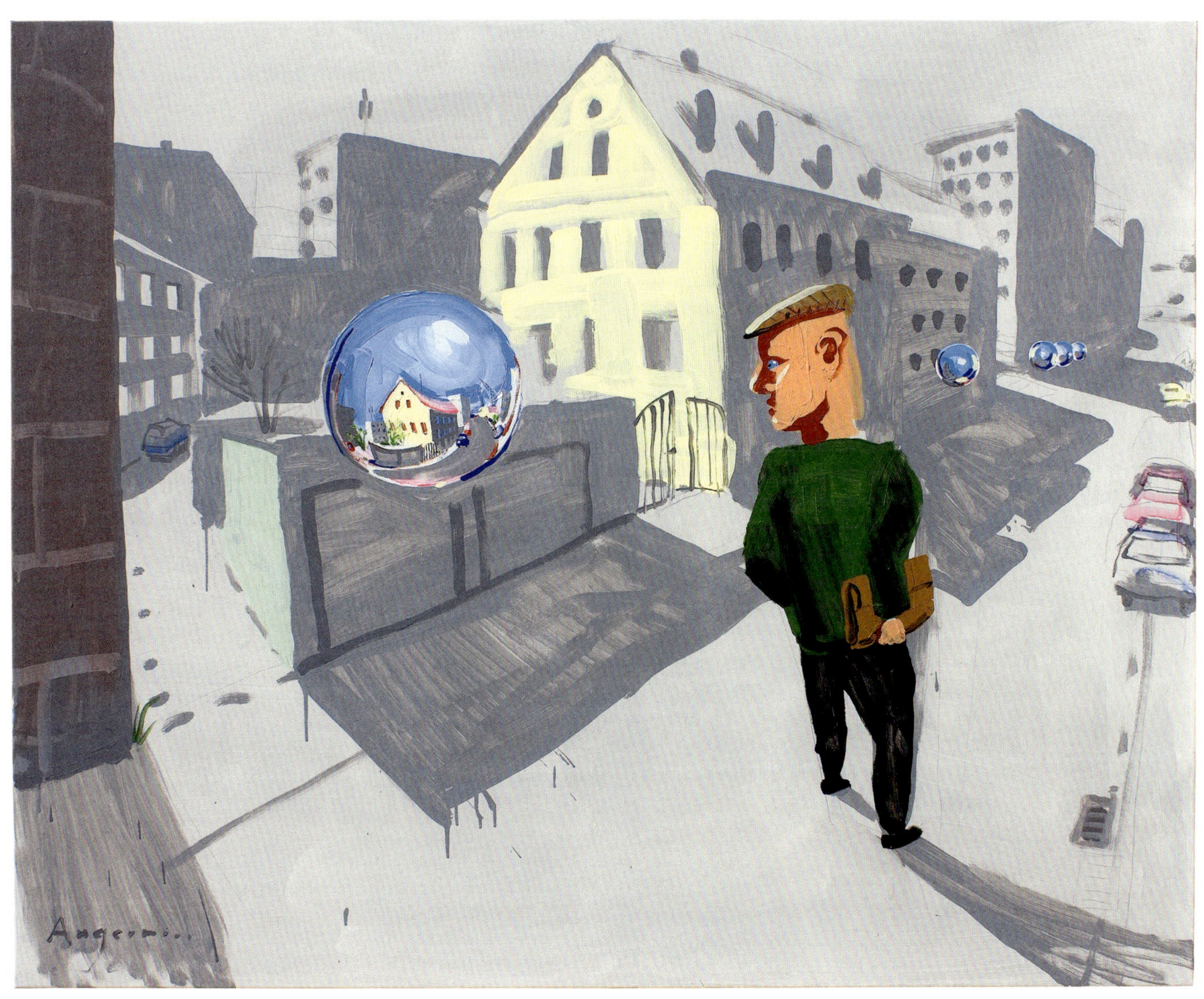

Streetview, 2011

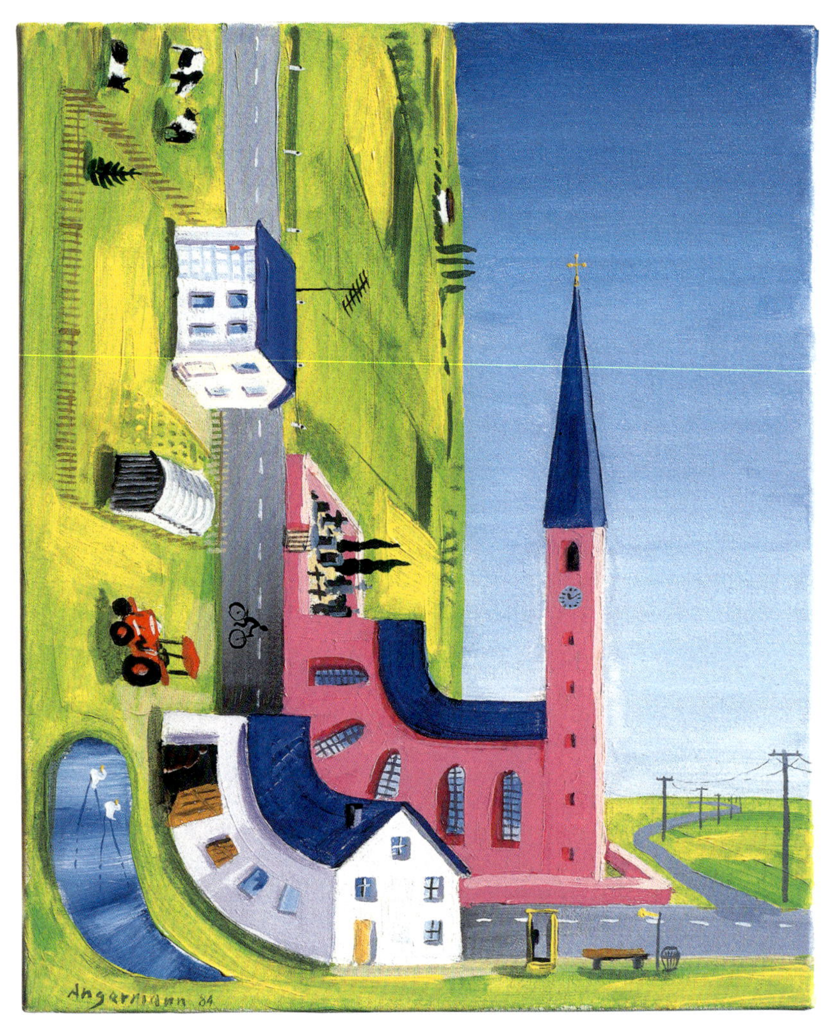

Krümmung 5 / Curve 5, 1984

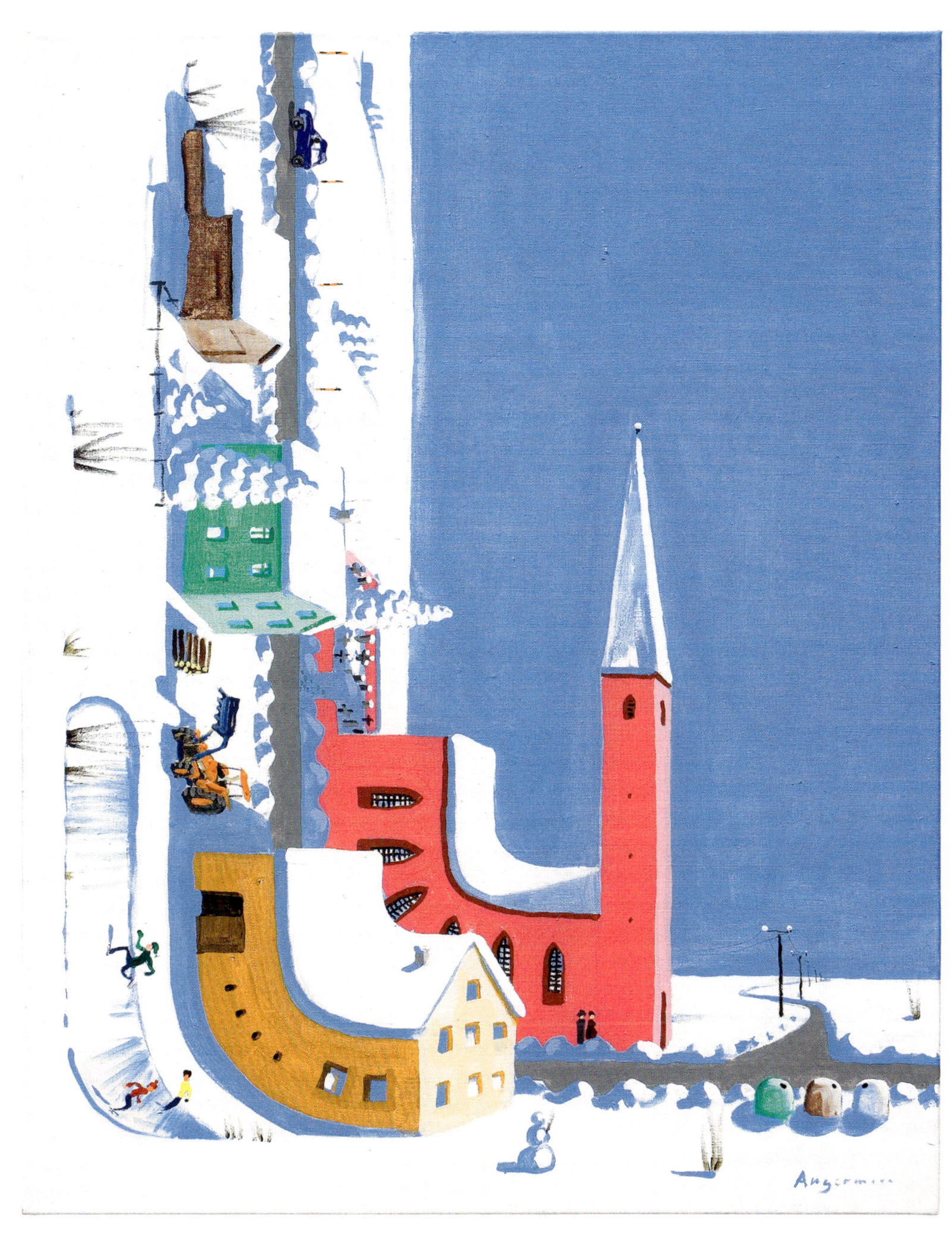

Krümmung (Winter) / Curve (Winter), 2013

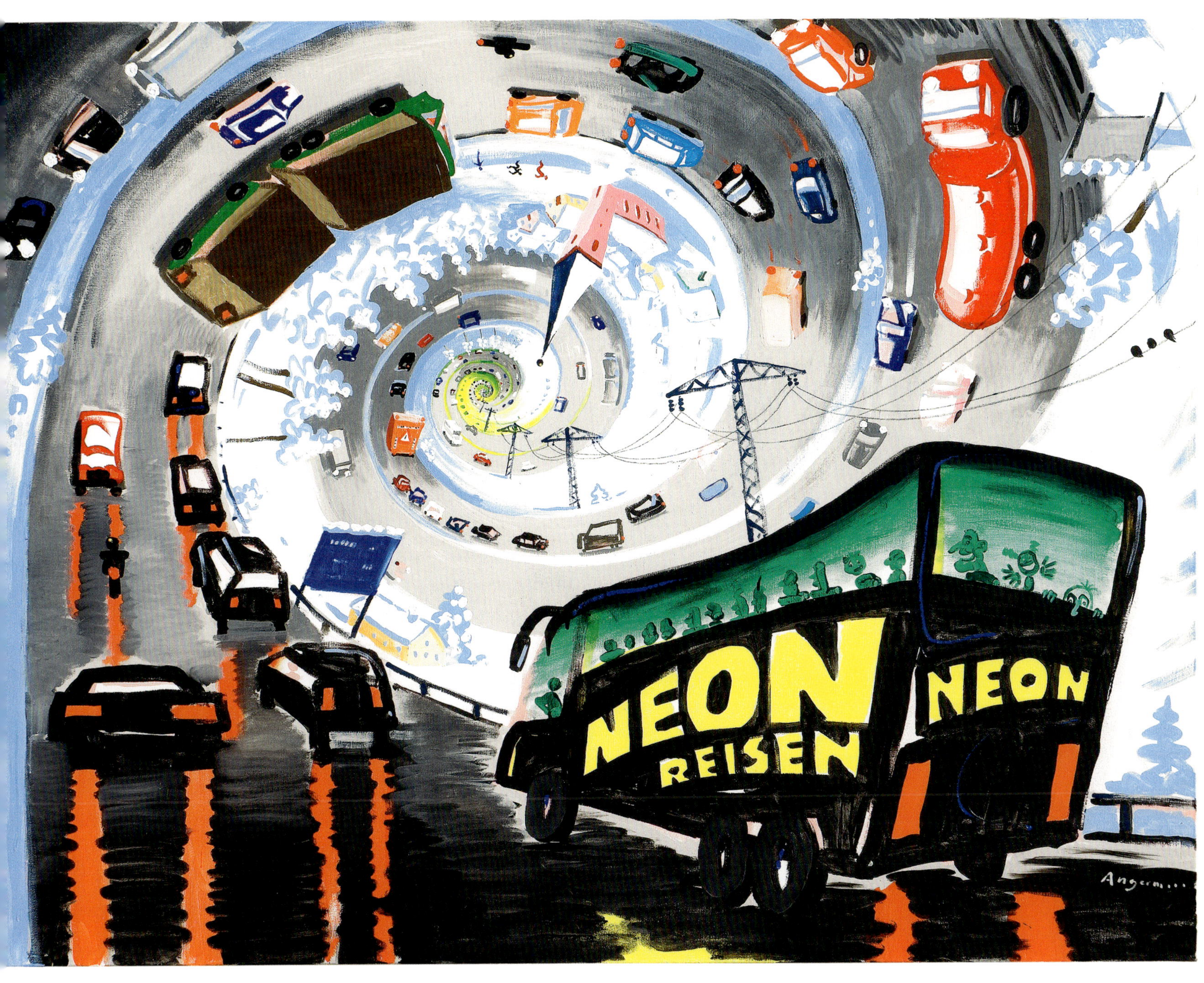

Spirale 2 / Spiral 2, 2013

Verzeichnis der Werke / List of Works

S. / p. 34
Drei junge Ahörner /
Three Young Maples
1959, Öl auf Pappe / oil
on cardboard, 42 × 30 cm
Courtesy der Künstler /
the artist

S. / p. 35
Selb
1962, Öl auf Holz / oil
on wood, 40 × 46 cm
Courtesy der Künstler /
the artist

S. / p. 36
Brainstorming 1
1968, Mischtechnik auf
Papier / mixed media on
paper, ca. 35 × 45 cm
Courtesy der Künstler /
the artist

S. / p. 37
Brainstorming 5
1968, Mischtechnik auf
Papier / mixed media on
paper, ca. 35 × 45 cm
Courtesy der Künstler /
the artist

S. / pp. 38–39
Große Zeitung /
Large Newspaper
1968, Mischtechnik auf
Papier / mixed media on
paper, 180 × 210 cm
Courtesy der Künstler /
the artist

S. / p. 40
Kleiner Mord /
Little Murder
1970, Öl auf Spanplatte /
oil on chipboard,
12 × 12 cm
Helmut Maringer

S. / p. 41
Feindbild/Image of the Foe
1970, Öl auf Hartfaser /
oil on hardboard,
40 × 50 cm
Courtesy der Künstler /
the artist

S. / p. 42
Hähnchen / Chicken
1971, Öl auf Hartfaser /
oil on hardboard,
31 × 45 cm
Neues Museum in
Nürnberg / Nuremberg.
Leihgabe der Stadt
Nürnberg / Loan of the
city of Nuremberg

S. / p. 43
Selbstportrait im Raum
111 / Self Portrait in
Room 111
1971, Öl auf Leinwand /
oil on canvas, 99 × 89 cm
Courtesy der Künstler /
the artist

S. / pp. 44–45
Zurück zur Kunst /
Back to Art
1973, Filzstift und
Mischtechnik auf Papier /
felt-tip pen and mixed
media on paper, 45 × 62 cm
Courtesy der Künstler /
the artist

S. / p. 47
Tatort / Crime Scene
1973 , Kasein auf
Leinwand / casein on
canvas, 180 × 200 cm
Privatbesitz / Private
collection

S. / p. 49
Schwarzenbach
1974, Kasein auf Nessel /
casein on nettle,
170 × 200 cm
Hans Angermann

S. / p. 51
Großes Froschbild /
Large Frog Painting
1974, Kasein auf Lein-
wand / casein on canvas,
170 × 200 cm
Hessisches Landesmuse-
um Darmstadt

S. / p. 53
Elsternbild /
Magpie Painting
1974, Kasein auf Lein-
wand / casein on canvas,
170 × 200 cm
Hessisches Landesmuse-
um Darmstadt

S. / p. 55
Für Renate / For Renate
1973/76, Kasein auf
Leinwand / casein on
canvas, 170 × 200 cm
Renate Angermann

S. / p. 56
Gregor Samsas Freunde 1 /
Gregor Samsa's Friends 1
1976, Öl auf Leinwand /
oil on canvas, 95 × 125 cm
Sammlung Hans Georg
Barsicke

S. / p. 57
Bärenbild 1 /
Bear Picture 1
1976, Öl auf Hartfaser /
oil on hardboard,
71 × 99 cm
Renate Angermann

S. / p. 58
Nekropolis / Necropolis
1976 , Kasein hinter Glas /
casein behind glass,
36 × 54 cm
Jan Knap

S. / p. 59
Armut, Wohlstand, Sex /
Poverty, Wealth, Sex
1977, Öl auf Nessel / oil
on nettle, 70 × 105 cm
Privatbesitz / Private
collection

S. / p. 61
Aus grauer Vorzeit /
From Time Immemorial
1979 , Kasein auf Nessel /
casein on nettle,
170 × 200 cm
Germanisches Natio-
nalmuseum, Nürnberg /
Nuremberg. Leihgabe
des Künstlers / Loan of
the artist

S. / p. 62
Saaletal 1
1979, Öl auf Leinwand /
oil on canvas, 170 × 200 cm
Centraal Museum, Utrecht

S. / pp. 64–65
Saaletal 3
1981, Dispersion auf
Leinwand / dispersion on
canvas, 270 × 450 cm
Deutsches Historisches
Museum, Berlin

S. / p. 67
Höhere Gewalt /
Force Majeure
1981, Öl auf Leinwand /
oil on canvas, 200 × 170 cm
Sammlung / Collection
Wildenberg

S. / p. 68
Flucht nach Ägypten /
Flight into Egypt
in Zusammenarbeit mit /
collaboration with Jan Knap
1981, Dispersion auf
Leinwand / dispersion on
canvas, 185 × 225 cm
Privatbesitz / Private
collection

S. / pp. 70–73
Tapeten / Wallpapers
1983, Mischtechnik auf
Tapete / mixed media on
wallpaper, je / each
40 × 40 cm
Nr. / No. 2, 4, 7, 8, 10, 16:
Sammlung Deutsche
Bank / Deutsche Bank
Collection
Courtesy der Künstler /
the artist

S. / p. 75
Die Jüngste Sekunde /
The Final Second
1983, Dispersion auf
Leinwand / dispersion on
canvas, 170 × 200 cm
Privatbesitz / Private
collection

S. / p. 77
Warm und Trocken 1 /
Warm and Dry 1
1983, Öl auf Leinwand /
oil on canvas, 170 × 200 cm
Hessisches Landesmuseum
Darmstadt

S. / p. 78
Kleingeschaidt
1984, Dispersion auf
Leinwand / dispersion on
canvas, 170 × 200 cm
Privatbesitz / Private
collection

S. / p. 79
Selbst mit Opa /
Self with Granddad
1985, Dispersion auf
Leinwand / dispersion on
canvas, 170 × 200 cm
Privatbesitz / Private
collection

S. / p. 80
Stadtparkweiher in
Nürnberg / Municipal
Gardens in Nuremberg
1986, Acryl auf
Leinwand / acrylic on
canvas, 60 × 60 cm
Sammlung / Collection
Tiberio Catellani

S. / p. 118
Selbst als Kleinsche
Flasche / Self as Klein
Bottle
1987, Öl auf Leinwand /
oil on canvas, 105 × 150 cm
Muzeum umění Olomouc /
The Olomouc Museum of Art

S. / p. 119
Spirale 1 / Spiral 1
1988, Öl auf Leinwand /
oil on canvas, 170 × 200 cm
Privatbesitz / Private
collection

S. / p. 120
Bären daheim /
Bears at Home
1988, Öl auf Leinwand /
oil on canvas, 170 × 200 cm
Rainer Schwalm

S. / p. 121
Yermo
1988, Öl auf Leinwand /
oil on canvas, 120 × 150 cm
Privatbesitz / Private
collection

S. / p. 122
Bärenpicknick /
Bears' Picnic
1988, Öl auf Leinwand /
oil on canvas, 170 × 200 cm
Sammlung Deutsche
Bank / Deutsche Bank
Collection

S. / p. 125
Turmbau zu Babel 1 /
Tower of Babylon 1
1989, Öl auf Leinwand /
oil on canvas, 240 × 170 cm
Bärbel Bach

S. / p. 126
Abteil / Train Compartment
1989, Acryl auf
Leinwand / acrylic on
canvas, 130 × 150 cm
Privatbesitz / Private
collection

S. / p. 127
Absturz / Crash
1989, Öl auf Leinwand /
oil on canvas, 170 × 200 cm
Muzeum umění Olomouc /
The Olomouc Museum of Art

S. / p. 128
Geisterfahrer / Ghost Driver
1989, Öl auf Leinwand /
oil on canvas, 170 × 200 cm
Privatbesitz / Private
collection

S. / p. 131
August 1
1989, Öl auf Leinwand /
oil on canvas, 170 × 200 cm
Neues Museum in Nürn-
berg / Nuremberg. Leihgabe
der Stadt Nürnberg / Loan
of the city of Nuremberg

S. / p. 132
Februar (Walberla) /
February (Walberla)
1993, Öl auf Leinwand /
oil on canvas, 50 × 70 cm
Privatbesitz / Private
collection

S. / p. 133
Mai (Walberla) /
May (Walberla)
1990, Öl auf Leinwand /
oil on canvas, 170 × 200 cm
Neues Museum in
Nürnberg / Nuremberg.
Geschenk von / Gift of Karl
Gerhard Schmidt, 2006

S. / p. 134
Der warme Februar 1990 /
The Warm February 1990
1990, Öl auf Leinwand /
oil on canvas, 240 × 170 cm
Privatbesitz / Private
collection

S. / p. 137
Nocturno / Nocturne
1990, Öl auf Leinwand /
oil on canvas, 185 × 245 cm
Privatbesitz / Private
collection

S. / p. 138
Dezember 1 / December 1
1990, Öl auf Leinwand /
oil on canvas, 170 × 200 cm
Privatbesitz / Private
collection

S. / p. 140
Schiefer 2 / Slate 2
1991, Öl auf Leinwand /
oil on canvas, 170 × 200 cm
Privatbesitz / Private
collection

S. / p. 141
Familienkrach 1 /
Family Row 1
1991, Acryl auf
Leinwand / acrylic on
canvas, 150 × 180 cm
Privatbesitz / Private
collection

S. / p. 143
Jungbrunnen 1 /
Fountain of Youth 1
1991, Öl auf Leinwand /
oil on canvas, 170 × 200 cm
Familie Pillenstein

S. / p. 144
Stahlplastik / Steel Sculpture
1992, Öl auf Leinwand /
oil on canvas, 40 × 50 cm
Privatbesitz / Private
collection

S. / p. 145
Stehender Verkehr 2 /
Standing Traffic 2
1992, Acryl auf Lein-
wand / acrylic on canvas,
240 × 170 cm
Privatbesitz / Private
collection

S. / p. 146
Juli (Biergarten) /
July (Beer Garden)
1992, Öl auf Leinwand /
oil on canvas, 170 × 200 cm
Privatbesitz / Private
collection

S. / p. 147
Heimweg 1 / Way Home 1
1992, Öl auf Leinwand /
oil on canvas, 120 × 150 cm
Privatbesitz / Private
collection

S. / p. 148
Regnitz 2
1993, Öl auf Leinwand /
oil on canvas, 70 × 50 cm
Atelier- und Galeriehaus,
M. u. H.-F. Defet Stiftung,
Nürnberg

S. / p. 149
Zwei Brücken bei Arles /
Two Bridges near Arles
1993, Öl auf Leinwand /
oil on canvas, 50 × 40 cm
Thomas Kocheisen und
Ulrike Hullmann

S. / p. 150
Kraftwerk Frauenaurach /
Frauenaurach Power Station
1994, Öl auf Leinwand /
oil on canvas, 40 × 50 cm
Courtesy der Künstler /
the artist

S. / p. 150
Der Bau des Hühnerstalls /
The Construction of the
Chicken Coop
1997, Öl auf Leinwand /
oil on canvas, 60 × 80 cm
Courtesy der Künstler /
the artist

S. / p. 151
Stadtpark Nürnberg 2 /
Municipal Park Nuremberg 2
1996, Öl auf Leinwand /
oil on canvas, 140 × 170 cm
Bayerische Staatsgemälde-
sammlungen, München

S. / p. 152
Reiher / Heron
1995, Öl auf Leinwand /
oil on canvas, 60 × 80 cm
Atelier- und Galeriehaus,
M. u. H.-F. Defet Stiftung,
Nürnberg

S. / p. 153
Am alten Kanal 4 /
By the Old Canal 4
1994, Öl auf Leinwand /
oil on canvas, 60 × 80 cm
Privatbesitz / Private
collection

S. / p. 155
Sechs Wullis im Gegenlicht /
Six Backlit Haylages
1997, Öl auf Leinwand /
oil on canvas, 170 × 200 cm
Max Angermann

S. / p. 156
Weltbild / World Picture
1997, Öl auf Leinwand /
oil on canvas, 170 × 200 cm
Privatbesitz / Private
collection

S. / p. 157
A9
1998, Öl auf Leinwand /
oil on canvas, 40 × 50 cm
Privatbesitz / Private
collection

S. / p. 159
Zwei Skifahrer im
Bärenkostüm / Two Skiers
in Bear Outfits
1998, Öl auf Leinwand /
oil on canvas, 170 × 200 cm
Privatbesitz / Private
collection

Peter Angermann
Biografie / Biography

1945

geboren in Rehau, Bayern, Deutschland / born in Rehau,
Bavaria, Germany

1966–1968

Studium der Malerei an der Akademie der Bildenden Künste in
Nürnberg bei Gerhard Wendland / Student of Gerhard Wendland at the Academy of Fine Arts in Nuremberg

1968–1972

Studium an der Kunstakademie Düsseldorf bei Joseph Beuys /
Student of Joseph Beuys at the Düsseldorf Art Academy

1979

Gründung der Gruppe NORMAL mit Milan Kunc und Jan Knap /
Founding of the group NORMAL with Milan Kunc and Jan Knap

1981

Lisa und David Lauber-Preis für Malerei / Lisa and David
Lauber Award for Painting

1986

Gastdozent an der Iceland Academy of the Arts, Reykjavik /
Guest Lecturer at the Iceland Academy of the Arts, Reykjavik

1992–1993

Gastprofessur für Malerei an der Gesamthochschule Kassel /
Visiting professor for painting at the Gesamthochschule, Kassel

1996–2002

Professor für Malerei an der Städelschule, Frankfurt/Main /
Professor for painting at the Städelschule, Frankfurt/Main

2002–2010

Professor für Malerei an der Akademie der Bildenden Kunste in
Nürnberg / Professor for painting at the Academy of Fine Arts
in Nuremberg

Lebt und arbeitet in Thurndorf und Nürnberg / Lives and works
in Thurndorf and Nuremberg

Einzelausstellungen / Solo Exhibitions

1975
Galerie Hartmut Beck, Erlangen

1976
Galerie Erhard Kick, Nürnberg / Nuremberg

1977
Galerie Defet, Nürnberg / Nuremberg

1978
Galerie Martin Figuli, Düsseldorf

1979
Galerie Traude Näke, Nürnberg / Nuremberg
Galerie Bikulimu, Hersbruck
Normal, Galerie Hartmut Beck, Erlangen

1981
Normaler Realismus, Galerie Eva Keppel, Düsseldorf
Galerie 't Venster, Rotterdam
Lisa und David Lauber-Preis, Norishalle Nürnberg / Nuremberg

1982
Galerie Schoof, Heidelberg (mit / with John Hummel)
Schilderijen en tekeningen, Galerie Swart, Amsterdam
Galerie Delta, Rotterdam
Leonardo & Walt Disney betrachten das Abendland, Galerie Eva Keppel, Düsseldorf; Galerie Hartmut Beck, Erlangen

1983
Zeichnungen 1973–1982, Galerie Hartmut Beck, Erlangen; Galerie Beck und Freudenthaler, Bad Honnef
Paintings, Dana Reich Gallery, San Francisco
Galerie Förtsch, Berlin
BarBar, Stockholm

1984
Living Art Museum, Reykjavik
Corridor Galerie, Reykjavik
Reese Bullen Gallery – Humboldt State University, Arcata, Kalifornien / California
Galerie Hartmut Beck, Erlangen

1985
Galerie Hans-Jürgen Müller, Köln / Cologne
Vitrine 002, Köln / Cologne
Galerie Traude Näke, Nürnberg / Nuremberg

1986
Galerie Michael Horbach, Köln / Cologne
Galerie Kaess-Weiss, Stuttgart
Living Art Museum, Reykjavik
Galerie Ryszard Varisella, Nürnberg / Nuremberg

1987
Third Eye Centre, Glasgow (mit / with Michael Reiter)
Computermosaik, U-Bahnhof Hohe Marter, Nürnberg / Nuremberg
Galerie Ryszard Varisella, Nürnberg / Nuremberg

1988
Galerie Brigitta Rosenberg, Zürich / Zurich (mit / with Helgi Fridjónsson)
Galería Estampa, Madrid

1989
Ölbilder, Galerie Ryszard Varisella, Frankfurt/Main
Galleri Bengt Adlers, Malmö
Hanna und Gerhard Hornung, Höchstadt an der Aisch
Galleria Toselli, Mailand / Milan

1990
Galerie Ryszard Varisella, Frankfurt/Main

1991
Beursschouwburg, Brüssel / Brussels
Galleria Toselli, Mailand / Milan

1992
Galerie Delta, Rotterdam
YIUP – Eine Ausstellung von Peter Angermann mit Papierarbeiten aus den Jahren 1968–1970, Galerie Traude Näke, Nürnberg / Nuremberg
Akte 17/1991, Galerie Hartmut Beck, Erlangen
Kunstverein Kassel
Galerie Lucien Bilinelli, Brüssel / Brussels
Galerie Hartmut Beck, Erlangen

1993
Pleinair – Malerei 1991–1993, Galerie Defet, Nürnberg / Nuremberg
Opere recenti, Studio d'Arte Raffaelli, Trient / Trento

1994
Rathaus, Rehau
Epilog für einen betrunkenen Drucker – Übermalungen, Galerie
Hartmut Beck, Erlangen
Serien – Siebdrucke und Zeichnungen, Galerie Brochier,
München / Munich
Galleria Cardi, Mailand / Milan
Galleria Toselli, Mailand / Milan

1995
Paesaggi, Studio d'Arte Raffaelli, Arte Fiera, Bologna
Opere recenti, Galleria Confini Arte Contemporanea, Cuneo
Studio Cristofori, Bologna
Galerie Hartmut Beck, Erlangen
Malerei 1973–1995, Kunsthalle Nürnberg / Nuremberg
Galleria Nazionale di San Marino
Kulturverein Winterstein
Galerie Brochier, München / Munich

1996
Neue Landschaften, Galerie Defet, Nürnberg / Nuremberg
Einstand, Städelschule, Frankfurt/Main

1997
Kunstverein Hof
Studio G, Mailand / Milan

1998
Galerie Delta, Rotterdam
Die Offizielle Polkakapelle, Galerie Fruchtig, Frankfurt/Main
Galerie Traude Näke, Nürnberg / Nuremberg
Schloss Kreuth, Heideck

1999
Ca' di Fra', Mailand / Milan
Galleria Alter, Turin
Foyer Oper, Nürnberg / Opera foyer, Nuremberg

2000
Stochastix, Galerie Hartmut Beck, Erlangen
Die Offizielle Polkakapelle, Yec 'het mad, Nürnberg / Nuremberg

2001
Galerie Defet, Nürnberg / Nuremberg

Fachhochschule Amberg-Weiden
dontmiss, Frankfurt/Main

2002
Galerie Hartmut Beck, Erlangen
Galerie Sona Safajan, Bayreuth

2003
Ca' di Fra', Mailand / Milan
Heimatmalerei, Campus Galerie, Bayreuth; Kunstverein
Weiden; Kunstverein Kronach

2004
Galerie Delta, Rotterdam
Galerie Anita Beckers, Frankfurt/Main
Bernsteinzimmer, Nürnberg / Nuremberg

2005
Galerie Sima, Nürnberg / Nuremberg
Kunstverein Heidenheim

2007
Galerie Witteveen, Amsterdam

2008
Autonomoney, Kunstverein Ansbach
Galerie Sima, Nürnberg / Nuremberg
Ca' di Fra', Mailand / Milan

2009
Autonomoney, Museen der Stadt Bamberg
Gallery at the White Unicorn, Klatovy

2010
Gallery Won, Seoul
MBC Gallery M, Daegu, Südkorea / South Korea
Urlaub für immer, Kunstverein Kirchzarten
Galerie Caesar, Olmütz / Olomouc

2011
Kunstförderverein Weinheim
Gemeinschaftshaus Langwasser, Nürnberg / Nuremberg

2012
Galerie im Woferlhof, Bad Kötzting
Urlaub für immer, Kunstverein Linz am Rhein
Bespoke, Düsseldorf

2013
Licht am Horizont, Museum Haus Lange, Krefeld

Ausgewählte Gruppenausstellungen / Selected Group Exhibitions

1959

Hofer Kunstausstellung, Hof

1962

Gruppe Nordfranken, Hof, Marktredwitz

1969

YIUP – Permanente Ausstellung, Raum 13, Kunstakademie
Düsseldorf

1971

YIUP-Gruppe, *Between*, Kunsthalle Düsseldorf

1979

Peter Angermann, Blalla Hallmann, Erhard Kick, Fränkische
Galerie Nürnberg / Nuremberg

1980

Normal, Galerie Hajo Müller, Köln / Cologne
Times Square Show, Times Square, New York
Normal, Galerie Defet, Nürnberg / Nuremberg
*11e Biennale de Paris. Manifestation internationale des jeunes
artistes*, Musée d'Art Moderne de la Ville de Paris
Après le Classicisme, Musée d'Art et d'Industrie, Saint Etienne

1981

Aljofre Barocco, Sala Dante del Teatro Comunale, Salone di
Palazzo Ducezio, Noto
Angermann, Tatafiore, Van 't Slot, Winnewisser, Galerie Eva
Keppel, Düsseldorf
Rundschau Deutschland, Lothringer Strasse 13, München /
Munich
Bildwechsel – Neue Malerei in Deutschland, Akademie der
Künste, Berlin
Szenen der Volkskunst, Württembergischer Kunstverein, Stuttgart
LIS '81 – Lisbon International Show, Galeria Nacional de Arte
Moderna, Lissabon / Lisbon
Normal, Galleria Pellegrino, Bologna

*Normal – Peter Angermann, John Hummel, Jan Knap, Milan
Kunc*, Museo Civico d'Arte Contemporanea, Gibellina
Normal, Neue Galerie – Sammlung Ludwig, Aachen
Positionen und Tendenzen – Kunstszene Nürnberg, Kunstverein
Nürnberg / Nuremberg
Giovane Arte Internazionale, Galleria Giuli, Lecco
Kunstanschläge 2, Galerie Magers, Bonn
11e Biennale de Paris a Nice, Galerie d'Art Contemporain,
Galerie des Pondettes, Nizza / Nice

1982

Arteder 82. Muestra Internacional de Obra Gráfica, Pabellón
municipal de la feria, Bilbao
Grand Hotel, Centro d'Arte Contemporanea, Syrakus / Syracuse
Art Festival, Living Art Museum, Reykjavik
Sommerausstellung 1982, Kunsthalle Wilhelmshaven
Ecole Normale and Friends, Frauenmuseum, Bonn; Schranne
am Marktplatz, Feuchtwangen
Trivial – ein Signal. Junge deutsche Kunst I, Städtische Galerie
Regensburg

1983

Kunst nu, Groninger Museum, Groningen
Kunstausstellung, Kunst + Diakonie e. V., Wehr-Öflingen
Normal, Galerie Nörballe, Kopenhagen
Neue Bilder, Galerie Michael Haas, Berlin
Sternbilder, Kunstverein Brühl
Das überflüssige Portrait, Förderkreis Kulturzentrum Berlin

1984

Wer überlebt, winkt, Neue Gesellschaft für Bildende Kunst, Berlin
Kunstlandschaft Bundesrepublik, Kunstverein Köln
Von hier aus – Zwei Monate neue deutsche Kunst in Düsseldorf,
Messegelände Halle 13, Düsseldorf
Tiefe Blicke, Hessisches Landesmuseum Darmstadt

1985

Brunnurinn, Living Art Museum, Reykjavik

KIS '85 – Kunsan International Show, Institute of
Contemporary Arts, Kunsan National University
5 Jahre Lisa und David Lauber-Preis, Kunsthaus Nürnberg /
Nuremberg

1986
Morgenröte, Galerie Ryszard Varisella, Nürnberg / Nuremberg
Im Zeichen der Burg, Galerie Ryszard Varisella, Nürnberg /
Nuremberg

1987
Vom Essen und Trinken, Kunstverein Wuppertal
Sex und Tod, Planet, Düsseldorf
IPPNW, Hospitalhof, Stuttgart
Exotik, Galerie Kaess-Weiss, Stuttgart
Owi lacht, Galerie Karin Sachs, München / Munich

1988
Das Kind, Galerie Horbach, Köln / Cologne
Atlantis, Galerie der Stadt Stuttgart
Eros & Arch, Torch Gallery for Contemporary Art, Amsterdam
Botschaften, Kunst + Diakonie e. V., Wehr-Öflingen
Arbeit in Geschichte – Geschichte in Arbeit, Kunstverein Hamburg

1989
Nutidskunst, Silkeborg Kunstmuseum, Kopenhagen
Fränkische Künstler, Kunsthalle Nürnberg / Nuremberg; Städti-
sche Galerie Krakau / Municipal Gallery, Krakow; Städtische
Galerie Skopje / Municipal Gallery, Skopje
Kunstausstellung, Kunst + Diakonie e. V., Wehr-Öflingen
Angermann, Knap, Kunc, La Bertesca, Genua / Genoa
Museumsskizze, Kunsthalle Nürnberg / Nuremberg
Angermann, Knap, Kunc, Galerie Kaess-Weiss, Stuttgart

1990
Endlich, Neue Gesellschaft für Bildende Kunst, Lapidarium, Berlin

1991
Los toros desde afuera, Diputacion Provincial de Valencia
Bärenlese. Zum Wesen des Teddys, Ruhrlandmuseum Essen

1992
Gegenwartskunst für Jedermann, Griffelkunst e. V., Kunsthalle
Rostock
Die Künstlerpostkarte, Altonaer Museum, Hamburg

Bärenlese. Zum Wesen des Teddys, Naturhistorisches Museum Wien
Sette artisti in vetta, Studio d'Arte Raffaelli, Trient / Trento
ordine & disordine, Zelig, Bari
Freunde und Verwandte, Kunsthalle Nürnberg / Nuremberg

1993
Gegenwartskunst für Jedermann, Griffelkunst e. V., Archäologi-
sches Museum Hamburg
La Montagna dipinta, Castel Telvana, Civezzano
Wege, Kunst + Diakonie e. V., Wehr-Öflingen
Hemdendienstbilder: Angermann, Schemm, Reeder, Galerie
Traude Näke, Nürnberg / Nuremberg
TeleCartoon, Postmuseum, Frankfurt/Main
Schnalle und Riemen, Galerie Röver, Nürnberg / Nuremberg
Angermann, Fridjónsson, Vautier, Trantenroth, Reeder, Galerie
Hartmut Beck, Erlangen
L'Arca di Noe, Trevi Flash Art Museum

1994
Für F.N. Nietzsche in der bildenden Kunst der letzten 30 Jahre,
Schloss Belvedere, Weimar
First International Triennal of Graphic Art, Muzeji Galerija
Bitola, Zavod
Aus der Sammlung, Kunsthalle Nürnberg / Nuremberg
Revoltella Estate, Museo Civico Revoltella, Triest / Trieste
Herbstsalon, Galerie Traude Näke, Nürnberg / Nuremberg
Stanze del Paesaggio, Palazzo Albertini, Forlì
Ritratto Autoritratto, Trevi Flash Art Museum
Peter Angermann – Milan Kunc – John van 't Slot, Galerie
Delta, Rotterdam

1995
Die Offizielle Polkakapelle, Yec 'het mad, Nürnberg / Nuremberg
Salut au Monde, Fries Museum, Leeuwarden

1996
Landschaft – mit dem Blick der 90er Jahre, Mittelrhein-Museum
Koblenz; Museum Schloss Burgk, Saale; Haus am Waldsee, Berlin
Romantico Contemporaneo 1996, Bentivoglio, Bologna
Divinità e misteri fisici, Juliet, Triest / Trieste
Schwabenheimer Kunstpfad 96, Schwabenheim, Mainz
Zoo, Kunsthaus Nürnberg / Nuremberg
The Burrell Collection, Kelvingrove Art Gallery and Museum, Glasgow

Spring, Galerie Traude Näke, Nürnberg / Nuremberg

Adicere Animos, Galleria Civica d'Arte Contemporanea, Cesena

1997

Sidhumanismi, Kjarvalsstadir, Reykjavik

Schöner Wohnen, Sensus, Uttenreuth

Weder gut noch böse: Kirche – Kunst – Diakonie. Die Sammlung Paul und Hanna Gräb, Galerie im Rathaus, München / Munich; Evangelischer Oberkirchenrat Karlsruhe; Evangelischer Oberkirchenrat Darmstadt; Kunstverein Kronach

Brot des Lebens, Diakonissenmutterhaus Münster

Q, Gallerie Omphalos, Bari

Malerei, Galerie Lindig in Paludetto, Nürnberg / Nuremberg

1998

Befreiung der Vernunft – Die Langheimer und ihre Künstlerfreunde, Galerie Klein, Bad Münstereifel

1999

Weder gut noch böse, Kunst + Diakonie e. V., Wehr-Öflingen; Kunstverein Kronach

2000

Landschaften eines Jahrhunderts – aus der Sammlung Deutsche Bank, Museum Küppersmühle für Moderne Kunst, Duisburg

Fließende Zeit, Kunst + Diakonie e. V., Wehr-Öflingen; Stadthalle und altes Schloss, Kronach

Contemporary Art from Germany, Capital Normal University Art Museum, Beijing

Normal, Ca' di Fra', Mailand / Milan

2001

The River and the City, Galerie Delta, Rotterdam

Landschaften eines Jahrhunderts – aus der Sammlung Deutsche Bank, Kunsthalle Jesuitenkirche, Aschaffenburg; Landesmuseum für Kunst und Kulturgeschichte, Oldenburg; Zeughaus Augsburg

Kunst für Kaliningrad – Königsberg, Museum Ostdeutsche Galerie Regensburg, Staatliche Kaliningrader Kunstgalerie, Kaliningrad

Berg, Bernsteinzimmer, Nürnberg / Nuremberg

2002

German Landscapes, SA National Gallery, Kapstadt / Cape Town

Die Erfindung der Stadt, Stadtmuseum Erlangen

Wunschbilder, Kunsthaus Nürnberg / Nuremberg

Die Sammlung Appelt, Bernsteinzimmer, Nürnberg / Nuremberg

Arbeiten auf Papier, Neues Museum in Nürnberg / Nuremberg

Die Sammlung Defet, Neues Museum in Nürnberg / Nuremberg

Autoritratto, Galerie Hartmut Beck, Erlangen

Internationales Verkanntentreffen, Endart, Berlin

Ils sont venu de si loin, Galerie Delta, Rotterdam

2003

Pegnitzer Kulturtage, Sparkasse Pegnitz

Dialoge, Kunst + Diakonie e. V., Wehr-Öflingen

50N04, Kunstmühle Mürsbach

2004

Michelys Show, Galerie mit der Blauen Tür, Nürnberg / Nuremberg

La boîte en valise, Kunstverein Weiden

Dialoge, Oktogon der Hochschule für Bildende Künste, Dresden

2005

La boîte en valise, Galerie AVU, Prag / Prague

Group Normal in Prague Biennal, Carlin Hall, Prag / Prague

Aste Invernali, Blindarte, Neapel / Naples

Hot Needle – Graphic Works of the 1980s, City Gallery, Prag / Prague

2006

Paint it loud – Musik in den anderen Künsten, Galerie Tedden, Düsseldorf

Ironischer Realismus, Galerie Tedden, Düsseldorf

Normal Group, Trevi Flash Art Museum; Museo Arte Contemporanea Isernia

Begegnungen, Kunst + Diakonie e. V., Wehr-Öflingen

2007

Ziemlich hoch – Das Alpine in der zeitgenössischen Kunst, Kunsthaus Kaufbeuren

Sex in Fürth, Kunsthaus Fürth

2008

Symposium Šumava / Böhmerwald 2008, Galerie Klatovy, Klenová

Rauschende Gäste. Die Sammlung Rausch und die Städelschule zu Gast im Hotel Marienbad, KW Institute for Contemporary Art, Berlin

Parallelwelten, Altes Schloss Bayreuth
Pas de Deux – Wie sich die Bilder gleichen, Städtische Galerie
Villa Zanders, Bergisch Gladbach
*To be a teacher is my greatest work of art. Joseph Beuys und seine
Schüler. Werke aus der Sammlung Deutsche Bank*, Kunstmuseum
Ahlen
*Napříč generacemi // Im Querschnitt – Zeitgenössische Kunst aus
den Partnerstädten*, Clam-Gallas-Palais, Prag / Prague

2009
100 Jahre – 100 Bilder. Deutsche Malerei im 20. Jahrhundert,
Landesmuseum Oldenburg
Astronauten zur Venus. Werke aus der Sammlung Appelt, Zen-
trifuge, Nürnberg / Nuremberg
*Joseph Beuys and His Students. Works from the Deutsche Bank
Collection*, Sakip Sabanci Museum, Istanbul
Caleidoscopio, duetart gallery, Varese
10 Jahre BAT CampusGalerie, Bayreuth
*Napříč generacemi // Im Querschnitt – Zeitgenössische Kunst aus
den Partnerstädten*, Kunsthaus im KunstKulturQuartier,
Nürnberg / Nuremberg

2010
Angermann mit Klasse, Blindeninstitut Rückersdorf
Nürnberger Tand, Kunsthalle Meiningen
Alles was erscheint, MBC Gallery M, Daegu, Südkorea / South
Korea
/+\=X, serial works studio, Kapstadt / Cape Town

2011
Faster and Slower Lines, Reykjavik Art Museum
Die Kunst des Sammelns, Kunsthaus Nürnberg / Nuremberg
20 Years After, Galerie Anita Beckers, Frankfurt/Main

2012
Böhmerwald Reflexionen, Galerie der Stadt Pilsen
Gastspiel 2012, Reiner Bergmann und Gäste, Kulturring C,
Fürth
Figura solare, Maniero Associazione Culturale, Rom
Dílna, Symposium, Schloss / Castle Mikulov
Grenzenlos, Focus Europa e. V., Marktredwitz
Zeitgenössische Kunst in Kalchreuth, Zehntscheune Kalchreuth
Der Ausstieg, Bernsteinzimmer, Nürnberg / Nuremberg

Schlachtpunk. Malerei der Achtziger Jahre, Kunsthalle Darmstadt
Der wilde Süden, Altes Schloss Wehr, Kunst + Diakonie e. V.,
Wehr-Öflingen
56. internationale Kinderbuchausstellung, Klingspor-Museum
Offenbach

Auswahlbibliografie / Selected Bibliography

1977
Peter Angermann – Hartmut Kuhnke, Ausst.-Kat. / exh. cat. Galerie Defet, Nürnberg / Nuremberg.

1980
Wolfgang Becker, *Peter Angermann – Bilder von 1973 bis 1980*, Ausst.-Kat. / exh. cat. Galerie Defet, Nürnberg / Nuremberg.
Après le Classicisme, Ausst.-Kat. / exh. cat. Musée d'Art et d'Industrie, Maison de la culture, Saint Etienne.
11e Biennale de Paris – Manifestation internationale des jeunes artistes, Ausst.-Kat. / exh. cat. Musée d'Art Moderne de la Ville de Paris, Centre Georges Pompidou, Paris.

1981
Wolfgang Becker, *Normal*, Ausst.-Kat. / exh. cat. Neue Galerie – Sammlung Ludwig, Aachen.
Hanspeter Heidrich, *Bildwechsel – Neue Malerei aus Deutschland*, Ausst.-Kat. / exh. cat. Akademie der Künste, Berlin.
Gerhard Mammel, *Positionen und Tendenzen – Kunstszene Nürnberg*, Ausst.-Kat. / exh. cat. Albrecht-Dürer-Gesellschaft Nürnberg.
Alfred Nemeczek, „Malerei '81: Die Sache mit den Wilden", in: *Art – Das Kunstmagazin*, Oktober / October.
Tilman Osterwold (Hrsg. / ed.), *Szenen der Volkskunst*, Ausst.-Kat. / ex. cat. Württembergischer Kunstverein Stuttgart.
Demetrio Paparoni, *Aljofre Barrocco*, Ausst.-Kat. / exh. cat. Sala Dante del Teatro Comunale, Salone di Palazzo Ducezio, Noto.
Demetrio Paparoni, *Normal – Peter Angermann, John Hummel, Jan Knap, Milan Kunc*, Ausst.-Kat. / exh. cat. Museo Civico d'Arte Contemporanea, Gibellina.
Annelie Pohlen, „Ernst machen mit dem Kitsch. Gruppe Normal in der Aachener Neuen Galerie Sammlung Ludwig", in: *Süddeutsche Zeitung*, 28. Oktober / October 28.
LIS '81 – Lisbon International Show.
International Exhibition of Drawings Portugal, Ausst.-Kat. / exh. cat. Galeria Nacional de Arte Moderna, Lissabon / Lisbon.

Rundschau Deutschland – Ausstellung in der Fabrik, Ausst.-Kat. / exh. cat. Lothringer Strasse 13, München / Munich.

1982
Hartmut Beck (Hrsg. / ed.), *Ecole Normale and Friends*, Ausst.-Kat. / exh. cat. Schranne am Marktplatz Feuchtwangen, Erlangen.
Veit Loers, *Trivial – ein Signal. Junge deutsche Kunst I*, Ausst.-Kat. / exh. cat. Städtische Galerie Regensburg.
Antje von Graevenitz, *Kunst nu: Kunst van nu in het Groninger Museum: aanwinsten 1978–1982. Kunst unserer Zeit: Kunst unserer Zeit im Groninger Museum: Neuerwerbungen 1978–1982*, Ausst.-Kat. / exh. cat. Groninger Museum, Groningen.
Bertram Müller, „Milan Kunc und die Gruppe ‚Normal' – Junge Wilde aus Düsseldorf – Grelle Erleuchtung aus dem Osten", in: *Rheinische Post*, 4. März / March 4.
Wolfgang Max Faust, Gerd de Vries, *Hunger nach Bildern – Deutsche Malerei der Gegenwart*, Köln / Cologne.
Demetrio Paparoni, *Thinking of the Europe*, Ausst.-Kat. / exh. cat. Living Art Museum Reykjavik.

1983
Paul Gräb (Hrsg. / ed.), *Kunstausstellung Wehr-Öflingen*, Ausst.-Kat. / exh. cat. Kunst + Diakonie e. V., Wehr-Öflingen.
Michael Haas (Hrsg. / ed.), *Neue Bilder*, Ausst.-Kat. / exh. cat. Galerie Michael Haas, Berlin.

1984
Thomas Deecke et al., *Kunstlandschaft Bundesrepublik, München und Bayern*, Ausst.-Kat. / exh. cat. Bonner Kunstverein; Brühler Kunstverein; Kölnischer Kunstverein, Stuttgart.
Kaspar König (Hrsg. / ed.), *Von hier aus – Zwei Monate neue deutsche Kunst in Düsseldorf*, Ausst.-Kat. / exh. cat. Messegelände Halle 13 Düsseldorf, Ostfildern.

1985
Sascha Anderson et al., *Tiefe Blicke – Kunst der achtziger Jahre aus der Bundesrepublik Deutschland, der DDR, Österreich und der Schweiz*, Köln / Cologne.

Karin Thomas, *Zweimal deutsche Kunst nach 1945 – 40 Jahre Nähe und Ferne*, Köln / Cologne.
Institute of Contemporary Arts (Hrsg. / ed.), *KIS '85 – Kunsan International Show*, Ausst.-Kat. / exh. cat. Institute of Contemporary Arts, Kunsan National University.

1986
Stephan Schmidt-Wulffen, *Peter Angermann – Landschaften*, Ausst.-Kat. / exh. cat. Galerie Michael Horbach, Köln / Cologne.
Peter Angermann, Blalla W. Hallmann, Erhard Kick, Ausst.-Kat. / exh. cat. Galerie Ryszard Varisella, Nürnberg / Nuremberg.

1987
Ursula Peters, Georg F. Schwarzbauer (Hrsg. / ed.), *Vom Essen und Trinken – Darstellungen in der Kunst der Gegenwart*, Ausst.-Kat. / exh. cat. Kunst- und Museumsverein Wuppertal.

1988
Peter Angermann, „Ein Gespräch mit Harry Schemm", in: *Apex. Zeitschrift für Kunst, Kultur, Fotografie*, 3.
Georg Bussmann (Hrsg. / ed.), *Arbeit in Geschichte – Geschichte in Arbeit*, Ausst.-Kat. / exh. cat. Kunstverein Hamburg, Berlin.
Paul Gräb, Karl-Christoph Epting (Hrsg. / eds.), *Botschaften*, Ausst.-Kat. / exh. cat. Kunst + Diakonie e. V., Schauenburg.
Leon Krier, *Atlantis*, Ausst.-Kat. / exh. cat. Galerie der Stadt Stuttgart.
Ursula Peters, *Peter Angermann*, Ausst.-Kat. / exh. cat. Galería Estampa, Madrid.

1989
Annie Bardon et al., *Kunsthalle Nürnberg – Museumsskizze*, Ausst.-Kat. / exh. cat. Kunsthalle Nürnberg / Nuremberg.
Angelica Horn, *Peter Angermann*, Ausst.-Kat. / exh. cat. Galerie Ryszard Varisella, Frankfurt/ Main; Galleria Toselli, Mailand / Milan.

1990
Peter Angermann im Gespräch mit Martin Blättner: „Ich bin nicht mein eigener Theoretiker", in: *Mitteilungen des Instituts für moderne Kunst Nürnberg*, 51/52.

Paul Gräb, Karl-Christoph Epting (Hrsg. / ed.),
Gerechtigkeit, Frieden, Bewahrung der Schöpfung,
Ausst.-Kat. / exh. cat. Kunst + Diakonie e. V.,
Karlsruhe.
Lucius Grisebach, *Kunsthalle Nürnberg. Aus der
Sammlung – Bilder und Objekte*, Ausst.-Kat. /
exh. cat. Kunsthalle Nürnberg / Nuremberg.
Peter Kampehl (Hrsg. / ed.), *Beispiele einer pri-
vaten Kunstförderung*, Nürnberg / Nuremberg.
Neue Gesellschaft für bildende Kunst (Hrsg. /
ed.), *Endlich – Postrevolutionäre Kunst im IV.
Reich*, Ausst.-Kat. / exh. cat. Lapidarium, Berlin.
Lisa Licitra Ponti, „La Torre di Babele di
Peter Angermann", in: *Domus*, 713, Februar /
February.

1991

Frédéric Cousinié, Pierre Daninos, *Los toros
desde afuera*, Ausst.-Kat. / exh. cat. Diputación
Provincial de Valencia.
Mathilde Jamin, Kania Rolf, *Bärenlese. Zum
Wesen des Teddys*, Ausst.-Kat. / exh. cat.
Ruhrlandmuseum Essen.

1992

Peter Angermann et al., *Freunde und Verwandte –
Künstler aus Nürnberg*, Ausst.-Kat. / exh. cat.
Kunsthalle Nürnberg / Nuremberg.

1993

Peter Angermann. Pleinair – Malerei 1991–1993,
Ausst.-Kat. / exh. cat. Galerie Defet,
Nürnberg / Nuremberg.
Fiorenzo Degasperi, *Peter Angermann*, Ausst.-
Kat. / exh. cat. Studio d'Arte Raffaelli, Trient /
Trento.
Paul Gräb, Karl-Christoph Epting (Hrsg. /
eds.), *Wege*, Ausst.-Kat. / exh. cat. Kunst +
Diakonie e. V., Karlsruhe.
Giancarlo Politi (Hrsg. / ed.), *L'Arca di Noe*,
Ausst.-Kat. / exh. cat. Trevi Flash Art Museum.

1994

Stefanoni Lecco (Hrsg. / ed.), *Peter
Angermann – La Voiture Verte*, Ausst.-Kat. /
exh. cat. Galleria Toselli, Mailand / Milan.
Lucius Grisebach, *Epilog für einen betrunkenen
Drucker*, München / Munich.
Michael Glasmeier, *Die Bücher der Künstler:
Publikationen und Editionen seit den sechziger
Jahren in Deutschland*, Ausst.-Kat. / exh. cat.
Institut für Auslandsbeziehungen, Stuttgart.
Stiftung Weimarer Klassik (Hrsg. / ed.),
*Für F.N. Nietzsche in der bildenden Kunst der
letzten 30 Jahre*, Ausst.-Kat. / exh. cat. Schloss
Belvedere, Weimar.

1995

Lucius Grisebach et al., *Peter Angermann –
Malerei 1973 bis 1995*, Ausst.-Kat. / exh. cat.
Kunsthalle Nürnberg / Nuremberg; Galleria
d'Arte Moderna e Contemporanea San Marino,
Nürnberg / Nuremberg.
Arends Toos et al., *Salut au Monde – Het Friese
landschap in de schilderkunst van 1900 tot nu /
Die friesische Landschaft in der Malerei von 1900
bis heute*, Ausst.-Kat. / exh. cat. Fries Museum,
Leeuwarden; Kunstsammlungen Böttcherstraße
Bremen; Städtische Galerie im Buntentor,
Bremen; Kulturgeschichtliches Museum
Osnabrück.

1996

Kathrin Becker (Hrsg. / ed.), *Landschaft – mit
dem Blick der 90er Jahre*, Ausst.-Kat. / exh. cat.
Mittelrhein-Museum Koblenz; Museum Schloss
Burgk; Haus am Waldsee, Berlin, Köln / Cologne.
Alice Rubbini, *Adicere animos: mostra multi-
mediale d'arte contemporanea e d'avanguardia*,
Ausst.-Kat. / exh. cat. Galleria Civica d'Arte
Contemporanea Cesena, Bologna.
Alice Rubbini, *Romantico contemporaneo*, Ausst.-
Kat. / exh. cat. Castello di Bentivoglio, Bologna.
Julian Spalding, Stefan Van Raay, *Gallery of
Modern Art. Glasgow: The First Years*, London.

1997

Paul Gräb, Karl-Christoph Epting (Hrsg. /
eds.), *Horizonte*, Ausst.-Kat. / exh. cat. Kunst +
Diakonie e. V., Wehr-Öflingen.
Angelica Horn, *Peter Angermann*, Ausst.-Kat. /
exh. cat. Galerie Ryszard Varisella, Frankfurt/
Main; Galleria Toselli, Mailand / Milan.
Ivo Kranzfelder (Hrsg. / ed.), *Weder gut noch
böse: Kirche – Kunst – Diakonie. Die Sammlung
Paul und Hanna Gräb*, Ausst.-Kat. / exh. cat.
Galerie im Rathaus München; Evangelischer
Oberkirchenrat Karlsruhe; Evangelischer
Oberkirchenrat Darmstadt; Kunstverein
Kronach, Wehr-Öflingen.

1998

Peter Angermann et al., *Befreiung der Vernunft.
Künstlerwitze von Künstlern – Die Langheimer
und ihre Künstlerfreunde*, Ausst.-Kat. / exh. cat.
Galerie Erhard Klein, Düsseldorf.

1999

Ariane Grigoteit, *Landschaften eines
Jahrhunderts – aus der Sammlung Deutsche Bank*,
Frankfurt/Main.

2000

Beatus Fischer (Hrsg. / ed.), *Fließende Zeit*,
Ausst.-Kat. / exh. cat. Kunst + Diakonie e. V.,
Wehr-Öflingen
Contemporary Art from Germany, Ausst.-Kat. /
exh. cat. Capital Normal University Art
Museum, Beijing.

2001

Thomas Heyden, *Peter Angermann – pleinair*,
Ausst.-Kat. / exh. cat. Galerie Defet,
Nürnberg / Nuremberg
Christian Mückl, „Der Alte geht doch bloß
spazieren, um zu malen – ein Besuch bei Peter
Angermann in der Oberpfalz", in: *Nürnberger
Zeitung*, 9. Juni / June 9.

2002

Thomas Engelhardt et al., *Die Erfindung
der Stadt. Von Babylon zur Global City: Eine
Ausstellung des Stadtmuseums Erlangen zum
1000jährigen Jubiläum der Stadt Erlangen 2002*,
Ausst.-Kat. / exh. cat. Stadtmuseum Erlangen.
Lucius Grisebach et al., *Defet – Eine Schenkung*,
Ausst.-Kat. / exh. cat. Neues Museum in
Nürnberg / Nuremberg.
*Wunschbilder 1 – Gemälde und Skulpturen für eine
neue Fränkische Galerie*, Ausst.-Kat. / exh. cat.
Kunsthaus Nürnberg / Nuremberg.

2003

Stephan A. Dudek, „Es geht darum, ein Bild zu
machen – Ein Gespräch mit dem Maler Peter
Angermann", in: *Rhein Main Presse*, 15. Juli /
July 15.
Gabriele Oberreuter, *Peter Angermann –
Heimatmalerei*, Ausst.-Kat. / exh. cat. BAT
CampusGalerie, Bayreuth.
Julian Spalding, *The Eclipse of Art. Tackling the
Crisis in Art Today*, München / Munich.
Johannes Stockmeier (Hrsg. / ed.), *Dialoge*,
Ausst.-Kat. / exh. cat. Kunst + Diakonie e. V.,
Kronach.

2004

Wolfgang Herzer (Hrsg. / ed.), *La boîte en valise
oder Die neue Welt liegt mitten in Europa*, Ausst.-
Kat. / exh. cat. Kunstverein Weiden.

2005

Luca Beatrice et al., *Normal Group*, Ausst.-Kat. /
exh. cat. Prague Biennale; Trevi Flash Art
Museum; Museo Arte Contemporanea Isernia,
Bologna.
Zdenek Felix, *Hot needle – graphic works of the 1980s*,
Ausst.-Kat. / exh. cat. City Gallery, Prag / Prague.

Christian Mückl, Magnus Zawodsky, „Schönheit ist, wenn's passt. 23 Fragen an den Maler Peter Angermann", in: *Nürnberger Zeitung*, 14. November / November 14.
Rob Perrée, „Anti-Avantgarde-Painting", in: *80+25=2005*, Ausst.-Kat. / exh. cat. Galerie Witteveen, Amsterdam.

2006
Peter Angermann (Hrsg. / ed.), *Fett auf mager. Studenten der Klasse Angermann 2006*, Nürnberg / Nuremberg.
Reinhard Valenta (Hrsg. / ed.), *Begegnungen*, Ausst.-Kat. / exh. cat. Kunst + Diakonie e. V., Wehr-Öflingen.

2007
Friedrich J. Bröder, Lucius Grisebach, *Kunst ist Kunst – Werke aus der Kunstsammlung des Neuen Museums in Nürnberg*, Nürnberg / Nuremberg.
Manfred Rothenberger, Anke Schlecht, *Rubin: Institut für moderne Kunst Nürnberg 1967–2007*, Ausst.-Kat. / exh. cat. Staatliches Museum für Kunst und Design, Nürnberg / Nuremberg.

2008
Nina Heydemann, Friedhelm Hütte, *To be a teacher is my greatest work of art: Joseph Beuys und seine Schüler – Werke aus der Sammlung Deutsche Bank*, Ausst.-Kat. / exh. cat. Kunstmuseum Ahlen, Frankfurt/Main.
Petra Hoftichová, Thomas May, *Napříč generacemi // Im Querschnitt. – Zeitgenössische Kunst aus den Partnerstädten*, Ausst.-Kat. / exh. cat. Clam-Gallas-Palais, Prag / Prague; Kunsthaus Nürnberg / Nuremberg.
Reinhard Kalb, „Votivbilder zwischen Traum und Albtraum. Neue Bilder von Peter Angermann", in: *Nürnberger Zeitung*, 16. September / September 16.
Ursula Peters, „Sagenhafte Tiere aus grauer Vorzeit. Ein Gemälde von Peter Angermann", in: *Kulturgut. Aus der Forschung des Germanischen Nationalmuseums*, 17, April–Juni / April–June.
Johannes Stüttgen, *Der ganze Riemen. Joseph Beuys – der Auftritt als Lehrer an der Staatlichen Kunstakademie Düsseldorf 1966–1972*, Köln / Cologne.

2009
Ahu Antmen, Friedhelm Hütte, *Joseph Beuys ve Öğrencileri – Deutsche Bank Koleksiyonu'ndan Seçmeler / Joseph Beuys and his Students – Works from the Deutsche Bank Collection*, Ausst.-Kat. / exh. cat. Sakip Sabanci Museum, Istanbul.
Amelie Himmel et al., *Astronauten zur Venus – Werke aus der Sammlung Appelt*, Ausst.-Kat. / exh. cat. Zentrifuge Kommunikation Kunst und Kultur e. V., Nürnberg / Nuremberg.
Bernd Küster (Hrsg. / ed.), *100 Jahre – 100 Bilder: Deutsche Malerei des 20. Jahrhunderts*, Ausst.-Kat. / exh. cat. Landesmuseum Oldenburg, Vastorf.
Ursula Peters, „Geschöpfe des Wassers, des Himmels und der Erde bei Peter Angermann und Antonius Höckelmann", in: *Vom Ansehen der Tiere – Kulturgeschichtliche Spaziergänge im Germanischen Nationalmuseum*, Nürnberg / Nuremberg.
Karl Schawelka, *Peter Angermann – Autonomoney*, Ausst.-Kat. / exh. cat. Galerie Klatovy, Klenová; Museen der Stadt Bamberg.
Katarina Uhlirova, „Peter Angermann", in: *art+antiques*, Juni / June.

2010
Kevin Coyne, *Peter Angermann*, Ausst.-Kat. / exh. cat. MBC Gallery M, Daegu, Südkorea / South Korea.
Wolfgang Grosholz, „Mit Mountainbike und Staffelei ab in die Natur: Peter Angermann stellt Malerei im Kunstverein aus", in: *Badische Zeitung*, 2. Oktober / October 2.
Brigitte Kölle, *Es geht voran. Kunst der 80er Jahre. Eine Düsseldorfer Perspektive*, Ausst.-Kat. / exh. cat. K21, Düsseldorf, München / Munich.
Julian Spalding, *The Best Art You've Never Seen. 101 Hidden Treasures from around the World*, London.

2011
Peter Angermann, Aloisia Föllmer, *Peter Angermann*, Ausst.-Kat. / exh. cat. Kunstförderverein Weinheim e. V.
Dieter Begemann et al., *Kunstwelten. 100 Künstler – 100 Perspektiven – 1000 Welten*, Witten.
Nicola Vitale, *Figura solare – Un rinnovamento radicale dell'arte. Inizio di un'epoca dell'essere*, Genua, Mailand / Genoa, Milan.

2012
Peter Joch, Klaus-D. Pohl, *Schlachtpunk – Malerei der Achtziger Jahre*, Ausst.-Kat. / exh. cat. Hessisches Landesmuseum Darmstadt; Kunsthalle Darmstadt, Mannheim.
Nicola Vitale, „Figura Solare", in: *Juliet Art Magazine*, 157, April–Mai / April–May.
Joost Swarte, „Swarte éternellement surpris par Angermann", in: *Casemate*, 47, April.

Danksagung / Acknowledgements

Peter Angermann dankt allen, die am Zustandekommen dieser Monografie mitgewirkt haben,
insbesondere / Peter Angermann would like to thank everyone who helped in the realisation of
this monograph, in particular:

Renate Angermann
Stefan Barmann
Ernst Christian Dümmler
Christiane Ebner
Matthias Egersdörfer
Sam Frank
Malcolm Green
Martin Hentschel
Jürgen Musolf
Dan Reeder
Katrin Sauerländer
Harald Schmidt
Julian Spalding

Gefördert durch / Supported by 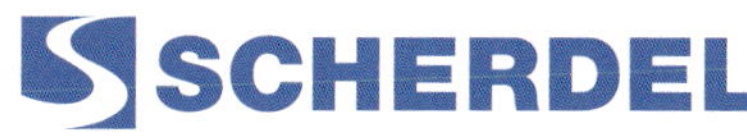

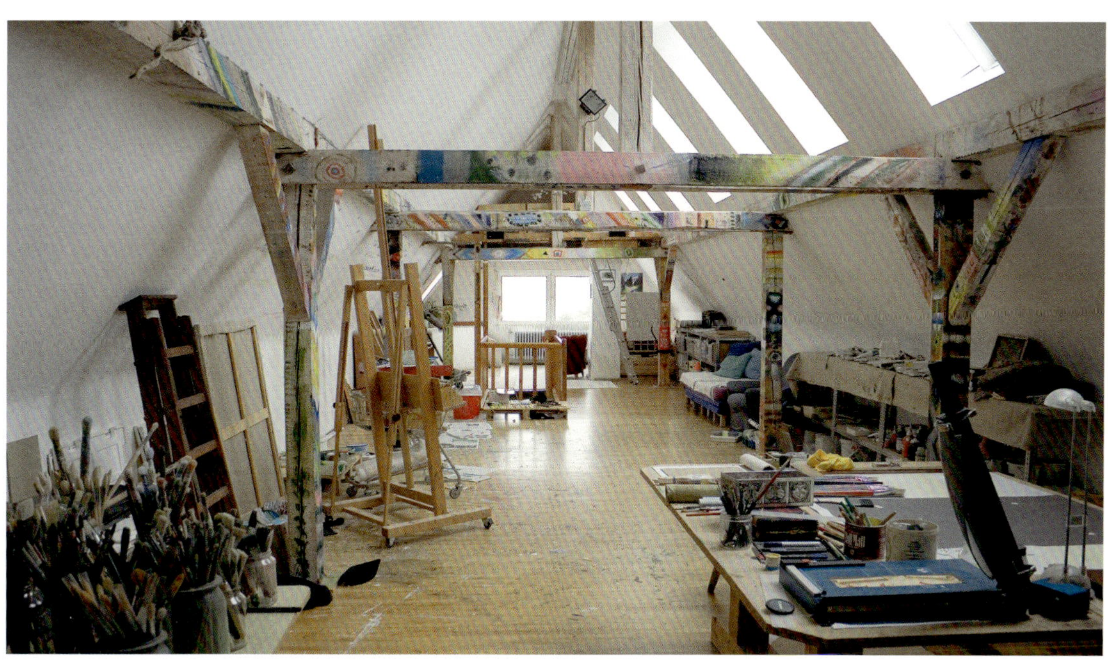

Impressum / Colophon

Diese Monografie erscheint anlässlich der Ausstellung /
This monograph is published in conjunction with the
exhibition

Peter Angermann ____ Licht am Horizont

Ausstellungsdaten / Exhibition Schedule
Kunstmuseen Krefeld, Museum Haus Lange
28. April – 1. September 2013
April 28 – September 1, 2013

Ausstellung / Exhibition

Kurator / Curator
Martin Hentschel

Transport, Finanzen / Transport, Finances
Marion Roggelin

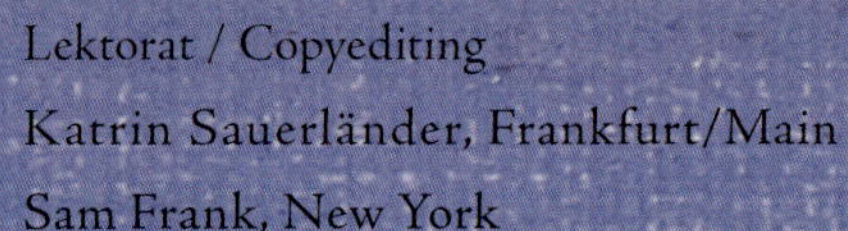

Ausstellungsaufbau / Installation of the Exhibition
Thomas Larisch, Andreas Nörenberg, Jürgen Schmitz

Restaurator / Conservator
Sebastian Köhler

Kunstmuseen Krefeld
Administration:
Dujardinstraße 1
47829 Krefeld
T. +49 21 51 9 75 58-0
F. +49 21 51 9 75 58-222
www.kunstmuseenkrefeld.de

Katalog / Catalogue

Herausgeber, Redaktion / Editor, Editorial Work
Martin Hentschel

Bibliografie / Bibliography
Alejandro Daniels

Übersetzungen / Translations
Peter Angermann (Spalding, Englisch–Deutsch / English–
German, überarbeitet von / revised by Stefan Barmann)
Malcolm Green, Berlin (Hentschel, Interview, Deutsch–
Englisch / German–English)

Lektorat / Copyediting
Katrin Sauerländer, Frankfurt/Main
Sam Frank, New York

Bildtafeln / Plates
Peter Angermann
Ernst Christian Dümmler
Werner Kumpf
Jürgen Musolf
Peter Salek
Sammlung Deutsche Bank / Deutsche Bank Collection

Textabbildungen / Illustrations
Peter Angermann, S. / pp. 24, 112–114, 186, 187, 196
Renate Angermann, S. / p. 100
Hans Henin, S. / pp. 85, 190
Martin Hentschel, S. / p. 22
Hanns Herpich, S. / p. 84
Pressearchiv Nürnberg, S. / pp. 182, 183
Peter Salek, S. / pp. 108, 109

Gestaltung / Design
Ernst Christian Dümmler, Nürnberg

Lithografie / Lithography
Repro Studio Schmidt, Nürnberg
Ernst Christian Dümmler, Nürnberg

Gesamtherstellung / Production
DZA Druckerei zu Altenburg GmbH

Bibliografische Information der Deutschen
Nationalbibliothek
Die Deutsche Nationalbibliothek verzeichnet diese
Publikation in der Deutschen Nationalbibliografie;
detaillierte bibliografische Daten sind im Internet über
http://dnb.d-nb.de abrufbar.

Bibliographic information published by the Deutsche
Nationalbibliothek
The Deutsche Nationalbibliothek lists this publication in
the Deutsche Nationalbibliografie; detailed bibliographic
data are available in the Internet at http://dnb.d-nb.de.

Distributed in the United Kingdom
Cornerhouse Publications
70 Oxford Street, Manchester M1 5 NH, UK
phone +44-161-200 15 03, fax +44-161-200 15 04

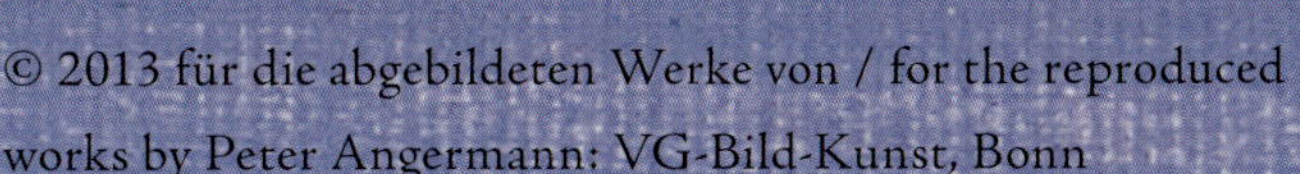

Verlag für moderne Kunst Nürnberg GmbH
Königstraße 73
90402 Nürnberg
www.vfmk.de

Distributed outside Europe
D.A.P./Distributed Art Publishers, Inc., New York
155 Sixth Avenue, 2nd Floor, New York, NY 10013

Website Peter Angermann:
www.polka.de

ISBN 978-3-86984-439-8